P9-CRQ-799

Red Flags or Red Herrings?

Also by Susan Engel

Real Kids: Creating Meaning in Everyday Life

Context Is Everything: The Nature of Memory

The Stories Children Tell: Making Sense of the Narratives of Childhood

Red Flags *or* Red Herrings?

Predicting Who Your Child Will Become

Susan Engel

ATRIA BOOKS
New York London Toronto Sydney

ATRIA BOOKS
A Division of Simon & Schuster, Inc.
1230 Avenue of the Americas
New York, NY 10020

First Atria Books hardcover edition February 2011

ATRIA BOOKS and colophon are trademarks of Simon & Schuster, Inc.

For information about special discounts for bulk purchases, please contact Simon & Schuster Special Sales at 1-866-506-1949 or business@simonandschuster.com.

The Simon & Schuster Speakers Bureau can bring authors to your live event. For more information or to book an event contact the Simon & Schuster Speakers Bureau at 1-866-248-3049 or visit our website at www.simonspeakers.com.

Designed by Jill Putorti

Manufactured in the United States of America

10 9 8 7 6 5 4 3 2 1

Library of Congress Cataloging-in-Publication Data
Engel, Susan.
Red flags or red herrings? : predicting who your child will become / by Susan Engel.
p. cm.
1. Personality development. 2. Character. 3. Child psychology. 4. Child development. I. Title.
BF723.P4E54 2011
155.4—dc22

2010016957

ISBN 978-1-4391-5011-5
ISBN 978-1-4391-5588-2 (ebook)

For Tinka, Kathy, and Jenno

Contents

Author's Note

You cannot dictate who your children will become. But you can get a pretty good sense of who they are and where they are headed. By noticing what they do, say, and feel, you can begin to see the story that is unfolding before your eyes. Like all good narratives, your child's story contains some red herrings—things that might alarm you but don't mean much. There's more good news. There aren't as many red flags in most children's stories as you might think. It's rare that any one thing a child does is a warning sign. More often, problems reveal themselves as a thread within the story, a thread that becomes visible over time. When there are problems, there are gentle ways to help. Every child's life tells a story. This book offers you a way of finding out what that story is and when you can revise the story just a little bit.

Red Flags or Red Herrings?

Introduction

A Road Map to Your Child's Future

I got my first pair of evening slippers when I was three, a birthday gift from my six-year-old sister. They were sparkly gold plastic high-heeled mules, with little pink poofs on the toes. I'd sashay around the living room in them, listening to the click of the plastic, feeling glamorous. I liked to wear them to nursery school, along with a large black leather purse I dragged around with me. It had first belonged to an elderly relative and contained lots of things I might need during the day: lipstick, candy, pencils, stuffed animals, Scotch tape, and sometimes a book or two.

According to my family, from the time I was two years old, I'd spend hours by myself dressing up in other people's discarded fancy dresses, telling stories, and outlining, to anyone who would listen, my secret lives. On any given day, I might be a mother of fourteen who also managed a busy medical practice. I loved the part where I would get out of my station wagon, loaded down with grocery bags, my stethoscope swinging around my neck. I'd pretend to soothe one of my babies on my hip, while holding a phone cradled between ear and shoulder, giving a diagnosis over the phone. I was harried and competent, and so many needy people depended on me. But other days, I was an immortal princess who had been married to a handsome strong king for a thousand years. I could visit with him only now and then, when he appeared magically in the night, to court me all over again. Sometimes I was the maverick head of a major company, who managed a large staff and strode into meetings wearing black high heels, holding a clipboard. At other times, however, I was a starving orphan who lived in the woods and had only animals for friends. I could get very caught up in the pathos of that character. My fantasies weren't confined to marvelous identities acted out in the privacy and solitude of my bedroom, either. Sometimes I tried to bring others into my imaginary world.

My grandmother Helen lived in a small white farmhouse at the edge of a potato farm, her home since she married in 1927. I visited her almost every day, walking down a little dirt path that led from my house at one end of the farm to hers at the other end. She'd toast me Wonder bread, spread it with oleo, and I'd chatter to her. She was a wonderful audience, smiling and nodding, ready to sit there with me for hours.

One day, when I was about six, I arrived and plunked myself down on one of her blue plastic kitchen chairs. It was probably about seven in the morning. I explained that I had some bad news. In a mournful voice, I told her that I was suffering from a rare disease. I lifted my hands from my lap and laid them out on the red plastic checkered cloth that covered her kitchen table, so that she could see the odd semi-shiny veneer, cracked in places, that covered my skin. I explained that the disease required me to peel that top shiny layer of skin off my hands every few hours, even though it was extremely painful. I demonstrated by pulling at one of the edges, grimacing in stoic agony as the translucent material lifted from the top of my hand. Tolerant and adoring, she'd watch sympathetically, clucking her tongue at how awful it must be for me. It was Elmer's glue, which I had carefully painted across my hand and allowed to dry before walking down the path to share my condition with my grandmother. I can remember the disbelieving glee that I felt when she seemed to fall for my fabulous account. I loved temporarily inhabiting that suffering victim, and I loved the thought that others would fall for my story.

The joke in my family is that someone passing by my bedroom door would hear lots of people talking. Looking in to find out who my visitors were, an observer would see just one little girl, pale and thin, sitting alone, sometimes in a darkened room, creating an imaginary world peopled by admirers, comrades, enemies, and support staff.

However, this funny little story has a twist. Sometime during my teens, I found out that when I was little, my father was concerned that all of those imaginary friends foreshadowed schizophrenia. When I talked to myself, he worried that I had a fragile hold on reality. He was alarmed that I didn't know the difference between the real world and make-believe and that I spent too much time pretending. He anxiously watched for signs that my fantasy life was getting the better of me. His aunt had suffered from schizophrenia, although her diagnosis had been kept secret for most of his childhood. Perhaps my behavior triggered his fear that someone else in the family would also be afflicted with mental illness. Was my father right? Did those early escapes from reality presage something more debilitating?

As things turned out, I am riddled with anxieties and, perhaps as a result, almost unbearably controlling. I tell my husband what to say to the kids, I tell my grown children what to say in job interviews, and I wake my sixteen-year-old son, even though his alarm clock has gone off, just to guarantee he will get to school on time. When guests visit our home, I rush down to the kitchen before anyone else wakes up, just to make sure that breakfast goes the way I think it should. I have all kinds of fears. I cannot board a plane without Xanax. I don't like to be the passenger in other people's cars. I've never met a superstition I didn't embrace. Every single evening, I stop whatever I am doing so that I can wish on the first star and ensure that my children will stay healthy. Just as I did when I was young, I still mentally rewrite the sad endings of novels I like. I've had my share of troubles, too—estrangements, disappointments, and regrets. But other than my quirks and the neuroses from which they spring, my connection to reality is pretty solid. I've worked my whole adult life, been married to the same man for thirty years, and raised three sons. The usual barometers of mental health point in the right direction.

Those wild gatherings of imaginary friends and narrative performances when I was little predicted something, but they did not predict mental illness. My love of fictive lives stayed with me. I studied literature in college and am still an avid reader; I love novels most of all. Much of my research has concerned the stories children tell and the worlds they create in their play. I have spent plenty of time thinking about alternative worlds, but scientists tend to call this counterfactual thinking. Most researchers do it.

My vivid fantasy life in early childhood might have foreshadowed my interest in psychology, but it wasn't a red flag for mental illness. Although my father's prediction turned out to be wrong, it's understandable that he was uneasy. Most parents feel anxious at one point or another about how their children will turn out. In those uncertain moments, what are they to do? Often, parents feel lost, as if all they can do is read tea leaves. Some lean on folk wisdom they have inherited from others, and it might not, in fact, be very wise. Yet developmental psychology can provide parents with a helpful road map for identifying and interpreting clues about who their children will become.

Finding Each Child's Pattern

I fell in love with developmental psychology when I was a sophomore in college. I was dazzled by the clever experiments that revealed how children thought. I loved the idea that there was a pattern and an order to development that could be deciphered through observation. I loved the contrasting theories that illuminated such different aspects of what children did and said. Seemingly small patches of behavior offered clues about how a child was thinking and feeling. Taken together, those clues provided a blueprint for growth and change. I had already spent years watching children play and talk (my much younger sister and the children I had taught in the summer program I ran during my teens). Now research was offering me a way to think about the patterns that governed what I had noticed.

Yet once I became a mother, the world of children looked very different to me. I no longer saw moments of behavior simply as a demonstration of a psychological principle. But I did begin to notice, with a sharpened focus, all kinds of details about my kids, and my friends' kids. One little girl I knew was high-strung from the moment she was born. She fell asleep crying and woke up crying. When she did sleep, she stuck one finger straight up in the air. She learned to talk with vehemence and rattled off long, breathless sentences about everything. Which of these things was an indication about her future, and how did the clues fit together? One little two-year-old friend of my son used to come home with us from the park and spend the afternoons at our house. From the moment he set foot in our loft, he would race around and around our kitchen table, letting out shrill screams for what seemed like hours on end, as if this were the most fun game ever. When he would eventually get tired, he would stop running, and a blank, inscrutable look would cover his face as he just stood quietly, watching whatever my son was doing. *What kind of a guy will he turn out to be?* I wondered.

As my immediate world became peopled with babies and children, my younger sister and I would play a guessing game. We would imagine the little boys and girls in our extended family thirty years later. What kind of grown-up would each of them turn out to be? One niece spent several years of her childhood dressed like her boy cousins, even wearing boys' boxers under her pants. She also insisted on peeing standing up. She was strong-willed and dynamic, a real bossy boots, and easily excited. My sister predicted that this niece would become the head of a big record company and would wear a pinstriped three-piece suit to work every day. Another niece had a quiet, beguiling manner. She was ultra-feminine, almost languorous, even as a little girl. She loved pretty things, and we guessed that she would grow up to be a fashion designer. We playfully thought we could see the seeds of their future selves.

For many years, my interest in children seemed to follow two parallel paths: the children I knew and watched, who seemed to be brimming with intriguing quirks, and the world of research, which was bent on lifting patterns from the confusing debris of specific children and particular situations. As a mother, I noticed the incidents and idiosyncrasies that made each child so interesting. As a psychologist, I thought about trends and benchmarks.

As strange as it might seem, I never thought my life as a mother and the friend of other mothers had anything much to do with my work as a psychologist. I lived among real kids, but I studied behaviors that proved and disproved general theories. I never dwelled on the possibility that I knew anything as a psychologist that could help me predict what my children or their friends would be like when they got older.

That changed suddenly in 2008, during a conversation with my sister. We were gossiping about the son of one of our childhood neighbors, a young man who had just celebrated his twentieth birthday. His early family life, we thought, had all of the ingredients that would surely lead to trouble. His father was a substance abuser with a spotty and troubled work life. His mother's hold on reality was tenuous. His parents had broken ties with many of their family members. They had few friends and were always feuding with neighbors. They mistrusted everyone around them. They seemed plagued by physical ailments that had no clear cause or cure. And when he was young, the son seemed muted, anxious, and often sad. We would have bet our bottom dollar that this boy would bear the marks of such problematic family life. Yet, against all odds, as a twenty-year-old, he was thriving. My sister reported to me how warm, smart, and engaged he now was. He was doing well in a good college, he loved his courses, he enjoyed the new friends he was making, and he was dating a really nice young woman. Who knew? On the face of it, his childhood had seemed filled with arrows pointing toward disaster.

As we discussed this, I laughed wryly and said, "Development is a mystery, isn't it?" This book starts with that comment, because it took me off guard and forced an idea that had been bubbling around in my head finally to take shape. I thought to myself, *Now, wait just a minute here. I've been a developmental psychologist for almost thirty years. Development is not a mystery. It's a crystal ball. But you need to know how to read it.*

When I thought about that neighbor, I realized that along with all of those worrisome signs were other, more significant qualities. The young man had had a very strong bond with his mother even as an infant. His parents had adored him and been very consistent in their attention to him. They were smart, and he was smart. He was good at things. The family had fun together, spent time doing things together, and showed love for one another. I shouldn't have been surprised that he seemed to have grown into a happy, able young man. I had let myself get distracted by red herrings and ignored equally clear signs that he would probably be fine.

The idea for this book came from that conversation, which led me to rethink the ways in which developmental research could help us see and understand the paths of real children. I wanted to show parents that the findings of well-done research could help them see their children with more subtlety and understanding.

The heart of the book comes from my experience as a mother and a friend to other parents. I have seen that each of us looks into the face of our little baby with joy but also with apprehension and uncertainty. What will her life be like? What will *she* be like?

A very close friend of mine had a little boy whom she worried about during nursery school. He spilled his milk every night at dinner, played too roughly with toys, and frequently broke lamps and dishes. His elbows were everywhere. He didn't sit, he bounced. Although he was kind and loving, he often clobbered other children or knocked them over. He played too hard, leaving tears and wagging fingers in his wake. In nursery school, he had only one buddy. He would often come home with his Charlie Brown mouth turned down, telling his mom that his friend had rejected him or that some little boy had been mean to him.

When it came time for kindergarten, his mother fretted that he would be the kid teachers wouldn't like, the rambunctious boy who found lessons difficult to concentrate on, and, on top of all that, a loner. As they were heading out the door that first morning of school in September, the little boy suddenly said, "Wait a minute. I need something." His mother stood watching as he raced to his shelf of toys, grabbed a small action figure that punched its fist when you pushed a button, strode over to her, and said, "I'm ready now." When they got to school, he walked in calmly, the small figure visible in his hand. Within thirty seconds, four little boys had gathered around him to admire the toy. He was off and running.

His mom thought to herself, *Phew. He's gonna be fine.* Then she called me on the phone and said anxiously, "Can I count on this? Does it mean he'll always know how to navigate a group?"

In the best moments of your child's life, you want reassurance that he will always be this ebullient/clever/determined/appealing. At the worst moments, however, you want reassurance that your child can change and is likely to. I recall going to visit a younger friend a few years ago, the mother of a smart and dynamic four-year-old named Rosie. Rosie was a handful. She had a big vocabulary and was a sponge for adult phrases. She often behaved as if others worked for her. As I walked through the door, she was thrashing around the house, screaming at her mother, "You are not the boss of me! I hate you. You don't love me, and you never have. Don't tell me what to do. I am the boss of myself!" Rosie's harried mother looked up at me with a stricken look on her face. "Is she going to be this way forever?"

I had to take some time to answer that question, because children are as complex as the adults they will become. Rosie was not simply bossy and stormy. She was also bright and highly attuned to what others were thinking. She was full of zest for life. She soaked up what was going on around her, and even at four, she was like a laser beam zeroing in on people's interactions, quickly learning what she should say to persuade others to do what she wanted. Which aspect of life was Rosie's mother trying to predict? As a grown-up, Rosie would probably come on strong—she might continue to put her own needs ahead of the needs of others. She might always tangle with people. But she would also have passionate close relationships, and no doubt, she'd use her vitality and intellect to become very successful in some career. But it's easy to see why Rosie's mom felt anguished. All of us gaze at our children in adoration or exasperation and can't help but try to envision the future that lies ahead for them.

My first son, Jake, was born when I was twenty-four. I thought

I had never felt that kind of love before. I couldn't stop kissing him and staring at him. I can remember holding him in a rocking chair, in our loft in New York City, and murmuring to him, "I knew I was going to have a baby. But I had no idea it would be *you*. I'm so glad it turned out to be you and not someone else, Jakey boy." Even as a tiny baby, he was, I realized, already a complex and distinctive person, brimming with qualities that, at that time, only peeked out but soon enough would define him.

He loomed so large in my life that first year. Everything he did seemed important and vivid. The way he nursed, his cries at night, the things that made him laugh, enthralled him, and terrified him, all seemed like crucial clues about who he was. It's just now, twenty-six years later, that I understand that some of the things I paid attention to when he was young were clues, and some were not. Other behaviors and qualities were pointing toward his future, but I didn't know it.

I also felt awed by the responsibility of being his mom. At three months, Jake still wasn't sleeping through the night, as my mother and Dr. Spock assured me all good babies would. He was still waking up in the middle of the night when he was six months old, still not sleeping well at nine months. When he was twelve months old, I let him cry for an hour and a half before bringing him to our bed. Was it bad that I picked him up in the middle of the night, or was it worse that I had let him cry for ninety minutes? Would either have a lasting effect? When he was two and a half and happily snuggling into our bed each night for a good night's sleep, a colleague at the school where I taught shook her head, sucked her teeth, and said knowingly, "If you don't get them to sleep alone when they're babies, you'll never get them out of your bed." I felt sick. Had I already screwed him up for life? Would he ever become independent? Would I ever again sleep alone in bed with my husband? Then my pediatrician, a slightly older mother, said to me, "Eventually, almost everyone figures out how to get through the night alone. Not that anyone ever wants to." With those casual words, she helped me shake off the emphatically dire predictions others had so eagerly offered me.

People's common hunches about human development are often wrong. We carry around strong intuitions, often based on nothing more than our own experiences, about children and their likely paths in life. Many of us have ironclad views on just what a child must have, or be, in order to turn into a healthy and good adult. One parent thinks good sleep habits are the key to a happy childhood, another thinks constant adult attention is the only way to ensure well-being, and a third parent is certain that if you allow a child to give up on things, he is doomed to a life of failure.

You might think that children must have discipline in order to grow up as productive members of society, or you might think that as long as a child is swaddled in love, nothing else can hurt her, and she will turn out to be a happy, caring adult. You might think that children who get lots of positive feedback are going to be confident grown-ups or that children with serious illness are certain to be riddled with neuroses later on. We make assumptions about which characteristics will follow a child as he or she grows up and which are simply passing phases of development. We assume that a defiant fifteen-year-old boy is just going through adolescence but an unsociable nine-year-old is in for trouble. Most people think they can spot the kid headed for turbulence and the one bound for success. But those intuitions are often wrong.

Red Herrings

A mother recently told me that the summer when her son Nate was seven years old, they went on holiday with extended family. Nate got into an argument with his five-year-old cousin, Tess, and smacked her across the back. Tense and disapproving, the little girl's father, Bill, warned with absolute certainty that Nate showed clear signs of developing into a violent teenager. Bill was a teacher who had worked in tough neighborhoods in Harlem and the Bronx, and he "knew" that kind of kid. By college, Nate had grown into a shy, cerebral literature major, with a small group of close friends who demonstrated against the war in Iraq. He loved violent movies and wrote his thesis on the horror-film genre. But as far as anyone knew, he hadn't hit anyone since before puberty. It can be hard to know, except in hindsight, when a child's unusual behavior is just a quirk with little long-term significance and when behaviors provide signposts for what's to come.

People mispredict children's futures all the time, and not everything can be determined. Exposing our mistaken assumptions about stability is an equally important part of the story that this book will tell. For instance, as new research shows, obstreperous behavior in early childhood does not predict academic difficulty in elementary and middle school. In one study, teacher and parent reports on three-year-olds were compared with various measures of school adjustment when those same children were in middle school. The children described as being difficult and loud and having low impulse control or in other ways being disruptive were no more likely to have problems in middle school than the other children. By the time she is in seventh grade, a rowdy three-year-old will not look different from other children, even though many teachers assume that the unruly preschooler is throwing up a red flag.

When my son Jake was three, his nursery-school teacher told me that he frequently seemed to have trouble finding something he wanted to do and sticking with it. It was a Montessori classroom, and the teacher set great store by the children's ability to choose a set of materials and play with them for a sustained period of time. It seemed to her that Jake was drifting through the room, picking up something for a few moments, putting it down, and moving on to something else. I began to wonder whether this meant he would lack self-direction and motivation. Would he be able to stick with things? Would he always need someone telling him what to do? His teacher's concerns sent me into a small tailspin, casting a slight shadow that I couldn't quite shake off.

A year later, in kindergarten, his teacher told me that she was concerned because he didn't pay attention when they sat at the table learning numbers and letters. A few weeks after I got this worrisome feedback, my mother visited his classroom for Grandparents' Day. She came home, shook her head, and said, "No wonder he drifts away during lesson time. It's boring."

I began to rethink my earlier worry. He was a child whose passions already consumed him. He could spend hours developing elaborate imaginary games involving his favorite superhero, Green Lantern. He spent whole summers directing his siblings and cousins in an extended and complex game of something they called "Baby Animal." Years later, he would direct them in even more complex films that he planned, filmed, and edited for large groups of friends and family to view. Meanwhile, he became an artist, working alone for months on end on a single sculpture. It wasn't his lack of self-direction that explained his vague wandering in the Montessori room. It was the lack of materials that really grabbed him.

Jake, like all of us, has had his struggles. But concentration, perseverance, and involvement are not among them. These were red herrings. The clues about his future were lying there, right next to the red herrings. They often are.

The Vital Clue

My youngest son, Sam, could already tell a wickedly funny dirty joke at two and a half. Precocious and outgoing, he stood up one night at a beach picnic and delivered a joke about three mice: "The three mice are sitting around talking about how tough and strong they are. The first one says, 'Ya know those poison pellets they put out for us to eat, so we'll die? I eat 'em up all the time. They're better'n candy.' The second mouse says, 'Well, you know those mousetraps they've left all over the house? I do bench presses with 'em every morning and night.' The third mouse gets up and starts to walk away. The two others call out, 'Hey, you didn't say anything. Where you going?'" At this point, my toddler turned and sauntered from the fire on his sixteen-inch legs, delivering the punch line over his shoulder, in his high, clear voice, " 'I'm going to fuck the cat.'"

My stepfather, a farmer who was raised a Methodist, laughed till tears squirted out of his eyes. And from that day on, he called Sam "The Reverend." Here's the catch. Sam, now a teenager, frequently gives public lectures around the country. His talks are inspirational, and in them, he urges young people to do good works in their communities. His grandfather saw his command of the audience and his urge to communicate. Although the nickname was a joke about a two-year-old child's profanity, it also captured a vital clue about a quality that would last through his adolescence and beyond.

Underneath our hopes and worries, we parents want to know which signs predict the future and which do not. We also want to know which of our own actions will have an influence on our children's lives and which will not. We're not the only ones trying to figure out the paths that connect our children's lives to their future. Psychologists have spent the past one hundred years trying to figure this out as well.

Children Are Clay

The American behaviorist John Watson famously claimed in the early twentieth century, "Give me a dozen healthy infants, well-formed, and my own specified world to bring them up in and I'll guarantee to take any one at random and train him to become any type of specialist I might select—doctor, lawyer, artist, merchant-chief, and, yes, even beggar-man and thief, regardless of his talents, penchants, tendencies, abilities, vocations, and race of his ancestors." He boldly asserted an idea that lay buried in the minds of many: that you could mold a child's future by the way you raised him. Countless people still believe this, although they might not even know it.

A few years ago, an old friend was complimenting me on my three sons, how well they had "turned out." She said this with some surprise and admitted that when they were little, she thought they were totally out of control. "You had no rules at all. Sam swore in the grocery store. He never wore clothes. They ate candy morning, noon, and night. You let them fight. I thought they were totally wild." I disagreed, suggesting that my rules might not have been about things like swearing or keeping their clothes on or saying thank you to a grown-up but had more to do with working hard at things and being kind. She thought about that for a moment and then said, "But what? Did you punish them when they weren't kind? Did they have a consequence when they didn't throw themselves into a project?" I was baffled. What was she talking about? Then I realized that her implicit model of development was showing through. Perhaps without even knowing it, she was basing her ideas on a behaviorist theory of child development: the traits that will emerge over time in a child are the ones that are regularly rewarded, while undesirable behaviors that are punished will disappear.

Although most psychologists no longer think Watson's undiluted behaviorism provides a good account of development, many researchers have shown that experiences in early life do shape the future adult—and not just in the obvious ways most of us assume. For instance, studies have shown that the number and kind of conversations children have with their parents when they are toddlers and preschoolers have a formative influence on the ability to read at five or six. Thus, we now know that a measure of a young child's family conversations allows us to predict something about that child's long-term academic success. But not every experience leaves an indelible impression on a child.

A friend who is a young mother of two recently confided in me, "You're not going to like this story. Finn came home from school the other day and walked straight through the kitchen onto the patio outside. He opened his book and began to read. No snack. No chatter. I finally asked him whether something had happened at school. He reluctantly admitted that he had gotten in trouble for throwing a candy wrapper across the room at snack time. It seems another little boy, something of a rabble rouser, had been egging Finn on to try to toss it into the garbage and make the basket. But Finn knows they aren't supposed to be rowdy at snack time. I don't want him to be the kind of child who gets into trouble with the teacher. He needs to learn how to control those issues. We are giving him a consequence. I told him how glad I was that he told me the truth but that there would be no play dates for a week."

She was right. I didn't like the story too much. That was partly because I think throwing a candy wrapper into a garbage can as if he were playing basketball is pretty harmless and was probably funny at the time. And it was partly because I think lively, exuberant children should be allowed their unpredictable moments. Mostly, however, parents can't mold a child's personality to fit their preconceived notions, no matter how consistent and carefully thought through their parenting style is.

Finn might be the kind of kid who likes rabble rousers and who periodically bursts out. Little his mother does will change those qualities. As I told her, "You can't make him exactly what you think he should be. You might be able to control him, but that doesn't mean you can control who he will become."

Children Are Seeds

Sometimes it is not that the conditions of a child's life hold the key to his or her future but rather that the child already contains his or her future self. In the old musical *The Fantasticks*, a frustrated father bewailing the way his almost grown child is acting thinks wistfully of how much more predictable and easy it is to grow a garden. He sings, "Plant a radish, get a radish." This view says that if you know what you start out with, you will have a good idea of what you'll get in the long run. As it turns out, there is some truth to this with human beings as well as with radishes.

Research has identified several characteristics that show up early in infancy or childhood and don't change much over a child's life. In contrast to Watson's view, these characteristics predict the future precisely because they are fairly impervious to features of the environment such as child rearing or schooling. Certain kinds of information about a baby provide us with a pretty good picture of what's in store for that child later on.

Take, for example, the way a young child plays. Whether a child prefers to turn small objects into characters and use them to enact a scenario or prefers to use small figures to make patterns tells us something about the kinds of conversations she will have when she is older and even what kind of reader she will be. Researchers have also found that the way a child plays offers a glimpse into her ability to think about other people's perspectives and imagine alternative outcomes to situations. One psychologist, Daryl Bem, has argued that a child's play style is the first indicator of his sexual orientation. Boys who play more like girls spend more time with girls, thus making boys the exotic objects of their erotic interest. Taken together, numerous studies have suggested that a child's play offers intriguing clues about specific aspects of her future self. Moreover, there is little a parent can do to affect her play style.

Some predictors are more mysterious than others. Consider Thomas Bouchard's research examining the role of biology in shaping a child's intelligence. Bouchard and his colleagues studied a group of twins who had been given up for adoption. They assessed the children's intelligence when they were in preschool, in middle school, and again in adolescence. The researchers also collected the IQ scores of the children's adoptive parents. When they were little, the children's IQ scores were more similar to those of their adoptive parents than to those of their twin siblings to whom they were genetically similar. However, by the time a set of twins were teenagers, their IQs were similar to each other and less like the IQs of their adoptive parents.

The most compelling explanation for this finding, and the one most researchers accept, is that IQ is driven by genes. In other words, a great deal of the variation among people's IQs can be traced to variation in the IQs of their parents. Very young children reflect the influence of the parents raising them, but as they age, the influence of their immediate environment wanes, and the genetic influence of their biological parents gains the upper hand. Along some dimensions, information about a biological parent provides an excellent forecast of the child's future.

The Alchemy of Genes and Environment

Yet even when we are able to identify genetic information about a child, it rarely provides a straightforward or simple blueprint for predicting psychological development. For instance, one important new study has found reliable links between the number of books, tools, art objects, and spaces for free play found in a child's home and a child's academic success in grade school. In this case, the physical environment, and what it might convey about interactions at home, is a crucial ingredient in shaping a child's intellectual capacity.

The current preoccupation with pinning down the relative contributions of nature and nurture has led to a mistaken notion that whatever is genetic is unchangeable and whatever is environmental is changeable. Yet research has consistently demonstrated that most attributes reflect a complex and dynamic interaction between genes and environment. The psychological effects of the environment can often be intractable, while expression of a genetic trait can be powerfully molded by experience.

When the Major League baseball player Jerry Hairston Jr. was two years old, his father, Jerry Hairston Sr., who had played in Major League baseball, and his grandfather, Sam Hairston, who had played in the Negro League, were having their photograph taken. Sam Hairston stopped the photographer. He said, "Bring Jerry Junior over here. I want my grandson in this picture. He's going to play for the Major Leagues someday." Sam Hairston was right. In 2009, Jerry Hairston Jr. was hired to play for the New York Yankees and helped them win the 2009 World Series.

What made Sam's prediction come true? He might have assumed that his grandson had inherited certain characteristics that would give him the same outstanding ability his father and grandfather clearly possessed. But which characteristics? A strong arm? Exceptional hand-eye coordination? Huge ambition? It's also just as likely that Jerry's baseball success came from the fact that he grew up in a family immersed in and dedicated to baseball. He probably saw, heard, and played more baseball than most children. His same strengths and talents, if he'd been born to a family of dancers, would have expressed themselves quite differently. And someone with those same strengths and talents whose family had no athletic ability or connections within the sports world might have ended up working as a gym teacher.

Unsimple Patterns

It's easy to think that some kids are lucky enough to have it all, while others will face one struggle after another. And it's true that during a child's first eighteen years, there are certain qualities that set the child on a happy pathway. Success and happiness often seem self-perpetuating, and so do failure and sadness. The cranky child stirs up conflict, often doing or saying something that rubs others the wrong way. He brings out the worst in others, and before you know it, he has every reason to believe that other people just aren't nice to him. The good-looking child who gets along easily with others and is sunny keeps encountering nice people who want to help him—enough to make anyone feel cheerful most of the time.

If you take even a cursory glance at the psychological characteristics found to be most stable, the ones that can be measured in a baby and remain pretty much the same over the next twenty years, it would be easy to think that forecasting a child's future is fairly straightforward. It might seem at first that a few good qualities predict everything wonderful, and a few limitations predict a lousy life. Take, for instance, the research on agreeability, a highly stable characteristic not hard to decipher. Agreeable people are easy to deal with, they take things in their stride, and they have a generally upbeat outlook on things. It seems obvious that children who are very agreeable, on the whole, are better off than children who are not. The agreeable child attracts friends. Having friends gives her a chance to become good at having friends, which ensures that she will always find friends. Being agreeable makes it easier to get along with your parents. And the better you get along with your parents, the more benefit you'll get from family life.

But development is a little more complex than that. We all know someone who has risen to the top of her field but spent years in unhappy love affairs. We all know someone who has a lasting, loving marriage but feels like a failure at work. Although a few characteristics are very important and surprisingly stable, each of us is made up of myriad qualities, and each of us lives in a particular set of circumstances that shape those qualities. Imagine three kids, none of whom makes friends easily. One of them has three close siblings and spends a lot of time with her family. The second is an only child whose parents don't have many friends of their own. The third, on closer inspection, does have strong friendships, but the friendships are rife with conflict. These three kids are on different paths leading to very different adult lives—and it's probably only the second child who will be lonely later in life.

This book is about figuring out which clues mean something and which do not. Every child's life contains patterns that point toward the future. But each child's pattern is quirky, not quite like anyone else's. This book offers a way to read the clues and decipher the pattern.

Each of the following chapters examines one central quality—an aspect of life that can seem hard to decipher when children are little and yet is of central importance as they grow up. Chapter 1 discusses how to spot your child's intelligence. This is a dimension of human behavior that has been hotly debated in recent years but almost always in the context of politics and educational policy. However, intelligence is not just a subject for policy makers and those concerned with social justice. Everyone values intelligence in their daily lives. It matters to all of us whether we are very smart or not so. This is as true for the bricklayer as it is for the mathematician.

Chapter 2 looks at the other quality that most worries parents during the early years: their child's ability to make friends. Like intelligence, sociability seems to have enormous stability, but, also as in the case of intelligence, there is more to making friends than meets the eye. There are different ways to make friends and different ways not to. Some young children spend a lot of time alone and will be fine as they grow up. Others might have an unhealthy friendship, throwing up a big red flag for later difficulties.

Chapter 3 examines a quality most people believe they value, even if you wouldn't know it from the way they behave: goodness. Very few parents feel that their children were just born bad, but if you have a child who is mean to others, cheats in sports, or lies to you, there might well come a day when you wonder whether she is going to be a good person when she grows up. Of course, there are different levels of goodness. Some people simply don't break rules and try not to be cruel, while far fewer of us consistently put other people's well-being ahead of our own. From a very early age, some children seem attuned to the needs of others, while others seem to have a keen sense of justice. But there are also several ways parents can have a powerful impact on how moral their children become.

In chapter 4, I head into somewhat trickier territory. Some of the things we yearn for and dread about our children's futures are not so easily defined or measured, but they matter a great deal. Even if we rarely admit it, most of us want our children to be successful, and we might consciously struggle with what that means. When my children were little, I imagined them doing great deeds. Now, as they enter adulthood and I peer at old age, I think of this somewhat differently. I care much less about their great deeds and not at all about fame or fortune. My longings have been tempered by age and the vagaries of real life. Now I want my sons to do well at something they love. What do I mean by doing well? Earning money, finding acknowledgment, and seeing the value of their labor. Mostly, I want them to be able to wake up most days happy to go to work. I want them to find pleasure in the work they do day in and day out. And I want them to earn money at whatever that is. The signs of someone bound for success are there in childhood if you know what to look for. But just as intriguing are the things you can do to encourage success, and these are not altogether obvious.

As your children enter adolescence, you begin to think about their love lives. My youngest son first fell in love at an early age. Sam was four when he was stricken by a six-year-old named Macy. He would blush every time her name was mentioned. He wrote her notes. He dreamily recalled their two-minute interactions on the playground. I myself almost got married at five, to a next-door neighbor, but at the last minute, I couldn't go through with the wedding. However, the roots of love don't lie in these early crushes. Love is a snowball that you begin making with your mother. Chapter 5 describes the nature of this snowball.

Parents I talk to worry about specific things—whatever has been troublesome for them or whatever has raised a red flag in their child's young life. But eventually, most parents will say, "I just want him to be happy." And life is agony for those of us who have watched our child be deeply unhappy or sad over a long period of time. The very worst moments of my life have been when one of my children was devastated by disappointment. If I could find a potion that would buffer my children against crushing defeat or give them the strength to rebound from setbacks, that's the potion I would pay big money for. Most of us want desperately to know what it would take to ensure that our children will be cheerful and content as they grow up. It turns out that although you cannot change a person's basic outlook on life, you can nudge it in a sunnier direction. I examine this in Chapter 6.

Two types of people will probably read this book. Some of you, I hope, are simply interested in the fascinating patterns that make us all who we are. You might even find yourself or your childhood in these pages. But many of you are reading this book because you have young children and want to know what lies ahead for them. You might also want to know what you can do to change the course of your child's future.

Children are born with certain powerful tendencies that shape their future. In addition, each child is born into a family, a neighborhood, and a set of circumstances that exert an equally powerful (and often unchangeable) influence. But none of this means that a child's path is set in stone. In each case, there are ways a parent can respond that will help a child draw on her strengths and minimize her weaknesses. Yet you cannot custom-tailor your child's personality.

In recent years, a dangerous myth has sneaked into our collective consciousness. It's a sophisticated modern version of John

Watson: we think that if we just do things well enough with our kids (use the right punishments, choose the right schools, encourage at the right moments), we can make them all into smart, successful, happy individuals. That is not the case. There is no perfect parent, and there is no recipe for parenting. Development, just like relationships, is complicated and unruly. Every gardener knows that you can put three plants in the same patch of the garden, feed them the same plant food, water them on the same schedule, and they'll still come out differently. The same is true of children. Thank God.

When babies in the United States are born, they are given a score, called the APGAR. That score rates them on several important dimensions (skin tone, sound of cry, and so on). In theory, the higher the score (from one to ten), the more likely it is that the child will thrive and grow in the days and weeks following birth. The APGAR score is an excellent predictor of early health. We don't have a psychological APGAR, especially not one that will predict a child's long-term development. Nor do babies come with labels that say, "Makes friends easily, smart but unmotivated." What we do have is a wide body of research that indicates the experiences and behaviors that are stable and those that are not. We know more than ever about which aspects of a child's early circumstances matter and how they matter. We know quite a bit about the things parents can do to influence their children, for better or for worse. There are plenty of good data telling us what clues predict a child's potential, when we shouldn't worry at all, and what we can do to nudge a child off a bad path and onto a healthier path. Each child's life contains clues that, when put together into a story, point the way toward her future.

1

Intelligence: As Smart As the Day You Were Born

At three, Stevie was jubilant and inventive, a lively little guy. He had a wiry, lithe body, brown, cheery eyes, and wide cheeks. In a photograph taken of him when he was four, he is lounging on the limb of a tall tree, his arms draped casually and comfortably over a branch. He looks spry and savvy, as if he knows what the photographer sees and gets a kick out of it. What doesn't show is any sign of the fierce intensity that later became such an integral part of his intelligence—for better and for worse.

His nursery-school teacher wrote this about him in his midyear evaluation: "Stevie loves to paint and enjoys experimenting with new techniques. Last week, he tried using two paint brushes at once. He is an avid block builder and often spends hours making complicated structures. He enjoys helping our janitor clean the room at the end of the day and almost always helps move the chairs and sweep the floor. Stevie needs to learn that teasing is not a good way to make friends."

A year later, the art teacher from the same school sent home a note to Stevie's mother: "I would like to talk to you briefly about Stevie. Until now, he has always loved arts and crafts so much. He's been one of the most prolific students in the woodworking area, but recently, he seems to have lost interest. He appears completely indifferent to what he makes. He seems like a different child—even his hand-eye coordination has slipped backward. He doesn't seem to have the interesting ideas for projects that he did just a few months ago, and his wood projects are carelessly put together."

Stevie's mother, Francis, was concerned. Highly intelligent, well educated, and extremely ambitious, Francis assumed that all three of her children would excel at school. It was a given, from her perspective, that her children had superior intellectual ability. Both she and her husband were smart and came from academically oriented families. Her husband was a well-regarded doctor in Boston, with a medical degree from Johns Hopkins University. Francis was a freelance book editor who had been the president of her class at a top women's college. They read constantly, discussed the news at dinner, went to art museums, and traveled. Stevie's older sister and brother were top students. What was wrong with him? Perhaps he just wasn't as smart as the rest of the family.

Who's Smart

Is there anyone who doesn't want his or her child to be smart? Whether you live in a family of schoolteachers or a neighborhood of factory workers and farmers, everyone values intelligence. There are few jobs where it doesn't matter, and most of us intuitively know that smarter people do better in all kinds of settings. They get more done, have better ideas, learn things more quickly, are better at their jobs, are often more fun to be with, and can solve unexpected problems.

Years ago, psychologist Robert Sternberg set out to learn what ordinary people think about intelligence. He sent his students at Yale out into the streets of New Haven to ask passersby what they thought were the essential characteristics that make someone intelligent. In particular, he wanted to know if people from different walks of life would agree or disagree about the qualities that make up smartness. It turned out that almost everyone found it easy to answer the question. To a great extent, at least within our culture, people tended to agree.

Whether we are highly educated or not, whether we work in offices or factories, almost all of us feel, even if we don't admit it, that we know whether someone is smart or not soon after meeting him or her. On what do we base this? We look for humor, savvy, verbal skill, competence within a domain, and a general air of "quickness." And as it turns out, our collective intuition about who is smart, and why, falls for the most part right in line with what psychological research has to say on the topic.

Herbert Crovitz, a social psychologist at Princeton University in the 1960s, used to tell his students, "Theories do two things: they account for the data, and they make people happy." As it turns out, theories of intelligence do one or the other but usually not both. And in the past two decades, theories that make people happy have gained some ground over theories that best account for the data. Many people in our society resist thinking of intelligence as a narrow, quantifiable characteristic. They find the traditional view of intelligence, conveyed by IQ tests, to be too restrictive. In my psychology classes at Williams, few students will say openly that intelligence is the ability to do math and comprehend texts, the very abilities that got them into a college like Williams. They worry that such a definition is elitist and are quick to point out that one can be intelligent in many ways. My students are like many across the country who are drawn to the idea that being "book smart" is only one way to be intelligent.

Howard Gardner, a psychologist at Harvard University, provided an alluring alternative to traditional views of intelligence when he published *Frames of Mind* in 1984. In it, he railed against the narrow-minded idea that the full range of people's mental acuity could be measured by something as academic as a traditional IQ test. He argued that there are not one but seven kinds of intelligence (logico-mathematical, spatial, verbal, musical, bodily kinesthetic, interpersonal, and intrapersonal) and that there are a range of ways to express intelligence. A child who is wonderful at dance but has a small vocabulary and trouble with numbers would be considered to have high bodily kinesthetic intelligence but low logico-mathematical and verbal intelligence.

As Gardner's idea began to take hold, teachers embraced the idea that they could use it to identify the particular kind of intelligence each child had. Teachers felt that Gardner's scheme helped them fine-tune their curriculum to fit the particular kind of intelligence each child possessed. As the theory got diluted within schools, some teachers simply used the idea of multiple intelligences as a way to help each child feel smart, even when he or she didn't excel at traditional school tasks. This egalitarian conception of intelligence has taken hold like wildfire, and in every town in America, you can hear teachers talk about the specific kinds of intelligence their students possess. "He might not be good at math, but he sure is smart when he's on the basketball court." "She struggles with English class, but she's so artistic; her visual intelligence is outstanding." Or the most common form: "He might be book-smart, but he's street-dumb." The theory of multiple intelligences makes people happy. But does it explain the data?

The Smartness Thermometer

Ever since psychologists began formally measuring things, they've been trying to measure intelligence. Until Howard Gardner introduced *multiple intelligences* into the common lexicon, people tended to use the term *IQ* as a stand-in for *intelligence.* The intelligence quotient is a mathematical expression, devised in France at the turn of the twentieth century by Alfred Binet. He developed the test to help the French school system identify children who were retarded or significantly slower than others in their age group. His goal was to make sure that "slower" children were not punished for their inability to learn. The original IQ (as well as almost all subsequent forms of it) was based on a very simple concept in psychological assessment: Ask children of a certain age a series of questions. The number of questions they get correct is then divided by their chronological age. Thus, although a given ten-year-old might answer more questions than a seven-year-old, the younger child might well have a higher intelligence quotient. Using the test to compare children depends on a much-trusted practice among researchers: norming. This means that in order to evaluate a given child's IQ, you have to compare it to the average (mean) score of children that age. As a result, each child of a given age is being compared with what is considered normal or typical of all the other children in that age group.

What kinds of questions do IQ tests involve? The test is divided into several components, each asking questions that tap into a specific kind of thinking. In one part, children are asked to say what is missing from a picture (a door knob from a picture of a room that includes a door, for instance). Another component requires children to recall a string of numbers. Another involves moving around a collection of colored blocks so that they form a pattern presented on a card. Another asks children to answer questions about famous books, presidents, the weather, and different parts of the country. Although the test has been criticized for favoring children who live certain kinds of lives (if a child looks at a picture of someone riding a horse and doesn't know that the missing piece is the stirrup, it might well be because the child has lived her whole life in the inner city, with little access to books about riding). On the other hand, many of the questions test more content-free abilities, such as memory span. However, even these supposedly content-free questions might well favor children with certain kinds of experiences.

In the early 1960s, Sylvia Scribner and her colleagues set out to show the invisible bias in intelligence tests. Scribner was sure that something about school experience was helping some children do better even on parts of IQ tests that had been considered relatively culture-free. Her previous work in nonliterate communities had shown her that children who go to school regularly seem to acquire, without even realizing it, specific techniques that might help them do well on the kinds of memory tasks used in IQ tests. Sure enough, when she and her colleagues asked students to recall a fairly long list of words, such as *apple, banana, desk, hat, plum, shoe, chair,* and *sweater,* the children who had missed a lot of school days because of poverty, migrant work schedules, and segregation seemed to struggle. Scribner knew, from her literacy work, that learning to read leads people to conceptualize in a different way. Thus, the school children were using categories to chunk the items, making it easier to remember them: first the fruits, then all the furniture, then all the tools. Unschooled children didn't have this strategy at their disposal. However, when Scribner provided the category names ("Tell me all the kinds of fruit on the list, now all the pieces of furniture, now the clothing"), the children with little schooling performed similarly to the others. It seemed, then, that memory span per se did not differ between the two groups. Instead, what differed was the savvy to use category labels as a mnemonic, a skill found in school.

Scribner's research, which was really so simple, dealt a serious blow to the notion that any aspect of the IQ test, even the most seemingly culture-free part, was the same for all children. However, for all of its weaknesses and built-in biases, it taps into something pretty steady and real. But it's been hard for psychologists and lay people to put their finger on just what the test measured.

That is, until psychologist Joseph Fagan published a paper in the 1980s arguing that traditional IQ tests, the kind developed by Binet and modified by David Wechsler, created the illusion of coherence where there wasn't really any. That is, traditional IQ tests measure concrete knowledge ("What is the capital of Pennsylvania?") with more basic processing skills (remembering a list of words). Researchers have found again and again that while each person taking the test might do better on some parts of the test than others (For instance, I always do terribly at creating a visual pattern to match a picture, but I do well at analogies), there is, generally speaking, a lot of consistency—in other words, a high correlation between components of the test. The person who gets a higher score than others her age on one part is likely to get a higher score than others on most of the other parts of the test. It is easy to see how scientists, and ultimately the general public, came to think of this test as actually measuring a particular quality of mind or even a physical part of the brain.

Psychologists have even given this imagined underlying quality a name: *g* (for "general intelligence"). If you're high in g, you are smart, and if you are high in g, you are likely to do well on many components of the test. Fagan didn't disagree that intelligence might ultimately be a single quality of mind, but he wanted a test that would actually focus on just that quality, the ability that produces g. So he zeroed in on the single characteristic he thought underlay the myriad of abilities we push together and call intelligence.

Fagan argued that what makes one person do better on an IQ test and seem smarter in real life as well is what he called speed of processing. We are all familiar with that concept from our computers: the faster the processor, the more the computer can do. It's the same with the human brain. The faster it can take in information, the more information it can take in. Hence two children might be exposed to the same environment, but the one who can take in more will know more. Fagan's point was that speed of processing is a much simpler, more precise, and more value-free characteristic, which might actually explain the correlation between items on traditional IQ scores. But how do you directly measure something like speed of processing?

This is pretty easy, as it turns out. From birth, babies stare at something until they become used to it—in other words, until they have processed it. Then they look for new stimuli. Fagan showed babies two pictures projected onto a screen in front of them. Then he measured how long it took them to absorb (become familiar with, or process) the first picture before turning their heads to look at the second picture. Of course, it's possible that some children simply have shorter attention spans than others. And yet the important thing about Fagan's test was that there was enormous consistency between his infant test and more traditional IQ tests. Babies who processed visual information quickly on Fagan's test also did well on IQ tests when they were in elementary school.

Fagan's IQ test cannot be bought over the counter, but that doesn't mean parents aren't looking for signs of their babies' intellectual potential. Most parents think their baby is smart unless they see signs of trouble. In particular, there are two points when parents tend to worry about their children's intellectual acumen: when they learn to talk and when they start getting evaluated in school.

Stevie learned to talk at the usual age for a third child and a boy. By the time he was two, he could name many familiar objects, and by the time he was two and a half, he could speak in phrases, and he learned new words rapidly. So far, he seemed as smart as the other bright pennies in his family. He only began hitting a snag when he went to school. When your child has trouble with schoolwork, it's only natural to wonder, even if you don't admit it, if it's a sign that he's not as smart as you had hoped.

Recently, my husband was skiing at our local slope in Great Barrington, Massachusetts. It was a Wednesday, and usually on weekdays, the only other skiers are local people sneaking in a few hours or children coming en masse from one of our nearby public schools. But on this day, my husband found himself riding up on a chairlift with a man in his late forties and his twelve-year-old son. They had taken time off from work and school to celebrate the day the son was adopted from Korea. As they glided up the side of the mountain, the boy and his father began discussing what trail they would ski on next.

The boy said, "Let's try the triple after this."

The father answered, somewhat uncertainly, "OK. But I am not sure I know how to get over there."

The boy quickly replied, "I know how to get there."

The father said skeptically, "How could you possibly know? We only have been here once before, and that was a year ago."

The boy answered, "I memorized the map."

The father smiled and shook his head. "How is it that you can memorize a whole map so easily, but you can't seem to do math in school?"

The boy said, "Because school is boring."

Here was a clear example of a child whose intellectual abilities weren't in sync with school tasks. When a child has trouble in school, does it mean he isn't bright?

Do Smart Kids Get Good Grades, or Do Good Grades Create Smart Kids?

Here we come to a dicey problem. On the one hand, school success is caused by intelligence. If two children come from the same socioeconomic background, have roughly similar childhood situations, and attend the same school, the one who is smarter is likely to do better—in school and in life beyond school—than the one who is less smart. And yet the caveats to this prediction are important. Some very bright children don't do well in school because they have specific learning disabilities, emotional problems get in their way, or, like the boy on the chairlift, they find school boring. In any of these cases, a very bright child can underperform in school.

On the other hand, if your son scores well on a math test when he is five or six, he is likely to get good grades in fifth grade. Equally important, if he scores better than most of the children in his kindergarten class, he is likely to get better grades than his classmates in fifth grade. The research is very clear on this, and it should come as no surprise. A child who is bright and comfortably applies himself to a math test as a five-year-old is not only going to be just as bright when he is eleven years old, but he is, in all likelihood, still going to be interested in doing well on tests, able and eager to focus on the task at hand and follow instructions. The Peabody Picture Vocabulary test, used to assess the verbal skills of preschoolers, is a very good indicator of a child's grades in elementary school. There is no mysterious trail leading from a good evaluation in kindergarten to high grades in middle school. The same abilities and motivation that led to the good kindergarten performance also explain the good algebra grade. But do those good scores in preschool and high grades in elementary school tell us anything about a child's intelligence?

The answer is a bit complicated. Early math and verbal scores predict later academic success, and academic success is correlated with IQ. But that doesn't necessarily mean that the five-year-old with the good math score is going to be smarter than the five-year-old who doesn't get as high a math score. For instance, some children do well in school because they are highly attuned to the expectations of adults—they are dutiful, eager to please, and able to focus on achieving the things expected of them in school.

Take, for instance, a young biologist named Elise. She graduated magna cum laude from an Ivy League university and received her PhD in sociology from a top graduate program. She was awarded tenure at one of the best colleges in the country when she was only thirty-two years old because she was successful as a teacher and did high-quality research that got published in the better journals in her field. However, she insists that this is much less because of her intellectual powers than her determination to do everything she needed to succeed. When she was a child, her parents made it clear that they expected good grades. Her mother insisted on looking over every assignment before it was handed in and made her fix mistakes. She had no interest in challenging the assignments or trying something outside the requirements. She was aggravated when other students distracted the teacher from the planned lecture. She hated vague assignments. But she was diligent and highly attuned to figuring out what each teacher wanted from her. She was a perfectionist and had great attention for detail. Good wasn't good enough for her. She felt compelled to do whatever it took to get the highest grade. She behaved well in class. She was a teacher's dream. At each stage of her career, she replicated that approach.

Robert Sternberg, the psychologist who asked the man on the street what it meant to be smart, has also argued that there are three kinds of intelligence: analytic, practical, and creative. He would probably find that Elise scored high in two of his three kinds: analytic (her ability to learn information and use it to solve new problems) and practical (she knew how to figure out what was required of her to reach her goal). In the end, that practical intelligence is as powerful for Elise as her analytic intelligence. But the point is, Elise's experiences in school pushed her forward. By the time someone is in college, it's not always easy to figure out whether academic success is rooted in intelligence or in earlier academic success. In other words, being smart might cause children to do well at school, but doing well at school also causes children to continue doing well at school.

For many children, the desire and ability to conform to expectations is as big a part of their success in school as their intellect and might well carry them even farther. Academic success tends to be self-perpetuating. And by the same token, the child who does not do well in school might continue to have trouble. She might not do her homework. She might question every assignment. She might skip classes. She might act surly in school. All of these qualities can affect her grade, and yet she might in fact be very smart. On the one hand, you can say she is bright but just doesn't do well in school. However, over time, a child who is not treated as if she is bright might begin to function as if she is not bright. As a result, by the time she is an adult, she might not have the knowledge and skills she could have acquired by participating more fully in school, which in fact would allow her to do the things intelligent people do. In other words, by the time a person is thirty years old, her functional intellect is no longer simply a matter of potential—it's a matter of what she has actually learned and done.

IQ might or might not capture all we would wish about the ineffable but powerful quality we call intelligence. However, it predicts a lot, and it's surprisingly stable—it doesn't change much over a person's lifetime.

The Resilient IQ

One of the simplest and most compelling facts about IQ tests is that the measure is so sturdy. If you give a child a proper IQ test (say, the Stanford-Binet or the Wechsler) when he is five and test him again when he is eighteen, he is likely to get a similar score. More important, if you give a group of ten children the test when they are five, each of them is likely to get the same score, in relation to the others, when he or she is eighteen. In other words, even though children know more as they get older and change in significant ways (double their size, learn to read and write and do math, and acquire whole bodies of knowledge about topics such as baseball, dinosaurs, car mechanics, or American history), whatever it is that is captured by an IQ test remains pretty much the same. Kids think they get smarter in school. They don't. They just acquire knowledge and skills.

One of the most thorough and elegant demonstrations of the stability of IQ was conducted by a group of scientists in New Zealand in the late 1960s, although that is not what they set out to study. Obstetric medicine and care had improved dramatically in the previous decades. Many more babies were surviving childbirth, particularly babies who experienced problems just prior to and during delivery. Doctors began to worry, however, that these children were prone to greater problems as they grew up. Perhaps by decreasing infant mortality, new medical practices had led to increased childhood morbidity. The theory was that the problems that might have caused difficulties during birth were now creating problems later down the road when these babies were a bit older. In an effort to track the well-being of this new population of babies, a group of doctors and psychologists in New Zealand decided to try to follow a large cohort of babies all born in one place at one time. The researchers followed the fate of 1,037 babies, all born at the Queen Mary Hospital in Dunedin between April 1, 1972, and March 31, 1973. Almost all of the babies chosen for the study have been visited, observed, and tested every few years right up to the present. Many of those babies now have babies of their own who are being observed and interviewed. One of the extraordinary features of this endeavor is that so many of the children remained in the study.

As anyone who has ever done longitudinal research will tell you, the hardest part is keeping your subjects in the study. Most studies of this kind suffer from attrition. Say a scientist recruits one hundred babies for her study. By the time the babies are ten years old, fifty of the families might have moved away, twenty more might refuse to be part of follow-up assessments, and before you know it, the researcher has only thirty subjects to work with and, as a result, can say almost nothing about broad trends. So it is particularly impressive that when the Dunedin kids were twenty-one years old, almost all of them were still around and happy to answer the researchers' questions, take the required tests, and participate in interviews. Ninety-three percent participated in a daylong assessment. Only nineteen refused to participate, and another nine couldn't be tracked down.

In the Dunedin study, doctors were able to learn a great deal about the health patterns of the children as they grew up. They began to see which kinds of illnesses were the sequelae of improved pre- and perinatal care. But as it turned out, they also learned quite a lot about the children's intelligence.

They first assessed the children's IQ when they were young, as part of a complete battery of baseline measures. Then, to be consistent, they measured the children's IQ every three years, through adolescence and early adulthood. And here's the simple but startling fact: when it came to performance on an IQ score, the overwhelming majority of the children (930 out of 1,037) stayed pretty much the same. The researchers first thought that they had found straightforward evidence that IQ does not change. However, the beauty and difficulty of large data sets is that you always get some noise.

The psychologists couldn't ignore the 107 children whose IQ seemed to fluctuate wildly across a twelve-year time span. Was this evidence, after all, that IQ is not so stable? To complicate matters more, the fluctuations in children's scores did not follow a simple pattern. Some scores dropped precipitously, while others seemed to surge upward. Perhaps IQ was more malleable than people thought. Then the psychologists took a closer look.

They realized that most of the kids whose scores got markedly better or worse during the study actually ended up about where they started. Among those 107 were children whose scores rose between the time they were five and eight but then dropped between the age of eight and adolescence. By the time those 107 children were in their teens, they had almost all returned to their original baseline scores. If you had tested a child only twice, you might see a surprising gain or loss in IQ. You might think you had found proof that children can lose their intelligence or get smarter. But the beauty of the Dunedin study was that researchers showed that over the long haul of childhood and adolescence, while there might be peaks and valleys, kids pretty much test where they began. If a child's IQ stays the same, the question is why. Is it because, like eye color, intelligence is inherited, or is it because, like taste in food, what you experience when you are little becomes imprinted on you? Just the fact that something is resilient doesn't tell you much about where it comes from.

Anyone who has adopted a child knows the quiver of uncertainty, however subtle, that makes you wonder whether your baby will "turn out" like you or like the biological parent neither of you will ever see. Karen had given birth to two children with her first husband and now wanted to raise a child with her second husband, a powerful creative director of television programs. They adopted Maude before she was even born. Karen was there for the birth and cut the umbilical cord, wrapping Maude up and giving her her first bottle. Neither Maude nor Karen saw the biological mother again. When Maude was little, she was full of energy, and she learned her first words before she was fourteen months old. She had a sparkle in her eye and a loud, happy laugh, and she seemed surprisingly like her father. She even looked like him. They doted on Maude, filling her life with toys, interesting trips, stories, friends, good food, and books. When Maude was a preschooler, she seemed every bit her parents' daughter. So Karen and her husband weren't sure what to make of it when Maude began to have trouble in school. She loved the work, was eager to try everything, and carried herself like someone who thinks she is at the top of her class. Then it was time for her to be tested, because her parents wanted to send her to a private high school, which required an aptitude test. Although she had seemed so bright and adept during her first years of school, her parents were confused and dismayed to learn that Maude's scores were very low, much lower than their own or than those of Karen's biological children from her previous marriage. Although in so many ways she was like her parents, her IQ was not. How could this be?

The most compelling explanation comes from a study of twins separated at birth and given up for adoption. When these children were tested in early childhood, their IQs tended to match the IQs of their adoptive parents. The subjects were more like the people they lived with than the people with whom they shared genes. But by the time the children in the study had become teenagers, they more closely resembled their identical twins than they did their adoptive parents. The researchers' explanation was that environmental influences of parents temporarily lifted the children's IQs but that this influence didn't last. As the children aged, the expression of their intelligence seemed less dependent on what was going on around them day to day (the conversations people had, the activities they were encouraged to engage in, the kinds of schools they went to). Instead, it seemed that biology was taking over, and their IQs inched toward a level that much more closely resembled the long-lost siblings with the exact same genetics, even when the two had been raised in very different circumstances. Maude probably had an IQ more similar to the IQs of her biological parents than to those of her adoptive parents, but the disparity only showed up as she entered adolescence.

The research on IQ tells a pretty unambiguous story: children's IQs and the intelligence IQ tests measure are stable and heavily determined by a child's genes. And yet, as we have seen, there are factors that can either temporarily disguise a child's true intellectual ability or in some way inflate or depress it. If you think your child is more intelligent than tests or academic performance suggest, what might explain the discrepancy?

What Gets in the Way

Many years ago, when I was teaching at a fairly progressive independent school in New York City, there was a four-year-old boy, Alec, who came in for the usual interview and admissions assessment—a combination of a shortened IQ test and some open-ended play in the admissions office. Alec had been touted as very bright, and his parents were sure this was the right school for him. And yet he did miserably in all aspects of the admission process. He did not get a high score on the test, he was uncommunicative in the interview, and his playing seemed immature, lacking the kind of complexity that is often seen as an expression of intelligence. Alec was denied admission. However, a teacher at the school later learned from a friend of the family that when Alec had gotten home that day, he had complained bitterly to his mother about his sore feet. It turned out his mother had mistakenly put him in a pair of shoes that were two sizes too small. The poor little boy had spent the whole time at the new school thinking about his aching feet, not old enough to realize that he could let someone know something was wrong. His performance in that interview was not a good measure of his real abilities. Anyone's intellect can be temporarily masked by some glitch of circumstance, and in the long run, such momentary setbacks won't alter the path of a child's intellectual development. A very smart teenager who does poorly on the SAT because he has a headache will do well the next time he takes it. And yet some glitches can have a long-lasting impact.

Hank, a four-and-a-half-year-old boy with bright red hair and an impish face, was exactly the kind of bright child bound to get into trouble at school. He had lots of physical energy and enormous physical skill. Let him outside with some mud puddles or put him near a climbing toy, and he'd be happy for hours. The first time he saw snow (on a visit to Massachusetts from California, where he lived), he spent four hours outside inventing different routes from the top of the hill to the bottom and constructing different kinds of jumps for the sled. If anyone handed him a complicated toy that involved moving parts, he would focus on it quietly for long stretches of time, trying out the different ways the toy could work. But he was also the little guy who unwittingly knocked over the glass of juice at the lunch table every single day. He often got chastised by other parents for things like pushing another child off the sandbox ledge in a moment of exuberance, although he did it not from anger but out of boisterousness. He was the little boy who tapped his pencil against the edge of the desk as the grown-up read a story aloud, fidgeting restlessly in his seat. As his mother said about him, "He can be rough, but he's never mean."

Hank had all the signs of high intellect. He took in information quickly and synthesized bits and pieces of knowledge he'd gathered from different settings. He could look at a picture of a shape and make the same shape using small plastic pieces, create a new kind of slingshot from branches, and devise a new set of rules for a dart game. As Howard Gardner would say, Hank could solve problems and make things that were interesting and valuable to the people around him. And Hank wasn't always fidgety and restless. He listened carefully when he was interested in something and seemed to zero in on the important information. A child like Hank shows his intelligence in slivers, like small fish darting through a stream of more unruly behavior. The signs can be easy to miss. Once when he was two, he sat on a couch watching television with his aunt Laura. She leaned toward him to ask a question about the cartoon on the screen but saw that he was gazing intently at her mouth.

"Laura, you're old," he said.

She laughed, a little thrown. "What?"

"You're old. Your teeth are lello. Lello means old."

It would be easy to miss the mental acuity that went into his logic, which in form resembled a syllogism. Yellow is a sign of age. Laura's teeth were yellow. Laura must be old. Hank's ability to analyze information and think logically was a clear sign of his sharp intellect. But those flashes of intellect were often obscured by his bouncy, slightly clueless energy.

He was just the kind of kid who could seem naughty and over time, because of that, be seen as not smart by a teacher. One day when Hank was four and a half, his aunt was trying to help him put his winter boots on. She kneeled down in front of him. As she began to tug at the first boot, Hank, looking down at her bent head, began to tug at her hair.

"Hank," she said in a slightly exasperated tone, her head bent in the effort of getting on the boot, "that hurts. Stop pulling my hair."

Hank tugged harder.

"Hey," Aunt Laura said sharply. "Cut it out."

Hank kept a steady tension on her hair for another two seconds before lowering his hands.

"Listen, Buddy. I'm helping you get ready to go sledding. But what you're doing really hurts." An experienced mom, Aunt Laura looked him right in the eye. "If you pull my hair one more time, I won't help you put your boots on."

Slight, lovable, goodwilled Hank looked her steadily in the eye and gave a hard yank.

One can easily see how behavior like this alienates grown-ups. Once alienated, they back away from a child, offering less help, less encouragement, less of the very attention that seems to help children make the most of their potential. It is easy to see that teachers would be aggravated by Hank's physical energy. When other children were happily filling in the questions on a worksheet, Hank would be looking out the window at the bird fight happening on a limb of a nearby tree.

Most teachers and many parents worry when a child is obstreperous. The young child who won't sit down when the teacher rings her little bell, who stares off into space when the other children are filling in worksheets, who talks during a group discussion or jumps up and starts fiddling with the thermometer during a meeting can look like trouble. But on its own, unruliness in kindergarten does not predict academic trouble later on. Research shows that all other things being equal, these children are just as successful as other children when it comes to grades in elementary school. However, those kinds of unruliness can lead to trouble if they frustrate teachers enough.

Years ago, in a pivotal demonstration of how this can play out, Harvard social psychologist Robert Rosenthal and his collaborator Eleanor Jacobsen, a schoolteacher, showed how malleable a teacher's view of a child really is. Rosenthal and Jacobsen gave children in a Chicago public school a paper-and-pencil test that is closely correlated with IQ. However, they told the teachers that it was part of a subtle and obscure test of children's thinking. They then mentioned casually that some of the children were real intellectual "bloomers," likely to make substantial intellectual strides in the coming months. Amazingly, those children, who had actually been chosen at random, did make significant intellectual strides.

When all of the kids were tested again at the end of the year, the children who had been tagged as "bloomers" had made significant gains on the IQ test. So, lesson number one: when teachers expect children to be smart, for whatever reason, children often become smarter. It's important to note that Rosenthal and Jacobsen spent a great deal of time in those classrooms and could detect no obvious or concrete difference in the way those bloomers were treated. In other words, there was no simple explanation for the phenomenon—teachers didn't give harder work to those kids or spend more time at their desks or even call on them more often. The expectations adults have of a child are, it seems, both enormously powerful and somewhat invisible.

You will recall that when Joseph Fagan tested the speed with which infants could absorb visual information, he had an excellent idea of how smart they would seem as seven-year-olds. But Fagan's test had an advantage over the more traditional scores. Whereas IQ tests seemed to favor certain ethnic and racial groups, Fagan's test did not. Some babies were quicker to turn their attention from one picture to another, but there were no differences as a function of what racial group a baby belonged to. This stands in stark contrast to the persistent finding that the average IQ score of a group of black children is almost always lower than the average IQ score of a group of white children. Keep in mind that the overall correlation between Fagan's test in infancy and more traditional IQ scores when the children were older was high. Yet the correlation did not hold up for all of the children. Either some of the white children were doing better as they got older, or some of the black children were doing worse as they got older, hence the group differences among older children, where none was found in infancy. What might explain this confusing pattern?

We're beginning to find out why the IQ test might be a weaker measure of intelligence for black children than it is for white children. In the past ten years or so, psychologists have learned something very important about what might depress the IQ scores of some students and how to remedy it. The gap between the average score of a group of black students and the average score of a group of white students has diminished somewhat in recent years. But it hasn't gone away or even halved. There are only two explanations for this, broadly speaking. The one promoted by Charles Murray and Richard Herrnstein in their book *The Bell Curve* is that underlying differences in ability account for the gap, and nothing will change that. But many psychologists (as well as geneticists) doubt this explanation, not simply because it is politically and socially distasteful but rather because it represents bad science. To begin with, we know next to nothing, so far, about the genetic underpinnings of intelligence. Intelligence might well be the expression of a cluster of abilities and skills caused by a wide variety of genes, rather than a single attribute determined by a single gene. Second, we know very little about the relationship between the genetic basis of race and intelligence. In other words, even though skin color is inherited and IQ also seems to a great extent to be inherited, those two facts tell us nothing about whether intelligence and skin color have any underlying genetic relationship. The difference in IQ between racial groups might be a result of something altogether different. This point is so important and so often misunderstood that it is worth illustrating with a few examples.

If you compare men who have had heart attacks with those who haven't, it turns out that the average height in the group who had heart attacks is lower than the average height of those who haven't. Does this mean that short men have more heart attacks than tall men? Does it mean that the gene for height comes hand-in-hand with a gene for blood pressure, cholesterol levels, or a predisposition to heart attacks? No. It means that older men are more likely to get heart attacks than younger men, and men shrink as they age. So what looks like a clue to an underlying genetic link is, in fact, nothing of the kind. Take a second example. People who live in temperate climates tend to get more colds in the winter. Thus, many of us come to believe that the cold weather actually causes sickness. Climate and colds are related, but not because one causes the other. Instead, one leads to the other. In cold weather, we spend more time with other people in close, unventilated spaces. Our immune systems become weakened because of the stress of staying warm. The winter weather does help explain our increased sickness, but it doesn't cause the common cold. Having black skin might mean you are less likely to get a high score on an

IQ test, but that doesn't mean that black people are not as smart as white people.

We are a long way from knowing what it is exactly about intelligence that is genetic and just as far from knowing what gene or genes might explain a person's intelligence. But imagine that you are a researcher who doubts that the lower IQ scores of black children can be explained as a genetic difference. What would you do? You'd begin to try to identify other explanations for the difference. And that is just what researchers have been doing in the past fifteen years or so.

Some of the causes of group differences in IQ have been hidden in plain sight, just waiting to be identified. Claude Steele, from Stanford University, knew that stereotypes not only influence the behavior of the stereotyper, but they also have a huge effect on those who have been stereotyped. He reasoned that a powerful social stereotype affects people in the stereotyped group, even when no stereotyping or prejudice is active or present. In other words, stereotyping is "in the air" and shapes people all the time. When it comes to students taking important tests that measure their ability and might determine their future, the threat of potential stereotyping is particularly menacing. Steele and his colleagues reasoned this way: black students might worry, when in a testing situation, that if they do not do well, they will strengthen people's erroneous stereotypes. Worrying about this keeps them from doing their best on the test. In the kind of demonstration every researcher longs for, Steele tried a very simple manipulation. He removed the threat by telling students at the beginning of the test that this particular test had never shown any differences between groups. He learned a few startling and important things. Removing the threat in that simple way dramatically improved the scores of black students taking the test.

Thus, while an IQ test might in fact accurately reflect a white student's intellectual ability, it might not be as good a measure of a black student's intellect. The fact that the black students' test scores could be improved with such a simple yet specific intervention is quite stunning. Since Steele's early studies showing this, researchers have followed up with equally important findings.

Steven Spencer and his colleagues reasoned that even if you assume that black students are not showing their true potential in a standard testing situation, that doesn't explain why those students continue to underperform in school. Spencer and his colleagues decided to try to remove the "threat in the air" from students' ongoing academic experiences. If those kinds of threats make it hard for a student to show his true ability on a test, why wouldn't they also hinder his performance in classes throughout school? Spencer contacted black students who had been accepted at Yale and told them that if they came to Yale, they would be part of an honors group within the college. During the next four years at Yale, the students in this group spent time together, talked about the issues facing black students on campus, and stayed connected. He tracked their success at Yale, compared with other black students with similar entering test scores who were not included in the group. Lo and behold, the black students in the group fared better when it came to grades than the others.

In a second version of this intervention, conducted at a junior high school in Connecticut, students were asked four times during the year to write a story about a personal value. These students also did better than students matched on race and test scores who did not write the essays. It seems that by supporting a minority student's sense of identity, you reduce the impact of stereotype threat.

Many students might not show their true potential during a test of their cognitive ability. Black students are not the only ones to experience stereotype threat. And there might be other invisible threats that depress a child's expression of cognitive ability. For those who run schools and design college admissions requirements, identifying those kinds of inhibitors and removing them are hugely important. But here's the twist: barring any powerful interventions, the same conditions that might influence a child's test score or his apparent intellectual ability when he is four years old are likely to go on shaping him throughout childhood.

People tend to think that internal characteristics are constant and somewhat impervious to change—the more biologically rooted the characteristic, the more resilient we think it is. For instance, although it is something of a fashion for adults to trace their neuroses to the kinds of parents they had, you rarely hear anyone suggest that the relationship a baby has with his mother might have something to do with how smart he will be. Yet it turns out that it does. Recent studies have shown that babies who are cuddled, touched, and even massaged as infants become smarter than babies who are not handled this way. Adele Diamond, eager to pinpoint exactly how important cuddling and touch might be to healthy development, found that keeping a mother rat from licking her pups for even an hour increases the pups' stress, causing the release of hormones that seem to inhibit their ability to learn. Simply put, rat pups who aren't licked are not as smart as pups who are. Does this mean that the more you cuddle your child, the smarter she will be? No, but it does mean that certain kinds of deprivation depress or limit a child from realizing her full potential. These kinds of studies remind us that what seems purely biological is not. Even the most intrinsic capacities are influenced by specific experiences, and biology is not set in stone. The inverse is also true. It would be wrong to assume that environment is always flexible. Biological characteristics can be changed, but environmental influences are often resistant to change.

As you will recall, psychologists Rosenthal and Jacobsen tested all of the children before identifying some as intellectual bloomers. Some of the children who had not been in the randomly selected group labeled as bloomers did make gains over the year in their IQ scores. These children were rated less favorably by the teachers at the end of the year. Teachers don't like to have their expectations violated. Again and again, educator Lisa Delpit encountered white teachers frustrated by the unruliness of their black students. Behavior that might otherwise be interpreted as engaged and enthusiastic is seen by the teacher through the lens of low expectations. Suddenly, an eagerly waving hand becomes a sign that a child cannot contain herself. A long, enthusiastic story about an adventure at home becomes a sign of a chaotic family or evidence that the child hasn't learned at home how to construct a good story. When a teacher responds to a child as if she is incapable, it is not simply that the child might feel bad about herself. The teacher often doesn't give that child the feedback she needs to expand her skills.

Sarah Michaels provides devastating examples of this in her research looking at how teachers respond to the stories children tell at circle time. When white children in a Boston classroom told stories, they conformed to the white teacher's idea of what a story should be. As a result, the teacher would nod and smile as the child spoke and then ask interested questions such as "Really, and what did your parents say when you popped out from behind the couch?" or "Did your brother know he was going to be alone in the boat?" Just the kind of questions that would lead the child to try to expand her thinking skills by filling in details, adding linguistic complexity, and providing perspective. On the other hand, when black children told stories that didn't fit the teacher's model of a story, the teacher would frown and hesitate. Sometimes, not knowing how to build on such an unfamiliar type of story, a teacher would say nothing at all. In some cases, rather than asking questions or showing interest, the teacher would simply correct the child's grammar. Michaels's research showed how these seemingly casual activities were providing white children but not black children with opportunities to expand their skills. It is easy to see how a teacher's mindset can, in turn, shape and mold a child's ensuing academic experience. So, although IQ is sturdy, negative expectations can become self-fulfilling prophecies. Race is one big source of negative expectations. So is poverty. On the face of it, research seems to indicate that rich kids are, on the whole, smarter than poor kids. But if you dig a little into the research, a slightly different picture emerges.

Are Rich Kids Smarter?

Charles Murray of the infamous *Bell Curve* argued that smarter people have better jobs and make more money. Thus, from his perspective, it is not that wealth leads to certain behaviors or benefits that help children do well in school and maximize their intellectual potential. Instead, he argues, smarter people will always be richer than those who are less smart, because their intellect brings them success. But this is a ridiculous argument, since it is premised on the notion of a completely fair society in which intellect alone leads to professional and economic success. And yet researchers have found again and again that children who live in families with more financial resources have higher IQs. Why would this be true?

One large-scale study showed that children with more books, more art on their walls, more rooms, and, strangest of all, more *tools* in the home are likely to have higher IQ scores and do better in school. That should mean that if you go into a toddler's home and find lots of books, tools, and rooms, it's a good bet that the child growing up in that house will get higher scores on school-readiness tests at age five and get better marks in third grade than a similar child growing up in a house without as many books and tools. But does that mean that if a parent, eager to help her child flourish, buys more books, hangs more paintings on the wall, and borrows some tools, her little girl will get better test scores? A close look at the data suggests that those objects are a proxy for a kind of behavior that does explain differences in IQ—and that behavior is conversation.

Children who live in homes with more wealth talk differently and more with their parents than children who grow up with less money. Todd Hart and Betty Risley compared middle-class families to families living at or below the poverty line by tape-recording the interactions of forty-two families from the time the children were nine months old until they were three years old. Children whose parents were well educated and held professional-level jobs heard about 2,100 words per hour. Welfare children heard about 600 words an hour. By the time the subjects in the study were four years old, the middle-class children of professional families heard as many as 48 million words. In contrast, children in families on welfare heard as few as 13 million words.

The difference in language environment goes beyond sheer numbers. Children from families with more money heard a different kind of talk from that heard by children with less money. Parents from the wealthier families were more likely to talk about the world around them, to identify what was interesting, and to discuss what was worth noticing and worth remembering. Some parents seemed to provide their children with a running narration of experience and also encouraged their children to narrate experience. This measure, which Hart and Risley called "extra talk (non-business talk)," taken when children were three years old, had a 77-percent correlation with the Peabody Picture Vocabulary test at third grade. In other words, families that engaged in a lot of "extra talk" had children who were much more likely to succeed in school.

It is not clear why families with greater wealth do this more than families without money. It might be because families with more money tend to have gone to better schools and to have spent more time in school. Or it might be that families with more money are more likely to have jobs that involve a higher level of education and require more conversation, more exchange of information, and possibly more time in deliberation.

In one of the oddest theories about intelligence, Robert Zajonc argued that birth order was the single strongest determinant of a person's IQ. Firstborn children, he argued, are likely to be smarter than later-born children. At first blush, this seems almost silly. How could your position within a family explain anything about your intelligence? Do a woman's eggs get weaker as she produces more babies? But Zajonc's explanation for his prediction makes some sense and fits with other data.

Zajonc argued that the firstborn is likely to have the highest IQ within a family because he or she benefits from a richer intellectual environment than subsequent children. Imagine, he argued, that the average combined IQ of two adult parents is 200. The firstborn child received all the benefit of that combined IQ. But the next child, and those who come after, have to share that intellectual environment. So the firstborn gets to grow up in a 200 IQ environment, while the later-born children are developing in a 100 IQ environment (200, the parents' IQ score, divided by two children). The formula is so simple it's almost hokey. But the logic behind it is backed up by other research. It is not that somehow the parental genes for intelligence get thinner or weaker with each child. Instead, each child, in theory, experiences a more diluted intellectual environment. Think of it in terms of any big family you know. The parents probably talked quite a bit to their firstborn, discussing what their little boy could see out the window, answering his questions about why his milk turned pink when he ate Lucky Charms, and asking him what was going to happen to the ice cube if he left it lying on the floor. But the third or fourth child in a busy household is much less likely to hear and be part of those kinds of exchanges. So, in fact, later-born children grow up in a somewhat weaker intellectual environment.

Interestingly enough, Zajonc's formula predicts that a child who is born a long time after the last one benefits from his position in the family. Why would this be so? Because if you have three much older siblings, your intellectual environment reflects the IQ of five grown-ups, not two diluted ones. Your much older brother and sister talk to you the way an adult would.

Zajonc's research is so parsimonious it is hard to accept. Everyone can think of exceptions—the twenty-four-year-old who is brighter than her twenty-five-year-old brother, the one born eight years later who is not as bright as his three much older siblings, and so on. But the logic behind his formula fits perfectly with all of the data showing that children benefit from conversation. When parents use talk as a way of reflecting on and making sense of the world around them, a child's intelligence benefits. And the data suggest that families with economic resources engage in more of this kind of conversation. So being rich does not make you smart, but having more wealth might be tied to having more conversation, which contributes significantly to a child's intelligence. In other words, the bank account itself does not explain wealthier children's advantage in school—what the bank account provides explains it.

Children do benefit from the intellectual environment created at home—and for children who grow up with their biological families, that environment tends to be an expression or an amplification of their genes. As I described earlier, smart families are likely to create smart environments. This is not only true for parents. Developmental psychologist Sandra Scarr followed adopted children as they grew up and found that children create their own environments—she called it "niche picking." Imagine two children within a family who seem, from day one, to be really different. One child, Emmanuel, learns to talk at an early age and loves words. It is clear almost immediately that he is attuned to the conversations around him and quick to use new vocabulary, try out verbal expressions, and tell stories. His brother, Dwight, seems more visual right from the beginning. Whenever he can, he uses toys to make patterns, buildings, and other visual displays. He seems to notice details in whatever room he enters. Even if Emmanuel and Dwight share the same parents and the same bedroom, go to the same family celebrations, attend the same nursery school, and spend their weekends on the same playground, they will experience substantively different environments. While Emmanuel listens to his parents' conversation, sits in rapt attention while his uncle tells a story, and creates elaborate stories when he is with his playmates, Dwight is oblivious to the conversation, spending his time instead taking all of the silverware and making a giant pattern with it, watching his grandfather repair the cabinet, and making patterns with colored blocks. These two children are, in effect, creating their own intellectual environment. Whatever it was they were born with, in terms of cognitive ability and style, leads them to notice, seek out, and immerse themselves in particular facets of the world around them. Emmanuel will grow up in a more language-rich environment than Dwight, who, in contrast, will grow up in a more visually rich environment than his brother.

Understanding what makes up a child's intelligence does not require parsing out the genetic component and the environmental component. Genes only express themselves within a particular environment. You can't be smart without questions, tools, and people to be smart with. But the questions, tools, and people you pick up on are shaped, in part, by your intelligence. Especially in the case of children who are raised by their biological parents, the IQs they get through their genes are often merely amplified by the IQs that surround them in their homes. The smart mom who has a large vocabulary provides her child not only with her genes but also with the kind of language-rich environment that enhances her child's native capacity.

Sign of Intelligence

What does this all mean for your child? To begin with, it means that your child's intelligence is likely to be similar to yours (and by the way, most research shows that people are likely to marry someone of similar intelligence, so you needn't fret too much about whether your child will get your wonderful IQ or your mate's lowly IQ).

It also means that in many ways, you need not try to disentangle what your child brings in the way of intellectual capabilities from what you provide her with. All things considered, these are likely to be of a piece. There are some dramatic exceptions—children who might have tested very highly on Fagan's test of infant speed of processing but who grow up without fundamental resources such as adequate nutrition or regular attendance at a reasonable school are likely to seem less intelligent than they otherwise would. After a while, if you seem less intelligent, you are less intelligent. IQ is not simply a capacity; it is a pathway. Each step leads you farther in one direction and away from another. The child who feels smart seeks out stimulating aspects of the environment. The child who feels that others don't think he's smart begins to inhibit his performance, further lowering other people's expectations, and so on.

I have said a lot about the stability of a child's intelligence. But I have said little about how a parent knows whether his child is smart or not. After all, as I mentioned earlier, many, if not most, children *seem* smart to their parents, and few people have their child's IQ tested, nor should they. It rarely helps. If your child is very bright, the chances are that you and his teachers already know it. Getting a number can only send you into a tizzy of needless enrichment activities, pushing teachers in ways that don't help, or aggravating your friends by finding subtle ways to tell them how high your child's IQ is. If your child's IQ score is lower than yours, or than most kids', you might unwittingly transmit that information to your child. And as we have seen, lowered expectations usually only make matters worse. For most kids, most of the time, IQ tests aren't necessary. You usually can tell if a child is smart, if you know what to pay attention to. Children who learn new information easily, can solve problems, can create objects and ideas, and can understand complex situations are smart. Children who struggle with more than one of these challenges are less smart.

The one caveat to this is when a child is having trouble in school and you want to know whether it is because she has a learning disability. IQ scores, handled properly, can sort out the difference between a problem learning to read and a general intellectual deficit, which brings us back to Stevie.

Stevie took in information quickly, especially visual information. He could look at a structure and quickly build one just like it. He could watch someone put a toy together and quickly take over adding new parts himself. He could walk into a room and tell you, hours later, the color of the furniture or a picture that was hanging on the wall. When he wanted to make something, if he didn't have the right materials, he could find a substitute and finish his project. That is, he was quick to process information, he could solve problems, and he could fashion products valuable to his community. But this was only when he was interested in the problem he needed to solve or cared about the thing he was making.

Only recently have developmental researchers begun to take seriously the idea that interest is a crucial component of the learning process. When babies are given objects to play with, they spend more time and, more important, use a wider variety of gestures to explore an object for which they have shown a prior interest. In another study, children who got to read stories about domains in which they had demonstrated a sustained interest actually learned more about and from the story. Teachers often try to elicit interest in academic tasks by making sure stories and activities relate to things that are, in general, child-friendly (a story about a kid who gets hooked on drugs for the preteen, a math activity that involves counting koala bears instead of colored rods for first-graders). But scholars who focus on interest are talking about something that goes beyond making a topic lively or superficially relevant to children. Research has shown that from a very early age, children often show intense and sustained interest in one activity or domain (bridges, puzzles, or bugs, for example). And it's also becoming clear that children actually behave in smarter ways when they are using the materials or engaging in the activities that most interest them. In one elegant demonstration of this, Suzanne Hidi gave toddlers objects to play with. Some of the children were given objects in which they had shown a prior interest (cars, dolls, various puzzles), while others were given objects in which they had shown no particular prior interest. When the toddlers were allowed to play with things in which they had a prior interest, they played for longer and used a wider range of gestures. So, it's not just nice to let a kid learn what she is drawn to. It's the best way to help her develop her intellect and make use of her intellectual potential.

Unfortunately, Stevie didn't find it easy to focus on the things that interested him. But it wasn't because he had a hard time focusing. It was because everyone around him was telling him he should do better in school, read more, apply himself, and talk more. His teachers and his parents wanted him to excel at things that didn't interest him and disregarded the activities and materials that did interest him. If a child seems highly motivated and intelligent in some domain, trying to push him to be well rounded or to excel in a more obviously marketable or appealing arena probably won't do any good and might just keep him from pursuing the activities in which he really does shine. In Stevie's case, his stubbornness was his best friend and his worst enemy. He began to act as if he didn't care what teachers said about him. He began to channel his resistance into rebellion and a determination not to follow the conventional path the adults in his life preferred. By the time he was seven, his parents were extremely alarmed that he hadn't learned to read. His mother gave him a dictionary for his birthday, even though he showed a clear disinterest in reading and writing. "For our little scholar," her card read. Then she transferred him to a stricter school, a school he hated.

Stevie was smart. And he was also stubborn. He resisted his parents' rules. One school day, it snowed, and Stevie didn't have boots that fit. His mother insisted that he wear an old pair of his sister's ski boots. He felt ashamed—he'd look silly arriving at his fourth-grade class in cumbersome ski boots. He walked out the front door as if he had agreed to his mother's injunction. But instead of continuing the five-block walk to his school, he wandered slowly around the block several times. After he had calculated that it was too late for him to go to school, he came back home. He had won. But his mother's sense that he wasn't up to snuff permeated the atmosphere. His teachers agreed, and Stevie began his journey away from anything with the whiff of schools or books on it.

With each year, his grades went down. Stevie became quieter, both at school and at home. A teacher in fourth grade wrote, "Steven needs to get hold of himself if he intends to achieve anything." His interests went underground, but they didn't go away. He began college at a conventional school—not the Ivy League school his parents would have preferred, which by then was inaccessible to him, but still a conventional academically oriented college. He hated it and transferred to art school. His parents refused to pay, appalled by his lack of academic focus. So he began working in a graphic design shop. By the time Stevie was twenty-five, he had succeeded on his own terms. He was an expert in graphic design, cabinetry, and printmaking. His intellect had taken the shape of the things he cared about. Along the way, however, the barrage of conventional expectations kept him from exploring things he might otherwise have delved into. The wall he built to keep out his critics also kept out interesting sources of information and inspiration and the expansion of his repertoire.

Stevie was smart when he was four, and he stayed smart. A child cannot get smart. Nor can he lose his smartness. However, a child's intellect takes shape in the company of other powerful forces. Some of those forces are inside the child (specific interest, motivation, and a sense of self-efficacy). Other forces exist outside the child (poverty level, social dynamics, and family events). If you had met Stevie when he was six, you might not have known that he was smart. You might not have known which clues to pay attention to. The clues about Stevie are buried in the stories of his childhood, but his parents missed those clues, which had repercussions.

Stevie's mother had been thrown by how different he seemed from her other children. And he could be so stubborn, so unwilling to do the things the other children seemed happy to do. When he didn't like what an adult asked him, he'd say, "Aren't talking," and fall into a long silence. To his mother, this was just more proof of Stevie's lack of verbal acumen.

When his kindergarten teacher noted that he had lost his steam for woodworking, his mom was dismayed. She believed that children need high standards, that even at five, it meant something when a child didn't do his best. And she was not sure what Stevie's best was anymore. The next afternoon, when he came home from school, she told him about the note.

"Miss Allen says you have lost interest in the woodworking area. That you don't try hard. She says you just smash two pieces of wood together and don't even hammer in the nail carefully. I know you are good with the hammer. What's going on?"

Stevie shrugged and looked away. He didn't like being questioned this way. "Nothing," he answered.

His mother felt sure that he just needed to be pushed, held to high standards, and she had a sharp tongue. She didn't believe in talking down to young children. She herself had been guided by a mixture of behaviorism and Dr. Spock (be firm and reasonable, and your reasonable child will accept your rules).

"Stevie, you have to try your best at school. I can't believe you are satisfied doing such shoddy work."

Stevie paused, still looking away. His mother came on strong, and he had learned to recede within, to disconnect from her. He answered diffidently, "I said I wanted to make a dog house for Sparky. Miss Allen said I couldn't. She said that was too big a project. So every day, I just tack together two pieces of wood and bring them home. Soon I'll have enough wood here at home to make the dog house."

Red Herrings

What would you do if you were Stevie's parent? His mother saw worrisome signs: disinterest in his work, a detachment from school, an unwillingness to cooperate with the goals adults set for him, and difficulty with reading. But the reassuring signs were there, too: Stevie was born smart. He had intelligent parents. He lived in a house filled with books, art, and tools and the conversations for which those things are a token. He had the stubbornness to seek out access to the activities and materials in which he had an interest.

A child who is fundamentally bright is very likely going to stay that way. And it would have done Stevie's parents a lot of good to relax a little about him—focusing on his great strengths instead of the red herrings. In fact, to the extent that their worry expressed itself as a low expectation ("Stevie's not that smart"), it might have become a self-fulfilling expectation for Stevie. Let's put it this way: the best thing for a child is to be around adults who think he is likely to bloom intellectually. Most of the time, when parents feel disappointed in a child's performance in school, what comes across to the child is the disappointment, not the sense that he or she is actually capable of more. What children often seem to sense is that their parents are worried that they are not smart. Teachers who think a child is not smart are also likely to have a dampening effect on a child's future academic success. And this brings us to the heart of the matter. For all intents and purposes, whether your child is smart or not, she's likely to stay that way. But how adults respond to her can make it easy for her intellect to find avenues of expression. This can lead her down a path of intellectual realization or can put roadblocks in her way that make her feel, and then behave, less intelligently than she might be capable of.

And why does it matter if your child is smart? Remember that the first intelligence test was created simply to make sure that children who were unusually slow were not punished for having trouble learning. Geniuses almost always announce themselves—you don't need to be tested to show that you are forty points smarter than other people. And as Malcolm Gladwell has argued in his book *Outliers,* above a certain level of intelligence, the difference doesn't, for the most part, matter when it comes to outstanding achievement. Children who get the highest IQ scores are not necessarily destined for a life of greatness, and children who have average intelligence are not doomed to an average life.

As I will explain in Chapter 5, success depends on a lot of things besides intelligence. However, it would be silly to discount intelligence altogether. In our society, the child who has an IQ score of 140 is going to be attracted to math or books in a way that a child with an IQ of 115 might not be. But the point is that you don't need to subject your child to an expensive and tiresome test to find this out. Most children who have an IQ score of 140 act as if they do. They seek out information, they like learning things, they solve problems more easily and creatively than others, and they analyze situations with acuity. Parents might simply learn what that looks like in the six-year-old, for two reasons. First, if your child is subjected to negative stereotypes, you can push against those stereotypes. Hank's mother had better make sure his teachers know the difference between unruly and stupid. He might knock the glass over, tap his finger during a lesson, or defy an adult's request, but none of these has anything to do with his intellect. A teacher had better know that her unconscious negative stereotype about black children needs to be examined and that she needs to take concrete steps to counteract that stereotype.

Second, on the positive side, the more aware you are of your child's expressions of intellectual liveliness, the more likely you are to encourage her, giving her a chance at a positive self-fulfilling prophecy. But here we need to draw a line. There is currently an epidemic, particularly in the white middle class, of parents eager to identify their children as gifted. Everyone wants his or her child to be in the program for gifted and talented children at school. It's not always clear whether it's because these parents think their children's needs are not being met in the regular classroom, whether they have a hunch that livelier and more engaging activities, things that would be appealing to any child, are going on in the gifted and talented program, or whether they want to make sure their children have an edge over everyone else when it comes to college. But in truth, not that many children are gifted, if gifted means exceptional. By definition, there are few exceptions. Few children fall outside the normal range of intelligence. Moreover, focusing on your child's exceptional ability encourages a kind of preciousness and competitiveness that isn't good for anyone.

Whether a child is of average intellect or on the high end, providing him with chances to pursue his interests, offering plenty of "nonbusiness" talk, and surrounding him with books that you and he actually read are the best support you can offer. The rest will take care of itself.

2

Friendships: The Fate of Lonely Children

One day when she was six years old, Abby came home from school and handed her mother, Meg, a picture she had made. Her drawing showed two large hearts and several smaller ones. She had drawn different kinds of lines connecting the hearts—some were solid, some jagged, and some broken.

"This is my heart," she said, pointing to one of the figures. "And this is Selena's," she continued, pointing to the second large heart. "The other hearts are our friends. These lines show you what my life is like."

All of the smaller hearts were connected by strong lines to Selena's heart. But all of the lines connecting the smaller hearts to Abby's were broken lines. The one line that directly connected Selena's heart to Abby's had a spear point on the end, and it was piercing Abby's heart, which was divided by fractured lines.

"My heart is shattered. Even if we make up, it can't be glued together again."

Abby was a smart and precocious little girl. Like her mother, who was an epidemiologist, Abby was quick to analyze a situation, detect inconsistencies, and construct a complex argument about something. She learned new information easily and excelled in her class work. Devastated by the social dynamics of first-grade girls, she used her keen mind to try to figure out her friendships. Her drawing offered a vivid picture of how Abby perceived her social world, which had always been vexed.

When Abby was little, she was not one of the cute, popular girls, and that didn't change much in the next few years. Even by eleven, she hadn't yet outgrown a slightly ungainly physique. Her hair lay flat against her neck, and when she spoke, you could tell she was self-conscious about her overbite. She often spoke a little too loudly at the dinner table, going on after others had lost interest in what she was saying. Her mother would remind her to let others have a chance to talk.

She did not have an easy time with other little girls. And to little boys, she was just invisible. In second and third grade, she was often left out at recess time, or she'd be invited to a party and then, when she arrived, excluded by the other girls. One friend, Gretchen, organized a yearly summer talent show where the girls competed against one another with song, dance, and other acts. Abby was always invited and then told by the other girls that her acts were lousy. Eventually, she began to believe them, but she still prepared an act each year, as if her life depended on it.

As is often the case with social dynamics like this, she was part of the problem. Quick to point out her friends' moral lapses, she would get visibly angry when they didn't treat her well. When she was ten, she was given the job of putting away the tennis rackets at the club where she took lessons and played. One day, she left a note in large capital letters on the blackboard in the tennis shed, addressed to a slightly older girl, one of the best and most popular players at the club: "JESSICA: YOU SHOULD TAKE BETTER CARE OF YOUR EQUIPMENT!"

It seems obvious, looking at this from the outside, that publicly chastising the older, more powerful girl was a bad way for Abby, a younger girl fairly new to the club, to break into the group. But Abby either didn't realize this or didn't care.

Abby's mother couldn't decide whether to point out to Abby that the blackboard message would probably backfire. And she wondered how significant it was that Abby had made such a blunder. Did the abrasive message on the board foreshadow an ongoing problem for Abby? Would Abby always have trouble with friends?

From the moment your child can walk and talk, you look for signs that she can get along with other kids. Some parents, probably the gregarious among us, simply expect that their children will like other children and be liked by them as well. Some parents, the shy or socially awkward, are a little more anxious and watchful than that. They monitor, out of the corner of their eyes, whether their child is invited to swing at the park or is standing at the center of the liveliest group at a birthday party. Any parent might feel a little twinge of anxiety if she arrives to pick up her three-year-old son at day care and finds him standing off by himself while the others are happily building blocks together. Is he destined to be a loner? Why don't the other kids invite him to play? Why does he isolate himself?

If you are a parent who feels that little twinge of worry when your child doesn't seem to be in the center of action, you're not alone, and you're not off base. Having friends is a hugely important part of childhood and one of the key indicators of a child's future well-being. A vast array of research has shown that children who have trouble with other children are more likely to have trouble as adults. Lonely and rejected children are at much greater risk for depression when they get older and, in fact, are at heightened risk for depression even when they are young. Aggressive children are at much greater risk for various kinds of problems with society when they are older. In other words, a child who doesn't have friends as a seven-year-old is less likely to have friends as a grown-up. She's also more likely to become depressed and/or to get into all kinds of trouble in adulthood.

If you have a child who is never chosen to be on a team during school sports, is often the one not invited to the birthday party, or has no one to sit with at lunch, it's pure agony—both for her and for you. As one eleven-year-old who was excluded, again and again, from the group of girls at her school said to her mother, "I'm not going. I'm not going to school ever again. I don't care if I can't go to college, if I never get a job. You can just forget it. Nothing would make it worth going back in to face those kids again. I'd rather die."

Not every child is so honest and articulate about his or her social struggles. And it's not always easy to know when a child is simply going through a difficult stretch with his friends and when his behavior indicates a real problem. You may think that when he comes home sad or mad about his friends, he's overreacting or that his frustration will pass quickly. If he's made similar complaints since he was very little, you might just assume that this is what happens to all little kids. You might even vaguely remember it happening to you and wonder why he cares so much. You seemed to get through it, and you're OK, so you assume he will be, too.

Every child has fights now and then with friends or goes through a brief period when he feels left out or unfairly targeted by others. But for some children, this problem becomes persistent—a defining characteristic of daily life. Somewhere between 10 and 30 percent of all school children are chronic victims of peer aggression. Even more worrisome, as it turns out, about 25 percent of the children who are continually victimized are also physically aggressive toward others.

Is there any objective way to know whether a child is just having a bad day or really has trouble with friends? The concerned parent faces two obstacles in answering that question. The first is that it can be difficult to see your own child objectively. A six-year-old comes home sad because he wasn't chosen for the kickball team at recess. One father might be outraged and worried, immediately certain that his little boy is doomed, destined to be left out of the group of cool boys for the rest of his school days. Another father, faced with a son who seems quickly to drop out of each group he tries to join, year after year, in summer camp as well as school, explains away each incident as an isolated event.

But parents face a second obstacle when it comes to understanding what is going on in their children's social lives. How does an adult find out about a child's social standing? You hear about your child's day only from your child. You have no real way of knowing how she is viewed by others. And it's not just parents who find it hard to scope out a child's social position. Psychologists face the same challenge. If being liked by others is so essential to a child's well-being, how might researchers find out who is liked and who is not?

Measuring Friendship

Unfortunately, the most obvious method—asking—is not the most reliable way to find out. Children are not necessarily good sources of information about their own popularity (any more than adults are). Although moderately well-liked children usually know that they are, certain kinds of children who are not well liked seem oblivious to the fact. So self-reports might gloss over the very kids you'd most want to know about.

A second, seemingly obvious source of information about a child's social skills is teacher evaluations. It makes sense for a concerned parent to ask a teacher if the child seems to have friends at school, and good teachers often do have an accurate feel for who is liked and who is not liked. However, there are limits to this source of information. For one thing, plenty of teachers are not that in touch with their students and don't really know what's going on. For another, a lot of the social dynamics of school-aged children happen outside the teacher's view. Knowing this, Canadian psychologist Debra Pepler and her colleagues placed a video camera in a playground at a suburban school and fitted the school children with tiny microphones attached to their clothes. The kids kept this equipment on for days, no matter what they were doing, until they had forgotten they were wearing it. Pepler and her colleagues were able to gain a sneak peek into how kids really treat one another when they aren't being supervised. When it comes to finding out about children's fights, this seems incredibly important. Kids, like adults, are much less likely to pick on another child when they know an adult is watching. Pepler and her colleagues found that the most aggressive children (based on separate measures of social behavior) said mean or incendiary things to other kids once every three minutes and hit or physically taunted other children once every eight minutes. Mind you, the more popular, sociable children were no angels—engaging in verbal aggression once every five minutes and physical aggression once every eleven minutes. It's pretty clear that kids are mean to one another and that some kids have more trouble than others (as victims and/or as aggressors). But this only provides information about the most external level of the problem, the kinds of aggression that come out in moments of conflict on the playground. Clearly, there are subtler dynamics at work throughout the day, which might help explain the relationships Abby so vividly diagrammed in her drawing of hearts.

For years, psychologists were stumped. How could they get an objective measure of something as subjective as how much a child is liked or disliked by others in her classroom? The solution, it turns out, is reminiscent of James Thurber's classic children's book

Many Moons. When the king is desperate to fulfill his daughter Lenore's sickbed wish for the moon, he asks all of the kingdom's wisest men what to do. They come up with lots of complicated yet absurd solutions. Finally, the court jester makes a suggestion that seems ridiculously simple: ask Lenore how to do it. Sure enough, asking Lenore solves the problem. In the 1980s, researchers, eager to know how children were viewed by one another, came up with a similar solution: ask the children what they think about one another.

In the past twenty years, psychologists have developed an intriguing and somewhat controversial way to measure a child's social standing, called sociometrics. To some extent, the measure just transforms what most kids naturally do anyway into a formal procedure, gauging a particular child's social worth by computing just how much the other kids like him or her. The experimenter asks each child in a given classroom to name the children he or she likes best and least. As it turns out, there is often a pattern: children in a group tend to agree on who is most likable, who is least likable, and who isn't worth rating at all.

But this popularity measure is not without its critics. Two potential weaknesses stand out in particular. First of all, there is a statistical weakness. What if a child is very popular with some kids and not at all popular with others? She will get pretty much the same score as a child who is moderately popular with everyone. And it doesn't take much knowledge of children to know that those two kids have a very different experience of daily life.

The other problem is a bit harder to get a handle on. Some parents (and ethical review boards) worry that gathering these data stirs up trouble and encourages kids to label one another. Perhaps when the experimenter asks a child who is really popular in her class, some little girl will begin to ruminate on how unpopular she is. However, the worry that such research stirs up problems ignores the reality of children's social lives. Most children don't go a full morning without thinking about and discussing who is good-looking, who is smart, who is gross, and who is cool. Children evaluate one another all the time. And of course, even if conducting such a study causes passing discomfort to a few children, it's worth it if it allows researchers to figure out how to keep bullies from bullying and rejected children from getting left out.

The Loner

Studies using sociometrics have revealed some striking, though not altogether surprising, patterns. Children who are consistently rated as unappealing and unpopular by their classmates have real problems—problems that persist. If your daughter is rejected by the other children at school again and again, she is not only likely to be miserable while she is enduring such brutal rejection, but she is also at risk for emotional problems later in her life. Children who are rejected are more likely to become seriously depressed as they get older.

When Sasha's third-grade teacher would look out the window during recess to check on his students, the first thing he would check to see was whether Sasha was finally playing with some of the other children or still standing alone. Each day, he would spot her, leaning on the pole of the swing set, twirling the rope on one of the swings. It wasn't easy to tell whether she was lost in a daydream, idly enjoying the breeze and the movement of the swing as she twisted it, or waiting, tentative and anxious, for one of the little clusters of kids to invite her in. When the children paired up to work on a mosaic project, there were just enough for twelve pairs. Yet the twenty-third child joined another pair rather than work with Sasha.

The teacher, Mr. Sanjit, had been talking with Sasha's mother all year. Sasha's parents knew she didn't have friends and felt angry that the school allowed her to feel so left out. Mr. Sanjit didn't quite know how to handle it. In his eight years of teaching, he had come to feel that you couldn't do much to change a kid's style of interacting. Watching different groups of children year after year, he saw that some children seemed to have a built-in mechanism for doing or saying just the wrong thing to other kids.

Mr. Sanjit had suggested to Sasha's mother that Sasha didn't seem to know how to connect to the other children. She would say things that just missed the mark. The other kids found her odd. When you are nine years old, being funny, energetic, and clued in to the reactions of other children is your ticket of admission. But it was as if the group was singing in C major and Sasha was singing in D minor. One day, after a difficult math lesson, Mr. Sanjit put on a CD of "The Macarena" and suggested that they enjoy the music for a little while. The children jumped up with glee and began dancing. Many of them knew the specific moves for the music and began to dance in unison. Even the ones who didn't know "The Macarena" got the beat and began swinging their butts, mirroring one another's moves. To the other kids, this was an invitation to party, something they had in common. But it was as if Sasha didn't recognize the invitation. She twirled around with a gentle sway to her body, as if she were hearing waltz music, slightly apart from the others. Mr. Sanjit would never have allowed the other children to make fun of her. But they didn't need to. They just ignored her. And that can be almost as bad.

Sasha's parents were very frustrated with Mr. Sanjit. Why didn't he do something to make things better for Sasha? And that raises a big question. Can teachers change the way children treat one another?

Can Teachers Fix Friendships?

There is no question that a teacher can create a certain atmosphere in his classroom. He can make it clear that overt meanness is not tolerated. Vivian Paley, the legendary nursery-school teacher and author from the Lab School in Chicago, made a rule one year in her preschool classroom: You can't say you can't play. A teacher widely known for encouraging play, imagination, and the free expression of children's inner thoughts, Paley decided to tell the children there was one thing she insisted on that year: the children could not exclude anyone from their play. If two children were in the dress-up corner playing Mommy and Daddy and another child wandered over hoping to join, they had to find a way to include her. It took a lot of time and energy not only to enforce the rule but also to help the children figure out how to resist exclusion and incorporate others into their stories and games. Paley claimed that by the end of the year, the children were kinder and more inclusive to one another. By creating a simple but dramatic rule, one that spoke in actions, not in talk, she created a norm and changed the way the children related to one another. Perhaps most teachers expect children to be mean and therefore subtly tolerate it in ways that perpetuate the meanness. If, on the other hand, a teacher assumes that children want to be decent to one another and simply need some gentle steering along the way, it can have a big impact.

The fifteen children in the second-grade class at the Hoboken, New Jersey, public school were a harmonious bunch. They seemed to like one another, and they liked their young teacher, Catlin Preston. He described them as a focused group, ready to plunge into school life. They held lively discussions during meeting time, solved problems, shared tasks, and worked at the wide array of projects and materials available to them in his small chock-filled classroom—observing the pet rats, making muffins for snack time, solving math problems, building with blocks in the block area, and writing poems on a computer.

"They were not an unruly group, as I've had other years, and they seemed unusually cohesive, right from the start," he said.

That is why he was so surprised when, in November, he became aware of the "Mortal Enemy Club." About six of the kids had formed a club during their daily recess time outdoors, away from Catlin's watchful eye. The primary purpose of the Mortal Enemy Club was to spy on and exclude one particular child. To be honest, the teacher couldn't see much ill will or fighting stemming from the club. But parents knew about the club, and they were upset. They called him to complain. He agreed that exclusive clubs could lead to no good.

Catlin typically used the children's work time to wander around the room, offering a word of advice or a helping hand, but mostly, he used this time to observe. Holding a clipboard and a digital camera, he walked from one activity area to another, jotting down what children were doing and talking about. Sometimes he photographed their work (for instance, a tall block skyscraper, a marble maze constructed from small plastic interlocking pieces, or a painting) so that they could show the other children what they had made during the meeting time that followed work time.

After learning about the club, Catlin did a little extra nosing around, asking the kids a few questions, listening to their conversations, and watching. He learned that a little boy had started the Mortal Enemy Club several weeks earlier because he was sure that one of his buddies had stolen a ship made from Legos while playing at his house. The members of the club would spy on the accused thief by following him around to watch his activities. If the little boy spoke to any of the spies, asking what they wanted, they would turn and quickly, silently walk away. Catlin said the club was not obvious to a casual observer: "You had to have heard about it, or pay careful attention, to see it in action."

Three thoughts guided Catlin as he mulled over how to end the club. Because the class had seemed to be such a well-functioning group in the first place, he felt confident that they could get past the problem without too much intervention. He also knew that the little boy who was the target of Mortal Enemy Club was "forceful, a gung-ho kid, not fragile." Finally, Catlin reminded himself of a premise he felt was central to working with elementary-school children: each of them is a "reasonable person." From what he had seen and heard, the club members were just "caught inside their own motivation." To them, it made very good sense to organize together against a "Lego thief," to show their solidarity with one another and express their disapproval of the other boy. "It just hadn't occurred to them to think about the effect their club might have on the outsider," Catlin said. Seven-year-olds can be inconsistent. When a child acts aggressively, that doesn't mean he actually wants another child to feel bad.

Catlin decided to count on their reasonableness and talk with them. But he wanted to surprise his students a little and make them think in a new way. "So I called a meeting of the club members and invited the 'enemy' to join us. I might not have done that," he said, "if the boy himself hadn't seemed so sturdy."

Once they were gathered on the rug in the meeting area, Catlin asked the boy whether he was aware of the club.

"I knew about the club, and I knew why they started it," the second-grader said. When asked how it made him feel, he shrugged and answered, "It made me feel lousy." But he didn't seem overly upset. Then the little boy looked directly at the other kids and added, "I didn't steal the ship. I only took it apart. If you had ever asked me, I would have told you."

Catlin addressed the club members: "What would you do if I told you right now that there was a new club, whose whole point was to keep you out?"

That was all it took, Catlin said. The kids seemed a bit taken aback by his question, and they readily agreed to dissolve the Mortal Enemy Club.

Things were fine for about six weeks. No clubs. Then a new little girl, Shonda, joined the class. She had played with some of the kids in an after-school program and was already friends with quite a few of them. However, within a week of her arrival in the class, Catlin found out that a group of students had started the "I Hate Shonda Club." They didn't actually exclude her from anything. They just periodically reminded one another of their club membership. Once again, a meeting was held, and the outsider was invited in. That was in January. During the spring, some of the children formed rock-finding clubs and animal clubs. But as far as Catlin could tell, there were no more enemies.

The children in Catlin's classroom seemed to lapse periodically into the kind of ganging up that many of us remember or read about in *Lord of the Flies.* With some well-timed intervention by a teacher the children loved and admired, the kids were easily guided toward a more gentle and inclusive way of operating. The Mortal Enemy Club incident was a red herring for those in the club and those outside it—it signaled little about the club members or their victim.

But Sasha, on the other hand, was left out again and again. And while a skilled adult can steer a group of kids away from bullying, that doesn't mean a teacher can make children like a kid they don't like. And here is one of the most painful truths for parents of a child who is left out: almost invariably, the child is doing something that is causing her to be left out. But what do children like Sasha do that makes other kids exclude them?

With some kids, like Sasha, it's not easy to put your finger on the behavior that pushes other children away. She wasn't mean, she wasn't loud, she didn't look for trouble in any way. She just seemed tuned out. Psychologists refer to these children as rejected-withdrawn. When teachers have a student like Sasha, they often have a hard time knowing whether she pulls herself away from the group or the other kids keep her out. The bad vibe is subtle for kids like Sasha. But the effects are not subtle. As they get older, children like Sasha are at a much greater risk for depression. What researchers haven't figured out is whether underlying depression causes the problem in the first place or the social isolation they suffer causes the later depression. However, some preliminary work with interviews and diaries suggests that children like Sasha experience real sadness and isolation even when they are young. She might have seemed unaware of what was going on around her, but she probably was very much aware of how her separation from the group was making her feel. Even when Sasha wasn't wandering around the edges of the classroom, she seemed droopy and slightly sad.

Mr. Sanjit encouraged Sasha's parents to invite a child over after school to play with her. Sometimes a kid like Sasha can forge a bond with one child, which acts like a bridge when they are back in school—a passageway to more group interaction. But—and here's the kicker—as often as not, a child who has trouble relating to other children has a parent who also has trouble relating to other people. Often, they don't even know how to help their child make friends.

Steve Asher described a parent who approached him after he gave a public lecture on children's friendships. The father was concerned because his child was being left out at school, and the teacher had recommended that the parents try to help their son make friends.

Asher said to the father, "So, what does your son like to do when he's with other kids his age?"

The father said, "How would I know that?" He seemed perplexed about how one would go about making such a judgment.

As Asher talked to the father more, it became clear that he had no clue about his son's social life and little idea about what might go into finding new friends or developing interests that would attract new friends. How could he help his son when he wasn't so sure how to make friends himself?

Sasha's parents made a few attempts to invite other little girls over. But those dates didn't seem to extend themselves. When I asked Mr. Sanjit about it, he said the parents seemed to invite kids at random, not necessarily the ones Sasha might actually get along with. He got no sense of what the girls did at Sasha's house, partly because the parents didn't have a sense of it, either. Sasha didn't become better friends with those girls in school, and she didn't seem to change her way of operating in the classroom. The get-togethers didn't change anything. Sasha remained alone. Eventually, she left the school. The last Mr. Sanjit heard, she was having similar difficulties in her next school. And she went on seeming depressed.

If Sasha's parents had created situations in which she could become friends with another little girl or two, away from the school environment, it might have helped. If they had found out from Mr. Sanjit who might become a friend for Sasha and invited that child over for projects and small outings, situations where they could gently guide the girls to become closer, it might have created a scaffold on which Sasha could build. But because they were somewhat clueless themselves socially, such help was not in the cards. In their situation, the best thing probably would have been to take Sasha to a child therapist, someone warm and skilled at forging a bond with children. It's possible that by creating a friendship with a therapist, Sasha would build up a base from which to connect to other children.

Lonely Bullies

Not all children who are left out are sad and quiet like Sasha. Some rejected children also behave, oddly enough, like bullies. And these kids have even bigger problems in store for them. Harold was big for his age—athletic but also kind of thick—the type of kid who would knock over a chair rushing to get to the seat he wanted. When he was in preschool, he always had long columns of green mucus streaming from his nose. His hair flopped over his eyes, and his shirt always looked as if he had just been rolling in the mud. Harold made other kids cry at least twice a day. It seemed to his second-grade teacher, Miss Levin, that just when another child might make a friendly overture, Harold would instead begin to threaten and intimidate some other child, often one who seemed obviously smaller or more timid than he. He was what psychologists call rejected/aggressive. Children didn't want to play with him, and he, in turn, antagonized them. Kids like Harold don't have many friends and they're not popular or admired. They are not the tough, cool guy, like the character Iceman in the movie *Top Gun*. They are just mean and scary, and they are disliked by the others. When Harold was sixteen, he was arrested for driving under the influence. When he was seventeen, his girlfriend got pregnant. When he was eighteen, he was arrested for beating someone up while traveling across the country. Bullies who are also rejected have around a 70 percent chance of getting in trouble with the law by the time they are young adults.

Kids with these problems aren't difficult to spot. Any teacher worth his or her salt knows exactly who is left out of the game at recess, who isn't chosen to work on the science team, and who eats lunch alone. Any teacher can identify the Sashas, quiet and withdrawn, and the Harolds, creating constant friction and trouble.

Invisible Trouble

Plenty of kids are not well accepted in school, and yet no one sounds the alarm bell. These kids can be emitting signs of trouble that no one is picking up. Unfortunately, this can lead adults to miss a vital opportunity to help a child.

Andy was just that kind of kid. Even at four, while he liked other children and they seemed to like him well enough, he was beginning to show signs of the trouble to come. Once, at a friend's house, he and his buddy wanted to build a tree house. They found a hammer and some nails. While his friend diligently, if unsuccessfully, tried to hammer a strip of wood to the trunk of a tree, Andy became absorbed in wildly smashing the nails into the dirt. It was as if he lost sight of the shared goal and lost interest in being part of a duo—two attributes essential to making and keeping friends when you are young.

But Andy was one of five siblings, with only two years between any two of them. Their parents were loving but slightly overwhelmed and distracted. They loved their own casual style. Once at a birthday party, a toddler's mother reached out to keep her eighteen-month-old from careening over the low edge of the deck. Andy's mother gently and authoritatively held her friend's hand. "Don't jump in. Let him explore. Let him find out for himself," she said. In the abstract, her advice seemed calm and wise. Relax. Let kids be who they are. But her impulse was not in the abstract. It was in the context of a son who already was showing subtle signs of social isolation.

As Andy got older, he seemed bright but out of sync with others. However, he didn't get into fights, and he didn't complain that children were mean to him. He raised no red flags. If he had been in a classroom where a psychologist had been collecting sociometric data, he surely would have come up as a neglected child—not the kid other children seriously disliked and not the one they loved or admired, just not someone other kids sought out. In Andy's case, this mild lack of acceptance might have been a wrinkle that got ironed out with time, if it weren't for his other difficulties.

Years later, as a sixteen-year-old, after he had been caught stealing a pair of basketball shoes from a local store, his mother recalled that when he was young, he would wander away from her. With no warning, he'd slip away, taking off by himself down the street. At the time, she thought it was the sign of an independent spirit. It went with his almost translucent skin and black curls. He was spritelike, quirky, and a bit dreamy, she thought. But she also recalled that the few times she sent him to his room for misbehaving, he'd climb out the second-story window and lower himself to the ground with ropes he'd found and tied together.

When Andy was caught with the stolen shoes, his mother happened to be shopping next door at another store. The policeman, who knew her, came and got her and explained what had happened. She promised she'd deal with her son, and the policeman agreed to let it go. Andy put back the shoes, and she and Andy left. Once they were in the car, Andy turned to his mother and said, "But now will you buy me the shoes?"

It's not hard, now that Andy is in his twenties and struggling mightily, to see that all the signs were there when he was young. But one can also see how easy it would have been to miss those signals. He didn't get into a lot of trouble when he was young, he wasn't a bully, and he wasn't picked on. The red flags were fleeting and obscured by daily life, which washed over his family and kept them from zeroing in on his emerging difficulties.

Andy's odd behaviors, once slight and easy to pass off as eccentricities, became more than that as he entered adolescence. By the time he was fifteen, he had been arrested, caught again and again with liquor and drugs, and had had several car accidents. But his parents thought, "Lots of teens drink too much and take risks with cars. His judgment isn't the best, so he gets caught while others get away with it. But he's not really all that different from other kids, right?"

They were comforted by the fact that he had a close relationship with a girl and had one really good buddy. Here is where they misread the cues altogether. The research shows that for kids who are not accepted by other kids, having one or two intense friendships might guard against future depression, but it doesn't necessarily indicate that things are OK. In fact, a rejected kid who has one good friend is more likely than other rejected kids to face future problems with the law. Kids who get into trouble and are outside the mainstream often gravitate toward other kids who get into trouble. And that's just what happened to Andy. He made close friends with a boy who loved to get high and skip school.

In another study of children who were either unpopular or had no friends, Asher found that often when a rejected kid has one good buddy, the quality of the friendship is fairly low. What does that look like? Good friendships, even among preadolescents, involve a fair amount of validation, help, exchange of intimate information, and low levels of conflict and betrayal. But when an unpopular kid makes friends with another unpopular kid, the same social problems each has with others begin to bubble up between them.

Andy's parents were grateful that he had a buddy—they spoke about how reassuring it was that Andy had an ally, a friend with whom he seemed close. It never occurred to them that Andy's friend was making things worse.

By the time Andy was sixteen, he was in so much trouble that his parents dropped him off at a rehabilitation program for teens in California. He spent the next few years moving from one program to another—three in all. He finally made his way to college, although he continued to get into serious trouble with the law for drugs, speeding, and disorderly conduct. This trajectory is classic, cited in study after study. Children who have trouble with peers tend to have other kinds of trouble as they get older. What, if anything, could his parents have done differently had they interpreted Andy's childhood behaviors as the red flags that they were?

Friendship 101

Asher has been studying children's friendships for thirty years. He's looked at kids who are kept out of the group and kids who simply are not sought after. He's looked at close friends, and he's looked at kids who have lots of friendly acquaintances. He's watched children interact, and he's questioned them one by one. He's observed kids' friendships evolve and dissolve over a period of years, and he's tried to intervene and change the course for kids with problems. And that brings us to the million-dollar question for those who do research on peer relations: Can children who have trouble with peers be coached? Can they change?

As Asher and others have shown, kids who are chronically rejected often do things that seem to get them rejected. They tease inappropriately, they promote themselves in just the wrong way, their timing is off, and they push when they shouldn't. Sometimes their difficulties are hard to change. Kids who are not athletic are less popular than kids who are, and kids who are funny are more liked than kids who are not. These are not qualities one can coach into a kid. But as John Coie has argued, a lack of these qualities is not in itself the kiss of death. Some plain, unfunny kids seem to make the most of their best qualities, read the pulse of the group, and find a way in. The kids who have trouble are typically the ones who don't know how to read the group. The kid who really has trouble often is the one who handles an initial experience of exclusion badly. Popular kids pay attention to signals from the others, and they adapt their behavior accordingly. Rejected kids do not. Children who are liked tend to be interested in what other kids are doing and saying. They share information about themselves and solicit information about the other kids. They are interested in making joint activities fun. Kids who don't seem to have these skills make a bad beginning worse. Thus, what begins as a slight difficulty meeting others or joining a group leads to other problems. Because they misread cues and miss opportunities to connect to other kids, they end up missing opportunities to practice friendship, which leads to further isolation and unhappiness as they get older.

However, Karen Bierman, among others, has found that kids can get better at becoming part of the group in just a few coaching sessions, especially when they are young. They can get better at showing interest in what other kids say and think. They can learn to focus more on having fun with other kids and less on proving themselves. They can learn to let the other kids know they are having fun. In one study, Bierman and her colleagues set up social training sessions for children who were unpopular. Each child who was unpopular (based on sociometric scores and on reports of teachers and the children themselves) was teamed with two well-accepted children from the classroom. These three kids spent a total of ten sessions together engaged in a variety of activities (drawing, talking, and so on). Half of these groups also received direct coaching from an adult. For the other half, an adult was present and supportive of their interactions but offered no specific directives about how to interact.

The coaching consisted of teaching children how to say positive things to the other kids, how to listen and acknowledge what the others said, and how to suppress the urge to be disagreeable and argumentative. Children who interacted with more popular peers and were coached by an adult did seem to become more accepted over time, even after the study was over. However, it wasn't clear that they actually became more popular or had more friends. Taken purely as research, this sheds light on what might go wrong for some kids and suggests that there are two critical factors for improvement: the chance to interact with more popular kids and some direct instruction in the behaviors that seem to cause the problems. But it's not clear what this offers to parents, because, as it turns out, it's often not only the kids who need help.

Marlene Sandstrom has been studying friendships since she was eight years old and in the third grade. She vividly remembers when a new boy joined her class in a public school in suburban New Jersey.

"Oh, boy," she said. "He was kept out from day one. He never got in. I could see that the other kids weren't all that nice. But it wasn't just that. I could tell, even then, even though I was only a kid myself, that he was just slightly off in every encounter. It was fascinating yet painful to watch. What was keeping him from fitting in? I couldn't stop thinking about it."

Fifteen years later, as a doctoral student in clinical psychology at Duke University, she worked with one of the founders of the study of peer relations, John Coie, and did her doctoral research on how parents might influence their children's peer status. Like others in her field, she got all of the children who were her test subjects to nominate classmates who were most liked and most disliked. Then she followed the kids who were most disliked. Those students whose parents got involved—by helping them join after-school activities and other kinds of groups—were much more likely to be accepted by peers one year later. The quick answer from Sandstrom's work: kids can get better, and parents can play a role. But her research highlighted a puzzle. Do the kids whose parents get involved do better because they get the chance to practice new skills or because if you're that kind of kid and you're lucky enough to have a parent perceptive enough and involved enough to help, you're already in better shape than the kid without that kind of parent?

Asher's research has something to say about this. In one set of studies, he and his colleagues actually involved rejected kids in some training groups. The children were taught how to ask other kids about themselves, how to make someone feel welcome when he or she came into the room, how to suggest a new game, and how to share interesting and appropriate information about themselves. A year later, rejected kids who had been part of his training groups were more well liked by other children in the classroom, suggesting that you can help a kid become more popular.

Asher is quick to say that we don't yet know if you can also help a kid make stronger, better friendships. A socially awkward child can learn to do the things that come naturally to the other children, and it has some payoff. These children get higher ratings on sociometric measures after the training and might well find themselves more accepted. It's not clear, however, that this kind of training leads to a change in the quality of a child's friendships.

You can learn how to act in a group, but that doesn't necessarily mean you can learn how to be a friend. But since being accepted and having close friends are not the same thing, the training is worth something. While everyone assumes that all good things befall the popular kid and all bad things befall the kid who is not popular, the data show something different. Children who are not popular but are also not rejected by the group seem to do pretty well over time. They report a fair amount of satisfaction with their daily lives. They can do well in school, and as they get older, they often get better at making and keeping friends.

One of the problems for kids like Sasha and Andy is that without help, they begin to identify themselves as unpopular—they feel like losers, and then they act even more like losers. But therein lies a good avenue for intervention. When kids can be made to feel that their interactions with other kids have gone well, they become more appealing. Coie and his students demonstrated this with a startling experiment. Children who had been identified as rejected through peer nominations were introduced briefly to two boys with average peer status. A few days later, some of the rejected boys were told that those two boys they had met a few days before really liked them and were looking forward to getting together again. Other rejected boys were not given that positive feedback. Then each of these rejected boys was given some time with the two boys again. Kids who were given the positive feedback were subsequently rated as more likable than the kids who were not given that feedback. In other words, when rejected kids are given the sense that they have made a good impression on others, they behave in a more appealing way. This should come as no surprise. In a similar study of adult attractiveness, a team of social psychologists asked subjects to talk on a phone to a stranger (another subject in the study). The stranger was shown a photograph of the telephone partner, but some were shown a picture of a very attractive member of the opposite sex, while others were shown a photograph of a very unattractive person. Those conversations were recorded. When a third subject listened to the original subject's voice during that conversation and rated how much he would like to meet the person whose voice he was listening to, he was much more interested in meeting subjects who had been talking to someone who believed they were attractive. Bottom line: if you feel attractive, you act attractive. And if others think you are appealing, it leads you to be more appealing.

Matt always had one or two good friends at a time. He was the kind of little boy who loved to have the same friend over each weekend. Together they would develop elaborate play scenarios involving superheroes and bad guys. They ran lemonade stands and made fortresses in the woods near their home. When he moved to a new school in third grade, Matt again made a few best friends. In fifth grade, those buddies gravitated toward soccer and hockey, things Matt had no interest in. So he found himself two new friends—kids who liked to talk, draw cartoons, and plan movies. But by the time he was in middle school, Matt felt lonely and unhappy. He was the only Jewish kid in the class. He read more than the others. The questions he asked the teachers were different from those the other kids asked. He got into feuds with a few classmates over things like gun control and the president. By the spring of his seventh-grade year, he felt isolated from everyone in his grade. In the winter of his eighth-grade year, a girl with whom he had had some conflict gave a party and invited everyone but him. He felt he had not one real friend in the whole school, and he was downright miserable.

Research shows that kids who feel rejected at school and who also don't have a close friend suffer a kind of loneliness that dominates their every waking moment. Many adults who were rejected either still feel that loneliness or can easily recall a time in their own childhood when they did. It's one of the most negative and powerful of all childhood experiences. Parents often don't even realize what their kids are going through. And even if they do, they aren't always sure how to help.

The Parent Steps In

Matt's parents began to look into other schools for him—the two nearby public schools to which he had access and a few private schools. His grandmother suggested that maybe it was something about him that was causing the problem, that perhaps he was rubbing the other kids the wrong way and would carry this problem with him wherever he went. His parents, worried and distraught to see him suffer, wondered how they would know if the problem was simply a bad fit between him and the group or something he would cause in any class.

Not knowing what else to try, they sent Matt to a different public school in a nearby town with a different demographic. The school had more kids from families who read books and more kids with parents who had white-collar jobs. There were more Jews and more kids who did as well as Matt at schoolwork. Most important, there were kids who hadn't known him in the seventh grade, which meant, among other things, more kids with whom he felt he could make a fresh start. He had a new buddy within a week. He had a new group of friends within two months and a steady girlfriend within three months. With a new peer group and a fresh start, he had a chance to shift his self-concept, and in his case, that made all the difference.

But switching schools is not the answer for every child suffering with social problems. Researchers have long wondered what many parents have wondered. Is it possible for an unpopular kid to change his reputation once he's been cast out? Do rejected kids repeat history wherever they go? Coie and his colleagues devised an ingenious method for disentangling the chicken-egg problem of a child and her social group. First, they went into the fourth-grade classrooms of a public school district in Durham, North Carolina, to find out who was popular, who was rejected, and who was neglected. Each boy who was characterized as rejected or neglected by the sociometrics was then recruited to participate in a six-week after-school program. Each child was placed in a group of unfamiliar children—all of the other children had received a neutral or positive rating in their original classrooms. Thus, each child who was chronically ignored or rejected was spending time playing with a new group of kids who were fairly popular. After each playgroup session, a different adult gave a ride home to the kids in the group. In the car, the driver would casually ask how things were going with the after-school activities. This gave the researchers a chance to gather information about the social dynamics without making the children too self-conscious or aware of the purpose of the program. What they found was both discouraging and encouraging. Ignored boys were able to turn over a new leaf—they used play time with this new small group as an opportunity to change their own social profiles. Kids reported liking the ignored boys, finding them interesting, and often noticing them more than kids in their regular classroom. However, rejected children didn't find the same success. They seemed to repeat the behavior that had made them unpopular at school, and the other children in their after-school groups reported the same kind of negative reactions that rejected children tend to get from their classmates. This study explains why a kid like Matt blossomed with a change of schools but why other children might not.

For instance, it had no effect on Abby, who moved to a new school for sixth grade. Not only did she continue to have conflict with friends, often feeling hurt by the girls she liked the most, but as the new girl in sixth grade, she found herself with a whole new set of problems. She wanted to be friends with the cool girls in her new classroom. But they hadn't really invited her to join them yet;

they were still thinking it over. Meanwhile, a girl in the class who knew Abby from the tennis club was eager to be her best friend. However, the cool girls made it clear that if Abby hung out with the "loser girl," they would never allow her into their clique. Abby had come home distraught over this plight.

Her mother, Meg, was in a quandary. "I don't want her to suffer. It's breaking my heart to see her so worried about who her friends will be. I can't stand to see her excluded yet again. I want to give her advice that will help her be more popular, but my own mother is appalled that I would do such a thing. She keeps telling me not to worry so much about her friendships. She warned me that I should worry more about whether Abby grows up with a strong moral compass. My mother says this is the time to teach her to put the welfare of others ahead of her own, to stick up for the weak. She's sure Abby's social life will sort itself out but that if I don't guide her to be selfless now, she'll become callous and self-interested. Help me. What should I tell Abby?"

The problem Meg faced will ring a bell with many parents. Who wants to see their child excluded or put down? And who wants to push a young child to behave in ways that might lock the child into unpopularity for years to come?

Meg hedged it. She encouraged Abby to find a way to be friendly to the loser girl but to explain that she was eager to make friends with lots of kids and wanted to spend time with that other group as well. As the year progressed, Abby forged ahead, finding herself deeper and deeper in what some have called "girl world"—filled with heated IM exchanges, changes of alliance, bad rumors, and ecstatic gatherings in town.

Toward the end of Abby's eighth-grade year, Meg was at a meeting of parent volunteers for the school. One mom called out, "How are Abby and Julio doing?"

"Who?" Meg asked.

It seemed that everyone but Meg knew that Abby had a boyfriend. Julio was a boy in her grade. They walked down the hall together between classes. They were known as a couple, a topic of discussion during nightly IM sessions. Once at a school dance, they kissed—a quick peck on the lips (all this Abby told Meg when she finally learned about it). When Meg asked Abby why she hadn't told her, Abby said, "When I asked you how old I had to be to have a boyfriend, you said eighteen. I thought you wouldn't let me go out with Julio."

What is most striking about this piece of the story is why Abby asked her mother how old she had to be. Many kids would not. Abby cared what her mother thought. She might have been trying to open up the topic when she asked her mother the question. Meg said her answer of eighteen gave Abby an out if Abby didn't feel ready to date. Meg didn't recognize the question for what it was. But that didn't really matter. What mattered was that Abby, highly aware of rules, both the ones she conformed to and the ones she circumvented, cared about her mother's rules.

I told Meg that I thought it was great that Abby had a boyfriend in eighth grade. It gave her bankable currency when it came to the other girls. Meg seemed happy to hear my interpretation. She smiled, relieved to think that Abby was no longer facing heartache each day.

"Yup" she said, with a small smile, "Abby is slowly but steadily working her way up the social ladder." She paused, and a rueful expression veiled her smile. "And she's becoming more conforming every minute."

But not all children can simply decide to do what it takes to become more popular and then do it. In one of the clearest pieces of research to emerge in the last fifty years, Jerome Kagan at Harvard has shown that shyness is one of the most persistent and long-lasting of human characteristics. But his story begins in the 1960s, when Stella Chess first argued that not all of a child's personality depended on the mistakes parents made. In response to the Freudian zeitgeist, in which parents were sure that their children's every foible was the result of some invisible but powerful interaction with them, Chess, a child psychiatrist, began to explore the possibility that babies arrive in the world with some pretty powerful characteristics, which play a big role in determining a child's future life. Chess and her colleagues asked parents to keep diaries of their babies, noting things such as the baby's response to a new food, how the baby fell asleep and woke up, and how she dealt with changes in routine (remember, this was in an era when modern U.S. parents were told again and again that a routine was essential to a baby's well-being).

In their classic book, *Your Child Is a Person*, Herbert Birch, Stella Chess, and Audrey Thomas argued that from birth, each baby has a temperament, a style of responding to the world, which influences every experience she has. Birch, Chess, and Thomas said that every child could be characterized as one of the following three temperamental types: easy, difficult, and slow to warm up. The easy baby falls asleep calmly, responds to new experiences (such as a new food) in a relaxed and open manner, and in other ways goes through the day with equanimity. Difficult babies, on the other hand, seem fussy and tense about any kind of change—waking up, tasting a new food, or entering a new place. The slow-to-warm-up classification is fairly self-explanatory, describing the baby who cautiously sticks her tongue out and warily tastes a new food, perhaps pauses, tries it again, and finally eats it. It's not hard to see how these basic ways of interacting might shape a child's experience. And any parent knows that you tend to respond differently to the calm, open baby from how you respond to the one who seems to get upset and tense again and again. In other words, the baby's temperament not only shapes her own behavior, but it also ends up shaping her emotional environment.

Forty years after *Your Child Is a Person* was published, Kagan picked up the thread of temperament. He began to tease apart what Birch, Chess, and Thomas were on to. From Kagan's experimental perspective, what parents say about their children was notoriously unreliable. The mom who says her baby cries all the time is just as likely to be exaggerating as the mom who says her baby loves every new experience. So, to find a more rigorous measure of a baby's temperament, Kagan invited mothers to bring their babies into the lab. After placing each child in one of those tilted baby seats that can be set on a table and rocked gently, he filmed them. After the baby had a chance to settle in, the experimenter dangled a toy that hung from a rod, sort of like a hand-held mobile. This type of toy is pleasing and interesting, the kind that parents often attach to their children's cribs and strollers. But this was a brand-new toy, one the baby had not seen before. In films of these babies, it is quite easy to see how differently each baby responds to the new toy. Some sit in the chair calmly. When the hanging toy is brought into their view, their eyes might widen for a moment, and they halt their characteristic exercising motions (the ones that make many four-month-olds look as if they are in a perpetual aerobics class). Little bands placed on their wrists show that their pulse temporarily changes, and their skin might produce slightly more moisture—the new toy makes them sweat. But after a few moments, most babies settle back down, their pulse returns to normal, and their kicking resumes. They might visually explore the mobile, but after those first moments, they are not overly perturbed by it. Kagan called these children "low reactive," meaning that they are relatively relaxed and able to take new experiences in stride. Some number of babies, however, have a very different response to the new toy. They become agitated, and instead of quickly settling back to normal, their agitation seems to be self-perpetuating. Their initial surprise and tension worries and upsets them, and before you know it, they are crying and unable to calm down. Kagan called these babies "high reactive."

When Kagan and his students observed the babies four years later, the two styles were still quite apparent, although they manifested themselves somewhat differently. Low reactive babies were the ones who eagerly entered a new classroom, joined a group of children playing on a playground, and seemed interested and happy when approached by a new child. The high reactive children, however, were the ones to stand back reluctantly at the door of a new classroom, hesitant to enter, unwilling to jump into the fray. In a host of follow-up studies, Kagan and others have shown that the babies he called high reactive become shy children. He wasn't talking about a little bashfulness at a big party. He was talking about children who are overwhelmed by new experiences, particularly ones that involve other people, children who would remain on the edge of a playground, even when the kids were doing something really fun, rather than have to talk to children they don't know.

Anyone who is extremely shy or has a shy person in his or her family knows that shyness can govern a person's life. A shy child finds it hard to meet new friends, terrifying to change schools, and overwhelming to have to talk to the teacher. Walking into the cafeteria can create dread day after day. Shyness can keep children from pursuing their deepest interests. A casual look at the narratives teachers write about children will show that most adults (except for those who suffer from extreme shyness) expect children to grow out of this kind of timidity. "We hope Jack will try to be more outgoing next year." "Sara should get involved in more group activities at school." "This year, Carlo has spent an awful lot of time alone. Next year, we hope to work on this with him." And yet, by and large, shy children become shy teenagers and then shy adults. Expecting a child to outgrow shyness is sort of like expecting a child to outgrow eye color.

If You Can't Change the Child, Change the Path

Knowing how to help your child deal with social problems depends a great deal on what the story really is. Often, the most valuable thing a parent gets from talking to a therapist is the chance to piece together a detailed narrative. But you don't necessarily need a therapist in order to watch and listen and then put together a story for yourself, one that conveys what your child is experiencing. A quick glance, coming up with a summary view in which the conclusions are drawn first, often misses the most revealing elements of the narrative. Find someone to tell your story to—a friend or colleague who doesn't know too much about your child's daily life. Knowing what clues to include in your story makes a big difference.

Patrick's journey testifies to that. Patrick came from a family that seemed to have stepped right out of a story about modern middle-class America. His mom was a schoolteacher, his dad a social worker. They lived in a small rural area in upstate New York. Patrick's parents met in college, married, and proceeded in an orderly fashion to have a daughter, Meghan, and then Patrick. When someone called their home, the message said, "We can't come to the phone right now. We're either out at work or busy doing a kid project. Please leave a message for Catherine, Tim, Meghan, or Patrick." Their home had a modest and perfectly manicured garden, a different welcome sign for each season, and portraits of the family taken by a professional. Everything about their life seemed measured, planned, and moderate. Their social life revolved around the children's interests, church, and their extended family.

When Patrick was little, he attended day care and immediately made friends with a small cluster of other little boys, all of whom had siblings who went to school together and whose parents worked as teachers and social workers. As a four-year-old, Patrick's dark, shiny hair was cut in a perfect bowl shape around his head. He looked sweet and well kept and completely conventional.

The little gang of boys eventually moved on to elementary school together and began to play against one another in Little League baseball and on community basketball teams. That's when Patrick's troubles began. The charming roundness that had suited the page-boy haircut was suddenly a liability as the boys began to compete for traveling teams, shortstop position, and starting positions in basketball. Even at four, Patrick seemed slightly more sensitive and reactive than the other boys in the group. On a trip with one of them to a haunted house for kids at Halloween, he ran screaming from the display, terrified. On a flight home from a family vacation in Florida, he became so anxious he almost couldn't bear it. In the weeks following that trip, he became hysterical when he left a sweatshirt at a buddy's home, calling several times to make sure the sweatshirt was there and insisting that his mother drive him over to pick it up the very next morning. At the same time, differences among the kids in academics and athletics began to show up. Patrick wasn't chosen for the traveling team in basketball. And although he loved shortstop, he was made second baseman.

Despite this, his buddies still played with him, and he was invited over to their homes. The birthday parties always included him. And he made it onto every team. But the other kids began to rib him, often quite mercilessly, for his fears. When his feelings were hurt, he'd tell them so, and they teased him for that. They were in the process of adopting a tough-guy jock manner—most of them wouldn't drop that until their midteens, some never. Patrick took on no such mantle. By the time these boys were eleven, he was often getting the short straw. It seemed as if he wore a "Kick me" sign on the seat of his pants. When he invited one of the crowd to his house for a Memorial Day picnic, the friend stood him up, lured by the more appealing last-minute invitation to the cool boy's house. Patrick, easily wounded and longing for inclusion, cried and stayed in his room for the whole afternoon.

In sixth grade, his buddies were starters for the basketball team. He spent the season on the bench, too pudgy and slow to help the team. In eighth grade, two of the four boys ran for class president. Patrick was one of them. He lost in the first round. When his friend Ed made it to the final election, Patrick had a meltdown. He became so furious that his eyes bulged out and his veins popped on the side of his head. He fumed at Ed, shouting about how furious he would be if Ed won the election. His rivalry pushed him to go around the school for days lobbying against Ed, persuading other children not to vote for Ed, an act of betrayal Patrick would bitterly regret. Ed didn't invite Patrick over for weeks after that and discouraged other friends from including him. Patrick's rage at being bested only caused him further trouble with his friends.

One night, when Patrick was thirteen, all of the boys were at one house, engaged in their usual string of entertainments—a little Xbox, an hour or so on the blacktop playing basketball, breaks for chips and juice, periodic bursts of IM-ing various girls, time out for a movie they had watched twenty times before. At some point while roaming around his friend Elliot's basement, the boys discovered an old set of boxing equipment. Delighted by a new form of entertainment, they quickly put on the masks, mouth gear, and gloves and rushed outside to go at it. By this time, it was 11:00 on a warm summer night. Just before going to bed, Elliot's mother peeked outside to see if they were okay. Patrick, wearing one set of the gear, was sobbing with great ugly gulps, while one of the other boys, Keith, was jabbing and punching at him, taunting him, "Can't take it, can you? What are you, afraid? You a sissy? Huh? Huh? Afraid to get hurt?" The other boys sat by, watching with mean passivity. What had begun as a rowdy but innocent pastime had become a cruel chance to make Patrick feel terrible. And Patrick's response seemed to embody the larger problem. He stood there wailing, refusing to give up or leave the group but unable to shift the tone or turn the tables on his tormentor. He seemed stuck in the role of loser.

Watching Patrick struggle was agony for his parents. His mother offered encouragement and sometimes pointed out to him what he might have done that made things worse. His father struggled with Patrick's woes. He was desperate for Patrick to be good at basketball and baseball. Those were things he had loved when he was a boy. Those were things that made you stand out when you were young. So he got Patrick special baseball coaching after school. He sent him to summer sports programs. He offered to help coach the teams. He got mad at the coaches when Patrick wasn't given enough time on the court or a position in the batting order. Middle-class parents from the United States often think that when they do those things, they are simply advocating for their children. But most of the time, they are just making things worse. Patrick's "Kick me" sign seemed brighter than ever.

What Patrick needed was support to do the things he liked and that made him feel competent, because in those settings, he was likely to find friends and feel good about himself. One of his problems was that because he felt insecure in many of the activities he was supposed to love and be good at, he behaved in ways that irritated the other kids. When they showed their irritation, it only agitated Patrick more and made him perform worse, which further put off the other kids. And while kids need to feel supported when they are upset with other kids, it doesn't help them if their parents are always angry at the bad coach, the bad teacher, or the bad friend. Such "support" only encourages kids to feel resentful and misunderstood.

For better or for worse, Patrick didn't back off from his group of friends. He kept spending Saturdays with them, joining the same teams, and inviting them over. It seemed like a recipe for disaster. If you had skimmed over the details of Patrick's social biography at this point, it would have been easy to label him as socially at risk. He seemed headed down a bad path, doing all the things that made the original difficulties worse. The signs seemed to point clearly away from popularity and social success. But his life, like every child's life, was more complicated than that. Buried inside the big picture were small details that turned out to make all the difference. During those years, as he seemed to move farther into the category of "loser," he was still invited to the parties, he still played on the teams, and, perhaps most important, he still had a strong and happy friendship with one of the kids in his original group. Meanwhile, he began to focus seriously on a new skill, something those boys didn't share. He began to play the saxophone.

He also made a few friends who were not part of the original group. And although the group of friends never fully embraced him, his friendship with the one boy, Wilson, persisted and deepened. They got together in the summer, when the group wasn't a group. They did things together on weekends that didn't involve sports or those other boys. And Patrick got older. He lost weight. The bonds that held the boys as a gang loosened, and what remained was his close friendship with Wilson. Finally, being great at baseball and basketball didn't matter so much anymore. His interests lay in music. He developed an intense crush on a beautiful girl. He would never be the captain of the football team. He'd never be the cool boy who had kissed every girl in the class. But he was good at things, he had close friendships, and he knew who he was. He had weathered the storm.

Patrick was like a lot of kids—he had some trouble with friends. But he was never totally isolated. And although he might have had moments of frustration and rage at the way he felt treated by other kids, he also had fun with them.

A child doesn't need to be the king of the castle to thrive socially. Not all children are the most popular, and not all children have lots of friends. Your child doesn't need to be the first one chosen on the team or be the queen bee. If she is part of a group some of the time or has made a good friend, she is probably going to be fine. She will be fine even if at some point she has felt lonely in a new school or gone through a rough time in her early teens. Those kinds of momentary dramas can be very painful, but they don't last, and they don't predict much. They're just one of the perils of growing up, at least in our society.

But if you are worried, what can you do? Start by trying to get a fuller picture of what your child experiences and how she feels. Listen carefully to her descriptions of her day. The most valuable clues are probably buried in her stories (or her avoidance of certain kinds of stories, for instance, if she never mentions experiences that involve friends).

You don't have to hover and pepper your child with questions to find out if she feels connected to other kids. But if you have any reason to be concerned, watch and listen. Does she talk about particular friendships? Do you get any sense of what your daughter and her friends like about one another or like to do together? Does she play with kids outside of school? Does she look forward to eating lunch with a certain child each day? Do her friendships last more than a few weeks?

Parents of neglected or rejected children are often themselves somewhat tuned out and might be somewhat cut off from their children's everyday experience. If you are not used to creating intimacy with others, it can be hard to become intimately familiar with your child's daily life. On the other hand, there are plenty of parents in our society who treat their children's daily experience like a job to be mastered, and this doesn't help much, either. Interrogation usually doesn't work very well. The goal is to get a rich picture of your child's friendships, fights, and quandaries, not to become an investigator or take a deposition.

If, after watching and listening, you feel that your child is seriously lonely or constantly left out of the social scene at school, you can help in three ways. First, you can try to create situations in which she can make new friends. She can get involved with a different group of kids (preferably a small group) for some after-school activity, something she really likes and wants to do. Invite children she likes to do things with over on the weekends, outside of the dynamics of the regular classroom. Sometimes these bonds carry over into the school week and shift the social dynamics in class.

Second, if you have the sense that she continually makes the same mistakes in the way she approaches kids or deals with others in groups, you might consider getting her some help, the kind of peer intervention that has been successful in experiments. Finding a good version of this might not be so easy outside of university towns, however. Don't despair if your community doesn't provide such programs. A good counselor might work just as well. Family life, too, can help make up for what she isn't getting out of social life. One of the sad ironies of early peer neglect and rejection is that what these children miss out on is the very thing they need for later friendships. Research shows that making friends takes practice. Early experiences of intimacy and friendship lead to greater social skills later on. If your child isn't getting a chance to practice those skills at school, she will need plenty of opportunities to have fun with others, share confidences, work out conflicts, and be close to others while at home.

The third thing you can do might be the hardest of all. Be aware that life in groups is tough for her. Remind yourself that she doesn't mean to get into trouble with the other children. She can't help it that she puts people off. How does it help to know this if you can't do much about it? Parents underestimate the power of simply understanding what their children are going through. You can give her the compassion and support to buffer against those negative experiences.

Having compassion for your child's social difficulty does *not* mean justifying her actions when she is mean to other children. It is important to let her know that it is wrong and hurtful to bully others. Make it clear, in your own behavior with family members and friends, that thinking about the perspectives and feelings of others is extremely important. When it comes to social behavior, kids model themselves after their parents quite strongly.

What you can't do is simply turn your child into a kid who makes friends. So far, there isn't much evidence that a child who is chronically rejected can change all that much. Marlene Sandstrom tells the following story from her days as a graduate student working with John Coie, who was recording the behavior of some children in an elementary-school classroom. He could not help but notice one little boy who personified the geek and was always left out of everything. One day, this boy had a sign on his desk: "I'm a wild and crazy guy." Violating his usual rule of scientific disengagement, Coie wandered over to the little boy and said in a quiet voice, "I don't think that sign is such a good idea. If I were you, I'd take it down. I don't think the other kids will react well to it." The next day, when Coie returned to collect more data, he looked over and saw that the little boy had put up a new sign: "Pay no attention to that other sign." The poor little guy had only made matters worse. No research has shown that a child with such offbeat social instincts can be taught or lured into becoming socially attuned or better at making friends.

As Kagan's work has shown, a really shy kid is unlikely to become a party animal. One of the worst things parents can do, in their anxiety or disappointment that their child is not surrounded by friends, is to try to force the child into social situations. But that doesn't mean you have to give up on your child's social life or that she is doomed to unhappiness because of problems in her elementary years. The most important way to help is to understand that even if you cannot change her, you can change her path.

3

Goodness: Bernie Madoff's Mother

Goodness comes from somewhere, and so does badness. In 2009, Bernie Madoff was arrested for bilking thousands of people out of billions of dollars. That was the year lots of people turned out to be selfish and immoral, many of them working in high-profile jobs at big corporations such as AIG and Morgan Stanley. What made Madoff stand out is that he not only duped faceless strangers, whose only connection to him was as a name on an accounts page, but he also cheated employees he had worked with and invited to his home, and he stole money from friends who had known him and trusted him for years.

In their quest to figure out how this charismatic and successful guy could have engaged in such a massive wrong, journalists began to poke through his childhood. What they found was that Madoff grew up in a tight-knit Jewish community, Laurelton, in Queens, New York. He hung out with the other kids, having the same kinds of fun they had. He came from an intact family. He did well at school and had extracurricular interests (one schoolmate remembered Madoff's hilarious turn as a sheik in a school play, wearing his parents' bedsheets for a costume). He attended the University of Alabama for a year before transferring to Hofstra University, and he married his high school sweetheart, Ruth.

"Mr. Madoff spent the next year at Brooklyn Law School, attending classes in the morning and running his side business—installing and fixing sprinkler systems—in the afternoon and evening, recalled Joseph Kavanau, who attended law school with Mr. Madoff. When Mr. Kavanau married his wife, Jane, who was Mrs. Madoff's best friend from Queens, Mr. Madoff was the best man. 'Bernie was very industrious,' Mr. Kavanau explains. 'He was going to school and working at the same time. Mr. Madoff was never interested in practicing law,' Mr. Kavanau says. Instead, Mr. Madoff left law school and, using $5,000 saved from being a lifeguard and from his sprinkler business, joined the ranks of Wall Street in the 1960s."* Nothing seemed to foretell the massive immorality that lay ahead.

But one detail about his childhood stands out as a huge red flag. Madoff's mother, Sylvia, was also involved in finance. During the late 1950s and early '60s, she had her own brokerage firm, Gibraltar Securities. In 1963, the Securities and Exchange Commission investigated her firm, along with several others, for failing to file financial reports. Before they could revoke her registration, Sylvia withdrew it, and matters ended there.

When people speak of a person's moral fiber, they would be more accurate to imagine a moral braid, a twisted rope of several different strands. And there is no question that one of those strands is the behavior a child sees in his home. Sylvia Madoff

* Julie Creswell and Landon Thomas Jr., "The Talented Mr. Madoff," *New York Times*, January 24, 2009, p. B1.

might well have told her son to say thank you when a neighbor gave him dinner and to get up and give his grandmother a chair when she came to visit. She might have lectured him sternly if he ever got caught cheating on a spelling test. He was known for his periodic generosity to friends and employees, and it could well be that Sylvia praised her young son when he was kind to the little boy down the street who got teased by other kids. All of this is possible. Meanwhile, she herself might have been defrauding customers, sneaking past the regulatory commissions, or cheating the government, and if so, there would be a good chance it was rubbing off on Bernie.

Although the roots of immorality can be found growing in a child's home, the roots of goodness can be found growing right within the child.

The Good Egg

Oliver had a difficult start in life. His father walked out on his mother months before Oliver was born, leaving her on her own throughout her pregnancy and childbirth. She was from a middle-class, educated family, but by the time she had Oliver, she was so poor she was living in a shelter for unwed mothers. She had a difficult labor, and with no access to decent medical care, she died shortly following childbirth.

Oliver, a slender, pale boy, short for his age, spent his early years in a group home. When he was nine years old, he was taken in as a foster child by the kind of family that should never qualify as foster parents. His foster father was rough, demanding, and cruel. By the time he was nine, Oliver had had very little experience of kindness or parental affection. Most of the adults in the surrounding neighborhood believed that harsh punishment was the best way to discipline children. In his early years in the group home and then later in his foster home, there was not one adult who provided Oliver with the warm, authoritative parenting we now know is best for children. There wasn't one adult or friend who provided him with a role model in thoughtful or altruistic behavior.

Although the neighborhood was rough, it was also a community in which there was a lot of talk about godliness. There was a great deal of ranting and railing against sin, and when children misbehaved, they were often chastised for being sinners. But the truth was that the adults around Oliver rarely behaved in decent ways. What he saw, day in and day out, were grown-ups who put their own self-interest ahead of others, who were mistrustful of one another, and who assumed the worst about children.

When Oliver was ten years old, he met a slightly older boy named Jack. Jack, too, had had a rough childhood, but he seemed to have weathered it well. He was full of life, good at things, and savvy, and he seemed genuinely interested in who Oliver was. Oliver felt for the first time that he had a friend. Jack invited Oliver to his home, shared confidences with him, hung out with him, and introduced him to other kids and to his family. But here, too, Oliver came face-to-face with the duplicity and selfishness he had seen everywhere in his foster home. Jack's father, it turned out, was a petty thief who encouraged Jack and his friends to help him out in his nefarious schemes.

During his early teens, it seemed that Oliver couldn't get away from the very situations that have been shown, again and again, to push people toward immoral behavior. He had every motivation to lie and steal and little encouragement to do the right thing. The adults in his life provided perfect role models for cheating, and his peer group was every parent's nightmare, low achievers who had already chosen easy money and thrills over conventional accomplishment and community engagement. Oliver was surrounded by badness—the kind that often seems to shape a child. If you had known Oliver during these impressionable years, you might have predicted that he was doomed to the same kind of sordid, low life of those around him.

And yet, from the moment he could talk, Oliver seemed different from the people around him. He was honest and kind. He went out of his way for other people. He not only knew what was right, but he also did what was right. Although he hung out with kids who stole and committed other petty crimes, each time he was supposed to demonstrate his own prowess, he found a way not to steal. When he was about eleven, he fell in with a gang of kids trying to rob a house. All Oliver could think of was how he might warn the family that owned the house. He got caught doing it, but he succeeded in stopping the crime. Again and again, he behaved in ways that were good for others, even when it cost him personal comfort. No matter what pressures he faced to engage in selfish and hurtful behavior, Oliver's inner goodness steadily shone through. By the time he was a young teenager, it was clear that nothing could have thrown young Mr. Twist's moral compass out of whack. Some strands of the moral braid are part of the basic human architecture, and Charles Dickens dramatized that truth in his novel *Oliver Twist* as well as anyone could. But most children aren't as good as Oliver, who seemed immune to every sinister influence, with an unshakable urge to do the right thing.

Yet most of us don't turn out to be like Bernie Madoff, either. In real life, children aren't villains or heroes. Annie, for instance, was an inscrutable mixture of the two. Annie was the eldest of three children. Incredibly pretty, with slightly tilted blue eyes, a wide lush mouth, and almost white blond hair, she was as smart as a whip, brimming with talent and energy of all kinds. She spoke early and seemed eager for big, new words. At age four, she chastised her one-year-old brother for tasting her food when she was sick. "Hal, don't eat it. It might be confectionary."

She was adored by her parents, who loved her feistiness and precocity. She was the kind of exuberant and animated child teachers are drawn to. But she was also headstrong from the get-go. When her babysitter insisted that they leave the zoo one day, Annie sat down on her haunches and growled. She spoke to adults outside her family as if she were their peer. And somehow her willfulness seemed to go hand-in-hand with a determined sense of sneakiness as well.

Annie's aunt tells the following story: "We were sitting at the picnic table in the yard. It was early August, and the whole extended family of fifteen people was eating dinner together on one of the first nights of our annual summer reunion in Maine. Just as the adults and older children were leaning back to enjoy their second helping more slowly, I noticed that my two-year-old niece, Annie, had left the table. Where was she? We rushed to check the dangerous places (the road or the lake near the house) and then began to wonder where on earth she could have gone. Who knows what led me up the stairs to the bedroom where I was staying? There was Annie, busily doing something she didn't want me to see. She must have heard my steps on the wood stairs, because by the time I walked through the door, she was sitting on the floor near the bed, looking at me with an expression of furtive innocence. 'Annie,' I said, 'what are you doing up here, sweetie pie?' 'Nothing,' she answered. Her blue eyes were wide with feigned blankness and surprise at my question.

"I don't know what inkling drew me into the bathroom to peek inside the small cloth case in which I had brought my jewelry when I visited my parents' home. Empty. By then, my sister Jodie, Annie's mother, had joined me in the bedroom. 'Annie,' she said with some force, 'what are you doing up here?' 'Nothing,' Annie answered, shaking her head vigorously, her voice slightly raised, reflecting her surprise that we were questioning her. It was clear that she took umbrage at our suspicion. 'Nothing, Mommy.' I whispered to my sister, 'I think she took my jewelry.' Jodie peered down at her little daughter. She had only been a mom for two years, but she already had a bead on her little girl. Annie's eyes darted toward the hiding spot—her underwear. Sure enough, we saw a small bulge with sharp edges and little gold fasteners and a few beads peeking out of the hem of Annie's underpants. Jodie put out her hand, saying, 'Annie, give them to me right now.' I could hardly hold in my laughter. As we left the bedroom with Annie trailing behind, Jodie leaned over and hissed to me, 'My daughter's a jewelry thief.'"

What can you tell from a toddler's misdeeds about her moral fiber? Would Annie's naughtiness turn out to be a sign of things to come or just a red herring?

Each baby arrives with a leaning toward goodness or badness. We know, for instance, that some children are born with a strong predilection for trouble. At the extreme end, we call people like this sociopaths, people who seem to have literally no concern for the well-being of others, no sense of moral obligation, and no innate grasp of the difference between right and wrong. They seem, in other words, to have no conscience. And to some degree, the opposite is true as well. At eighteen months old, many babies seem to have a natural impulse that does, in fact, contribute to what we think of as moral behavior—they appear to feel the psychological distress of other babies.

The Root of Good Deeds

If you've ever watched two toddlers who have spent time together, perhaps in a family day-care setting or in a sandbox, you might have witnessed a version of the following scene. One of the children falls down, hurts herself, and begins sobbing. The other child, who had been busily playing nearby, hears the crying and looks over at his buddy. A worried look suffuses his face. He studies his friend's agonized sobs for a moment, gets up, marches over to her, reaches out, and offers her his own blankie. Anyone could see that he is hoping the blankie that comforts him so reliably will also help his friend feel better.

Psychologists view this as a clear indication that some toddlers feel empathy—they feel the distress of someone else and are moved to reduce that distress. Because he is still just a toddler, unable really to think about other people's thoughts, a young child will often offer his suffering friend the object that would comfort himself rather than the friend. In one classic example, a little boy saw his friend fall and dissolve into tears. Even though the crying child's mother was standing nearby, the little boy, stricken at his friend's distress, grabbed his own mother's hand and dragged her over to the other little boy.

The term *empathy* first appeared in the work of a German psychologist, Theodore Lipps, toward the end of the nineteenth century. The German word *Einfühling* literally means "feeling into another" and conveys the somewhat primitive, nonrational quality of empathy. Psychologists believe that empathy emerges before its more sophisticated cousins sympathy and perspective taking, both of which require a level of complex thinking that young children might not yet be capable of. You watch another person who has just heard terrible news, and you feel as if there is lead in *your* stomach. Your face has the same miserable pale cast that the other person's does. That's empathy. But even if you don't feel *Einfühling,* you can think through what another person is feeling. I've watched people in restaurants be high-handed and haughty with a waiter. If they paused for a moment and imagined what it would feel like to serve one hundred people in a hot, crowded room, they might see the situation differently and they just might change their tone. Even if such perspective taking doesn't occur spontaneously, people can deliberately lead themselves through such a mental exercise, although this is a different process from empathy.

To take someone's perspective and to feel concern for what you think they are feeling both require cognitive processes not available to young children. In other words, they can "feel into another person" before they can think about what someone else thinks or feels.

But as anyone with more than one child can attest, not all kids are equally empathic. Imagine the following experiment (not one you could actually carry out, of course). Put three toddlers in a playroom. Make one of those toddlers cry, and then watch the reaction of the other two. One might look very worried at the sight of her friend's tears and then come wobbling over to offer her crying friend her bottle. The other child might glance at the one who is crying, study him for a moment, and then go right back to playing. Researchers believe there are two components that contribute to a child's level of empathy: the intensity of emotion she feels in general and her ability to regulate those feelings. Children who have very intense emotional reactions but have a lot of trouble managing their feelings might actually avoid other children in distress as a way of avoiding their own discomfort. And children who don't tend to feel strong emotions might just not care that the other child is in pain.

This should come as no surprise. Adults clearly vary in their levels of empathy. Not all adults are equally upset when they see another person look sad or scared, and not all adults are equally quick to try to help the other person feel better. As with young children, some adults get very upset when they see another person hurt, but seeing the person's pain doesn't spur them to help.

In recent years, there has been a great flurry of activity aimed at increasing empathy in elementary and high school students, as a way of decreasing bullying and social exclusion. Can you teach an unempathic person to feel the pain of others? Is that a first step toward goodness?

Norma and Seymour Feshbach, psychologists at UCLA, believe so. Their approach hinges on the link they see between aggressive behavior and empathy. All of us have periodic urges to hurt or dominate another person. But if you feel empathy, you might rein in your aggressive urges, so as to avoid the pain you'd feel for having caused someone else distress.

The Feshbachs reasoned that if they could increase aggressive children's tendency to empathize with others, they might be able to teach children to be less aggressive. Their study involved more than eighty schoolchildren in the Los Angeles school system. First, they asked teachers in elementary schools to rate how helpful and kind the children in their classrooms were. Then the children were put into small work groups that met for one-hour sessions over a period of ten weeks. Each group contained some children who had been identified as highly aggressive and some who were in the normal range (from low to moderate). The children spent the "workshop" time playing various games designed to teach them how to feel what others were feeling and see the world from another's perspective. In empathy camp, the children looked at photographs of people's faces and tried to "name that feeling." In another game, the counselors described people who had been put into various situations and then asked the children to role-play. The kids drew pictures and told stories showing how the world looked from someone else's perspective. "What would the world look like to you if you were as small as a cat?" "What birthday present would make each member of your family happiest?" Over the course of the ten weeks, the tasks became increasingly abstract and complex. Instead of imagining how a friend would feel if her favorite toy was broken, the now seasoned campers were asked to imagine "What would your best friend do if he found a lost child in a department store?"

Meanwhile, the children in the control condition also participated in thirty hours of problem solving and games, but the games they engaged in were focused on learning about trees, water, and the weather. At the end of the ten weeks, teachers were asked to think over recent days and to rate their students again (without any knowledge of the groups the children had been in). The children who had participated in the empathy-training workshops were rated as kinder, more helpful, and more thoughtful toward others than those who had been learning about the natural world. Interestingly, the researchers reported that the children far preferred the nonempathy activities (those included in the control condition). As Norma Feshbach put it, "Empathy training is hard work."

Empathy is not all that different from baseball. As anyone who's watched tee-ball or mini-league can tell you, some kids are born with the ability to hit a ball. As early as age three, some kids know how to hold a bat, how to keep their eye on the ball, when to begin swinging, and how to use their bodies to send the ball flying in the right direction. For those kids, few words or lessons are needed. They don't need to be told the right batting stance or how to swing the bat—they just feel it and do it.

However, kids who lack that intuitive feeling can learn the components—they can practice watching the ball, someone can show them the right way to hold the bat, and they can learn how to adjust to different kinds of pitches and when to hold off and not swing at all. With good instruction and practice, those components can come together and enable a Little-Leaguer to do well at the game. That kind of kid might never have the feel for the game that naturally talented kids have, but he can still play baseball.

The Feshbachs' research suggests that those children who don't seem naturally to feel the pain of others can learn to recognize the feelings of others, imagine what they are going through, and identify with their circumstances. With practice and instruction, they can become empathic and, perhaps more important, less aggressive.

If Bernie Madoff had participated in an empathy workshop, it might have helped—but it wouldn't have been enough. If a toddler feels sad when her friend cries, that doesn't automatically mean that she will grow up to be an especially kind and ethical person, particularly when doing right comes at her own expense. Empathy might be a powerful building block for doing the right thing, but there is more to it than that. The proclivity to help others at one's own expense, otherwise known as altruism, is also a key component of what we think of as moral behavior.

Selfish Genes Cause Kindness

My stepfather was a man with a complicated moral code. A farmer, he would risk his life for a stranger drowning in the ocean and happily give away hundreds of dollars to someone down on his luck. But he would lie without batting an eyelid to keep others from interfering with his plans. He used to say, "Nice guys finish last." He'd wait a beat and then, to make sure we understood his cynical philosophy, add, "Survival of the fittest!" with a knowing nod. He assumed that this proclamation would remind us that the tougher, more ruthless person would always do the best. He was sure, as many people are, that Darwin's great discovery was that looking out for number one is the surest way to survive. If this were true, what on earth would make any of us go out on a limb for another person? Why would our kids acquire an impulse to put other people's needs first?

Psychologists and philosophers used to believe that altruism was a highly sophisticated behavior based on an exalted sense of the common good. It represented the triumph of human rational thought over our basic instincts. Yet some evolutionary psychologists have shown that monkeys, whales, and bats, among other species, regularly put the well-being of others ahead of their own needs.

What would make an animal put its own survival at risk for the good of another creature? Take a moment to consider how any behaviors (rather than a physical characteristic) might evolve. People prefer sweets because the ones who liked bitter food died eating poisons, while the ones with a sweet tooth gravitated toward high-calorie items. The ones drawn to high-calorie foods lived long enough to have babies who inherited their preference for sweet things. People with the cognitive capacity to invent and use tools were more likely to live in shelters and make weapons, which helped them survive animal attacks and bad weather. The tool users were much more likely to survive long enough to pass on their particular kind of cognition. The ones whose mental processes kept them from figuring out how to build a shelter or a weapon probably died before they had a chance to pass on their non-tool-use way of thinking.

But what possible advantage could there be in dying for the sake of another? Why would altruism give any organism, human or not, a leg up in survival? The answer, according to Richard Dawkins, is that it is our genes, not our individual selves, that need to survive. If helping another creature helps a species survive, the next generation of that species will contain more individuals who help. People with genes that cause them to help others live longer. Those who live longer have more opportunities to have babies and therefore pass on those helping genes. Selfish genes might cause unselfish behavior. This is why scientists have found that both people and animals are more likely to help out another when that other is closely related to them.

When Harald Euler and Barbara Weitzel asked adults to think back about their childhood and report how they were treated by their grandparents, they found that most people remembered kinder, more protective treatment from their maternal grandmothers than from their other grandparents. What does this have to do with the evolution of altruism? The more certain people are that their grandchildren are genetically related to them, the more likely they are to have an instinct to protect them. Your mother's mother had a lot of certainty that you were related to her, hence her great interest in your well-being (and the survival of her genetic material). Your father's father, on the other hand, could never be absolutely sure that you were genetically related to him (two different opportunities for a mixup). In one startling experiment, identical twins were much more cooperative to each other than were same-sex fraternal twins. In other words, two same-age brothers help each other a lot more when, by doing so, they are supporting the survival of 100 percent of their genes. Same-age brothers who share only 50 percent of their genes (fraternal twins) don't have as much incentive to help each other.

Selfishness Rears Its Ubiquitous Head

Although the urge to help others might be part of the equipment we come with, so, too, is the impulse to put oneself first, even when it hurts others. And if there are signs that babies have the seeds of goodness in them, it is even clearer that in our first years, selfishness runs rampant. Some of the most important developmental psychologists have described infants as solipsistic, autistic, and egocentric. In fact, Anna Freud famously claimed that if you put a toddler on a street corner in Cambridge, by the time she made her way to Harvard Square, she would have committed every crime known to mankind. We assume that babies are born heedless of the rights of others, consumed with the impulse to please themselves at all costs.

In a videotape I made years ago in a day-care center, a little boy named Daniel, with a huge mop of very dark brown hair, is rocking away with great energy on a small wooden rocking boat. Another little boy, Max, who is about two and a half years old and has a wide freckled face and inscrutable blue eyes, is playing nearby with some blocks. Suddenly, the rocking boat catches Max's attention. He drops the blocks and walks over to Daniel, who continues to rock away in the boat. Without saying a word, Max tries to knock Daniel out of the boat so that he can get in. Outraged, Daniel shouts, "Maaaxxxx! I'm rocking!" But Max doesn't seem to register Daniel's dismay. Max quietly and insistently pulls at Daniel until he's pushed him off balance and dragged him out of the boat. While Daniel marches over in tears to complain to a teacher, Max complacently climbs into the boat and begins to enjoy the ride.

Psychologists call Max's behavior, common in toddlers and preschoolers, instrumental aggression. Max isn't being mean in order to hurt someone or dominate others. He simply wants what he wants, and he won't hesitate to knock over anyone who comes between him and his object of desire. While young children do care about other people—offering them blankies or gently stroking a sibling who has been hurt—the dominating force that energizes them is the drive to fulfill their own needs and desires.

Sigmund Freud argued that throughout life, the drive to please oneself guides and explains much behavior, but that over time, one learns to temper it in order to live with others. He also argued that we develop a conscience by internalizing the mores of our parents—becoming like them is safer than trying to defy them. While the specifics of Freud's explanation have not held up to scrutiny, research has amply documented the enormous power of people's urge to satisfy their desires. When your young child seems driven by a selfish demon within, it does not mean he is doomed to a life of heartlessness or greed. It means he is not yet able to wrestle his impulses to the ground. Human development takes time and, with any luck, involves the guidance of moral parents.

When Max knocked the little boy off the rocking toy, Daniel, grief-stricken, stomped over to the teacher to protest the injustice. Then the teacher did what adults from time immemorial have done when children displayed their raw need to run roughshod over others in order to please themselves. She chastised Max. "That wasn't nice, Max. Daniel was riding the boat. What do you say when you've hurt someone?" The urge that most adults feel to chastise is just as natural as the urge the child feels to get what he wants at all costs.

Children grow up in a world of others and usually find early on that they are not allowed simply to take or do whatever they want. If they are especially attuned to the expectations of adults—if they are eager to please others and win approval—they quickly come face-to-face with a dilemma: how can they get what they want without displeasing those around them?

That was certainly the bind Annie found herself in. By the time Annie was six years old, her attraction to surreptitious adventures had expanded. She climbed out the window of her bedroom, under the guidance of a nine-year-old friend, so that they could sneak off to the park across the street. A year later, her mother discovered her hiding in her parents' closet, phone book and telephone in hand, making prank calls to unsuspecting strangers. Again, her older friend was there with her, offering suggestions. Upon getting caught, Annie again insisted that they had done nothing wrong. She seemed instinctively to know the strategy so many adults have used when caught in the wrong: "That's my story, and I'm sticking to it."

"Annie doesn't care how she makes other people feel," her father lamented. "Where does that come from?"

What made her behavior more baffling was that it was certainly not a family trait. Hal, three years younger than Annie, had red hair and a pale, narrow face. Although he was often exuberant, he had a voice that could express woe like nobody's business. Hal seemed to have been born concerned about the feelings of others. When he was two, he insisted that Annie couldn't join him on a special trip to the store their mother had invited him on. Annie was crestfallen. For once, he had outdone her. But when he got into the car, his long narrow mouth turned down like Charlie Brown's. "I don't like what I just said to Annie," he said. He made his mother turn around and pick Annie up so she could go, too.

When Annie was six and Hal was three, they learned the rhyme "Sticks and stones can break my bones, but words will never hurt me." Annie leaned her head to one side and said, "That's true. Words don't hurt me." She gazed at her mother with her light blue eyes, calm and inscrutable. She looked as pretty as a picture and impermeable.

But Hal's eyes widened. "Words can hurt *me*!"

His sensitivity, his compassion for others, and his eagerness to help didn't rub off on Annie. Instead, Hal's thoughtfulness seemed, in the family constellation, to make up for Annie's lack of empathy.

Then came the clincher. Annie, now seven, was sharing a bedroom with Hal, now four, and their eighteen-month-old brother, Nate. Their parents had hatched this sleeping arrangement because none of the kids was a good sleeper. Perhaps, they thought, if the children had one another's company, they'd stay out of their parents' room. Hal's room became the sleeping room. Annie's room became the playroom for all. The plan seemed to be working wonders. All three kids were sleeping better than they ever had. But suddenly, three months into the new arrangement, the baby started waking in the middle of the night, crying loudly. When their mom, Jodie, went in to see what was wrong, she found the baby agitated and Annie wide awake, wanting conversation and comfort. Jodie worried that the baby was waking Annie up. Maybe she should change things around. Then, after a few weeks of this, when Jodie was at her wits' end, Annie leaned in toward her mother and confided, "I've been waking up Nate. I knew that if he cried, you'd come in. I wanted to see you."

That morning, Jodie called her older sister, desperate, and announced on the phone, "Annie is selfish. And she's sneaky. What am I going to do? I've already tried stars, checks, losing TV rights for sneakiness, and offering a trip to the ice cream store for acts of unselfishness."

Her sister, a schoolteacher, reminded her, "Discipline isn't a form of control. It's a process of education."

Way back, after the stolen jewelry incident, Jodie had been on the lookout for opportunities to instill a stronger conscience in her slightly ruthless little girl. Jodie seemed to know intuitively that Annie needed lots of what psychologist Martin Hoffman calls parenting by induction, the process by which parents help children think about how their actions make other people feel. When parents are encouraged to use this approach with children, they often get it slightly wrong. Once, after speaking to a group of parents about this, I overheard one of the dads say to his son, "If you don't share your bike, the other kids won't want to play with you." This is not what Hoffman had in mind, since the parent was simply reminding the child to think about his own interests. Encouraging thoughtful behavior works better when you say, "Think how it feels to your friend when he doesn't get a turn," thereby directing your child's attention to the feelings of others.

There are so many things developmental psychologists don't yet know, but one thing the research has shown quite clearly is that when it comes to raising children who are thoughtful, the way a parent disciplines the child has a huge impact.

One day, Annie and her mother went to see a pottery exhibit by a cousin who attended college nearby. In her typically exuberant manner, which sometimes seemed heedless of the things and people around her, Annie began twirling around the gallery. In a flash, she had knocked into one of the pedestals, sending it crashing to the floor, along with the large ceramic jug that had been placed on it. She had broken a college senior's thesis project, smashing it into a million little pieces. Annie collapsed onto the floor in alarmed tears and shame. Used to mishaps like this from her lively and somewhat unconstrained little girl, Jodie knelt down to console Annie and enlist her help in cleaning up. But Jodie took it one step farther. She and Annie wrote a note for the student, expressing their apologies and regrets about the broken jug.

A number of studies have shown that when you criticize a child for hurting another or take away a privilege or a valued item when the child has been unkind, it does no good. When your child grabs a toy from another kid at the playground, giving her a time-out will not help her learn to share. Punishment doesn't work.

Yet not all rewards work equally well, either. In one study, toddlers were put in a room with an adult who was engaged in other tasks. At some point, the adult dropped a pen or a piece of paper and then reached for it, making it clear that he was having trouble reaching it. The idea was to see if the toddler would come over and help the grown-up reach the object or do nothing. Toddlers who helped the adult moved on to the second phase of the study. In this phase, they were once again placed in a room with a grown-up who needed help. But a third of the children received praise for their help: "That's really nice." Another third received a small cube, part of a larger toy they had previously found very appealing. The final third received no reward. Instead, the adult merely took the fallen object the toddler had helped reach and went back to the original activity. During a subsequent series of play sessions, each child went through five versions of this, always with the same kind of feedback. Which type of response led to the most helping over the long run? You might think that the children who received a toy would be the most likely to continue helping adults. Not so. The children who received praise were much more likely to continue helping the adult than the children who received rewards. Perhaps more surprising, the children who received no feedback were almost twice as likely to continue as the ones who received a prize. In other words, rewards can undermine intrinsic motivation. The findings of this study remind us that, like many complex characteristics, goodness cannot simply be trained into a person.

But this issue has more layers than an onion. While it's clear that praise works better than prizes, not all praise is the same. The difference is seemingly subtle. Telling a child that it was good that he shared his cookies might get him to share more of his cookies right then and there. But it won't have as powerful an effect as letting the child know you believe his actions reveal that he is a good person.

In one study, a group of seven- and eight-year-olds were brought to a trailer set up outside their school in Toronto. The first time they came to the trailer, they were told that the experimenter wanted their opinion on a new toy, a bowling game. They were told that when they had scored seventy to eighty points, they could take two marbles from a bowl of marbles, which would be traded for a prize at the end of the game. The children were also told that they could put one of their marbles into a bowl for poor children (a bowl was on the table with a picture of two "indigent-looking children" and a sign that said, "Help Poor Children") so that the poor children could have toys as well.

While the children played the game, the experimenter stood slightly off to the side to prompt a child if he or she didn't spontaneously give a marble to the donation bowl. If the child didn't donate, the experimenter would say something like, "Remember, you can give one of your marbles to the poor children if you want to." When they were done with the game, the experimenter made one of three comments to each child. The first attributed goodness to the child: "Gee, you shared quite a bit. I guess you're the kind of person who likes to help others whenever you can. Yes, you are a very nice and helpful person." Other children were offered old-fashioned reinforcement for their good deed: "Gee, you shared quite a bit. It was good that you gave some of your marbles to those poor children. Yes, that was a nice and helpful thing to do." And finally, as in all good experiments, some children served as the control condition and received a comparatively neutral comment: "Gee, you shared quite a bit." After the statement, the children were left alone to play another game while the experimenter watched through a one-way mirror to see how much each child donated.

After the second game, each child chose a prize and was given twelve colored pencils as an additional prize for participating. They were told that they could donate some pencils for children in the school who had not gotten to participate. At that point in the experiment, the children who had received both forms of praise donated more pencils than the children who had simply been told, “Gee, you shared quite a bit.” If the experiment had stopped there, the researchers could easily have thought that praise encourages good deeds and that it doesn’t matter what form the praise takes. But the experiment didn’t stop there.

One week later, the children returned to the trailer and participated in a task involving folding cardboard cards so they could be used as roofs for toy houses. The experimenter remained present while the children folded four cards each. Again, children heard one of three comments: “Thanks for folding the cards. You know, you are certainly a nice person. I bet you’re someone who is helpful whenever possible.” Or “Thanks for folding the cards. You know, that was certainly a nice thing to do. It was good that you helped me with my work here today.” Or the bland “Thanks for folding the cards.” The experimenter then gave each child a Viewmaster toy and said that he or she could either play with the toy or fold cards for the next five minutes while the experimenter made a phone call.

Two weeks later, the experimenter came to visit the children in their classrooms. She announced that she was collecting drawings and craft materials for sick children in the hospital. Children were given paper for drawing and asked to put their artwork in a bag to be collected in two days. The children who had been given the sense that their previous actions reflected a truly good inner self were far more likely to draw pictures for the sick children.

The moral of the story: When children are encouraged to believe they are good, they are more likely to be good. Taken together, this study and the study in which children were praised or not praised for helping an adult remind us that goodness is not a surface behavior that can easily be trained into or out of a child. Children who have the impulse to help do so because of that impulse, not because of any feedback they get. Moreover, appealing to the child's inner sense of her core goodness affects her more than more transitory pleasures such as simple praise for a specific good deed.

But not all good deeds begin in the gut or the heart. Some begin in the head. When asked to talk about their moral impulses, some people say that they don't feel empathy—they don't feel a twinge in the gut or a lump in the throat hearing the plights of others. They're guided instead by what they think is right, a moral code that leads them to do the right thing—help others, be honest, and contribute to the common good. Seeing another child crying and offering him your bottle is just the beginning. The kinds of morality we judge others by in adulthood often involve far more deliberative rational acts than that. Bernie Madoff carried out his scam over more than a twenty-year period. People who join the Peace Corps think about it for a while before they do it.

What did Madoff talk about at the dinner table when he was young? And was it different from what Warren Buffett talked about at his dinner table? Buffett provides an interesting contrast to Madoff. One of the richest men in the world, Buffett has given away a huge amount of his money. He regularly admits his mistakes and has frequently urged the government to impose higher taxes on people like himself. In 2006, he gave a vast amount of money to Bill Gates's foundation, eschewing the glamour and stature of having a foundation in his own name. Either Madoff or Buffett might or might not step off a curb to pull an old lady out of the way of a speeding cab, but when it comes to their moral thinking, they obviously differ. Did that difference start during their childhood?

How would you suss out a person's way of thinking about moral issues? Lawrence Kohlberg, considered the godfather of research on moral development, constructed stories that embodied moral dilemmas. He told the stories to children of different ages and asked for their response. He argued that their answers revealed their developmental level of moral reasoning. Children (and adults) find the stories he used intriguing and often not easy to respond to in a simple way. That is what makes them so useful in eliciting a person's train of moral thought. Kohlberg used many stories, but this is his most famous, the "Heinz Dilemma."

> In Europe, a woman was near death from cancer. One drug might save her, a form of radium that a druggist in the same town had recently discovered. The druggist was charging $2,000, ten times what the drug cost him to make. The sick woman's husband, Heinz, went to everyone he knew to borrow the money, but he could get together only about half of what it cost. He told the druggist that his wife was dying and asked him to sell it cheaper or let him pay later. But the druggist said no. The husband got desperate and broke into the man's store to steal the drug for his wife. Should the husband have done that? Why?

The answers children gave to Kohlberg's moral dilemmas led him to argue that all children developed in a particular sequence. Toddlers respond only to reward and punishment. They'll do anything and everything they want, as long as they can get away with it. The preschooler, though, begins to monitor her own behavior, eager to gain approval. She tries not to do the things that elicit a frown or her mother's disapproval. She is eager to help when she thinks this will earn a smile from her father or kind words from the teacher. As children enter elementary school and are capable of more complex abstract thought, Kohlberg argued that they begin to use a set of rules to guide their behavior, rules that reflect the conventions of their community. The schoolchild's morals are defined, then, by what is acceptable to others rather than any abstract set of principles. By the time teenagers are capable of abstract reasoning, Kohlberg argued, they are also capable of knowing the right thing to do, even when that means breaking the rules within a given institution or community. Stealing medicine to help a sick person who has no money might be illegal, but it might be the right thing to do. From Kohlberg's perspective, the more able one is to reflect and deliberate using abstract principles, the more sophisticated one's moral sense will be.

But in the years since Kohlberg devised his famous scenarios, it's become clear that what people say is the right thing to do doesn't always match up to their actions.

Psychologist Eugene Subbotsky told young children in Russia a story about a little boy who was asked to move some balls from a pail to a jar without using his hands. But once the grown-up left the room, the little boy had trouble, so he used his hands. Subbotsky asked the children in his study, "Was the little boy wrong to do that? Why?"

Almost all of the children thought it was wrong for the little boy to break the rules. But then Subbotsky put the children in the same situation as the boy in the story. He brought them into a little playroom and asked them to use a shovel to put some balls into a jar. The first time they did it, everything went smoothly. They could all accomplish the short, simple task. But the second time they had to do it, they were handed a convex shovel that made it nearly impossible to lift the balls. To succeed at their assignment, they would have to use their hands. About a third of the children lied afterward, pretending they hadn't used their hands. In other words, for some children, it is actually quite easy to pry apart their moral reasoning from their moral actions.

Adults are not all that different. Many of us spout off at the dinner table about what the right thing to do is, only to turn around and do the selfish, sneaky thing at the grocery store or in our office. Harvard's Joshua Greene believes that some scenarios hit our emotional hot spots more than others and that this might provide a clue about why we sometimes find it hard to do the right thing.

Greene and his colleagues use functional magnetic resonance imaging (fMRI) equipment to try to figure out what role emotion plays in people's moral reasoning. Greene's interest stems from an intriguing phenomenon. Consider the following dilemma. A runaway train is headed for five people who will be killed if it proceeds on its present course. The only way to save them is to hit a switch that will turn the train onto another set of tracks where it will kill one person instead of five. Should you turn the train onto the other track in order to save the five people at the expense of the one person? Most people say yes.

But then Greene considers a slightly different version of the dilemma. Again, a train threatens to kill five people. You are standing next to a large stranger on a footbridge that spans the tracks, between the oncoming train and the five people. In this scenario, the only way to save the five people is to push the stranger off the bridge onto the tracks below. He will die if you do this, but his body will stop the train from reaching the other five. Should you save the five others at the expense of one? Most people say no.

Greene presents these two versions of the dilemma to experimental subjects hooked up to fMRIs. It turns out that when people hear the second version, the parts of the brain associated with emotion light up more than when they hear the first version. In other words, our moral reasoning is influenced by how "hot" or emotional a situation is. What we think is right depends a bit on how involved our feelings are.

If hot issues push a different moral button from cold ones, what good does it do to talk with children about what is right and wrong? The answer is that it helps a lot. Children who are more able to attain Kohlberg's higher levels of moral reasoning are, in fact, more likely to be helpful, to donate money, and to engage in volunteer work. In addition, children who are more able to think about the perspective of another person (which is not the same thing as feeling what another person is feeling) are more benevolent than others.

Paul Harris and Karen Hussar wanted to explore how children think about the moral choices they make. They interviewed children who had chosen to become vegetarians although the rest of their families ate meat. What Harris and Hussar learned was intriguing and suggestive. Kids who have chosen not to eat meat seem to think about the pain animals endure when they are butchered more than do meat eaters (or those who grow up in vegetarian families). It seems that a vivid imagination is part of the mental equipment that supports moral choices, at least the kind of moral choice, such as vegetarianism, that unfolds over time and requires sustained consideration.

Harris and Hussar learned another thing as well. All of the children they studied condemned people who chose vegetarianism and then ate meat more than they disapproved of nonvegetarians. In other words, children seem to understand the idea of moral commitment. Helping children think about goodness makes a difference, not just because there is a logic underlying our moral principles, as Kohlberg suggested, but also because imagining the plights of others (whether they are people or animals), though considered an intellectual activity, might lead us to think and act differently in everyday life. Doing right is complex, and fairly young children seem to know it.

In one study, researchers told six- and seven-year-old children stories about a boy who took something from another child. Then they asked their young subjects two different questions: "Was it right?" "How would you feel if you were that character?" Many of the children said that although the act was wrong, the boy was happy that he got what he wanted. Researchers call this the "happy victimizer" phenomenon. It seems that even first-graders know that there are some things you might do that would make you feel lousy afterward and some acts that are morally wrong but might feel good. For children who don't feel bad when they hurt others or see others in pain, helping them to understand the principle of the matter makes a big difference.

Several months after Annie admitted to waking her brother in the night, Jodie called her sister again. "Did I tell you about Annie's career in drug dealing?" she asked.

At a weekly get-together with other families at the park, the kids played, the parents talked, and eventually, they all went to one family's house for pizza. They had been doing this since Annie was five. This time, Annie, now almost eight, and her buddies disappeared almost instantly. The parents figured they were off playing soccer on the open field at the park. But they had been gone a long time. When one of the mothers went to look for them, she found them huddled around Annie in the park shed. When she looked into the huddle, she saw that they were munching on sweets, a furtive yet glazed look on their faces. All of the children were forbidden by their parents to eat sweets. Annie had brought some of her money from home to the park. She knew that if she offered the other children candy, it would make her queen for the day. As she later admitted, she knew she shouldn't do it. But that didn't stop her. She slipped away on her own and went to spend the money at the park canteen buying her goodies. Then, when the parents weren't paying attention, she beckoned to the other kids, who gathered around her where the parents couldn't see. She doled out the candy, enjoying the hands reaching out to her, basking in her peers' admiration of her feat, happily enjoying her plan's success. When she was caught, she didn't seem at all sorry.

Jodie said to her sister, "Why is she such a sneak? Is she always going to be this way?"

Was Jodie right? Could a seven-year-old be sneaky? Was Annie already destined to grow up doing whatever she needed to satisfy her own desires?

The answer lay in the other pieces of Annie's story. When she was only a year old, Annie had developed a quirky habit. When she was very excited by something (a story, something she saw, a conversation), she would hold her two hands up and wave her fingers in the air, her upper lip extended and trembling as if she were channeling the tension in her mind right down into her mouth. Her godmother referred to the finger waving as "twizzling," perfectly capturing what it looked like and why she seemed to do it. Although her wide face, sprinkled with freckles, so often looked angelic, when she twizzled, she looked a little odd. Her parents periodically wondered if the uncontrollable finger waving might indicate some mild form of autism. Yet as Annie passed the two-year mark, it was clear that she connected to other people better than most. Because she was so precocious with language, she engaged family members and neighbors in all kinds of conversation and seemed to come to life with visitors. Once, during a community softball game in the park, she chose to sit with all the moms and gossip while the other children played. But on most days in the park, she was right in the midst of a gang of girls and boys. She had absolutely no trace of the characteristics associated with autism. On the contrary, she was extraordinarily endowed with intellect, gregariousness, coordination, humor, and good looks. What she also had, however, was a huge amount of drive. Annie liked excitement and was easily excited. Sneaking was just one of the many things that seemed to excite her.

Annie learned to read with ease. She loved to get the right answer at school and loved to be the one who followed the rules. She often stayed near the teacher, once offering to be her first-grade teacher's assistant. Each day when Annie got home from school, she happily pulled out the worksheets from her backpack and settled down to fill them in with energy and confidence.

By seven, she knew the pleasure of getting lost in a chapter book for hours. She gobbled up Nancy Drew mysteries and loved to discuss the small details that suggested a solution to the crime that Nancy was investigating.

When she and her aunt were on a trip to a museum of natural history, they encountered a huge dinosaur with a tiny head. A museum guide began to explain the connection between brain size and intelligence. Annie began to twizzle. She was as charged up by information as she was by sneaking.

In elementary school, some of Annie's great energy for shenanigans began to get funneled into doing well at school. She loved mastery, and, just as significant, she cared about pleasing adults, especially her teacher. Although she liked the feeling of being sneaky, she also liked to shine in the eyes of others. These forces began to shape and whittle her imperviousness to the feelings of others.

In a perfect world, your toddler would show strong signs of empathy. She would look worried when friends got hurt, help someone reach a fallen object, and in other ways exhibit her fledgling sense of caring. But she would also show you that she had the ability to manage or regulate her own emotions, so that rather than running away from other people's upsets, she would be motivated to help them. By the time she was in elementary school, she would have the intellectual capacity to think about what things looked like and sounded like from another person's perspective. And she would have benefited from your efforts to "induct" her into thinking about how her actions affected other people. There's one more thing the perfect world would provide her with: parents who themselves behave morally.

How often have you seen a parent yell at a child to be nice? You might even have done it yourself. It certainly won't surprise many readers to hear that their young children are heavily influenced by how their parents behave, but it's an easy thing to forget in the hurly-burly of everyday life with children. This explains why so many parents insist that their children share toys at the park and then rant at the dinner table about why they shouldn't have to take a pay cut just so Dick down the street can keep his job. I know a very wealthy family whose three daughters spent their childhood with every luxury. At the end of a weekend of swimming and sunbathing, the girls could simply step onto the family plane, barefoot in their bathing suits, to go back to their townhouse in New York City. They had a driver and private lessons in whatever interested them—surfing, figure skating, jazz dancing. They were surrounded by paid help. The children never saw their parents prepare a single meal. The parents were known for their ruthless dealings with the employees of the large, very successful business they owned. By the time the girls were teens, the eldest daughter seemed spoiled and high-handed with others. She expected others to work harder than she did, she wasn't all that kind to her friends, and she showed little concern for the larger world. Her parents were shocked and dismayed. But what had they expected?

When children see their parents putting other people first, they are much more likely to do so themselves. When they hear their parents mulling over how to balance their own needs with the needs of others or how to do what is morally right even when it comes at a personal cost, they internalize those arguments and actions and are much more likely to follow suit. In a society where many people believe they are supposed to knock over others to get to the first spot in line, it's easier said than done to set a moral example for your child. And as Stanford psychologist Bill Damon points out, these examples emerge in both large and small ways every single day: "What parents can do, and what they need to do, is set a moral compass. I don't mean lecturing them about what is right and wrong, or anything that direct, but being able to react and respond to whatever they observe in the child's behavior with a moral voice. It doesn't have to be heavy-handed or moralistic. What really makes a difference is when they are setting their goals in life, if they think whatever means will get me to this end, status and other self-oriented goals, if they really think anything goes, they really are at risk for bending the goals and standards—a lot of those kids will get into trouble.

"Making sure kids don't think the ends justify the means. I am convinced that Bernie Madoff did not get the kind of influence in his childhood that how you do things is more important than whether you succeed. I'll bet no one said to him, 'It's important to me that you are honest and compassionate and fair.' There are a million ways to communicate this to your kids."

When asked about their childhood, non-Jewish Germans who helped Jews during the Holocaust recalled having parents who had been deeply engaged in their communities, often risking personal comfort for larger principles. Not all of us are cut out to be heroes. But anyone who wants their children to grow up thinking and doing the right thing must provide a good example.

When Your Child Isn't Oliver

Jodie can't make Annie less headstrong, nor would she want to. And she cannot necessarily make Annie a more docile child with less va-va-voom. She can't give Annie a deeply felt, spontaneous sense of compassion. That's not what Annie came with. But Jodie can keep her own moral compass out on display, where Annie is reminded of it all the time. Jodie can stoke the fire of their strong emotional connection, so that Annie will want to please a mother who values kindness and altruism. That strong bond will also lead Annie to want to emulate her mother's good deeds and expressions of compassion.

Annie is smart, and Jodie can make the most of her daughter's intellect by reminding her to think and imagine what she might not feel when left to her own devices. She can help Annie develop habits and inclinations that offset her heedlessness or her lack of sympathy, such as the habit of cleaning up her messes (literally and figuratively), of apologizing, and of righting the wrongs she has done.

When Annie was nine, she went to the zoo with her aunt, the same one from whom she had stolen the jewelry seven years before. Annie went running up to the pen with the animals children could feed and then went running back to her aunt, fist out: "I need quarters. Quarters. Give me quarters." She was still bossy and ready to push for what she wanted. Her aunt handed her several quarters and sat down to watch.

Annie rushed back to the little dispenser where kids were dropping in coins for handfuls of corn. A little boy, perhaps four years old, with pudgy little legs and a slightly bewildered look on his face, was standing at the dispenser, trying to figure out how it worked. His fingers were short and fat, and he was taking a long time trying to get the dial to turn. Annie's hands twitched with impatience. She wanted to use her quarters; she wanted to feed those animals. She began to push forward in the line, shoulder-to-shoulder with the little boy.

Her aunt slid closer to the edge of the bench. Annie put her hand on the little boy. Her aunt leaned forward, ready to call out to stop Annie from pushing the little boy aside, ready to remind her that he deserved a turn and that Annie would have to wait. But then she heard what her niece was saying to the little boy: "Here. Want me to help? You turn the dial like this. Yeah, that's it. Now, let the corn fall into your hand. Yay. You did it. Now you can feed the goat! Take another turn if you want."

Misdeeds are red herrings. All kids misbehave. Testing authority, satisfying one's own needs, seeking pleasure, and putting oneself ahead of others are all natural and healthy characteristics of early childhood. As Freud so eloquently pointed out, growing up is, at heart, the task of learning to redirect your passions so that you can satisfy your needs while being part of a group. On the other hand, some young children, like Annie, begin to show a pattern that suggests that they are no Oliver Twist. They are less empathic than others, more determined to satisfy their own needs at any cost, less willing to be guided by an internal sense of right and wrong. If a child is over the age of five and still behaving this way, it might be a red flag.

Luckily, morality comes from outside as well as from within. You can set a good example by doing good in obvious ways (giving away money, volunteering, speaking out against injustice, standing up for others). But you also need to set an example in subtler ways, thinking out loud about how others feel and sacrificing your own pleasure for someone else's. You can pull a somewhat selfish child toward goodness.

There is a flip side to this. Children who already feel empathic—who tend to think about moral principles and act on them—don't need to be pushed farther in that direction. Nor do they need endless praise for doing what comes naturally to them. Good children usually stay that way. Less good children can become more so.

4

Success: Who Wants to Be a Millionaire?

One mom's triumph is another mom's disappointment. By the time my friend's first son, Ian, was twelve months old, he already loved toys that had doors and levers. He could spend more than an hour at a time sitting on the floor, carefully opening and closing each little panel on his favorite painted wooden activity board.

One day, his grandmother looked on smiling and said, "Look at him play with that thing. He's going to be an engineer!"

His mother laughed and countered, "Yeah, or a doorman."

By the time a child is old enough actually to do things (open doors, draw, dribble a basketball, read the letters on traffic signs, or put together Legos), most parents find themselves daydreaming about the child's future triumphs or perhaps wondering whether the child will have any future triumphs at all.

When I meet with groups of parents who have children in elementary school, I often begin by asking them what they want for their children in the long run. Middle-class parents almost always begin the same way: "I want my child to be happy." Sometimes they will say they want their children to "love learning." But eventually, those wishes and the easygoing, tender looks with which they are expressed give way to a wish parents are more reluctant to articulate: they want their children to be successful. They never say this straight out; instead, they talk about grades, skills, a competitive edge, or college admissions. But most of these specific goals represent a more general notion of success.

One forty-two-year-old father meeting with other parents at a suburban school captured the contrast in just a few sentences: "I want Tess to be happy. You know, I mean, I just want whatever she wants. As for school, the main thing is to like learning. I mean, I hated school when I was a kid. I want Tess to like coming to school. I mean, sure, she needs to get those skills down. I want her to have choices. What if it turns out she wants to be a nuclear scientist? She's gonna need to know her math to make that choice. I mean, I don't care so much what grades she gets, but if she gets to high school and she can't ace the test, where's that gonna leave her?"

We love to hear that success is unpredictable. Most of these same parents rush to read the article that recounts how even though Bill Gates didn't finish college, he is one of the richest men in the world or that Albert Einstein did badly in his elementary-school math class. We find it reassuring to think that great success might emerge late in life and appear to spring from nowhere. However, those extreme examples don't shed much light on anything. The kind of success most of us wish for our kids cannot be defined by those who become so famous we all know about them. While parents might secretly dream that their child will be a millionaire or a genius, deep in our hearts, we know it's not likely. Most of us have more modest hopes—that our children will do well at something, win the good opinion of others, and earn money, influence, or power through their accomplishments. It's not clear that those uncommon stories of outstanding ability have much to say that will help us understand the more common kinds of success our kids might actually achieve.

Several years ago, I took a small charter plane from my hometown in western Massachusetts to the eastern end of Long Island. I am a terrified airplane passenger, dependent on antianxiety drugs such as Xanax and lots of reassurance. To my worried eyes, the pilot who greeted me in the tiny terminal was just the right age. In his early forties, he seemed old enough to have done a lot of flying but young enough so I could count on his fast reflexes and the low probability that he would have a heart attack in flight. In order to distract myself and to forge a bond with the man on whom my life depended for the next forty-five minutes, I began asking him about himself. Lo and behold, he had been a student at Wesleyan, where my own son would soon be attending college. Even then, in my preflight daze, it seemed a bit incongruous to me that a Wesleyan grad would be a pilot for a tiny rural airport. Wesleyan, home to maverick filmmakers, caustic art critics, and bold left-wing activists—a charter pilot?

I asked him how he had gotten from Wesleyan to the cockpit. He said that everyone from his neighborhood was thrilled when he was accepted at Wesleyan. He came from a rural farm family, and everyone thought Wesleyan was a step up, a passport into a world of greater wealth, broader horizons, and bigger challenges. Everyone assumed that he would use this great opportunity to launch himself into business, medicine, or law.

"I tried to do what I thought everyone wanted me to do. I took two premed classes. I attended a special seminar for students interested in becoming lawyers." He knew those were the proper uses of a Wesleyan education. "But," he said with a shrug, "they just weren't for me. I just couldn't muster the interest. I didn't want to be a doctor or a lawyer. I wanted to fly. That's what I had always wanted to do."

Soon after college, he began flight school. And what started as a part-time hobby quickly became his life's work.

"I always figured," he told me calmly as he checked his flight instruments and began to navigate the plane onto the runway, "that if you work hard, you should be able to make a living doing whatever it is you love, no matter how unusual it is."

Thirty thousand feet above land, the roar of the plane engine muting his words, I felt a flash of clarity. I thought, if my child can make a living doing something he loves, I will surely feel he is a success. But what does it take for a child to become an adult who will make money doing something he loves?

If you walk into the St. Paul's preschool in Stockbridge, Massachusetts, the low hum of four-year-old boys and girls, deep in the work of childhood, envelops you. Once you settle in and begin to watch, individual children come into focus, and you realize they are not all doing the same thing. In 1990, I spent several weeks observing and filming the teachers and children at St. Paul's. I was there to collect data for a study of children's play, but I found myself keeping a kind of video journal of two of the children. I wasn't looking to keep track of those kids, nor did I seek them out because of any judgments I had made about them. Filming them didn't have anything to do with the study that had brought me there. I simply found my camera's eye wandering to certain children again and again.

One little boy, Raymond, sported thick, unruly brown hair covering a head that looked just a little large for his slender body, and his voice was unusually gravelly for a four-year-old. He walked into the preschool every day with a warm grin and a slightly quizzical expression on his face. He stepped into the swarm of activity with good cheer, as if he was hoping to hear something funny or interesting. He clearly liked the adults and would often talk enthusiastically with one of his teachers for a few moments, offering vivid descriptions of something that had happened at home. It was easy to see that the adults found him delightful, interesting, articulate, warm, and enthusiastic.

But within moments of chatting, while other kids launched themselves into making airports with wood blocks or setting up elaborate scenarios of households and hospitals in the dress-up corner, Raymond would thread his way through the small groups, heading purposefully for the painting area. When he got to the easel, he rarely hesitated but took up a brush and immediately began dipping it into one of the jars of paint. He never seemed uncertain about where to put the first mark. He didn't pause or glance away lost in thought. He simply began dipping his brush into the paint and applying the colors in unhesitant brush strokes to the white surface. With each application of paint, his tongue would move furiously in and out of his mouth, as if it were the engine powering his actions. While he painted, he seemed quite oblivious to the raucous sounds around him. Once in a while, his face would become suffused with frustration. He would rip the piece of paper off the easel, crunch it up angrily, and toss it into the wastepaper basket. What happened then was the most interesting part of the sequence. Teary-eyed and red-faced, Raymond would begin painting again, more intently and energetically than ever.

I visited St. Paul's on and off for that whole year. From September through June, Raymond would begin his day dipping a brush into red, yellow, green, and purple tempera, pulling the brush across the paper, absorbed in the lines he created on the page. But he wasn't equally absorbed during other parts of the day. One of the teachers told me that she had noted in Raymond's half-year narrative evaluation that he had trouble paying attention during circle time. I watched him when the group was gathered on the rug for their daily meeting. He did often get up and quietly wander away when the teacher was talking about the calendar, the weather, or the letter of the week. He would silently fiddle with objects that were shelved nearby or pass his hand lightly over various books that seemed to catch his eye. Sometimes he'd just look out the window. He wasn't obstreperous, just, it seemed to me, uninterested.

When Raymond was a bit older, his intensity about art was sometimes a problem for him and for his family. In fourth grade, Raymond came home and announced that he was supposed to make a project that involved research on a topic of his choice. He had decided, he told his mother, that he would make a pop-up book about the life cycle of a maple tree. His parents had no idea where this idea came from, but they didn't pay much attention, figuring that he would use the box of paper, crayons, scissors, and glue that they kept in their kitchen for anyone in the family to use. His mother assumed, she told me later, that he would bring home a book about maple trees and then create the pages he wanted for his book. She was all set to buy whatever extra material he might need—some rings to hold the pages together or perhaps some special paper. After he first mentioned it, he didn't talk about it again, and she forgot about it.

Two days before the assignment was due, Raymond had finally finished his research and was ready, he declared, to begin making the book. He began to lay out the pages as he had envisioned them, each more elaborate and ambitious than the one before. Raymond wanted one page to be a disk the reader could rotate, revealing a different limb of the tree for each season. Several pages involved shapes that sprang up in three dimensions. On another page, the reader was to pull a string and make the tree grow tall, beyond the edge of the paper. This was no ordinary book. Bringing Raymond's plans to fruition involved various unusual kinds of paper, nothing his family had at home. He wanted to find bark that could be glued onto the tree trunk and glue that would cement the seeds he planned to paste on, but that wouldn't show under the seed. He needed to invent new methods to attach things to a page that would make the figures move and shift as planned and still look smooth and pretty.

A nice project turned into a heated, tempestuous marathon of gluing and cutting. Each page required several failed attempts. Eventually he was in tears, yelling at his mother, who, she says, was yelling back. "His nose was running, his finger was bleeding, there was ripped paper everywhere, and drips from a glue gun drying on every surface. I screamed at him that I just wasn't going back to town for more paper one more time. I swore at him. I was so impatient. His plans seemed way too ambitious to me. Why couldn't he just draw a nice picture like the other kids?"

Raymond's mother thought they would kill each other before the day was over. But they didn't, and Raymond's book was outstanding. The teacher told Raymond and his mother that she had never seen anything like it. Not all children have such perseverance.

Cody's arrival at St. Paul's each morning was quite different from Raymond's. Cody had inky black hair that was so shiny it practically glistened and beautiful large brown eyes. His small frame was tighter and more muscular than Raymond's. He entered the classroom with a jaunty gait and a calm sense of self-assurance. But his route around the main room at St. Paul's told a different story. Cody's eyes would instantly scan the different clusters of kids. Several boys and girls would often call out greetings to him. He was popular, the kind of kid others wanted to include in their play. He rarely spoke much to the teachers, more interested in jumping into the goings-on at the sand table, the Matchbox car races, or the group effort to make a really tall skyscraper. Activities didn't draw Cody in—other children did.

When the children were asked to decide where to spend their "work" period, Cody would sometimes have difficulty making a decision. He'd often begin at the carpentry table, where he'd pick up a hammer and begin pounding in a nail. But within a few moments, his enthusiasm would pale. His eyes would begin wandering, looking to see where his friend Alec was. He'd lay down the hammer (or the paintbrush, the book, or the puzzle piece) and leave to see if another area of the room would offer more appeal.

Cody was bright as a whip—that showed through when stories were read aloud and he asked sharp questions or at circle time when he told his own stories. He could add numbers accurately and swiftly, and he learned to read with ease. When the children were introduced to a new activity or worked with small pieces (Legos, gadgets, magnifying glasses), Cody was always among the first to figure things out. But nothing really kept his interest for long.

Every September, Cody was excited about school. He missed his friends during the summertime. But as eager as he was to see the other kids at school, around October, he began to feel bored and disenchanted. School sucked. There was nothing to do. The assignments were too easy, and they were dull.

When he was nine, his parents moved him from the public school to a private school, certain that in a more enriched atmosphere, he'd begin to discover what topics he cared about. At first, he was thrilled. He made friends immediately, teachers found him appealing, and he seemed enthusiastic about his classes. But by the spring of that year, he began to feel that school was just no good. In seventh grade, he switched schools again, and then again in ninth grade. He slid through high school, passing but not excelling at anything.

Cody and his parents often spoke of his love for sports. He had a lithe, athletic build and took to soccer, basketball, and baseball easily. In preschool, he was always out in the yard, eager to be a part of any game. He signed up for Little League, soccer team, and the community basketball program. He loved to buy the right shoes for each activity and had lots of pairs. When he was ten years old, the other kids started outpacing him. Some of them were bigger, some came from families with dads who coached, and many practiced for hours every day after school. He became more and more frustrated with each team he was on. He and his parents felt that they had bad luck when it came to the coaches. He never seemed to get enough time on the field to show how good he was. The coach often favored some other kid. By the time he was a freshman in high school, he had quit team sports.

During the last two years of high school, Cody really just went through the motions. He liked his friends, he started dating a girl, and he loved to hang out. He got into a small college in his home state that didn't require good grades or extracurricular accomplishments. But he soon found it boring—he felt he had already moved beyond what college could offer. He dropped out after two years, deciding instead to wait tables and live independently. Attractive, with friends, and good at his job, he was fine. But he still hadn't become the master of anything.

There is no question that practice and hard work lead to success. But even among those who work hard, one or two always go farther and do more than the others. Imagine a group of twenty people who all do the same kind of work, whether it be basketball, farming, music, or mathematics. Assume that these twenty people grew up in the same community, come from the same social class, and were born within a few years of one another (in other words, they are part of the same cohort). Now, imagine that they all had the same basic educational opportunities and all worked equally hard, whether because they shared the same cultural values about work or because these twenty kids were the ones who particularly loved basketball (or farming or mathematics or music). Even with all of those shared circumstances, some of the twenty will do better than others. Examples of this abound. One basketball player makes more shots, dominates other players, and sees the whole court better than the other players, even if all of them make two hundred baskets a day, lift weights year-round, and practice rebounding daily for two hours. One farmer gauges the first frost more reliably than another, gets more milk from his cows, loses fewer animals to infection, and produces a bigger crop. What explains that kind of difference between individuals? We often look to talent to explain why one person rises to the top. It is easy to look at the stars in any field (Derek Jeter, the Beatles, Freeman Dyson) for some sense of what makes a person stand out in his or her chosen field. But outstanding talent is all too rare and therefore can't explain the kind of individual differences in success that abound among the average population. Something else accounts for the distance between those who get by and those who flourish.

The Urge to Do Well

When my son Will was four years old, he already loved to play basketball, although we were mystified about where this interest came from. He'd stay out on our blacktop for hours dribbling the ball. His older brother Jake would wander by, sometimes taking a shot, sometimes lounging on the porch, reading a book and watching his brother's relentless activity. One day, I heard Will talking in his high, earnest voice to his big brother. I could tell from the stream of sound that he was dribbling the ball as he spoke and following Jake, who was walking toward the hammock with a book.

"Jake, Jake, do you wanna know something, Jake? Wanna know something? Wanna know how you get good at something? There's only one way. You have to practice and practice and never take a break, and that's the only way to get good at something."

Several months later, I found myself sitting near Will while he practiced his four-year-old version of long jumps on our lawn. He was already very athletic but had the short, solid legs of a preschooler. He had found two branches and was using one to mark a starting line and the other as his target. He took several leaps from the starting line to the target. When he had successfully landed just past the target stick three or four times, he moved the target stick about six inches farther away and tried again. When he had conquered this as well, he moved the stick a good two feet farther along. He stood for a moment at the starting line, bending his legs a few times, as if to prepare his body for the leap.

Suddenly, he paused and called out to me, "Mom! Mom! Do you think I can get from here to there? Do you think I can make it?"

I took a quick glance at the distance between the two sticks and responded emphatically, "Whew, that's a long distance. Nope, I don't think you'll get that far."

My small, dark-eyed, chubby-cheeked son gave me a withering glance and said in his most disapproving tone, "You're just saying that so that you can be excited when I do it." After shooting me one more glowering look, he walked over and pushed the target another two feet away.

Somehow, even as a four-year-old, Will had a great desire to improve. Motivation, long understood to be one of the corner stones of success, has presented teachers, parents, and researchers with a tantalizing mystery for years.

Step inside almost any classroom in this country, and you will hear and see teachers trying to motivate their students. In some classes, children earn a star every time they answer all of the questions on a quiz correctly. Some teachers offer elaborate reward systems—for instance, awarding children a piece of candy if they earn a certain number of checks on a chart. As students get older, teachers are likely to use good grades as a motivator. In college, many professors feel that the promise of a good test score will motivate their students to read the books they assign. The powerful intuition underlying these common acts is that rewards are a good motivator. And in one sense, this is true. You can get some children to work hard for a star, a candy, or a grade. But being motivated for a particular task and being a motivated person are not the same thing. The logic behind offering stars and candy flies in the face of the process by which children develop an internal drive to do well.

To see why, consider the following experiment conducted years ago by Richard Nesbitt and his colleagues at Stanford. The experimenters brought markers (a kind the children had not seen before) and paper to groups of children in a local nursery school. In one group, children were told that if they used the markers to make pictures, they would get a certificate with a star and a ribbon on it. Another group of children were not told this, but when they were finished, they unexpectedly received the ribbon and star awards. A third group of children were offered the drawing materials, but no mention was made of possible awards, and none were received.

Most kids like to draw, so you might expect that the kids who also received a reward for their drawings would be twice as interested in making more pictures. And yet the opposite was true. A couple of weeks later, when the researchers returned to the nursery school, they found that the children who had expected a reward for their first pictures had spent much less time drawing in the subsequent weeks. The researchers also asked adults who had not been part of the research team to rate the children's artwork. The drawings of those who had worked toward a reward were deemed to be of lower quality than those of the children in the other two groups. The lesson psychologists drew from this study is that extrinsic motivation lessens a person's intrinsic interest in an activity. This might be particularly true when the activity holds some natural appeal. In other words, if children naturally like doing something, offering stars or candies might actually cause them to like the activity less.

And yet, as Raymond discovered at St. Paul's while making his paintings, even the most appealing activities can be frustrating and discouraging. The more you care about the thing you are doing, the more upset you might be when it doesn't go well. Anyone who has seen a child try unsuccessfully to make a skyscraper with blocks knows that even though something is pleasurable, that doesn't mean every minute of the process is fun.

But why do some children persist when the going gets tough, while others do not? Psychologist Carol Dweck has made it part of her life's work to find out. She believes that some children feel helpless, while others feel sure that they can get better at things: "Helpless and mastery-oriented children are pursuing different goals in achievement situations, with helpless children seeking to document their ability, but failing to do so, and mastery-oriented children seeking to increase their ability, and looking for information that will help them do so."

When four-year-old Will rejected my cheesy ploy to let him impress me, he exemplified the mastery-oriented kind of motivation Dweck has identified: he preferred to try something genuinely difficult rather than merely appear to succeed. Of course, he wanted to impress me—but only if he did something that was actually difficult. In a series of elegant studies, Dweck has shown that children can be sorted into two groups: those who focus on their performance and those who seem more interested in achievement.

In one line of experiments, Dweck offered children the choice between an easy and a difficult version of a task. Children who were focused on performing were likely to choose the easier task, whereas children who focused on achievement preferred the harder task because the "stretch" felt so good for such kids. In the long run, needless to say, children who are achievement-oriented will do better than children who are performance-oriented. Even though picking the easier task might ensure "shining" during some pivotal moment (for example, during an interview for college or work or in a tryout for a team), children who are drawn to challenge make more progress in school and in life.

But the problem, as Dweck sees it, is more layered than this, because it's not self-evident why some children are focused on mastery and others on performance. Watch a child begin to work on a mildly demanding task (such as solving all of the math problems on a worksheet, building a small machine, or crossing a bridge made of ropes), and you might overhear her mumble, whisper, or moan, "I'm not good at this," "This is too hard for me," or simply, "I can't." On the other hand, some children respond in another way altogether: "It's a little easier this time," or, "I'm just gonna make it halfway this time, all the way next time." It seems that underlying the two kinds of motivation are two different ideas children have about what might explain their abilities. Those offhand comments reflect two very different implicit theories of ability. The first Dweck calls the "entity" theory of ability. Some children seem to believe that you either have an ability or you don't, as if it were an entity within you. Such kids often assume that if you have the ability, you were born with it. Other children have what Dweck calls an "incremental" theory of ability. They assume that they can get better at a given skill or activity, bit by bit. Children with an entity theory are much more vulnerable to a performance orientation.

Imagine, for a moment, a seven-year-old girl who sits down to solve some addition problems assigned by her second-grade teacher. If she has an entity theory of ability and she's good at math, she's likely to feel confident but won't necessarily push herself when she gets to more difficult problems. She might figure that she's good enough to get by, and that's enough. However, if she's struggled with addition in the past and believes that ability is an all-or-nothing capacity, she's not likely to spend a lot of time trying to do well on the problems or get extra practice. She might figure that won't get her anywhere. She'd rather take the easier problems and do well on them than take the harder problems and show how bad she is at math.

On the other hand, if your child believes that people can get better at things bit by bit, the challenge is worthwhile. By reaching a little beyond what she can already do, she might well get better. The seven-year-old with an incremental theory of ability is less focused on how easy math has been in the past and more interested in how much better she can get if she keeps trying. This individual difference shows up in all kinds of settings—school, playground, gym, even within the family context.

If you listen in on parents and teachers talking to young children, you can hear these two different approaches in action. A little boy brings home a spelling test from school. Eight words are spelled correctly, and four are wrong. One parent says, "Look at that. Good job. You are a great speller." This comment expresses and encourages an entity theory of ability. The parent is drawing her child's attention to his ability as if it were a steady talent. Another parent says, "Look at that. Good job. You got two more right than last time. All that practicing paid off." This parent is drawing the child's attention to the progress you can achieve with effort, encouraging his child to use an incremental theory of ability.

Dweck has shown that a child's theory of his ability can be influenced. In one experiment, Dweck and her colleagues recruited low-performing seventh-grade students from a New York City public school. Each child participated in one of two eight-week motivational workshops that met once a week for twenty-five minutes. All of the children were taught something about learning and the brain. But the children in the experimental group received four sessions that focused on the message that intelligence is malleable, that connections in the brain are made from learning, and that students are in charge of making those connections happen. To balance this "extra" experience, the subjects in the control group instead received lessons and discussion regarding memory. After the workshops, the researchers asked the students' teachers to report on any students showing change in motivation in math class. Children who had learned that practicing can change the brain seemed more motivated, more interested in trying, and more engaged in their lessons. Just as telling, the math grades of the students who had learned that abilities can change began to climb.

Researchers are not the only ones who can influence a child's theory of ability. Parents can influence their children's motivation through things as low-key as comments that highlight the value of progress and the benefit of effort. On the other hand, families that talk all the time about talent are likely to encourage their children to form an entity theory.

This difference manifests itself at a national level as well. In a classic study comparing educational patterns in the United States with those in China and Japan, Harold Stevenson and his colleague Shin-Ying Li interviewed parents about their children's education experience. It became apparent to Stevenson and Li that one of the clearest differences between China and the United States concerned the relative emphasis parents put on ability and effort. Asian parents tended to underemphasize their children's "natural" gifts and put great faith in the power of effort. They felt that success in school depended almost completely on diligence rather than talent. United States parents, on the other hand, tended to overestimate their children's academic talents and underestimate the value of effort. American parents, and teachers as well, were much less sure about the value of homework, for instance, whereas Asian parents and teachers thought homework was very important and contributed to children's academic success. Unsurprisingly, Asian children reported liking homework more than U.S. children. It is clear that some cultures encourage children to believe that trying pays off. The United States has not been one of those cultures. And yet within the United States, there are many kids with a powerful drive to do well.

Melissa was one of them.

Melissa remembers only one consuming interest from her childhood: getting good grades. Her family expected all four of their children to do well. Melissa attended a good public school in suburban New York, where she got the highest grades in her class and was the valedictorian. When she was waiting to hear from the colleges to which she had applied, she'd bike past the mailboxes of the other top students, peering into their mailboxes to see if they had received thick or thin envelopes. When she learned she had been deferred for early admission to Harvard, she was devastated. Then, in April, she was accepted at Stanford and Yale, as well as at Harvard. She remembers Harvard as one long marathon of studying, with regular breaks for primping with the other girls, drinking just enough to flirt with men, and working her way into and out of one romantic soap opera after another. She worked hard. But she doesn't remember being consumed by the topics she was studying or the professors whose lectures she attended. Yet she graduated summa cum laude and gained admission to one of the most selective graduate programs in the country for her academic field, chemistry. From there, her trajectory continued exactly as it had begun. She got the best postdoctoral position after graduate school and went straight into a tenure-track position at one of the most selective colleges in the country, where she got early tenure. Sure, she was smart. But she had something else as well.

Odd as it may seem, most psychologists are reluctant to make any broad generalizations about the nature of human development. Cautious and precise, researchers typically offer sixteen qualifications for any general statement about human behavior. Asked if it is true that younger siblings are more easygoing than older siblings, they will list all of the situations in which that is not the case. Presented with the proposition that boys and girls differ in certain cognitive tests, they will provide you with ten circumstances that nullify that difference. Yet if you listen closely enough, you can detect a few psychological patterns that psychologists always come back to.

If you sit down to lunch with a group of psychologists and listen to them talk casually, as they gossip about colleagues and friends, they will invariably, however unwittingly, mention a person's neuroticism or introversion or how easy he or she is to work with. When they use these terms, they are drawing on a concept that emerged almost one hundred years ago—the idea that everyone has certain personality traits that cause him or her to act in particular ways again and again and that explain his or her behavior across a wide range of situations. And if you pay attention to the specific qualities psychologists use in their own casual talk, you will begin to realize that they are invoking the explanatory power of five traits in particular: openness, conscientiousness, extroversion, agreeability, and neuroticism. These traits are so prevalent in the field of psychology that there is even an acronym for them: OCEAN. Thousands of experiments done over the span of a hundred years across the globe have shown that these five dimensions are easy to detect and surprisingly useful in forecasting a person's future.

Among the sturdiest of these is the one Melissa possessed so much of: conscientiousness. This all-important quality is not hard to measure, either. Typically, when researchers want to assess the conscientiousness of adult subjects, they simply ask individuals to rate, on a scale of one to five, how true various statements are about themselves:

- I am always prepared.
- I am exacting in my work.
- I follow a schedule.
- I get chores done right away.
- I like order.
- I pay attention to details.
- I leave my belongings around.
- I make a mess of things.
- I often forget to put things back in their proper place.
- I shirk my duties.

Interestingly, people seem to get this right about themselves. People who feel that the first six statements fit them closely but that the second four are off the mark tend to do well at school and at work. In contrast, subjects who say that the first six statements do not capture them well at all and that the last four describe them accurately tend to struggle professionally. They procrastinate, they have trouble following through on projects, and they waste time.

It's harder to imagine the five-year-old who could, or would, give you reliable answers to those same questions. And yet psychologists have been sure for a long time that very young children do show early signs of conscientiousness. So, how do you get an accurate assessment of a child's conscientiousness? You ask the people around her.

Jens Asendorpf and Marcel Van Akenwere followed 151 schoolchildren in Munich from the time they were four until they were twelve years old. They wanted to know whether it was possible to measure conscientiousness in preschoolers and whether young children who seemed very low or high in this dimension remained that way as they got older. When the children were four, their teachers were asked to rate each of them on the following dimensions:

- Is persistent in activities.
- Doesn't give up easily.
- Has high standards of performance for self.
- Is attentive and able to concentrate.
- Is planful, thinks ahead.
- Can be trusted, is dependable.
- Is competent, skillful.

Six years later, the children's parents were asked to rate them on those same dimensions. Another two years later, the researchers sought out friends of their young subjects and asked them for ratings. Asendorpf and Van Akenwere found that a child who was rated by his teachers as persistent, attentive, and trustworthy at four was likely to be rated the very same way by his parents when he was ten. He was also likely to be rated that same way by his friends when he was twelve years old. Perhaps more important, those children who were seen as conscientious by their teachers, parents, and friends were also likely to do better in school.

In every study, even where there are strong, clear patterns, some shifting around occurs. A few of the kids who were rated as highly conscientious in Asendorpf and Van Akenwere's data didn't do so well in school later on. A few of the kids who teachers thought were not conscientious were rated as highly conscientious by their parents. Good researchers pay as much attention to those jagged lines as they do to the straight ones. When Asendorpf and Van Akenwere looked closely at the discrepancies, they found that when the teachers' ratings of the younger children didn't agree with the parental ratings, it was the teachers' ratings that predicted later school success. One way of interpreting this is that teachers are better judges of a child than his parents are. But it also suggests that the signs of school success are just as easy to see in a four-year-old as they are in a ten-year-old (remember, the teachers first rated the children when they were four, and the parents first rated the children when they were ten). The child who is able to focus on a task and keep a clear sense of her priorities, who is able to delay fun in order to fulfill her obligations for school, and who wants to meet the expectations of the adult world tends to be headed for school success, and children exhibit these qualities when they are four years old.

While it's not all that surprising that the child who plans and pays attention is likely to get good grades, it is somewhat more surprising to see that this quality might have a bigger effect than other important indicators, such as a child's intellect, her family's commitment to education, and the particular teachers she is assigned to. Think of it this way: if you went into a preschool classroom and could choose only one quality to use as a way of predicting who would thrive in high school, your best bet would be conscientiousness.

Another child might have had Melissa's particular aptitudes and a lot of ability, but without Melissa's patience, focus, and eagerness to meet the expectations of adults, another child would not have ended up where Melissa did. Sean certainly didn't.

There are lots of good stories from Sean's childhood. His family called him Gosling because of his white-blond crew-cut and cherubic cheeks. When he was eight, he won a state prize for one of his short stories. When his baby sister fell and got a deep gash across her chin, it was Sean, age ten, who held and comforted her, bleeding and crying, all the way to the hospital. By the time he was twelve, he had organized a community soccer game on the town green. When he was fourteen years old, a sophisticated, beautiful older girl from the neighborhood fell madly in love with him. When he was sixteen, he put together a literary magazine of young voices from the L.A. ghetto. As Sean grew up, these anecdotes seemed to his family to create a map indicating where his life was headed. Sunny, vibrant, smart, warm, and reliable, he seemed to be on a path headed directly toward success.

Other stories, less flattering, were barely remembered or quickly dismissed. He took a quarter off his father's bureau when he was six, refusing to admit it afterward. He used someone else's credit card to make long-distance phone calls in high school, and he failed French, even though his aptitude scores were the highest in his class. One of the discarded stories goes like this: when Sean was three years old, his mother, Joan, took him along with her to visit her old friend Alice, who happened to be a child therapist. Holding his mother's hand, Sean bounced happily into Alice's office, plunking himself down in the corner, where Alice kept toys for her young patients. Sean played contentedly while his mother and her friend chatted.

As they said good-bye, Alice pulled Joan aside and said, "I am not sure if you noticed, but while we were talking, Sean pocketed one of the small toys from the play area."

Joan shrugged and laughed, thinking to herself, *Alice is a psychiatrist. Doesn't she of all people know that three-year-olds don't follow all the grown-up rules? It means nothing.*

Joan all but forgot this passing moment, a tiny bit of driftwood in the ocean of experiences that made up family life. The stories of Sean's appeal and ability seemed more salient and seemed to go together, until many years later, when Joan began racking her brain to understand what had gone wrong. By the time Sean was in his early thirties, he had been fired from every job he had been hired for. In constant financial crisis, he was addicted to both gambling and drugs. He lied and stole. Sean probably would have rated low in conscientiousness. But there were other hints that Sean might be not only low in conscientiousness but also high in a characteristic that can cause a lot of trouble.

As I described in chapter 2, Jerome Kagan's research has showed that even when they are babies, we can identify those who will be easygoing later on and those who will react too strongly to new experiences.

The big story Kagan told concerned the strength and stability of shyness (a.k.a. inhibition). But there is another chapter to the story of that research. While most of the children who were classified as uninhibited turned out to be garden-variety kids—comfortable joining a new classroom, trying a new activity, or meeting new people—some of those easygoing kids were *extremely* uninhibited. And *those* children turned out to have a different kind of problem when they got older. Children who had "high temperamental exuberance" as toddlers had low impulse control as teenagers, leading to problems such as drinking, gambling, and lying. And high exuberance turns out to be even more stable over time than inhibition.

Even as a little boy, Sean had been bursting with outgoing energy. But he also kept secrets. He smiled, he pleased, and then he did something he shouldn't while no one was looking. What seemed like vitality was in fact the first sign of impulsivity. In Sean's case, glimmers of impulsivity and the sneakiness it led to were overshadowed by his many appealing strengths. No one really saw that episodes such as the toy pocketing formed a pattern of red flags marking out a path toward future trouble.

These two dimensions, conscientiousness and impulsivity, mark a continuum of sorts, and they seem to provide a startlingly good lens through which to see a child's future ability to get and keep a good job. And yet that's not always enough.

All through Melissa's steady and impressive climb toward the golden ring of her academic career—tenure at an excellent college—she looked at those around her with envy. Why didn't she love what she was doing the way they did? She felt like a fraud. After each major accomplishment, she felt empty, not sure what to set as her next goal. She did excellent research, which got published in all of the best scientific journals. But within weeks of publication of each article, she would forget what the results of her study were. In fact, often just after she collected the data, when some other avid scientist would stay in his or her office until midnight just to go over the results, Melissa would put the data in a drawer and not look at it for weeks. She could never quite lose herself in the work itself. Her parents were proud of her. She had a good salary and the prestige of an excellent job. She was invited to conferences and put on committees at her college. She had intelligence, drive, and diligence. So, from one perspective, she had great success—she embodied the power of childhood conscientiousness to put a child on the path to achievement. And yet something was missing.

"I don't wake up thinking about my research," she said. "I stop thinking about this stuff the moment I leave the office. I never can remember the results of my old research. My brother, who is an economist, thinks it's just weird."

Soon after she got tenure, she felt flat. What would motivate her now? By the time she was thirty-eight, she dreamed of what she would do when she retired. She had lots of conscientiousness but not quite enough of something else. And that something else turns out to be critically important. She claimed she didn't have a passionate interest in the work itself. Remarkably, this vital component of success has only recently begun to attract the attention of researchers.

Developmental psychologist Judy Deloache became interested in what she calls young children's "extremely intense interests" (EII) when her own children were small. She describes the origins of this new work as follows:

> First, I had a little boy who had a fascination with vehicles. One of his earliest words was "cu," (short u, as in duck), which meant car. A little later came "cuck," meaning truck. Whenever we were driving around, he would invest lots of attention in other vehicles—lots of "cu" and "cuck" alerts. His fascination started to ebb after his second birthday, and there wasn't much evidence of it by age three.
>
> Equally interesting were two children of some of my best friends many years ago. Both are college students now. One had an intense interest—balls. This is one of the most common EIIs among boys. Everywhere he went, he was always on the lookout for anything spherical—gum balls in a machine, light fixtures, actual balls, etc. His parents acceded to his passion and purchased many, many balls for him. They were always underfoot in their house when we went over for our weekly dinner with them.
>
> The other child had a much less common EII—brushes. The first evidence of his passionate interest in brushes was his recurrent desire to sweep—to use a broom. This gen-

> eralized to brushes of all kinds. His parents bought a huge number of brushes for him; at one point he had toothbrushes in every room of the house so he was never without one.
>
> Knowing these two children with these Extremely Intense Interests at the same time made a lasting impression on me. I did an initial very preliminary study that convinced me that there was something of general interest to be investigated. However, not until a few years ago did I initiate a formal study into it.

It has taken researchers and educators a strangely long time to realize that when a child is interested in something, he learns it better. This inexplicable gap in our inquiries into learning has persisted, despite the fact that researcher Daniel Berlyne demonstrated almost fifty years ago that people remember an item more easily if they learn it in order to satisfy their curiosity. More recently, two psychologists, K. Ann Renninger and Suzanne Hidi, have been slowly but surely trying to pin down the role interest might have in a child's emerging academic competence.

Parents who take time to watch their baby and toddler play will notice that some toys, or groups of toys, are more alluring than others. One child is excited every time he sees a toy car or truck, and another spends hour after hour with small action figures. But does it really matter whether a child has a chance to play with the toys he likes best? It seems so. As described in chapter one, when Renninger and her colleagues offered a baby a toy in which he had shown prior interest, the baby spent longer exploring the toy and used a wider range of actions on the toy. In other words, he stretched his cognitive repertoire when he was interested in the toy. In another experiment, psychologists divided fourth graders into two kinds of study groups. Some of the children were asked to work collaboratively in small groups, learning the material harmoniously. The other children were also put into small groups, but they were encouraged to focus on controversial aspects of the material and argue with one another, debating the topic. At the end of several days the children were tested for their knowledge of the material. Children who had been encouraged to get really invested and discuss aspects that had grabbed their interest not only learned more, they were also much more likely to give up a recess period to watch a film on the topic. This seems so obvious as to be laughable. Don't we all know it's easier to learn stuff we want to learn? Yet we have continued to ignore this fact when thinking about schools and learning. However, it is not simply that interest leads to learning. Interest might be the very component that leads someone from doing what is required to going beyond what is required.

Stefi always had friends. It seemed that from the time she was three until she was fifteen years old, all she cared about were her friends and decorating herself. She always did her work. Her mother, Robin, said, "You never needed to check on Stefi. She'd come home from school, go to her room, sit down at her desk, and do each assignment one after another. And each morning, she went to school with everything she needed to hand in. She has always gotten a B plus or A minus in every class. But you'd never know anything was happening in those classes. Not one night did she come home and say, 'We read the most amazing story,' or 'The teacher said the funniest thing today.' I didn't know what she cared about, except for friends, clothes, and her hairdo. She matured early. Once in eighth grade, she walked in for breakfast wearing this tight, low-cut blouse with her bosom just flowing over the top. I said, 'Stef, I don't think you should wear that to school. You'll be sitting in math class, and the math teacher will be staring at your boobs instead of the math problems, and all the boys in the class will be watching your boobs instead of thinking about math. I just don't think that's right.' Stef stared at me for a second, a totally blank look on her face, and said, 'I don't have math today.'

For the longest time, I really had no idea who was in there. Then, when she was fourteen, she went for the summer to an island off the coast of Canada to work with a group of teenagers running a summer program for young children. I felt she came back from that experience a different person. Suddenly, she could talk about ideas, and she understood abstract concepts. I felt like her brain had literally changed. This past summer, she started making purses using pieces of felt, beads, and feathers. Wherever she carried one of her purses, people asked her about them. She started to sell them. She has a thriving small business now. Then, in the fall, she found out about a course uptown on custom-designed pocketbooks. She signed up, and every Saturday, she gets herself up there first thing, to take the class. People keep asking to buy her bags and purses. I really thought for the longest time that Stef was going to end up working in an accessories store. But suddenly, it seems as if she is a serious person with a lot of interests. And she's a real entrepreneur."

Robin thinks that Stef changed in some wonderful, dramatic way as she entered adolescence. That's how it must have felt to watch Stef morph from a child who seemed concerned only with her next party and her next purchase to a young woman who had direction, energy for work, and an eagerness to plunge in. As Stef was growing up, fashion and friends seemed like warning signs. To Robin, they signaled superficiality, an absence of real interest. Instead, they *were* the real interest. Stefi had initiative, just not for school or books. It was for friends and accessories. Once she had developed a more goal-oriented frame of mind (something that often only kicks in when children enter early adolescence), she put her interest to work. Actually, Stefi's mom was right about her all along. She did care more than anything else about decorating girls. She might well end up working in a shop. It will probably be a luxury women's boutique, and she will probably own it. The accessories and hairdos weren't a red flag. They were a signpost.

One of the most important accomplishments of adulthood is to love one's work. Loving what you do for a living is different from getting (and keeping) a job with a high salary or lots of status. Where does such love come from? A clue to this comes from a somewhat unexpected source: a complex study of the lives of adolescents.

In the early eighties, psychologist Mihaly Csikszentmihalyi set out to learn what no one had figured out: What is it teenagers are doing, thinking, and feeling as they go about their everyday lives? He recruited his young subjects from Chicago public schools. Each teen was given a beeper (this was before the age of BlackBerrys and iPhones) and a packet of forms. For one week, he or she would be beeped at random times throughout the day. Each time the teenager got beeped, he or she was supposed to fill out a few pages answering questions such as "What are you doing right now?" "Who are you with?" "On a scale of 1 to 10, how good do you feel?" "Draw a picture describing your state of mind," and "How focused do you feel?" The data provided a vivid and detailed picture of the highs and lows of teenage life.

Csikszentmihalyi was particularly interested in trying to figure out what might explain why some teenagers in certain situations reported feeling so energized and involved and at other times so aimless and disconnected, while other teenagers never reported feeling energized and involved. He focused on one particular phenomenon, which he termed "negentropy," a state of total engagement and focus on something that is socially meaningful and productive. When a person experiences negentropy, he is so involved with what he is doing that he loses any self-consciousness, feels at one with the activity, and becomes unaware of the passing of time. Csikszentmihalyi argued that students who regularly experienced negentropy were more likely to be well-adjusted, happy teenagers who made a smooth transition to adulthood. Kids who played the violin, did a sport they loved, or were involved in a chess club were the kinds of kids who regularly experienced negentropy. Key to their experience was the chance to devote themselves to something they really loved and were good at.

Some kids, often the ones who stand out, seem to have a kind of zest for life, an enthusiasm that lifts their skills and interests to a new level. Rebecca Shiner calls this "surgency." She and her colleagues studied a group of 205 children between the ages of eight and twelve, assessing not only their conscientiousness and motivational orientation but also what she thought were the four components of surgency: dominance, expressiveness, attentiveness, and self-reliance. The researchers returned to these same kids twenty years later and asked them to describe themselves and their daily lives. They found that children who had been motivated to gain mastery became adults who took pleasure in daily activities and worked hard to accomplish goals. Children who had high levels of surgency became adults who were persuasive, forceful, socially potent, and likely to derive pleasure from hard work.

Shiner found something else as well. Just as other researchers have shown, kids who are conscientious do well in school, and kids who do well in school are more likely to get good jobs and keep them. One of the reasons conscientious children do well in school and at work is that they tend to be very rule-abiding. And along with their tendency to follow rules, it turns out that they are likely to be highly self-controlled and tend to avoid risks. A conscientious child might be very successful in school, which is a good route to getting a job that has good status and good pay. Those are the kids who are likely to be good at their work later on. But they might also avoid taking the kinds of risks that lead to great accomplishment. This might explain why the Melissas of the world do very well in conventional terms but might not often break new ground in a given domain.

Do you want your child to earn a lot of money? Do you want her to have influence over others? Do you want her to do work that has an impact on people's lives? Do you want her to be really good at something? Do you want her to gain recognition from others? Probably the answer to all of these is yes. For most children, becoming Bill Gates or Michael Jordan is not likely. Short of that, however, there are big and important differences in the kinds of work-related success people find in adult life. Some people cannot seem to hold a job, others have steady work but never find the satisfaction and recognition they yearn for, and some eschew earning power but love what they do so much that it buffers them from other disappointments.

What are the behaviors that indicate a child is headed for success? Early ability, of course, is a good sign. But ability without motivation and conscientiousness rarely takes a child far. Children who seem eager to do well and are able to do well are on their way to success. When that is coupled with a great capacity for loving work—whether it's collecting dinosaurs, making tree houses, pitching a baseball, or solving mathematical puzzles—parents should relax. Such a child has the essential components of success.

What are the red flags? A child who finds it hard to persist, even at the things she enjoys, might find it harder to find work she likes and to do well at work she likes. Usually, this shows itself in small moments—the comments she makes while she attempts something challenging, her tendency to choose an easier rather than a harder goal, and her attention to her own talents rather than the progress she has made. And although children seem to come ready-made with a lot or a little of this quality, it is something that can, to some extent, be changed. You can help a child become more oriented toward improvement and less oriented toward instant (and easy) attainment. Even if you live in a culture such as ours that elevates talent and minimizes effort, your own comments and approach to daily life will influence the way a child views her efforts. When she struggles with something, commend her effort and remark on her improvement, rather than whether she is good at it or not. Stress the role of effort in your own work, and talk about the satisfaction you take in your progress rather than your victories.

What are the red herrings? Ironically enough, the easiest mistake parents can make in this regard is to be disappointed or alarmed if their child doesn't always win the prize, earn the best grade, or get chosen for the most elite team. Those early victories are great if you get them. But not getting them isn't a predictor of a lackluster or dismal future. And it actually tells you nothing about your child's tendency to thrive as she gets older. Prizes, outstanding accomplishments, and big wins in grade school do not predict success in adulthood. And the lack of those early victories does not predict failure.

Children who are encouraged to work hard at things they love are likely to find success, if not fame and fortune, when they are adults. Making sure that your child has a chance to work hard at things she loves is the best tool you can give her for carving future success.

5

Romance: The Origins of Love

This chapter begins in a funeral home. The funeral is for a man who has died at fifty-eight from a massive stroke. I am there because the dead man was the husband of someone with whom I work. An interim pastor is presiding over the funeral. The funeral home is in a small, depressed town in western Massachusetts, Adams. It used to have thriving mills and a lively main street. Now it has little that thrives. There is a tiny, ramshackle diner that has offered the same menu for fifty years. There is a large-chain grocery store, the Big Y, some empty factory buildings, several old dark-brick school buildings, a five-and-dime, and a motley assortment of other drab storefronts.

The people at the funeral are like the people in any small rural town—the men and women work in factories and local stores or at trades such as carpentry, plumbing, and masonry.

The pastor looks like a thousand other ministers—short white hair, a receding hairline, a white beard, and kind eyes set in pink, weathered skin. He is low-key and admits he doesn't know the family well. His sermon is simple and banal. It would be easy to tune out. But then, out of nowhere, in his ordinary homespun way, he mentions an idea that rests at the core of what we know about human love.

He says, "In the shepherd's prayer, the baby lamb asks what we all want to know. How can the shepherd who brought me into this world, who cared for me and looked over me, who brought me food and protected me from wolves and other predators, take me away? He will surely take my life away when he butchers me or offers me up for religious sacrifice. How can the one who gives me life take life away? This is what we all want to know." Then the pastor adds, "When young men and women come to me to seek my blessing because they want to marry, I always say to them, 'If you don't want to suffer, don't do this.' But of course, they have no choice. It's always too late. They already love each other. And every baby is already in love with its parents the day it is born."

The pastor has that dead right. But he has made one small yet crucial mistake. When babies are born, it's actually only their mother they are in love with. And that love turns out to be the starting gate for all future romance.

The First Romance

I often tell my introductory psychology students the story of Frederick II of Prussia. He wanted to find out which language was the original language of mankind. He commandeered a whole cohort of babies and decreed that they be raised by nurses who took care of every physical need but remained totally silent. That way, he figured, he would find out which language the children spontaneously spoke when they were free of adult influence. He was a clever experimentalist but obviously not very nice. The story goes that he never got the answer to his question, because all of the babies died. Silent wet nurses, it turned out, weren't enough for the babies. They needed something more. It took a couple of hundred more years for researchers to begin to understand just what it was those babies had been missing.

During World War II, a British doctor, John Bowlby, made the same discovery under somewhat different circumstances. Bowlby visited orphanages in London to check on the health and welfare of the babies orphaned because of German bombing. Strange as it now seems to us, Bowlby was stunned by the malaise of the babies, who were for the most part well cared for in basic medical and physical terms. They had been well fed, given safe, comfortable cribs, kept clean, and given decent medical care. Nevertheless, the babies were withdrawn, developmentally delayed, and small for their age. They suffered from what came to be known as failure to thrive. Bowlby realized that the babies were suffering from the absence of a mother figure, someone who loved them and could be loved by them, someone whose physical presence provided them with a sense of well-being. From his experiences in those orphanages came Bowlby's seminal trilogy: attachment, separation, and loss. He described the essential bond that forms between a child and his mother and the terrible toll it takes on a child to have that bond broken.

But it was Harry Harlow who used experiments to demonstrate vividly what happens when an infant cannot be close to a parent. He couldn't experiment with humans, of course. Instead, he isolated baby monkeys from their mothers. When these little motherless monkeys became juveniles, they couldn't get along with other monkeys. While monkeys raised with a mother would play, share food, and peacefully coexist in a small space, the motherless monkeys would alternate between huddling by themselves in a corner, rejecting any overtures from other monkeys, and attacking those who approached. We take it as a given now that Harlow's research demonstrated how essential it is for primates (including humans) to get something other than food and safety when they are born. But understanding that the bond is essential is only the first step.

It might not be enough simply to have an adult around a lot of the time. In a second famous experiment, Harlow placed baby monkeys in a cage with two parent surrogates. One was made of wire, but it offered nutrition—a bottle of milk attached to the wire. The other surrogate, placed in a different part of the cage, had no bottle but was covered in soft terrycloth. Harlow found that the babies would hurry over to the wire mother to drink milk and as quickly as possible, hurry back over to the terrycloth mother, where they would spend the bulk of their time trying to cozy up to the soft fabric-covered figure. The implication was obvious: babies crave comfort. But Harlow's monkeys faced a stark choice: soft terrycloth or wire. Even the soft surrogate offered a pale facsimile of emotional nurturing. Isn't there something more complex to the bond between mother and child than the emotional gratification gained from snuggling? Surely not all babies who grow up with their mothers are alike.

Mightn't there be better and worse mother-child relationships? Imagine any playgroup where a parent brings his or her child to play each week or any playground where parents bring their babies and toddlers. If you watch for a while, subtle differences will begin to take shape before your eyes. One mother seems to know what her baby's reaching gesture means—this time she wants the ball, this time she wants her bottle, this time she just wants a smile. Another mother keeps scanning her baby's face anxiously, looking for clues while the baby fusses and fusses, unable to make himself clear. One toddler rushes off to fling herself into the sandbox. Her father sits nearby talking with his friend. Every ten minutes or so, the little girl looks up. Her father meets her gaze and nods, and she happily returns to her work with trucks. Not all of those pairs are bonding in the same way. This is what Bowlby's disciple Mary Ainsworth wanted to know more about.

Her method for assessing the relationship between a mother and her child remains one of the most ingenious in psychological research. Figuring that not all mother-child pairs would be the same, she set out to examine differences in their emotional connections. Watching parents and their children in everyday situations is good for getting a sense of the variety of parent-child bonds. But it wouldn't provide an objective and reliable way of categorizing such pairs or of testing the stability of such differences over the course of childhood. You'd see one mother in a grocery store ignoring her baby while searching the aisles for cereal. How would you compare that to a mother who worked most of the day but spent twenty minutes totally focused on her child at bath time? And what if the day you watched a mother play with her child, siblings were in the room, diluting the relationship between your target baby and his mother?

Ainsworth's genius was to create a situation that would be the same for all of the mothers and babies she observed. But bringing a mother and a baby into a room to play for a few moments would not necessarily reveal the nature of their attachment. It would be hard to know what you were comparing. Which slice of interaction would you focus on? The moment they snuggled? Perhaps, as Tolstoy implied, all snuggles look pretty much the same. Would you watch them as they concentrated on playing a game? Maybe their level of education or intelligence would explain more about what went on than the quality of their relationship. If one pair spent the time cooing at each other, and the other spent the time looking at a book together, how would you evaluate their differences or similarities? And here is where Ainsworth was most inventive.

A close reader of her mentor, Bowlby, Ainsworth realized that a good attachment shows up best in the very moment it is threatened, when a mother leaves her baby. She reasoned that babies would differ in the way they reacted when their mothers left the room. She also figured that the second most revealing moment would come when the mother was reunited with her baby. Again, her hunch was that not all babies would deal with this in the same way and that the differences would show something about the kind of attachment each mother had with her child. And this is how the "strange situation paradigm" was born.

Each baby (ranging from nine to eighteen months) and mother participating in Ainsworth's research were brought into a room set up to look like a living room, with comfortable chairs, toys, and, in some versions of the study, an unfamiliar adult sitting in the room. After a few minutes, the mother got up and left the room. Ainsworth and her colleagues watched through a one-way mirror to see what would happen when the mother left. Most babies cried. Some cried inconsolably, while others cried for a few moments and then began to explore the toys near them. A few seemed not to notice or watched their mothers leave with little expression on their faces.

And here's a crucial point that flies in the face of much Western folk wisdom about child rearing. Contrary to popular opinion, it was not a good sign when a baby seemed calm or oblivious to her mother's departure. As much as we all admire the baby who easily goes to a stranger, from the perspective of Ainsworth, this suggests that the baby doesn't have an adequate connection to her mother. In other words, crying can be a good thing.

But not all unhappy babies are the same. After the mother had been out of the room for a few moments, she came back in. Ainsworth watched to see what happened then. The babies who had seemed not to care when their mothers left seemed equally unaffected when they came back in. These babies are not, as some might think, the calm, well-adjusted babies who are independent and comfortable with strangers. They were, in Ainsworth's worldview, lacking an essential bond with their mothers. Most of the babies were overjoyed when reunited with their mothers. They would crawl or walk right over to them, burying their faces in the mothers' necks or bosoms. But the love story doesn't end there. After just a few moments of cuddling, many babies would clamber off their mothers' laps and happily toddle off to play with the toys.

However, some babies who were distraught when their mothers left and delighted when they returned seemed unable to regain their equilibrium. These more riled-up babies would rush over and nuzzle their moms when they came back into the room. But the reunion lacked both the joy and the brevity of those other babies. They seemed conflicted. Some of them hugged their mothers but then, as if remembering their sadness, would pummel them. Some pinched their mothers. Some began whimpering, as if they still hadn't gotten over the upset of being left in the first place. These babies would crawl back over to the toys but keep turning to watch their mothers, as if to make sure they didn't leave again. They seemed to have trouble regaining their composure. These babies might return to playing with the toys, but they seemed distracted by the possibility that their mothers might leave again. And because they kept their eye on their mothers, they never really got reabsorbed in their play.

This ambivalent behavior on the part of some babies led to one of the pillars of attachment theory. The nature of a child's bond with his mother has consequences for the way that baby interacts with the world.

But Ainsworth observed a third kind of attachment as well. Some babies didn't care at all when their mothers left the room in the first place and seemed equally uninterested when they returned. Although it can be a relief to a young mother if her baby doesn't mind when she leaves for work, to developmental psychologists, that calm obliviousness reads as detachment. And detachment can spell trouble on the road to adulthood.

Even the best relationship between a baby and her mother is

not simple. The powerful love a well-attached baby feels from and for her parents bubbles with shifting feelings. No matter how close a baby and a mother are, they have conflicts; they yearn for each other and feel sick of each other. This first relationship forms the basis for all others, and inevitably it carries with it a mother lode of complex dynamics.

When my sister's daughter Maddie was four, she was angry at my sister for something. Maddie and my sister were sitting on a chair together, locked in a battle of wills. Finally, my sister said in a quiet but exasperated voice, "Maddie, that's it. You cannot go out to play right now with Erin. We're leaving soon to go grocery shopping, and there is no time. We're not discussing it anymore."

Maddie's face looked like a small storm—her mouth turned down, her eyebrows bunched together, and her eyelids were red from crying. Holding her mother's shirt with her little fists, she kicked her foot into her mother's back, nudging her mother off the chair, moaning tearfully, "Go away. I need you."

Mothers vs. Fathers

When Lenore was born, she was supposed to fix her parents' marriage. Aida and Sol had been unhappy together long before their wedding. But they were serious, thoughtful people, both from strong, middle-class, Jewish immigrant families, and they intended to make their family work. So first they had a daughter, and then they had two sons. In between, they each had a few affairs, as well as fairly sustained stints of psychotherapy. They fought about money. They fought about sex. They fought about the children. Sol wanted them to go to public school, and Aida wanted them in a more open environment. Aida wanted the children to play after school, and Sol thought they should have chores. Sol didn't like the way Aida flirted with other men. Aida didn't like the way Sol hovered over her with his constant air of superiority. These differences simmered under the surface. If you had met their family, you would have seen an intelligent, attractive, well-educated brood, a family that rode bikes together in the park, took weekend trips to the shore, and had long dinners with friends, filled with conversation about books and politics.

But underneath the veneer of urbane control, anger and discord rumbled. Sol loved his kids, but he didn't really like being with them. Aida loved her kids, but she liked her freedom, too. A closer look at the interactions within their lovely home would have shown that not all of the relationships were what they seemed to be. However, Aida and Sol didn't believe in angry displays in front of the children. Their tension lay deeper than that and took form only in the privacy of their respective therapy sessions or the bedroom, where they talked and talked and talked about their troubles.

When Aida's third child, Adam, was three, she had an affair with someone she met at a dinner party. But it was over within months, and Aida realized that she desperately wanted her family life to be happy. Maybe she should have one more child, a baby to cuddle and love, someone to cement their life together as a family. She and Sol had problems, but they shared a commitment to the life they had built. A child would refresh that and give them a new start.

When Lenore was born, tawny, with large brown eyes and a sunny temperament, Aida was sure this would set things right. Aida took a three-month leave from her job as an occupational therapist to care for her little Lenore. And what a delicious baby. Lenore would gaze up joyfully from her baby carriage as Aida happily strolled with her in the park and met friends to chat, sunbathe, and enjoy the silky-skinned new baby. Lenore was just the right baby for Aida, at just the right time. When Lenore cried, Aida's gentle, firm touch calmed her right down. When Aida spoke to Lenore, the baby gazed up happily at her mother's face. Aida felt she was looking down into a wonderful reflection of herself—the same deep brown hair and eyes, the same tilted nose. She was such an easy baby—easy to feed, easy to hold, and so ready to laugh. It was like looking down at herself, only better, because she was looking down at a baby who adored her.

Sol was another story. By the time Lenore was born, he was completely disaffected by family life and spent little time at home. And from the day she was born, Lenore was so clearly Aida's baby. Sol, on the other hand, adored their eldest child, a black-haired, blue-eyed girl named Miranda. Miranda and he were two peas in a pod, and from the time Miranda was a baby, she and her father understood each other. Miranda was the apple of Sol's eye. Not Lenore.

By the time Lenore was four years old, Sol and Aida were too unhappy to stay married. Aida and the children went to live in another part of Westchester, and Sol moved into a small apartment in New Jersey.

Lenore spent every Saturday night with her father. He was kind and attentive. They did nice things together—he read aloud to her, and they took walks through the park, went to puppet shows, and made visits to Aida's favorite cupcake store. Even so, she missed her mom. Her dad's small apartment was sterile and gloomy. The neighborhood seemed lonely to her. She never felt totally herself when she stayed with her father. He was somewhat formal with her, using big words when he spoke. "He wanted to discuss things. I wanted to play," is how Lenore recalls it. They just didn't click. But her time with her mom was the opposite. They liked the same food, they thought the same things were funny, and they made each other feel better. They were in sync.

In the years since Ainsworth set up the "strange situation paradigm," researchers have unearthed some powerful mechanisms that push mothers and their babies toward each other. Ainsworth couldn't have known how overdetermined that first love affair really is.

Babies come into the world equipped to like people. If you show a baby pictures of lines and dots in a random design and pictures that form the barest outlines of a facial configuration (squiggles and dots where eyes, nose, and mouth would be), the newborn will look longer at the pattern suggesting a face. Babies also prefer a symmetrical pattern to a nonsymmetrical one. They are hard-wired to like indications that they are looking at a person. All of this means that from the moment they are born, they are tuned toward others—no one more so than their mothers.

When researchers play the sound of a baby's mother on one side of her head and the sound of another female voice on the other side of her head, the baby will turn in the direction of her own mother's voice. Remarkably, a newborn baby seems to recognize her mother's smell. Within a few hours of life, she will turn toward clothing her mother has been wearing, rather than toward an object worn by someone else. Babies are wired to prefer their mothers above all others. And vice versa.

Mothers are wired to prefer their babies. When women give birth, they release a hormone called oxytocin. In recent years, neuroscientists have learned that the release of oxytocin triggers feelings of love and attachment. This seems to explain, in part, why women tend to feel that they love the man with whom they just experienced an orgasm (another cause of oxytocin release). The mother who has just given birth and is floating in an internal bath of oxytocin feels a wave of love looking at the newborn placed on her chest. This isn't all in her head. It's all through her body. The role of oxytocin in triggering maternal affection explains why the route to attachment is somewhat different for babies who are separated from their mothers at birth, raised by a father, or adopted. It is not that these other kinds of parent-child pairs don't bond, but it is true that they don't have the same natural boost of hormones. However, that initial burst of hormonally triggered attachment is only the first step.

Although the bond between mother and baby is hard-wired, sometime during those early months, what begins as an automatic preference evolves into a textured relationship, replete with fulfillment, unrequited love, and the kinds of subtle corrections that go into any romance.

For one mother, those early exchanges with her baby feel just right. She loves the fact that when he cries, she knows just what to do—she takes his legs and pushes them up against his tummy. He feels better and quiets down. She feels like a good mom. Another mother might find that, as euphoric as she felt in the hours after her little girl's birth, in the days that follow, her baby seems like an inscrutable stranger to her. She peers into her little girl's face, cooing and singing. She longs to see a smile in return. But the baby turns away. These sequences form a kind of dance.

When parent and baby click, it reflects what psychiatrist Daniel Stern called attunement. And some pairs are more attuned than others. In his early research on attunement, Stern and his colleagues filmed mothers interacting with their babies, who were seated in inclined infant seats so that they could "talk" to their parents. Viewing a split screen of the filmed data, showing the mother on the left and the baby on the right, Stern could measure just how closely each parent-child pair mirrored each other's sounds, gestures, and facial expressions. He found that most mothers and their babies are extraordinarily well coordinated. But he also found that some mothers were out of tune with their babies. For instance, a mother might keep looking at her baby and making sounds, while the baby turns his face away, avoiding more interaction. Some babies cannot tolerate the level of interaction the mother yearns for. In some cases, the tables are turned. The baby makes all kinds of sounds, with his eyes glued intently on his mother's face, clearly eager for a response. But the mother, perhaps lost in her own thoughts or finding it difficult to respond with the same animation as her baby, just gazes off in the middle distance.

Stern's camera work and microanalysis revealed very subtle hits and misses in the nonverbal conversations mothers and babies constantly engage in. His method allowed clinicians to identify mothers who displayed a lack of synchrony with their babies. They were certain that such a mismatch would cause difficulties in the vital bond between mother and baby. Stern and his colleagues worked with the pairs who had the most trouble. Their goal was to help mothers learn to match their own gestures, gaze, and vocalizations to those of their babies—sort of like teaching someone who wants to dance the tango how to follow the steps of her partner.

Years after Stern first identified this intricate pattern, researchers began to see that the quality of that dance had consequences they hadn't realized. For instance, researchers have found that babies who engage in lots of back-and-forth with their moms do better on a variety of cognitive tests when they first go to school. It seems that experience at such finely tuned back-and-forth exchanges leads to skills essential for talking, solving problems, and learning from others. When researchers have followed depressed mothers and their children from infancy, they notice that it can be hard for a mother who is depressed to pick up on her child's subtle invitations to "talk." She often misses the sound or expression the child uses to start conversations. Lacking a rich exchange with his mother turns out to limit the baby's own emotional repertoire as he grows. What might begin as an emotional problem for the mother can lead the child to have a long-lasting problem with relationships as he grows up.

If you've watched a baby gaze at her mother's face, you can easily spot the signs of true love. And although most scientists, as well as the general public, have all too happily rejected much of what Sigmund Freud told us, a few of his ideas have gained strength with time and better scientific methods. One of his strongest ideas had to do with the roots of love.

Freud told us that the roots of love are found in a mother's arms. Specifically, we first fulfill our need for pleasure at our mother's breast. As Freud and others noted, a baby who has just nursed has the sated, relaxed look of someone who has just had sex. And surely, the slightly suspended breath and rapt gaze of a baby whose mother is trying to win a smile from her evokes the passion of romantic infatuation, a feeling she might not have again until she's in her late teens.

When my first son was three, I became pregnant with our second child. I bought a book called *How Babies Are Made.* My son loved hearing me read that book aloud to him. We read it again and again, even after his little brother was born. One day, he picked it out of a pile, climbed onto the couch where I was sitting, and asked me to read it one more time. The new little baby was lying next to us, sleeping peacefully in his basket. When I got to the page that said, "When a man and a woman love each other very much, they lie close together, and the man puts his penis in the woman's vagina," and prepared to turn the page, my son rolled over from his seat next to me on the couch so that he was lying on my torso, and with his face very close to mine, he looked straight into my eyes and said, "Let's try it right now." After a split second of astonished confusion, I said, "Oh, well, little boys don't do that with their mommies. But when you grow up, you might meet someone you like very much, and you'll probably want to try it with that person." He flipped back to his seat on the couch next to me, shrugged airily, and said, "OK. I'll try it with Courtney tomorrow." Courtney was a four-year-old classmate in his preschool.

By the time he was four years old, he had a favorite game to play with me. "You be Guinevere, and I'll be the White Knight. I'll save you." I'm not sure what I did to "be Guinevere" or what it entailed to have him save me. As is so often the case, four-year-olds get as much out of planning and narrating their play as they do enacting it. Designating our respective roles—his as a powerful knight in shining armor and mine as the beautiful damsel in distress who would love him for his strength and daring—seemed very satisfying to him. That same year, soon after his little brother was born, he had a great idea for Halloween: "I'll be a king, and Will can be a little pig." I tell these stories when I teach college students, in order to bring to life what Freud was talking about when he said that every child goes through his or her own Oedipal drama. It's often less subtle or abstract than people might think. But although little girls might want to marry their daddies and little boys court their mothers, those romances do not predict much about how a particular child's love life will unfold.

When Lenore was thirteen, she still looked eleven. She hadn't gotten her period yet, and she was thin and flat-chested. Although she looked like a child, she had the daydreams of a teenager. She and her friends talked endlessly about boyfriends. She had the most vivid imagination among them and would describe the boy of her dreams in detail—what they would do on the first date, the note he would write to her the day after the first date, and how he would behave in the weeks to follow. She could envision her first romance in novelistic detail. But she still hadn't even held hands with a boy.

Meanwhile, her older sister, Miranda, was deep in the throes of a love affair, and her mother, newly separated from her stepfather, was spending a lot of time with the new man in her life. Lenore could see what love looked like, even if she hadn't come anywhere near it herself. She studied Miranda's romance, as if it provided her with a blueprint for her own future.

Lenore excelled easily at her suburban public school. Actually, the work was too easy—it didn't come close to tapping her enormous reserve of energy. Instead, that energy went into imagining life as she yearned to live it. She recalls, "I saw every movie that came to town. I read every new romance novel that I could get my hands on. I told long, elaborate stories to my friends about the love affairs I would someday have. The stories were so detailed and so vivid that half of the time, I convinced my friends that the men were real people I had already met. Meanwhile, here's what was actually happening. I came home from school each day at three, did my homework, ate dinner with my family, watched one hour of sitcoms, and went to bed. My mental life and my actual life had nothing to do with each other. The emptier my days, the fuller my daydreams of handsome men with exotic names."

But while other girls in her neighborhood were tasting their first kiss, letting boys feel their breasts, and considering going steady, Lenore hadn't even been to the movies with a boy.

When Lenore was eighteen, she went with her brothers to a party at the lake near their home. And that's where her dream came true. Ryan was twenty-three and very handsome. He had broad shoulders, thick blond hair, and an infectious laugh. She could tell he was used to flirting. She had been waiting all this time to charm and be charmed by a boy like this. This was it. It was happening! For three weeks, they met at nearby parties, swam at the lake, and lay in the hammock together. They also had sex. She felt she had been ready for this since she was nine. Lenore was in love. But it was now August and time for her to leave for college. They spoke on the phone three times each of her first seven days at college. Then she suddenly woke up on the eighth day and felt as if a fever had just broken.

"I still can't explain it," she told me. "During those three weeks, it was as if I was on a drug. When I was away from Ryan, I couldn't breathe. When I was with him, I couldn't really hear or see anyone else. The first night at college, I told my new roommate that I thought about him every second. I wrote him a passionate love letter. Then, a week later, boom. It was over. I didn't miss him. I didn't want to talk to him. I suddenly felt slightly disgusted by the whole thing." Lenore shook her head ruefully and said, "What a brat I was. I didn't write to him. I didn't call him. When he called,

I let the machine pick up. It's obvious to me now that even though I thought I was so grown up, I wasn't anywhere near ready to be in love or even have a boyfriend."

It wasn't that she had met someone else. She didn't want a real boyfriend. She preferred to lie in bed in her dorm at night, telling her roommate all about her current mad crush (one week the drama professor, another the varsity baseball player or the day student enrolled in her biology class). She preferred those late-night conversations about love to a living, breathing boy.

The Second Romance

In the middle of the twentieth century, Harry Stack Sullivan constructed a theory that explained how friendships might pave the way to romance. He argued that preadolescents formed what he called "chumships," close, intense friendships that allowed children to practice the intimacy of adult love. It didn't matter that most friendships during the preteens are between children of the same sex. Sullivan reassured parents that with "normal development," children would transfer the patterns and behaviors they had practiced with their chums to members of the opposite sex. Sullivan rarely mentioned that he himself was gay.

Almost all of the literature on adolescent love suggests that young teens unwittingly use their buddies to practice love. They spend time together, they fight and make up, they listen to one another, they reveal intimate thoughts and feelings, and they feel at times as if no one can understand them as well as their best friend. A close scrutiny of memoirs shows that wherever you see close friends in late childhood, there is a strong whiff of Eros. Even kids who don't remember talking about love, masturbating together, or practicing kissing one another remember a sense of connection to a best friend that had the same intensity we usually classify as passion.

Some psychologists have even argued that the love young children feel is basically the same as the passionate love of adulthood. To compare feelings of children with those of older adolescents and adults, Elaine Hatfield and her colleagues recruited 236 Hawaiian boys and girls ages four to eighteen. First, the researchers made sure that each child understood the concept of boyfriend/girlfriend. Then they asked each child to select one boyfriend or girlfriend to answer questions about. Each young subject was asked to complete what is called the Juvenile Love Scale, a list of questions adapted from a similar survey used to evaluate the feelings of adults describing their romantic partners. The children were asked to rate the truth of each statement—1 was very untrue, and 10 was very true.

1. I feel like things would always be sad and gloomy if I had to live without ______ forever.
2. I have kept thinking about ______ when I wanted to stop and couldn't.
3. I feel happy when I am doing something to make ______ happy.
4. I would rather be with ______ than anybody else.
5. I'd feel bad if I thought ______ liked somebody else better than me.
6. I want to know all I can about ______.
7. I'd like ______ to belong to me in every way.
8. I'd like it a lot if ______ played with me all the time.
9. If I could, when I grow up, I'd like to marry (live with) ______.
10. When ______ hugs me, my body feels warm all over.
11. I am always thinking about ______.
12. I want ______ to know me, what I am thinking, what scares me, what I am wishing for.
13. I look at ______ a lot to see if he (she) likes me.

14. When ______ is around, I really want to touch him (her) and be touched.
15. When I think ______ might be mad at me, I feel really sad.

In order to make sure that puberty itself does not cause children to begin feeling passionate love, the researchers rated each child on a puberty scale. They found that the scores of young children did not differ dramatically from scores of older children and that children of all ages demonstrated passionate love quite similar to the kinds of feelings adults have for someone with whom they are in love, regardless of whether they had facial hair or were menstruating. According to what these children said about their own feelings, they experienced passion pretty much the way adults do. For most kids, though, that passion does not pass straight from their mom to their lover but takes an important detour into the world of friends.

Bernie had lots of friends and a rotten home life. If you had met him when he was eleven, you would have made two completely opposite bets on his future love life, depending on the situation in which you saw him.

If you had seem him on a basketball court or cutting up with his buddies after school, you would have seen exactly the kind of chumship Sullivan was talking about. He loved his pals. They played sports together, they went swimming together, they stayed out past their curfew together, and they got into trouble together. He candidly recalled the "circle jerks," which seemed to be such a sordid but compelling element of boyhood friendships. He and his friends liked girls, but only for a few hours at a time. What they really liked was the bond they felt with one another. And Bernie was particularly popular. He had a flair for telling entertaining stories, he was funny, and he had endless energy for a good time.

"I was this real outgoing, talkative, gregarious little kid," he said. "There's a story everyone in the family loved to tell about me. Our family's place in upstate New York was on a lake, and the whole social life took place around boats. Lots of cousins and aunts and uncles own property. Each night, a different family member cooked dinner. We're talking thirty to fifty people. You'd get from one house to another by boat. The story they tell is that I was sitting out on the end of the dock greeting everybody as they arrived. This two-year-old saying, 'I'm Bernie. This is my grandmother's house.'" When he thinks about his teen years, all of the good memories are of the time he spent with his friends.

But if you had seen him at home, you would have seen a different picture. Bernie's early years seemed to come right out of a picture book (smart, successful dad, pretty devoted mother, and two younger sisters, living in a beautiful suburb of Philadelphia), but by the time he was eleven, everything had fallen apart. His parents had divorced. His mother, completely undone by the change in her circumstances, had become deeply involved in a religious cult. And Bernie's cozy life as a privileged and talented member of the middle class had been thrown out the window. Bernie had to go to work after school to help his mother pay the bills. Meanwhile, he felt increasingly estranged from her. He often had to run interference for his younger sister, who fought so much with their mom that she finally left the house to live with their father.

"When I was little, it was Utopia," he said. "My mom was very loving, very attentive, always there. She started a nursery school in our house. My mom was always having birthdays and parties for us—other kids were always at our house. But later, after they got divorced, everything changed. She couldn't handle three kids, and the divorce had broken her. That's the whole time the Jesus shit started to happen, and she became a necessary evil to me. She woke up every day wondering what the Lord would have her do that day. But she also became totally disengaged. She wouldn't consider seeing a movie or reading a book. She didn't know anything about music. She just didn't care about anything. I stopped being able to count on her at all. She couldn't cook anymore. And she didn't approve of how I was living my life because of her religious beliefs. But here's the sick part. Even though we had almost nothing in common, and even though I felt so angry at her, I made my mom proud. And that was our sick, twisted relationship. She felt that people admired her because of my achievements or successes. And I think that when I was little and my parents were still married, she felt I was the link that would tie her to her husband.

"But by the time I was twelve, she was the 'often person,' not the 'intimate person' in my life. By the time I was twenty-five, it became impossible to be around her at all. She wanted the 'picture' version of our relationship, not the real version. She was so out of touch she didn't even realize it had become a fraud. Actually, it was worse than that. She didn't even care that it was a fraud. She didn't care that I only came to church with her to meet girls. If I was sitting next to her in that pew, everything was good."

If an intimate relationship with a mother is so important to later love, things didn't look good for Bernie. Not only had his attachment to his mother become a sham, but his way of interacting with girls wasn't so promising, either. He'd spend hours courting a pretty girl (he recalled, "My favorite thing was getting a girl to change her mind"), only to grow quickly tired of her, yearning to hang out with his buddies from the basketball team or the golf club where he earned money in the summer. When he got to college, he had many conquests but no relationships. Not with girls, anyway. Girls were for sex. Boys were forever.

Then, when he was twenty-five, he met Edith at a business meeting. She was beautiful, as most of his girlfriends were. She was funny, too, and, like him, she was athletic and smart. Success had come easily to both of them. They both stood out in a crowd. And they stood out to each other. Bernie recalled feeling instantly smitten. His office mate remembers him coming home from the meeting and saying, "I gotta marry that girl."

Edith was taken with him immediately though reluctantly. She already had a boyfriend. Bernie was kind of brash. He watched sports on TV and used expressions like "Ma'am" and "Sure thing." She read edgy fiction and hated sentiment. Nevertheless, Bernie didn't let up, and she gave in to his relentless pursuit and her deep attraction.

They had one other thing going for them. It is not simply that Bernie and Edith felt a connection, a sense of similarity at a deep level. Chance was also on their side.

Finding the Time and Place for Love

George Burns and Gracie Allen were married for thirty-eight years, and the world got to see just how much they loved one another. Someone once asked Burns what the secret to such a long happy marriage was. Burns answered instantly, "Marry Gracie." But psychologists think something else is just as important as finding the right person. It's finding him or her at the right time in the right circumstances.

In 1974, psychologists Arthur Aron and Donald Dutton set out to test the hypothesis that people get confused between anxiety and arousal. How to test it? Ask people to cross a bridge! Aron and Dutton brought young single men (between the ages of eighteen and thirty-five) to cross over a wobbly suspension bridge with low cable handrails, which hung over a 230-foot drop. Another group of men were invited to cross a solid, wider bridge with handrails ten feet off the ground. After each young man had crossed his bridge but was still standing on the edge of the bridge, a female interviewer approached and asked him to complete a questionnaire with six irrelevant questions and then look at a drawing and tell a story about it. After each man had finished his questionnaire and drawing, the female experimenter gave him a phone number and told him to call if he wanted to know more about the study (to test the effect of having a woman interviewer, half of the wobbly high bridge subjects and half of the sturdy low bridge subjects were interviewed by a male experimenter). The stories written by the men were scored for sexual imagery on a scale of 1 to 5. Men on the wobbly bridge received an average score of 2.47, while those in the control group received just over a 1.41. With the male interviewer, the wobbly bridge group received a .80 score, and the control group received a .61. In addition, half of the eighteen men who had accepted the interviewer's phone number followed up with a phone call, whereas only two of sixteen in the control group did so. With the male interviewer, fewer men accepted the phone number, and only two of seven wobbly bridge men and one of six control bridge men called. The men aroused by crossing the scary bridge were much more likely to think about sex and to respond flirtatiously to the woman interviewer. When men (and possibly women) are in arousing situations, the arousal spreads—a feeling of anxiety or fear either sets off a feeling of desire or, more likely, is interpreted as being sexual arousal. Years later, Aron wrote articles urging long-married couples to try new and somewhat scary things together. He is still sure that when people are a little nervous, they get a big fat side benefit: they think they are excited romantically by the next person they see.

Bernie and Edith met during a high-stakes meeting between their two companies. Both were at a pivotal point in their very pressured high-climbing careers. The adrenaline might have been prompted by work, but it spread a rosy glow over the fledgling couple. However, that kind of fortuitous timing is only short-term. There is a longer-term kind of timing that might also affect the chances that a person will fall in love. Psychologist James Pennebaker and his colleagues named this phenomenon after an old country song, "The Girls Look Prettier at Closing Time," and set out to prove that the singer was correct.

The subjects for the study were fifty-two males and fifty-one females selected from three bars close to the campus of a university in the South. Experimenters entered the bars at 9:00 P.M., 10:30 P.M., and 12:00 midnight, which was half an hour before closing time. Experimenters asked people in the bar to rate members of the opposite sex who were also there, on a scale of 1 to 10. The closer it was to closing time, the higher the ratings were. The moral of that story: As you feel your time for getting a partner wanes, your available choices look better and better.

Bernie and Edith had good timing. They met when they were twenty-five—in our culture, that's just when people feel compelled to settle down with someone. Perhaps Bernie felt the bar was closing, which made Edith look not only beautiful but as if she was "the one" to him. But as we all know, there is a 50 percent divorce rate in this country. Bernie had a bad track record with women. The longest relationship he had had before Edith was six months. Would they last? John Gottman could have told them.

Gottman and his colleagues have been able to predict a couple's longevity from just a few moments of taped interaction. Couples who will weather the storm of daily married life seem to talk to each other differently from couples who won't make it.

In one study, Gottman and his colleagues recruited fifty-six married couples and asked them to talk about how satisfied they were with their marriages. They were also asked to describe how they met, courted, and decided to get married and how the marriage had changed. After three years, the researchers contacted the couples to find out how their marriages were going and examined the original interviews of the couples who had divorced. What they learned was quite startling. The men in marriages that did not last had shown low levels of fondness when they talked about their marriages but also when they talked to their wives. The husbands and wives in these couples rarely talked in terms of "we" and didn't express much feeling during the interviews. They were often negative and articulated their marital disappointments.

Gottman has used these and other data to argue that you can predict whether a couple will last based on the way they talk about their marriage and the way they talk to each other. Bernie and Edith argued a lot. They both often swore at each other. They freely mocked, challenged, and snapped at each other. Bernie flared up, looking like a fire-breathing dragon. Edith would roll her eyes, suck in her breath, and become distant. But when they talked with friends, their conversations were laced with things they had done together, funny stories about each other, and common references. They laughed at each other's jokes, were profoundly interested in each other, and looked at each other often. Their talk was filled with signs of marital stability, and the signs of conflict indicated nothing much at all.

When Bernie tells the story of his upbringing, it's surprising that he came out of it intact. He even feels that it is something of a miracle that he ended up in such a loving marriage. But buried in his narrative, amid all the dysfunction, is a slender thread connecting the stable love he experienced early on with his mother to his friendships that paved the way for courting Edith.

Meanwhile, Lenore seemed to be dying on the vine. Midway through Lenore's nineteenth year, she realized that all of her friends were dating. She had a worried feeling that something was wrong with her. She knew she was pretty. She recalled, "My mother always told me how pretty I was. And I looked like her. And everyone talked about how pretty she was, even her. But somehow I didn't attract boys the way my friends did. The pizzazz I had with girls, with adults, with children, with teachers, I just didn't have it when I was talking to guys. I felt flat, the same way I felt when I talked to my dad. I began to feel I'd never have a real boyfriend."

It has long been the case that psychologists tend to study the phenomena that lend themselves to good experiments, rather than what we find most important or fascinating to understand about human behavior. So it's no shock that the science of love has wavered and faltered. Perhaps surprisingly, a prominent expert in intelligence, Robert Sternberg, turned his attention for a period of time to the equally important matter of love. He has argued that love consists of three parts: intimacy, passion, and commitment.

In the best of all possible worlds, two people in a long-term relationship (say, marriage) feel connected on all three levels. They confide in each other, they feel known by each other, and they feel close. That's intimacy. They also desire each other, feel jealous when their partner appears to desire another, and feel excited by the presence of each other (at least some of the time). That's passion. Finally, they both feel they are in it for the long haul. This sense of loyalty—a plan to stay together—helps them weather the times they don't feel passion or intimacy. That's commitment. The question is, what leads one person to create this kind of loving bond and renders another incapable of the full package?

The answer, according to those who are interested in how people develop, is that love is just a grown-up form of attachment. A child's experience of first relationships paves the way for her adult love life.

However, it's not so easy to prove that there is a direct line leading from the way you felt in your mother's lap to the way you feel at age twenty-seven with the person you plan to marry. Ask anyone to talk about his or her love life and in the same breath to recall his or her earliest relationships, and you are just asking for rewritten histories, ones that create a continuous narrative whether there is one or not. People will recount stories of a distant, unloving mommy to help explain a crumbling marriage or a powerful, overwhelming father to explain why they could never meet the right guy. Those kinds of tales are usually just-so stories. Although these homespun stories might often be baseless, there is a connection between one's early relationships and grown-up love. The trick is identifying the real thread.

Phillip Shaver and his colleagues have chipped away at this elusive challenge from a number of angles. When they ask people to describe their earliest memories of their parents and their early life at home, the answers can be sorted into the three attachment styles first described by Ainsworth. And remarkably, the number of people falling into each of the three styles almost perfectly mirrors the breakdown of attachment styles found in the original research with toddlers. This suggests that though psychologists often think that self-reports are unreliable, in this case, people's accounts are accurate and quite revealing. When the same subjects described their adult relationships, a clear pattern emerged. Those whose earliest memories captured an anxious, ambivalent attachment were the same ones who described a nagging sense that their partners didn't love them enough and felt constantly distracted by the worry that their mates might be cheating on them. These were the adults who constantly hankered for more reassurance from their romantic partners. Sadly, people who have ambivalent attachments as babies often seek out mates who suffer from the same kinds of ambivalence. It's not hard to imagine that such couples are in for a tough time. The same is true for those who experience what Ainsworth termed "avoidant attachments." The baby who watches impassively as his mother leaves the room and barely acknowledges her return might well turn out to be the man who has difficulty creating intimacy with a lover, who has trouble forming a long-term attachment, and who avoids the kinds of closeness so important to long-lasting love.

Shaver's work only shows that there seems to be some stability between how a person recalls early relationships and how he or she experiences current romantic relationships. It doesn't prove that early stability guarantees happiness in later love life. But taken together, the data on early parent-child interaction and the little we have gleaned about what goes into successful adult love suggest that developing a capacity for closeness in early life has a huge impact on the closeness you can find in your love life. As psychologist Susan Golombok has pointed out in her book on parenting *(Parenting: What Really Counts)*, it is not the structure of family life that seems to matter as much as the quality of family life.

Growing up with a single parent might tell you little about your chances of a happy marriage. The quality of the relationship you had with that parent says a lot more. When you experience intimacy as a young child, you are good at it, and, just as important, you seek it in your grown-up love life.

Vera and Matthew met in their late twenties. They both had been briefly married to other people. They were smart, hardworking, and deeply immersed in their shared life working on educational films. All of their friends worked in film, and they loved nothing better than to gather with editors, cameramen, screenwriters, and set designers to talk shop and gossip. They both came from stable, strong families, and of course, they wanted to have children. They had a lot of trouble conceiving, but with medical intervention, they finally had a son, whom they named Alex. Alex was adorable, bright, and full of pep. Vera had waited a long time to have a child. The photographs of her with her little boy show her beaming with delight. But people are who they are. And Vera was cool and crisp. She found it hard to confide the details of her personal life, even to her closest friends. She wouldn't have considered changing her clothes in front of anyone, not her mother, her sister, or her friends. She thought it odd when friends kissed one another hello. There were huge gaps of information between members of the family. They didn't like to pry.

Vera was not one of those moms who took naps or baths with their babies. She had trouble nursing and put Alex on a bottle when he was three weeks old. She couldn't understand why other people had difficulty getting their babies to sleep. She had no trouble giving Alex a quick kiss and resolutely closing the door behind her. By three months, Alex slept through the night. As Alex and her friends' children got older, she found it strange that other little boys told their mothers all about what they did with their buddies, what their conversations at school were like, and what they were feeling. She thought it was better for children to have some distance from their parents, someone who could be an authority. When Alex was a teen, she commented to a friend that it was good to make rules that Alex didn't like—how else could he rebel and therefore grow up? She took him to the park, read books to him, and played games with him. However, if you watched them together when Alex was little, you could see that although she was loving and attentive, she was distant, and Alex seemed slightly oblivious to her comings and goings. It was hard to catch them absorbed in each other. He didn't flop against her when he was tired, and she didn't nuzzle his stomach with her head. When she mentioned her concerns about him, she might have been talking about an acquaintance or a character in a book, rather than her flesh and blood. The very slight reserve they had with each other was subtle, not easy to catch at first glance. As child psychiatrist Susanne King says, "What begins as a pretty basic kind of attachment needs a chance to grow into something more. Children need a chance to experience giving emotionally as well as getting."

When Alex was in high school, Vera and Matthew kept waiting for him to find a girlfriend. Although they had a sense that he had crushes, Vera didn't like to ask. She felt that was intrusive. And they had less and less sense of what his social life was like. When Alex went off to college, they were sure he'd find a sweetheart. He had roommates he seemed to like, he enjoyed his class work, and he did well. But no romances. After college, Alex moved to Boston. He got a job working in a bookstore and began to take graduate courses in English, which had been his major in college. But he didn't seem to have many friends. He met a girl in one of his classes, and he dated her for a few weeks. Matthew and Vera were relieved. But then, mysteriously, the relationship evaporated. Even Alex seemed uncertain what had gone wrong. At twenty-nine, he still hadn't had a close relationship that had lasted more than three months.

Meanwhile, Lenore was miserable. At twenty, she was the swan who had become an ugly duckling. Why didn't boys ask her out? Why wasn't she sexy? At eleven, her mind had been dancing with future lovers. Except for her truncated whirlwind romance with Ryan, she lived like a nun. No one approached her. How could a young woman already be an old maid? A therapist suggested that her trouble finding love had to do with the uneasy rapport she had with her father, maybe because her parents had divorced, maybe because her mother had been too competitive with her. Maybe maybe maybe.

When my eldest son was a toddler, I spent a lot of time in a New York City park with other young moms and their children. I remember one mother in particular who seemed to be perpetually angry, controlling her little boy's every move. She called him "Pudge." I confided to some of the other moms that I predicted he would not feel attractive as he grew up. She constantly reminded him what he should and shouldn't do in the playground: "Pudge, stop that right now. I told you we wouldn't stay if you kept grabbing other children's trucks. Pudge, take that out of your mouth. That's revolting." Watching this mother and her young son, I heard a small warning bell go off. With such constant criticism, how could this kid ever feel autonomous and confident when he was older? So much of their interaction was suffused with conflict. I wasn't the only one who didn't like what I saw. "Oh," the mothers on the bench said, "this doesn't bode well for Pudge's love life. He's doomed to marry the same kind of heckling micro-manager he's got now. Everyone marries his mother."

There was another mom in the park who walked in each day

holding her son's hand. They often skipped together as they neared the gate. He'd give her a kiss before running off to the swings. Sometimes he'd leave the play area and come back over to his mother sitting nearby on a bench. She always seemed to know ahead of time what he was coming for. The thermos of juice, the cookie, the other toy truck, or the mittens would be ready by the time he got there, as if she could read his mind. He'd give her another big wet kiss before heading back off to the swing sets. The other mothers would shake their heads at this pair: "Oh, boy. I feel sorry for his girlfriends. They're gonna be out on a date at a nice restaurant, and he's gonna want to get up to make a call to his mother, just to say hello. No one will ever measure up to Angel Mommy."

The first prediction is probably not true. People don't marry their mothers (or their fathers, for that matter). There isn't one shred of evidence for that old nut. And there isn't one theory that even makes sense of such a prediction. The second prediction is probably not true, either. A good relationship with a parent doesn't get in the way of love—it paves the way for love.

I read novels. So it's hard not to think of love in terms of the great love stories, which offer vivid pictures of the different kinds of love we might wish for our children. When we gaze adoringly and anxiously into our babies' eyes, we might not all have our hopes pinned on the same romantic future. Do you want your son to know the all-encompassing passion Heathcliff felt for Cathy? Do you want your daughter to feel the gentle, steady devotion that Jane Eyre felt for Mr. Rochester? Would you prefer she elicit the feelings Mildred drew from Philip in *Of Human Bondage*?

In our society, the majority of people end up finding a mate. That doesn't mean, however, that they have found love. And a passionate romance doesn't guarantee that your child will form a lasting, supportive, committed relationship, either. The road to love is filled with happenstance, good and bad luck, and the influence of outside forces.

But children who experience emotional closeness when they are young are much more likely to seek intimacy in adulthood and to be able to share themselves with others. If your child finds you to be emotionally reliable and consistent when she is little, if you and she like being with each other, if what begins as a bond becomes rapport, her romantic future is off to a good start. In fact, a loving reciprocal relationship with a primary parent is as close to a love potion as you can get.

When Lenore was twenty-three, she married Paul. During the years that followed, they faced plenty of tough times. Paul suffered untold stress when he was diagnosed with diabetes, and he became seriously depressed. After about ten years together, when Lenore changed jobs and Paul started a new business, they were so broke they almost lost their house. They fought and once came close to divorce. But they also raised four children and recently celebrated their thirty-fourth wedding anniversary. When asked if they are in love, Lenore smiles wryly. "We were in love. Absolutely. I totally remember those days. I think he does, too. And now we'd rather be together than apart. We still like to wake up in the same bed. We're good."

6

Happiness: The Path to Contentment

"For Sale: Baby shoes, never worn." If his suicide didn't make the point, his supposed one line memoir shows Ernest Hemingway's dim view of life. On the other hand, Elizabeth, the young heroine from Thomas Hardy's novel *The Mayor of Casterbridge,* seemed to earn the good fortune that a fundamentally happy child carves out for herself: "Her strong sense that neither she nor any human being deserved less than was given, did not blind her to the fact that there were others receiving less who had deserved much more. And in being forced to class herself among the fortunate she did not cease to wonder at the persistence of the unforeseen, when the one to whom such unbroken tranquility had been accorded in the adult stage was she whose youth had seemed to teach that happiness was but the occasional episode in a general drama of pain."

Why is one person happy with so little and another, talented and fortunate, miserable anyway? When you gaze at your baby and watch her play, can you tell whether she will grow up happy?

Even as a two-month-old, Lily liked peace and quiet. Her mother quickly realized that although she herself was naturally drawn to a slightly more rough-and-tumble style of parenting, it wouldn't work for her tiny girl. Lily liked to be lifted gently and lowered into her crib gently. She liked soft voices and a gentle up-and-down rocking motion. She was calm, happy to be held by anyone as long as they weren't loud. Gorgeous from the day she was born, she had a heart-shaped face, with gray eyes that ended in a small tilt and a lush, wide mouth. From the moment she could smile, adults and older children wanted to make her smile again. When something pleased her, a slow glow rose from her face, illuminating those around her.

Yet babies are not simpler than adults, and Lily was filled with seeming contradictions. Although she craved quiet and order, she was also zany. At three, she liked to dress in wild costumes—pants on her head, brightly striped knee socks, large leather shoes for bike riding, her uncle's yellow fishing gators for suppertime. She liked to make crazy faces and say raucously funny things in a crowd. There are photographs of her looking like a cross between the Artful Dodger and Tinkerbell. As soft and dreamy as she could appear, she was as tough as nails. She learned to swim, in a freezing-cold murky pond, before she was two, and she could navigate the rocks in a waterfall before she was four. No dog, however big, scared her. She liked sour foods and, with a belly laugh, would crunch into her favorite snack, a dill pickle.

When Lily learned to talk, she became even more entrancing to those around her. She added new syllables to the phrases she liked best—her uncle's dog Slash became "Slasher," and at noon, she often called out boisterously for "Lunchialia!" She had lots of easy charm, which she seemed to bestow effortlessly on the objects and people around her.

If you had met Lily when she was a toddler, you would have seen an easy, calm baby, full of smiles, equanimity, and an infectious sense of humor. And things seemed to go so well for her you would have bet money that she was a child destined for a cheery, happy life.

But no baby is an island. Every baby's temperament unfolds in a world of people and events. Lily came into the world a younger sister. Hazel, six years older, had been tempestuous from day one. She was full of life, but she was also full of vinegar. She hadn't been an easy baby, gassy and unsettled from the first. As Hazel grew older, she continued to demand a lot of attention, good and bad, from the adults around her. So, from the day Lily was born, she was the angelic foil to her high-strung sister.

Other aspects of Lily's life impinged on her as well. Don't they for everyone? When Lily was two years old, her family moved from San Francisco to a suburb a few hours away. Her mother gave up her full-time job in a community arts agency to work as a freelance graphic designer. Her father, a musician, took on a full-time job teaching music in a high school. Her older sister, Hazel, was ecstatic and loved their new house by a lake. Lily's parents were thrilled—this would be the first time they had actually owned a home, and they were exhausted from working and raising children in an expensive and noisy city.

But the transition was harder for Lily. At three, she was particularly vulnerable to change, and research shows that a move of homes and neighborhoods is one of the biggest adjustments a child can face. Lily had thrived on calm and routine and found the move disruptive and deeply disconcerting. She began to protest when her mother left her at day care. Those separations, so easy and unimportant when she was younger, suddenly seemed filled with anguish. As her mother kissed her good-bye at the door of the preschool, Lily's soft, wide mouth would turn down, and her eyes would turn a dark, murky gray. She'd complain huskily, "Why do you have to go? Why do you have to leave me?" Her mother, torn and unsettled, would leave her at day care, fretting all the while at how hard it was for her usually sunny child to handle this small routine.

Lily's protests rattled her mother. What had been a harmonious, flowing connection between Lily and her mother now seemed rife with small upsets. A cloud began to accumulate over their relationship and over Lily herself. If you met Lily when she was eight, you would never have been able to guess that her start in life had been so sunny.

Lily's teacher shook his head about her and said, "Lily comes into school as if she were carrying the weight of the world on her shoulders." Although she was beautiful, athletic, and good at her schoolwork, she often scowled or shrugged when family members asked her how school was. She complained about her teachers ("He's boring," "She's mean," "She never calls on me"). She was frequently aggrieved by her friends. The things that lit her up were few and far between. She developed a habit of shrugging diffidently when asked almost any kind of question. Her soft, low voice, which seemed when she was little to beckon, now deflected, sounding muted rather than husky. What had happened to her?

Happiness is the magic elixir of life. If you have lots of it, you can weather all kinds of terrible disappointment and even misfortune. If you don't have it, even the luckiest life feels gray. While academics endlessly debate the precise elements of happiness, most people know it when they feel it and often know it when they see it in others. You don't need to be a research psychologist to see that some people have a zest for life, a pervasive sense of well-being that lifts them above the general population, gives them a bounce in their step, and makes them really attractive to others. Franklin Delano Roosevelt was one of those people.

In a *New York Times* article about happy presidents, Lou Cannon described FDR's irrepressible good mood in the face of tremendous pressures: "In a little-remembered book, 'F.D.R., My Boss,' Mr. Roosevelt's secretary Grace Tully affectionately described how he cheerfully added to his stamp collection, dabbled in architecture, played cards and 'made a ritual of the cocktail hour' where serious talk was avoided during the depths of the Great Depression and World War II. Happiness was part of F.D.R.'s makeup. 'From the bottom of his heart he wants [people] to be as happy as he is,' wrote his adviser Raymond Moley."

Roosevelt had a lot of good fortune. He was rich. He was hugely successful. But he also was paralyzed from the waist down. He presided over one of the modern world's most devastating wars. He was responsible for the well-being of a society thrown into the worst economic depression ever recorded. His marriage was not happy, and he was unable to live with the woman he really loved. Nevertheless, he felt good. To paraphrase the Cowardly Lion, "What does he got that we don't got?"

The roots of his happiness can be traced all the way back to his childhood in Hyde Park, New York, on the Hudson, where he lived with his mother and father. In her biography of FDR, Jean Smith quotes him: " 'In thinking back to my earliest days,' he said many years later, 'I am impressed by the peacefulness and regularity of things both in respect to places and people. Up to the age of seven, Hyde Park was the center of my world.'" Smith writes, "America's confidence in FDR depended on Roosevelt's incredible confidence in himself, and that traced in large measure to the comfort and security of his childhood."

Stability and a pleasant home environment gave FDR a boost, and these factors are generally an antidote to life's ills. Children who come from stable, warm families have an advantage when it comes to their long-term prospects for happiness. But FDR had another weapon in his happiness arsenal: he made it easy for people to make him happy. Both his mother and his father recalled him being a delightful son, one they took great pride in but also enjoyed. "We never subjected the boy to a lot of don'ts," Mrs. Roosevelt wrote. "While certain rules established for his well-being had to be rigidly observed, we were never strict merely for the sake of being strict. In fact, we took a secret pride in the fact that Franklin instinctively never seemed to require that kind of handling." When he got to boarding school at Groton, he made friends easily, and the teachers liked him. But he had something else as well. Even as a little boy, he was enthusiastic about his interests, having begun stamp collecting by the age of ten. He had a gift for pleasure.

Several summers ago, I was visiting my childhood home on the eastern end of Long Island. My parents' house is on a small country lane with only three houses next to it and lots of open potato fields. Usually, it's very quiet there. But one morning, as I sat on a chair in my second-floor bedroom, high above the lawn, listening to the stillness of a sultry August day, I slowly became aware of an odd sound floating through the air into my window. It took me a few seconds to figure out what I was hearing. It was the voice of a little girl, maybe five years old. She was singing a tuneless little song, over and over again. I couldn't hear any words, just a little girl's singsong lilt and a five-sound phrase, repeated again and again with exactly the same cadence each time. "Da de DA de dah. Da de DA de dah. Da de DA de dah." The first two "da's" went up the scale, the third was the loud high point, and then came the final "de dah," which took her back down the scale. She was singing the way you do when no one is listening, when you are singing just for your own pleasure. Sometimes her voice would fade until I could barely hear her, and then it would rise again in volume, brimming with renewed enthusiasm and energy. As I strained to listen, I realized the young chanter wasn't just sitting under a tree—she was doing something. So I peered out the window to find out what. Through the bushes, I caught a view of the young singer. She was a slight girl of about five, with pale thin legs and arms. She was wearing faded shorts and a hot-pink T-shirt. Her brown hair fell to just below her chin and flopped when she jumped. She was leaping, with a kind of calm sobriety, between two tall trees. Each time she landed under one of the trees, she reached up and swatted at one of the low-hanging leaves, then turned to make her leap back to the other tree. That was the game. It must have been really fun. I sat there, listening to her leap and chant, for a good fifteen minutes. When I finally pulled myself away from the hypnotic allure of the little girl's game and went downstairs to join my family, she was still at it.

Her absorption in that small sequence captures the remarkable capacity young children possess for delighting in the smallest slices of life. Just recall the universal game of peekaboo with a nine-month-old. Imagine the baby's nervous and expectant excitement while she waits for your hands to come off your eyes as you say, for the thirty-fourth time, "Peekaboo!" Her surprised laughter contains an intensity that adults typically reserve for very special occasions.

But a child doesn't need to be playing a game to be thrilled by life. Seemingly mundane activities can be equally absorbing. Watch just about any toddler sip water from a cup. She grabs the cup with two fists, focused on her task. She brings the cup up to her mouth, widening her eyes as she peers at the liquid within. You can just imagine how inviting that small amount of water looks to her. She puts her lips around the edge of the cup, readying herself to taste. Each infinitesimal gesture, the ones that become so automatic we'll never give them another thought unless we are deprived of them because of illness or hardship, is carried out by the toddler in a deliberate way. She notices what she is doing. She marvels at the texture of cool liquid slipping into her mouth. You can see how she relishes the sensation of filling her mouth with the wet substance, and you can almost see her decide just how quickly to let it slide to the back of her mouth so that she can swallow it. The gulp looks almost as wonderful as the first taste. But the pleasure of sipping water does not lead to laughs and smiles. Children often take very seriously the things that make them most happy. For the young child, such pleasures are not giddy punctuations that contrast with the more serious or dull routines of everyday life—the routines contain a multitude of opportunities for the young child's delight.

What FDR, the little girl on the lawn, and any toddler sipping from a cup have in common might well be the quality we most yearn for later in life: the young child's ability to immerse herself in the pleasure of small things. Many of us, no matter what our childhood circumstances, can recall a kind of exquisite joy in ordinary moments that seems harder to come by as we age. The young child's capacity for intense pleasure is a seedling, something to be built on and nurtured rather than cast away. Yet by the age of four, the capacity to get a kick out of life has, for some, faded. Some preschoolers seem sadder than others. Lily did, for sure. Is a sad child doomed to a sad life? Can a glum child become happy?

Martin Seligman thinks so. While psychology has traditionally concerned itself with people's problems—depression, anxiety, shyness, and anger, just to name a few—Seligman, a research psychologist at the University of Pennsylvania, has spent recent years trying to understand why and how people feel good.

The science of happiness, however, poses an unusual research problem. While psychologists usually depend on surreptitious methods to find out what people really feel (by tricking their subjects into revealing thoughts and emotions thought to be inaccessible to consciousness), it's hard to imagine being happy and not knowing it. So, positive psychologists (the way Seligman prefers to describe psychologists who want to understand people's strengths) just ask their subjects how happy they are.

Seligman typically uses something called the Authentic Happiness Inventory. He invites subjects to sit down at a desk and answer a list of twenty-seven questions about their outlook on life. The score provides researchers with a measure of a person's overall sense of well-being. Participants in Seligman's studies are usually simply asked to rate themselves on a long list of questions that are designed to tap into a person's sense of self. A subject might answer the following kinds of questions:

(1)

A. I feel like a failure.
B. I do not feel like a winner.
C. I feel like I have succeeded more than most people.
D. As I look back on my life, all I see are victories.
E. I feel I am extraordinarily successful.

(2)

A. I am usually in a bad mood.
B. I am usually in a neutral mood.
C. I am usually in a good mood.
D. I am usually in a great mood.
E. I am usually in an unbelievably great mood.

(3)

A. When I am working, I pay more attention to what is going on around me than to what I am doing.
B. When I am working, I pay as much attention to what is going on around me as to what I am doing.
C. When I am working, I pay more attention to what I am doing than to what is going on around me.
D. When I am working, I rarely notice what is going on around me.
E. When I am working, I pay so much attention to what I am doing that the outside world practically ceases to exist.

Sure enough, the way a person scores on Seligman's questionnaires matches up pretty well with other indices of a person's well-being—

people who get a high happiness score tend to be viewed by others as quite happy. They also tend to make fewer visits to doctors, suffer less frequently from depression, do better at work, and report greater marital satisfaction. The results of those questionnaires, given to hundreds of people across the country, have provided researchers with some clues about the essential components of happiness.

Data from these studies have led Seligman and others to believe that how happy we feel stems in large part from how we think—a startling concept emerging after almost fifty years of behaviorism and psychoanalytic theory. In the 1960s and '70s, behaviorists and psychoanalysts dominated the way we understood people's emotions. Behaviorists thought sadness was a learned response and that if you could learn to act happy, you would come to feel happy. Psychoanalysts believed that depression was anger turned inward. The anger was presumed to have its origins in an earlier emotional loss of some sort. Freudian psychoanalysts thought depressed patients were overly dependent on love and approval from others and unable to deal with small disappointments.

In this climate, psychologists Aaron Beck began his research by trying to find empirical support for the psychoanalytic model of depression. He studied dream content in an attempt to prove the existence of internalized anger in depression. If such a construct existed, he expected depressed people to report higher degrees of hostility and anger in their dreams. His results showed that depressed and nondepressed people did not differ in the frequency with which they had angry dreams. Instead, he found that depressed people tended to have more dreams in which they are victims of rejection, disappointment, or criticism.

He also noticed that depressed patients were more negative and pessimistic about themselves and their performance than nondepressed patients. As Beck wrote, "the studies led to the conclusion that certain cognitive patterns could be responsible for the patients' tendency to make negatively biased judgments."

In addition, during his treatment of patients, Beck became aware that people experienced what he called "negative automatic thoughts," a second stream of thinking of which they were unaware. Beck had been with one patient who was telling him how angry he was with him. While exploring these feelings in the therapy session, the patient noted that he was also having self-critical thoughts about expressing the same feelings. Through therapeutic encounters like this, Beck came to the conclusion that patients were communicating with themselves at an automatic level all the time. These thoughts tended to be fleeting, specific, spontaneous, and consistent in theme and almost always involved a distortion of reality. Beck maintained that negative thinking was not merely a symptom of depression but its cause. He argued that depressed thinking is characterized by the "cognitive triad," a negative view of oneself, one's future, and the world. If a person sees the world in negative terms, he will constantly be confirming his own worst fears: *I'm bad, no one likes me, there's nothing I can do to make things better.* Beck argued that depressed people couldn't simply be retrained to act in happier ways; they needed to learn how to reinterpret the world.

Seligman, influenced by Beck, turned his attention to children who were depressed. He wanted to show that children who are gloomy, like depressed adults, explain the world differently from children who feel good. And he wanted to show that this explanatory style could be changed.

When asked to explain various imaginary scenarios, children reveal two clearly distinct patterns. Some explain good events in terms of global stable qualities about themselves. For instance, this kind of child thinks he got an A on a test because he is smart. Other children, however, assume that good events are mere chance, nothing to be counted on. When this kind of kid earns an A on a test, he's sure he just got lucky or that the particular test was unusually easy.

But the same child who sees good events in terms of stable, underlying strengths typically explains bad events in more specific and temporary terms. A child with a positive outlook might think she didn't get a part in the play because so many older kids tried out that year, while a downbeat child figures it's because she's no good at acting. Happy children explain life's events one way, and glummer children explain things in the opposite way.

Psychologists have developed a questionnaire that elicits these two patterns of explaining life's events. The most standard version of this assessment is called the Children's Attributional Style Questionnaire. The questionnaire contains forty-eight items. Each presents the child with a hypothetical situation, followed by two statements about why the event happened. For instance, the young subject might read, "You run in a race at school and lose," and choose from the two explanations, "I'm not athletic" or "I just didn't give it my all that day." The array of questions is carefully designed to reveal three different dimensions of a child's explanatory style.

Psychologists believe that both optimistic and pessimistic outlooks rest on three kinds of explanations children use to understand their own successes and disappointments: how responsible they feel for what has happened ("It was my fault"), how stable they think the cause of the event is ("I'm never good at that"), and how likely it is that the cause of the event will occur in other situations ("I'll never do well at that"). Optimistic children draw on the mirror image of those three kinds of explanations: they think they caused positive events to happen ("I did a great job"), that good things have stable causes ("I'm good at that"), and that the cause is likely to generalize to other situations ("I'll do well every time I do that").

Each of the forty-eight items on the questionnaire focuses on one of these three kinds of explanations, posing either a good or a bad event. For instance, one of the questions might be: "You break a glass in the kitchen. Choose a or b to explain what happened: (a) I am not careful enough. (b) Sometimes I am not careful enough." This choice identifies whether children think bad events are caused by permanent stable characteristics or by temporary characteristics. Another item on the questionnaire says: "You try out for a sports team and do not make it. Choose an explanation: (a) I am not good at sports. (b) The other kids who tried out are very good at sports." In this case, the child who answers, "I am not good at sports," attributes a bad event to herself, while the more optimistic child assumes that it was caused by factors outside herself. The questionnaire also gives children a chance to show how they interpret good events. For instance, one of the items says: "You make a new friend. Choose an explanation: (a) I am a nice person. (b) The people I meet are nice." The optimistic child who might well have assumed that bad events were caused by external factors might attribute this nice incident to her own good attributes, while the more pessimistic child, likely to think he caused his own bad luck, might well think making a new friend happened because of other people, not because of him. Children's answers to the forty-eight questions tend to be pretty consistent, hence the designation of a pessimistic or optimistic child.

Lily never completed the Children's Attributional Style Questionnaire, so we don't know how she would have scored. But when the painting she spent three weeks on in third grade wasn't chosen for the school exhibition, she shrugged. "I knew it wouldn't get in. I can't paint." When her father canceled the trip they were supposed to take together to Washington, D.C., when she was in fifth grade, her mouth turned down. But she didn't protest. She said softly, "It's OK. I knew we probably wouldn't go." She felt burdened by schoolwork, oppressed by the demands of teachers and the daily ebb and flow of social life. At home, she became a somewhat withdrawn observer of the louder, more vibrant exchanges between her older sister and her parents.

It's not obvious why Lily had developed such a negative outlook. She was born, like most children, with the ability to derive huge satisfaction in everyday life. But that was not all. She was also born with some of the other elements that predict happiness. Early on, she had a sunny disposition, good looks, humor, and what's known as low neuroticism. She didn't ruminate, she didn't dwell on grievances, and she didn't seem in her early years to be beset by the kind of indecision and ambivalence that plague neurotic people. Yet even so, as she entered elementary school, her sunny self became overshadowed by a vague sense of discontent with people and experiences. She seemed to draw less and less satisfaction from her work, whether it was writing, reading, soccer, or knitting. Nothing seemed to draw her in deeply. The less engaged she got, the gloomier she seemed. By the time she was twelve, it was a joke among her friends that if they asked Lily to make a decision about where to go for lunch, what dress to buy, or what movie they should see, she'd shrug and say in a low voice, "I don't mind."

Seligman is certain that kids like Lily can learn to think differently and that when they do, they begin to feel happier. Using Beck's framework for treating adult depression, Seligman set out to show that you could also shift a child's view of herself, her future, and her world—that you could teach unhappy children to have happy thoughts and that such thoughts would make them feel happier.

In his original study on the topic, Seligman and his colleagues enrolled a group of two hundred eleven- and twelve-year-old children from Philadelphia in a six-week after-school program. Children were chosen to participate because in questionnaires they filled out at their school, they reported feeling depressed and/or were experiencing problems at home, such as that their parents were fighting. Half of the students participated in small groups who spent the twelve weeks learning "coping skills." The goal was to teach the children how to identify their own negative beliefs and pessimistic explanations and come up with more positive accounts for the things that happened to them at home and at school.

Researchers have found that children who have a negative explanatory style are also more likely to feel that they have little effect on situations—they feel helpless. Happier children seem to feel more confident that they can change a situation, that they can determine their own level of success, and that they can come up with solutions to problems. Psychologists refer to this as a sense of self-efficacy. A recent description of the Dalai Lama provides a vivid portrait of just the things Seligman has been looking at all this time.

"Dream—nothing!" is one of the many things I've heard the Dalai Lama say to large audiences that seem to startle the unprepared. Just before I began an onstage conversation with him at New York Town Hall this spring, he told me, "If I had magical powers, I'd never need an operation!" and broke into guffaws as he thought of the three-hour gallbladder operation he'd been through, weeks after being in the hospital for another ailment. For a Buddhist, after all, our power lies nowhere but in ourselves.

We can't change the world except insofar as we change the way we look at the world, and, in fact, any one of us can make that change, in any direction, at any moment. The point of life, in the view of the Dalai Lama, is happiness, and that lies within our grasp, our untapped potential, with every breath.

Easy for him to say, you might scoff. He's a monk, he meditates for four hours as soon as he wakes up, and he's believed by his flock to be an incarnation of a god. Yet when you think back on his circumstances, you recall that he was made ruler of a large and fractious nation when he was only four years old. He was facing a civil war of sorts in Lhasa when he was just eleven, and when he was fifteen, he was made full political leader and had to start protecting his country against Mao Zedong and Zhou Enlai, leaders of the world's largest (and sometimes least tractable) nation.

This spring marked the completion of half a century for him in exile, trying to guide and serve 6 million Tibetans he hasn't seen in fifty years and to rally 150,000 exiled Tibetans who have in most cases never seen Tibet. This isn't an obvious recipe for producing a vividly contagious optimism.

Yet in thirty-five years of talking to the Dalai Lama and covering him everywhere from Zurich to Hiroshima, as a non-Buddhist, skeptical journalist, I've found him to be as deeply confident, and therefore sunny, as anyone I've met. And I've begun to think that his almost visible glow does not come from any mysterious or unique source. Indeed, mysteries and rumors of his own uniqueness are two of the things that cause him most instantly to erupt into warm laughter. The Dalai Lama I've seen is a realist (which is what makes his optimism more impressive and persuasive). And he's as practical as the man he calls his "boss."

The Buddha generally presented himself as more physician than metaphysician. "If an arrow is sticking out of your side," he famously said, "don't argue about where it came from or who made it; just pull it out. You make your way to happiness not by fretting about it or trafficking in New Age affirmations but simply by finding the cause of your suffering and then attending to it, as any doctor (of mind or body) might do."

Who knows where the Dalai Lama got his sense of self-efficacy? But Seligman believes this, too, can be taught to ordinary kids. The children in Seligman's study were also taught how to take more control of their own actions—to think about goals and consider alternative solutions to the problems that might come up each day. Finally, the workshop leaders taught them relaxation techniques and showed them how to be more assertive.

The experimenter worked hard to make the sessions fun and un-school-like. They used comic strips, role-playing, games, and videos to teach each core concept in their program. They created two characters, Hopeful Holly and her brother, Hopeful Howard.

Holly and Howard became known throughout the twelve-week sessions as the Silvers, because they could find the silver lining in even the darkest cloud. In a range of stories and scenarios the teachers presented to the children, the Silvers had to combat Gloomy Greg and Pessimistic Penny. The researchers also created characters for the other components of their program: Say-It-Straight Samantha, Bully Brenda, and Pushover Pete. Meanwhile, the children in the control condition were told that they were on a waiting list and could participate the next year. That way, all of the kids could ultimately have a chance to learn the coping skills, but meanwhile, the researchers could compare the children who had been through the twelve weeks of small-group sessions with similar children who had not experienced the training.

When Seligman and his colleagues went back to visit these children six months later and again two years later, they found that the children who had been in the experimental condition were doing better than the children in the control condition. They reported less unhappiness, and their teachers also described them as more cheerful and optimistic. Children who did not participate in the treatment group showed worse symptoms of unhappiness two years later than they had in the first place. In other words, if a child seems to be morose and negative when she is eleven, she is likely to get more so over time if she doesn't learn a new way to deal with everyday life, and children who get some help continue to benefit from the treatment a full two years later. Seligman is very gung-ho about his approach. He has used the basic model in a wide range of school districts—urban, rural, and suburban. He has moved on from using highly trained doctoral students to training teachers and parents to show kids how to think more positively, and he reports great success. He feels certain that in a relatively short period of time, you can retrain pessimistic children to think more optimistically and thereby become happier. Lily was smart and pretty and went to a good school. But according to Seligman, her negative thinking kept her from enjoying all of her good fortune.

The irony is that some kids seem to be born with such a strong dose of optimism that they can withstand disappointments much worse than the ones Lily encountered. Colin was one of those kids.

When Colin was fifteen years old, he became haunted by the feeling that he was going to hurt someone or perhaps already had. He recalls these dark feelings first emerging when he was at boarding school as a young teen. But he kept his troubles to himself. It was only after his first semester of college at the University of North Carolina that his scary thoughts began to dominate his life. He could no longer hide his problem from the people around him. Plagued by terrifying impulses and images, he couldn't eat, he couldn't sleep, and he certainly couldn't work or be with other people—in fact, he could barely talk. "I became catatonic," he recalled. Until then, his very typical-seeming family had almost no idea what he was going through.

Colin was one of four children. He had a twin brother, a sister five years older, and a brother ten years older than he. They were well off and lived in an affluent community in Virginia. His father was an attorney and extremely well connected politically. His mother was a homemaker. They had friends and a nice house. To have encountered the family in those days, you would have thought they were just another lucky American family. They had health, wealth, education, and a large intact family. Colin, too, seemed to have plenty going for him. "I did well in school. There was nothing about me that was particularly odd. I guess I was the family clown. My parents were good parents, though they were somewhat estranged from each other." Distant with each other, they were not particularly affectionate to their children, either. Colin said, "I don't ever remember being told that we were loved or hugged. What I needed as a child and what they were able to do was slightly off. I needed more direct nurturance than they were able to give."

Colin is not the first person to have grown up feeling that his parents didn't express their affection. If you think that lackluster parenting is the cause of a child's emotional problems, then you haven't really looked at the data. Many children grow up in families where parents don't show much affection to each other or don't acknowledge anger. Colin lived in a family much like others.

In telling me about his family, Colin described his siblings. "My twin was the social one. I was the student. When we were kids, I felt my brother did the social networking for both of us. I had a sister—she was five years older. She's dead. But I'll tell you about her later. And I had a brother who was ten years older. I always felt my sister and I were the low ones on the totem pole, the way my parents saw it."

Colin went on, until finally I interrupted him. "You said your sister is dead. What happened?"

Colin's voice is low-key, with the gentlest Southern lilt to it. He is one of those people who express complex and sophisticated thoughts in unusually simple, lucid terms. Even on the telephone, his modesty and sense of humility come through. He answered my question quietly. "My sister was murdered. She was being stalked by somebody. She had been doing some modeling for an art class, and one of the students took a fancy to her. I think that is the defining experience in my mother's life."

After about a year, Colin was forced to withdraw from college. He was almost completely immobilized and suffering delusions. Although they were emotionally restrained, his parents were not negligent. When Colin asked if he could see a psychiatrist, they agreed. The psychiatrist diagnosed him with schizophrenia and prescribed a regimen of heavy medication, including an antipsychotic. But Colin didn't get better. He got worse. On the advice of the doctor, Colin's parents sent him to a highly regarded residential hospital for people with mental illness, the Austen Riggs Center in Stockbridge, Massachusetts.

At Riggs, the therapists took him off the medication he had been taking. His therapist said to him, "I think when we get beneath the surface, we're going to find that the things you are feeling are feelings that everyone has."

"When I first got there," Colin said, "I didn't want to get better. But then I began to realize people liked me and wanted to do stuff with me, and I noticed that when we hiked or swam, people were happy, so I figured that if I was doing those activities, I must be happy, too."

Colin stayed at Riggs for a year and a half and stayed in the neighborhood for another two years so that he could continue intensive therapy. But he didn't just get better. He thrived. After leaving the Riggs community, he was admitted to a good liberal arts college as a transfer student. It was there he realized that he wanted to study psychology. He went on to attend one of the best PhD programs in the country, did an internship at the Yale Child Study Clinic and his clinical residency at McLean, a renowned mental hospital in Boston. Now in his fifties, Colin is a clinical psychologist who directs a treatment program for pregnant women who are addicts. He is also the doting father of a teenage daughter, although he is now divorced from his daughter's mother.

It would be nearly impossible for Colin to know for sure whether he did suffer from schizophrenia when he was a teen, but the odds are against it. Most people who are diagnosed with schizophrenia never get cured. Their symptoms might be alleviated, they might learn to cope with it, and they might even return to a somewhat normal life with the support of continual medication, but few leave it fully behind them, as Colin has. The only medication Colin has taken as an adult was the antidepressant prescribed to him briefly in the first months after he got divorced.

What happened to Colin in his late teens might always be

something of a mystery, but it's just as much of a mystery that he weathered such a psychological hurricane and came out the other side so well. Hearing about Colin's life, one cannot help but wonder how a man who has suffered such dramatic mental illness, has felt plagued by the darkest of thoughts, and has been almost completely incapacitated by his troubles can live such a happy, full adult life. It's impressive, but not surprising, that he might have found some modicum of stability, rid himself of his most terrible fantasies, finished his schooling, and achieved success professionally. But was he happy? I asked him.

"I'm a pretty happy soul. I've had to learn my way into this. The human spirit is pretty phenomenal. I'm fortunate. Many people have the problems I've had and don't get past them. It's all kind of bonus time for me. I've been very lucky," Colin replied.

Colin said that he doesn't remember all that much of his childhood, wryly adding, "Clinically speaking, that's interesting in and of itself. I don't think any dark thing happened. I was happy in the sense that I was born seeing the humor in things. My father said that was my saving grace." Although Colin remembers being pretty cheerful and having a good time, he added, "I wasn't exuberant the way one might like to see in kids. But not every kid is exuberant.

"I've come to realize over the years that my mother has given me a wonderful legacy of hope—she's a very cheerful person. There was no room for anger in my family. I was much more emotive than anyone else in the family. I was a little high-strung. It was extremely important to my father that I did well in school.

"My mother had this very abiding faith, and her sense that everything was going to work out gave me my own sense of optimism. The first thing I did after grad school was work with adolescents. I used to tell parents that the main goal for teens is just to get through the thing, period. The second thing is to try to become self-supporting. The third thing is to be as happy as one can reasonably expect to be. That's a kind of concave way to look at it. It's not just one joyful party. Working with the population I do, happiness is just a little thin on the ground. A colleague said to me, 'Colin, you're one of the most optimistic people I've ever known. You make me sick.' Another colleague said, 'I always believe that something good might happen.' When I asked her where she got that sense, she looked at me in disbelief. 'I learned that from you.'"

Colin remembered a therapist at Austen Riggs asking him if he had ever had suicidal thoughts. "I said, 'I feel like a rock precariously balanced on the point of a plateau.' I might have fallen off the point but not the plateau. I think that plateau was my sense of hope. My hope is part of my faith. I have a particular way of thinking about religion. To me, God is our collective sense of hope in the world. That's the entirety of my religious belief. I've spent time around people who don't believe in anything outside themselves, and I don't like that. That's the reason I go to church."

As with many people who report a fair level of happiness in adult life, Colin's belief in something larger than himself (what some call faith or spirituality) seems to be an ingredient in his optimism. Research shows that people who are religious tend to live longer lives and often report higher levels of personal satisfaction than nonreligious individuals. But as Colin says, this might be simply because religion provides people with a "collective sense of hope," rather than because a belief in a deity is, per se, uplifting. That sense of hope, it turns out, is a powerful vaccine against hardship.

In 1954, Emmy Werner set out to Kauai, Hawaii, to answer a question: What happens to children who grow up with all the odds against them? Werner went to Kauai as part of a group of pediatricians, psychologists, and public-health workers to gather information on one thousand children from conception to adulthood. Kauai is the westernmost county in the United States. It was home at the time to a population of about 28,000 diverse people—not only Caucasian but also of Chinese, Korean, Japanese, Portuguese, Puerto Rican, and Filipino descent. The island was mostly agricultural, and the people were known for their friendly, laid-back approach to life.

The researchers began their time on the island by obtaining a household census. Five nurses and one social worker listed the occupants of every home, along with personal data. Women of childbearing age were asked if they were pregnant. The research team left cards with all of the women, encouraging them to mail in the cards as soon as they suspected pregnancy. The goal of the researchers was to track pregnancies from the earliest date possible. As a result of the campaign to raise awareness about the study (which included letters mailed to the women, meetings with community leaders, advertisements on milk cartons, and organized mother-and-baby care classes), the team tracked 2,203 pregnancies in 1954, 1955, and 1956. The pregnancies resulted in more than 1,963 live births, which have since been tracked into adulthood. Among those children, Werner found many to be the products of teen pregnancies. These kids almost all grew up poor, without access to education or good medicine. Many of them lived in highly stressful family situations as well.

Twenty-three years after Werner arrived in Kauai, she published the answer to her question in a book titled *The Children of Kauai.* With the publication of that book, she created a new entry in our lexicon of child development: resiliency. Her data showed that some children who grow up in the toughest circumstances seem to thrive anyway. One of the factors that seems to buffer kids from poverty, stress, and inadequate family life is an optimistic outlook: "A potent protective factor among the high-risk individuals who grew into a successful adulthood was a faith that life made sense, that the odds could be overcome."

Colin certainly had that sense of hope. But he had something else: a sense of purpose. At one point, he recalled a family member asking him if he was learning a trade at Austen Riggs. He laughed and answered, "Yeah, as a matter of fact, I did learn a trade there: psychotherapy." Listening to Colin talk about his work as a therapist, it is quickly apparent that his ability to help other people is an essential part of who he is. And that, too, is an ingredient of happiness that might begin long before a person actually gets a job. In fact, it might begin in preschool.

When the little girl outside my parents' house was leaping and chanting, she was lost in a moment of aimless pleasure. But often children's most intense moments of pleasure come when they are engaged in a different form of activity altogether.

When my son Sam was about six, he asked if he could work at my husband's toy store on the weekends. Friends knowingly smiled and commented, "What kid wouldn't want to work in a toy store? He can spend all day trying out his favorite merchandise." But they had it wrong.

My husband came home after the first Saturday of Sam's new job. I asked how Sam had spent the day, and he told me, "He had to price about twenty boxes of merchandise. It usually takes the people who work for me about two days to get that much merchandise priced correctly. Sam had it done in about three hours. He's the most enthusiastic employee I've ever had. I'd give him a task, and he'd leap to it, finish it, then come over to me and say, 'What's next?'" Sam loved working. And why not? Adults need to feel useful, and so do children.

John Dewey argued back in the early twentieth century that children were bored at school because what they were learning seemed to have so little to do with the world that really mattered to them, the world of their parents and their community. In his classic piece, *School and Society*, Dewey argued that society had made school irrelevant. He claimed that children would want to learn more if what they were learning seemed meaningful—and by meaningful, he meant activities and skills that were a part of society. It was this idea that led him to argue that children should learn through "occupations," activities such as carpentry and sewing.

For the past century, educators have made a big to-do over the motivational and academic merits of Dewey's approach. Teachers who use real-world activities to teach skills (setting up stores to teach math, putting together a newspaper to teach writing, asking children to enact scenes from the past to learn history) are all showing the influence of Dewey's thinking. There is consensus that children seem to like school better when they do projects that bear some resemblance to the activities they see around them in the grown-up world. Not only do they like it better, but children also seem to learn more when what they are learning has some connection to the real world. And it is true that a vast array of research has demonstrated the power of Dewey's vision. When children work on projects that seem more closely related to the activities of the real world, they are more interested in the material, they are more excited to learn, and they seem to remember what they learn better. But if you watch children build wood structures, cook food, sew quilts, and write newspapers, it becomes quickly clear that the children aren't only more motivated to learn. They are also happier. Children like to feel useful.

Any parent who has asked a preschooler to help set the table or wash the car has seen the zeal with which most young children fling themselves into the pleasure of hard work. They like effort, they like activity, and from the moment they are born, most of them yearn to be part of the world around them.

In the early 1960s, cognitive psychologist Jerome Bruner thrust himself into a raging debate about the nature of early mental development. One group argued that young children were born with all of their mental abilities—most famously, Noam Chomsky claimed that children were born with the ability to speak grammatically. Another group argued that children needed to learn everything, mostly by being rewarded for correct actions, language, and responses. Bruner offered a third way of looking at development. He argued that what children are born with is a great desire to become part of the social world. Because of that innate desire, they learn whatever will get them "in"—they learn to talk, to engage in thinking patterns that are part of their community, to solve problems, and to participate in the rituals and routines they see around them.

Because children are wired to become part of the social world around them, they find it rewarding to contribute to daily life. And, as with so much else about young children, there is a cyclical pattern to this dynamic. When children do things that are valued by the people around them, they win the approval and appreciation of others, which only strengthens their natural urge to help out. Obviously, allowing children to contribute and feel useful has its limits. Children who are forced to do chores or schoolwork at the expense of play and time with friends are not happy and often are deprived of the very experiences they need most in order to develop. But here is where Dewey's idea has such relevance. When children do work that helps them learn and is meaningful to their community (whether it's their school community, their ethnic community, or their geographic community), they gain a kind of satisfaction and meaning from their efforts that is not possible when the work is simply a way of getting a good grade or earning the right to recess.

Lily's high school years were lackluster. And she seemed lackluster. She did okay in school, but nothing really grabbed her, and she didn't shine in any one course. When she was fourteen, she switched schools. She decided she wanted to play field hockey. But she didn't prepare for the tryouts. She didn't do exercises or run in order to get fit enough to do the routines required during the tryouts. She didn't practice the basic moves, and she didn't learn more about the game. Her parents told her she was a natural at field hockey, that it was great that she was going out for the sport, and that she was sure to do fine. They felt they were encouraging her and bolstering her self-esteem. But when it came time for the tryouts, she didn't look that good compared with the other children, even though she was easily as athletic. She *could* have been good at field hockey. But her seeming indifference had kept her from becoming good at it. Not making it onto the team made her feel worse and confirmed her interpretation of herself: she wasn't good enough, life wasn't fair, and you couldn't expect good things to happen. She explained her disappointment in global, pervasive, and stable terms, just as Seligman said. On top of that, not being on the team meant not playing field hockey every day, one less thing about which to feel good.

Lily had lots of friends. She seemed to shine with them. Buried in what had become her somewhat flat manner were little sparks of interest that offered clues about what might bring her out of her malaise. She loved to cook, and what really lit her up was to see people enjoy her homemade candy. Sensing Lily's need to be more engaged, her mother enrolled her in a candy-making class. She enjoyed it, but somehow it didn't catch fire, deepen her love of cooking, or open the door to more enthusiasm for life. She also loved to work with younger children. She enjoyed the feeling that she could take care of a baby and loved holding the hand of a toddler. She wanted others to depend on her. She babysat during the summers—she got a kick out of the money, and she liked it that the children asked their mothers to hire her rather than the other babysitters.

The summer after her sophomore year in high school, she decided that in addition to babysitting, she would scoop ice cream at a local shop. Her parents were worried that she was working too hard, that she wasn't going to have time to relax. But they had undergone a shift as well. By this time, her stormy older sister was having a really rough time. Hazel had decided that rather than going to college, she would spend a few years in Hawaii surfing and supporting herself with odd jobs. After two years, she moved back to San Francisco, feeling dissatisfied and lost. She no longer wanted to surf but had no clue how to move forward. What had seemed to Hazel and her parents to be the natural pleasures of adolescence turned out to feel more like a swamp of transitory satisfactions that kept her from actually moving forward with her life.

Once again, Lily's life was shaped in part by her sister. Her parents, not wanting to see Lily get marooned, began to insist that Lily work hard at school and encouraged her to find a few things she really loved and wanted to be good at. They began to take great pride in her hard work and her good grades. Lily longed not to relax but to throw herself into something. She wanted to feel exhausted, to feel useful, and to be good at things. The staff at the ice cream shop loved her. The customers loved her. In her senior year, Lily began singing in the school choir. Her beautiful voice was praised by all.

Lily's soft voice once again sounded content and alluring, rather than subdued. Her raucousness resurfaced. She wore a pretty diamond stud in one ear and a tiny mummy in the other. She caught people off guard and made them laugh—the angelic face and the sharp, ironic jokes were irresistible. She liked who she was. She went off to college pleased with life.

In order to appreciate how happy it makes children feel to be competent, imagine the opposite. Think for a moment of a child you've known who has struggled to read. The head hangs down, and the body sags. Each day of not being able to decipher the letters on the page brings dread. A child who cannot read feels miserable while he struggles at reading time. And many of the children who have trouble reading begin to feel sad at other times of the day as well. When reading is what every student around you is supposed to be able to do, when the world is offered up in signs, pages, and screens of words, a nonreader is reminded constantly of what he is not good at. His whole demeanor is a study in the opposite of happiness.

Like many children in kindergarten, Craig had learned to recognize common words from memory and to sound out simple words—the first steps toward reading. Most children catch on fairly easily after this, learning to use the meaning of words and sentences as a guide to greater fluency. But Craig, at nine years old and a third-grader at a school in rural Massachusetts, had never made that leap. While most children his age could read simple chapter books, he could not even read a picture book.

At the beginning of the school year, his teacher, Ms. Brennan, had paired the children and asked them to read aloud to one another. Craig would hesitate over the first words he did not recognize and then take so long to read anything that he and the partner would both give up or run out of time. Craig refused to read aloud to his teacher. He would chat and describe the picture, then spend long minutes sounding out the first few words until she provided them so he could move on.

He had been tested for vision, hearing, and reading disabilities, but none had been identified. His family was not highly educated, Ms. Brennan said, "not school people particularly, and I don't think there was lots of time at home for reading.

"He was an appealing child," she continued. "He'd come stand at the corner of my desk and chat with me about the foster kids who lived with his family. He talked a lot about his dog, something like a St. Bernard. He liked to draw. He'd walk up to my desk while I was busy with odd jobs and slip a drawing he had just made for me onto my desk. But he had a cautious, wary manner. He never acted reluctant or angry about reading time." She added that she suspected he found his difficulty in reading frustrating and that the frustration was itself part of the problem.

She developed a hunch about what was holding this child back.

First, she said, he was not getting enough practice reading, and learning to read and practicing reading are closely intertwined. Second, because he was not practicing, he was not improving, and that itself was undermining his self-confidence. He was so worried about sounding stupid in front of other people, she decided, that he clammed up. He was a strong little boy, and when he shut down, there was not much she could do. Ms. Brennan knew that not being able to read was a much bigger problem to Craig than he would admit.

In early October, Ms. Brennan announced that each day, the children would have half an hour to read alone. Choosing the place in the classroom to read was quickly as important to the pupils as choosing the book. They rushed to claim the best spots under a desk, against the radiator just under the window that looked out onto an internal quad, and the most popular place, near the teacher's small terrier, Barnaby, who came to school every day with her. During lessons and lunch, Barnaby was in his crate, but during reading time, he was out. In mid-November, Ms. Brennan realized that Craig had successfully avoided reading aloud for nine weeks of school. And so she suggested that he read near Barnaby, promising him first choice for that spot. She also suggested that rather than read just to himself, he read aloud to the dog. This proved to be the key. Every day until mid-April, the boy selected *Go Dog Go* by P. D. Eastman, settled himself near Barnaby, and recited the book to the dog while pointing to the words and looking over the pictures. By June, Craig was picking a wide range of picture books to read to Barnaby, popping out of his chair eagerly for read-aloud time. Learning to read gave Craig something important to feel genuinely happy about.

Some children seem born happy. They smile readily, they are easy to soothe, and right from the get-go, they approach life with gusto. Three qualities that contribute to a person's happiness are agreeableness, openness to experience, and low neuroticism.

These aren't qualities you can learn to have. You either have them or you don't. Although most of us don't think of our children in terms of these dimensions, it's not all that hard to get a rough sense of how your child fares with them.

Pippi Longstocking, one of the happiest people to bound across the pages of a book, certainly would have scored high on agreeableness and openness to experience and low on neuroticism. Perhaps unwittingly, writer Astrid Lindgren created a young girl who possessed the very qualities that seem to make some people prone to feel good. Although Pippi lives alone, with no parents or siblings (she never knew her mother, and she hasn't seen her father in years because he was lost at sea), she does not feel isolated. She shares her home with her pet monkey, Mr. Nillsen, and her horse. When she moves to the small Swedish village in which the story is set, she immediately makes friends with her conventional neighbors, young Tommy and Annika. But Pippi's ability to form connections goes beyond that. When burglars invade her house, she ends up dancing all night with them and making breakfast for them. She doesn't hesitate or ruminate about things and thus would get a low score on neuroticism. And although bad things have happened to her, she expects things to be good. She is optimistic.

If your child is born a Pippi, you'll know it early on. Those children, like my son Sam, seem to get a kick out of life, feel sure things will go well, and automatically interpret good things as stable and general, while seeing bad things as momentary hurdles that can be overcome. If your child is like that, you are lucky. Such a child can face a lot of disappointment and still bounce back.

But not every child is born a Pippi. Are gloomier children doomed to a life of sadness or negativity? The answer is unequivocally no. And that's because we now know that the way we think is a key ingredient of the way we feel. Positive interpretations lead to more happiness. And children can learn to think differently.

If you think your five-year-old gets less pleasure out of everyday life than other little boys and girls, and if you think she seems sad a lot of the time, one of the first things to do is get a reality check. Find out if other adults who are part of her life see her that way. Talk to a therapist who specializes in young children, and describe what she is like day in and day out. Young children who are clinically depressed should get help—it can make a big difference.

However, many children aren't clinically depressed, but they just tend to put a negative spin on things. If you yourself put a negative spin on things, you have a double job in front of you, because it's hard to get your child to see the world differently from how you do, and children learn a great deal by listening to how their parents talk. However, you can try to encourage your child to attribute disappointments to temporary, fixable, specific causes and explain good things in terms of enduring, stable causes that are likely to affect many aspects of their lives.

The other thing you can do that will help your child to be happy is to make sure that she gets to do things at which she is good. Being good at things makes kids happy.

Finally, and this might be the most important of all, accept the fact that not all children are jubilant. Happiness comes in many shades, and to some extent, we all are born with our happiness thermometers set at different points. Contentment, a sense of hope, and the ability to relish the things we do in everyday life are the components of happiness. A child could experience these components and still not seem to be bursting with joy. Lily will never be Pippi. One of the greatest gifts you can give your child is to know and accept who he or she is. If your child doesn't burst into smiles when you give her her favorite cookie or when a friend arrives to play, don't try to make her into a smiler. She might show her pleasure in subtler ways. If your child seems pensive or is often quiet, learn to recognize that as her way of experiencing life, not a lack of enthusiasm.

Sadness is a red flag. A child who doesn't seem to dive into any activity, who can't find anything she loves to do, or who seems flat about everyday life might be depressed. Children who think they are helpless to make good things happen to them or who expect bad things to happen to them are giving a clue about their general level of happiness. Listen to the way your child interprets his life. Pay attention to the way you interpret life, because that is what he is hearing as well.

While sadness is a red flag, disappointment is a red herring. If your child reacts strongly when something bad really does happen (she doesn't make it onto a team, someone she loves moves away, or she has a serious fight with a friend), that doesn't mean she is sad. Allow your child to feel bad, and trust her to get over it. Children can get through really tough times. A generally happy child can weather terrible sadness or frustration.

Being low-key is a red herring. A child doesn't have to be jubilant to be happy. She needs to feel a sense of optimism, she needs to feel that she can make things happen, she needs to feel that she is good at things, and she needs to feel connected to others. Lily began life with these qualities, and as she moved through adolescence, she regained them. So did Colin.

The good news, once again, is that a child who is basically optimistic is likely to remain that way. The other good news is that although you cannot turn Eeyore into Roo, you can help a child feel happier by helping him think differently about the world and finding things to do that he loves and is good at. And you can understand that children have different ways of showing happiness.

Conclusion

Accepting Fate, Rejecting Fatalism

Soon after I began writing this book, I was invited to give a talk to parents at a public elementary school in Los Angeles. I decided to try out some of the ideas I would be writing about. For about an hour, I spoke about children's future love lives, how to read the signs that indicate whether your child is smart, and how to tell whether your child will have friends when she is older. The parents were a varied bunch—some young first-time parents, others seasoned, most middle-class, from a mixture of ethnic and racial backgrounds. It was L.A., so most of them came in casually, with the look of people who take things lightly and might at any moment make a joke about one of their children. But as I spoke, apprehension began to emanate like a vapor from my audience. I could tell what each parent was worried about, because as I began each new topic, one or another person would suddenly lean forward a little, holding his or her torso more tightly, eyes widening slightly.

Because most of the parents in that school are middle-class, they spend time, money, and energy trying to be "good parents." They read books about parenting, they attend school functions, and they talk endlessly with their friends about child rearing. Like most parents everywhere, they care a lot about their children. In recent years, such parents have been made to feel that they can and should fix anything that's not just right about their children. And here I was, telling them that there are many qualities that not only show up early in life but also remain quite steady over time. They were torn between anguish at the idea that some difficulties cannot be "solved" and relief that some things can just be left alone.

After the prepared part of the talk, I invited them to ask questions. Hands shot up all over the auditorium. A slender, nervous-looking woman with long blond hair and hip faded blue jeans said, "I had to really rethink my social life when Hannah was born. I realized a lot of my friends weren't true friends. I went to a lot of parties, got high a lot, did stupid things. I didn't want her to grow up seeing me in that crowd. I really began to see that those people didn't mean anything to me. Now I spend a lot more time alone. I don't want Hannah to waste time with false people. But I mean, it's not that I don't want her to have friends. I just want her to make the right kind of friends."

It took me a while to figure out what she was telling me and a few more moments to figure out what she was asking. She was putting into words a common phenomenon. Often, when a parent regards her child, she sees two layers: her actual little boy or girl, standing just behind a transparent hologram of herself. It can be difficult for many parents to know which is which. It was hard for this woman to watch her child navigate the world of friendships clear of the shadow thrown by her own past social life. What she wanted to know from me was whether she could influence her daughter's friendships.

I listened for a while and suggested that her behavior would influence her child and that she could create certain kinds of opportunities for her child to bond with others, but she couldn't dictate what friends her child was drawn to or how her daughter interacted in groups. And although she could make some conscious decisions about her own social life, a lot of who we are is beyond our deliberate control. In the past seven years since her daughter was born, she couldn't possibly have become a different person. I couldn't tell if my answer made her feel better or worse.

Another mother came up to me at the end of the evening. In her late forties, she looked vigorous and animated. "I know Lucia is superbright. And we're very laid-back parents. I tell her all the time, 'You're doing a great job. Don't worry about the grade.' But I am beginning to think she needs extra help with her academic work. I mean, she spends a lot of time just lying around with her cat. Reading doesn't come all that easily to her. I don't want her to fall behind."

Stalling for time, I asked, "How old is she?"

The woman answered, "She's five. It's not that I'm worried about her. I know how bright she is. But still, I don't think her performance reflects her real abilities. I just wonder what I can do to help her." Her lyrics said, *No worries*. Her tune said, *I'm worried. I'm going to fix things.*

These parents were torn between wanting to find out what they could do to help their children grow up into happy, successful, popular people and wanting to know that it was all going to be fine no matter what they did. They yearned to hear that they didn't have the burden of "doing it right."

By the time your child is born, she is already a complex assortment of characteristics. It's almost impossible for the nonscientist to sort out a child's inherited characteristics from those she will develop because of the home she lives in or the parents she lives with. Even scientists are not yet ready to do this analysis with any certainty. After all, in most cases, parents give their children both their genes and an environment in which to grow up. The environment parents create is as much an expression of their own genes as it is a result of their deliberate choices or a reflection of their culture. Even when a child is raised by adoptive parents, it can be very hard to disentangle what the child brings to life from what she acquires through her experience. Children help create the environment that shapes them. The same environment is experienced differently by different children. The ways in which we raise our children are often no easier to alter than it would be to change their genes. The way we respond to our kids, the kind of behavior they see in us, the dynamics between parent and child, all of these forces, which have as big an impact on a child as her genes, are largely outside our conscious control. So, when it comes to helping your child live a happy and good life, it doesn't really matter where she got the qualities she got. What matters is what you can do to help her navigate the path that will lead her to her adult self.

When you sift through the vast sea of research on child development, two important ideas stand out. First, the clues about what kind of person your child will grow up to be are there if you know what to look for. Much of a child's future is evident early on, in nascent form. A child's true self is even more visible in the five-year-old than in the twelve-year-old. Most of this book has been about identifying what those clues look like and what they can tell you.

But once you know what to look for and how to interpret it, you still have to figure out what do. The research also shows that there is only so much you can change about your child. Many qualities are set very early in life. The ones that aren't can be nudged in ways that really matter, but you can't remake your child into a different person.

Recently, a good friend was admitting to me that she was sometimes too hard on her eight-year-old son. "Sometimes I really come down awfully hard on him. You'd be appalled."

"Oh," I said, "I doubt it. He knows how much you adore him."

"Yeah," she said, "but there are certain things I just can't stand. When he loses things at school, I get really upset. I do *not* want him to be scatterbrained and lose things. Ted can be a dreamer."

I broke in. "There's nothing wrong with being a dreamer, right?"

"Well, sure, but I don't want him to be a dreamer about everything."

I had just finished writing this book. I said, "You can't make him be the person you want him to be."

She gave me a crazy look—her eyes wide with fear, anxiety, anger at me for what I said, and defiance. She didn't want to give up on the thought that she could shape his dreaminess.

You can help a child who repels other kids learn how to tone it down and learn to say friendlier things to his peers. You can try to find or create situations where she is more likely to connect to another child. A child who puts a negative spin on everything can learn to see things through a rosier glass. If your child seems callous about the feelings of others, you can draw his attention to the way other people feel. But you cannot change a child's basic intelligence or make a shy child gregarious. You have to accept fate but reject fatalism.

As I have said throughout this book, knowing that many aspects of a child's character are stable is just as often good news as it is worrisome. Recently, I saw a friend for the first time in more than a year. She asked me how this book was coming along and said, "I just keep repeating to myself what you told me, 'Once smart, always smart. Once smart, always smart.'"

I tried not to laugh. Why would she be worried? She is smart, and so is her husband. Her son has given every sign that he, too, is smart. He solves problems easily, he learns and remembers information effortlessly, and he likes to think. He is growing up in a house with books, tools, and space to play in. He goes to a friendly school that's not too big, with grown-ups who like kids. Nevertheless, she needs to keep reassuring herself that he can't lose his smartness. She worries that if he is not in a challenging math class, he might lose intellectual ground. If he hangs out with jocks rather than nerds, he might somehow become duller. But what she feels is what most of us feel. Wouldn't it be great if we could just sigh and relax, secure that our child's good qualities are here to stay?

My friend's son is not going to get dumber. But he might become unmotivated or begin to feel that there's no point in trying things that are difficult. He might have the belief that if you don't succeed at first, you might as well turn to something different. And this is where my friend can have an influence. She can help her son find things he really cares about, and she can highlight the value of effort and the importance of incremental improvement. She can nudge, but she cannot remake.

Many behaviors are red herrings, things that seem alarming when you're in the thick of everyday life but don't necessarily mean much about who your child really is or where she's headed. Children tell you who they are through a million small things they do and say. The first step is to see the pattern, no matter how quirky it (and your child) may seem.

The second step is to know what you can and cannot change in your child. Keep in mind that you can guide a child in a better direction, but you cannot redesign her.

When my son Will was about seven years old, I could already see that he was moody. He was a powerful little boy—strong, athletic, and intense. In moments of joy and accomplishment, he radiated triumph and delight. But when angered or hurt, he would become enveloped by a storm cloud and often didn't know quite what to do with the rage and urge for revenge that overtook him. One day, he got into a fight with his brother Jake. He began ranting and railing, and I could see he was seconds away from leaping at Jake. I took him by the hand, and we went outside, where I asked him to tell me what he was so mad about. He began explaining the hurtful, terrible thing Jake had done (I no longer remember what it was). I hadn't let go of his hand yet, and as he spoke, the grip changed, and it was he who was holding my hand. Not just holding it but squeezing it hard. When he was done telling me why he was so upset, his small hand relaxed its hold. I looked down and saw deep red marks where his fingernails had dug into my skin.

I said, "Will, you're so angry. See how angry you are?" and drew his gaze to my hand.

He looked astonished and dismayed. He had had no idea how powerful his anger was.

I remember telling my mother that I was concerned about the intensity of his rage. She scoffed at that idea, reminding me how kind he was. So I shut up, but it stayed on my radar. Not long after that incident, Will was mad again. I reminded him that it was fine to be angry but not fine to hurt people. So he started yelling at his brother, saying angry, mean, rude things. I said it was fine to be angry but not to talk that way. Then I thought to myself, *Hey, make up your mind. Which is it? Can he feel anger, or can't he? If I don't allow him to express his anger in a way that has an impact, what good is it?* I suggested that he make some really dramatic, forceful drawings of the worst words he could think of and show them to people when he was mad. I reminded him that art could be a weapon.

He paused and then smiled. He ran for the markers and set to work, making huge neon 3-D posters of the raunchiest, most offensive words he could think of, with all kinds of vivid patterns around the letters. For days afterward, he triumphantly and vigorously held his swear words up to our faces when the need arose.

It was a lesson to me. I couldn't make Will into a person with a mild temper. Would I want to? But it was up to me to help him cope with his powerful responses, learn how to handle who he was.

As a teenager, Will was thoughtful, gentle, and insightful. When a boy in his second-grade class peed in his pants, Will was the one who told the other kids it was a new look—mottled jeans, all the rage. But he hadn't become a different person. When a boy taunted his best friend with racist slurs, Will punched the boy hard in the face. I once watched him play basketball. I was sitting as close to the court as you could get. The player from the other team who was defending Will became increasingly aggressive, provoking Will with elbows and ugly words. As Will walked off the court for the halftime break, I heard him say in a guttural voice, "I'm gonna ram it down that bitch's throat."

Later I commented to him about it, amused at how riled up he had been.

He stared at me blankly and said, "I didn't say that."

Just as when he was seven, at eighteen he could be gripped by violent emotion and in those moments didn't even realize how strong his anger was.

My mother periodically brings up my earlier concern from Will's childhood. She will laugh and say, "And you were worried that he didn't know how to handle his anger. Look at him. He's the most loving, thoughtful, tactful man."

Yes, he is. Will grew into someone whose enormous personal and physical power is matched by his gentleness. But he is still someone with a lot of strong feeling, someone who can be scary when angered. As an adult, he has told me about the moments when he could easily push an adversary into the ground. "But I ask myself, is it worth it? Would it be right?" Somewhere along the way, he found out how to live with his aggression. I don't think my noticing it when he was young hurt him—it gave me a chance to provide him a helping hand.

If you think you see a worrisome pattern, you can help change your child's path. Slightly. You can offer her new ways of interpreting bad and good events. You might be able help her learn new ways to approach friends. You can get help if your relationship with her is not as solid or close as it should be. You can try to be kind, principled, and hardworking yourself. You can savor joy in everyday life and have close relationships, hoping to set a good example. But you cannot make your child into a different person. Not everyone is gregarious, sunny, filled with ambition, or highly intelligent.

You might have been hoping that these pages would offer you a list of things to watch for. But there is no list that can capture your child—or any child, for that matter. As I said at the beginning, your child's life is a story. Few behaviors are red flags, and many are red herrings. Any one characteristic or incident in your son's or daughter's life has to be understood in terms of the other things he or she does and experiences. A lonely child who has intense interests and great ability is in a different situation from a lonely child who has no interests. A weakness is less of one in the context of other strengths.

On the other hand, a weakness that might seem insignificant on its own is of greater concern if you notice that it is part of a pattern. When something is a genuine red flag, it almost always appears in a series of red flags.

And remember that there are often plenty of subtle clues that things are better than you thought—a child who doesn't get wonderful grades but whose words and gestures reveal that he is very smart, a child who isn't the most popular but clearly has strong warm relationships with a few other kids, or a child who isn't Miss Sunshine but nevertheless seems to get a quiet kick out of everyday life. The good patterns are just as important to decipher. If you see a good pattern, it will help alleviate your alarm when your child hits a bump and allow you to enjoy the person you got.

Even if your child has a lot of trouble in one part of her life, you can help by building on her strengths. If a child tends toward gloominess but has strong, close relationships with other people, that's great. It will mitigate the pain of her low moods. Give her ample time and opportunity to enjoy her friendships and connect to others. Those friendships might not make her ebullient, but they will buffer her when joy is hard to come by. If your son is very smart but not all that driven, give him chances to do the things that feed his intellect. You cannot inject him with ambition, but you can encourage him to focus on the pleasures of work that excites his mind.

Back in that school in L.A., another parent came up to speak to me. He was very tall, with sandy hair and pale gray eyes. He walked with the lope of a former athlete. He and his wife, who was with him, were the parents of three young children. He spoke with a slight drawl in his voice, as if he had lived in the South. He said, "You know, it sounds an awful lot to me like you are talking about the serenity prayer used in AA."

I was thrown. What does parenting have to do with becoming sober? Warily, I said, "Really?"

The man answered, "Yeah. The prayer goes like this: 'Please grant me the strength to change what I can, the serenity to accept what I cannot, and the wisdom to know the difference.' It seems to me that you are telling us that there are some things you can change about your kid and other things that won't change, no matter what you do. And that you're better off accepting those things and working with them rather than butting your head against a wall."

I couldn't have said it better myself.

Selected Bibliography

Adolph, Karen E., & Robinson, Scott R. 2008. In defense of change processes. *Child Development,* Vol. 79, pp. 1648–53.

Ainsworth, Mary D. Salter, & Bell, Silvia M. 1970. Attachment, exploration, and separation: Illustrated by the behavior of one-year-olds in a strange situation. *Child Development,* Vol. 41, pp. 49–67.

Aron, Arthur, Paris, Meg, & Aron, Elaine N. 1995. Falling in love: prospective studies of self concept change. *Journal of Personality and Social Psychology,* Vol. 69, No. 6, pp. 1102–12.

Aron, Arthur, Fisher, Helen, Mashek, Debra J., Strong, Greg, Li, Haifang, & Brown, Lucy L. 2005. Reward, motivation, and emotion systems, associated with early-stage intense romantic love. *Journal of Neurophysiology,* Vol. 94, pp. 327–37.

Arsenio, William, & Lover, Anthony. Children's conceptions of sociomoral affect: Happy victimizers, mixed emotions, and other expectancies. In *Morality in Everyday Life: Developmental Perspectives,* Melanie Killen & Daniel Hart, eds. New York: Cambridge University Press, 1995.

Asendorpf, Jens B., & Van Aken, Marcel A.G. 2003. Validity of Big Five personality judgments in childhood: A 9 year longitudinal study. *European Journal of Personality,* Vol. 17, pp. 1–17.

Asher, Steven R., & Paquette, Julie A. 2003. Loneliness and peer relations in childhood. *Current Directions in Psychological Science,* Vol. 12, No. 3, p. 75.

Asher, Steven R., Paquette-MacEvoy, Julie, & McDonald, Kristina L. 2008. Children's peer relations, social competence, and school adjustment: A social tasks and social goals perspective. *Social Psychological Perspectives,* Vol. 15, pp. 357–90.

Asher, Steven R., Parker, Jeffrey G., & Walker, Diane L. Distinguishing friendship from acceptance: Implications for intervention and assessment. In *The Company They Keep: Friendship in Childhood and Adolescence,* Bukowski, W.M., A.F. Newcomb, W.W. Hartup, eds. New York: Cambridge University Press, 1996.

Bagwell, Catherine L., Bender, Sarah E., Andreassi, Cristina L., Kinoshita, Tracy L., Montarello, Staci A., & Muller, Jason G. 2005. Friendship quality and perceived relationship changes predict psychosocial adjustment in early adulthood. *Journal of Social and Personal Relationships,* Vol. 22, No. 2, pp. 235–54.

Bagwell, Catherine L., Schmidt, Michelle E., Newcomb, Andrew F., & Bukowski, William M. Friendship and peer rejection as predictors of adult adjustment. In *The Role of Friendship in Psychological Adjustment.* Nangle, Douglas W., & Cynthia A. Erdley, eds. U.S.A.:Jossey-Bass, 2001.

Beck, Aaron T., Rush, John A., Shaw, Brian F., & Emery, Gary. *Cognitive Theory of Depression.* New York: The Guilford Press, 1979.

Berscheid, Ellen, & Hatfield, Elaine. *Interpersonal Attraction,* 2nd ed. New York: Random House, 1969.

Bierman, Karen Linn. 1986. Process of change during social skills training with preadolescents and its relation to treatment outcome. *Child Development,* Vol. 57, pp. 230–40.

Blackwell, Lisa S., Trzesniewski, Kali H., & Dweck, Carol S. 2007. Implicit theories of intelligence predict achievement across an adolescent transition: A longitudinal study and an intervention. *Child Development,* Vol. 78, No. 1, p. 246–63.

Borghans, Lex, Duckworth, Angela Lee, Heckman, James J., & ter Weel, Bas. The economics and psychology of personality traits. Institute for the Study of Labor, Discussion Paper Series No. 3333.

Brehm, Sharon S., Kassin, Saul M., & Fein, Steven, eds. *Social Psychology,* 5th ed. Boston & New York: Houghton Mifflin Company, 2002.

Brendgen, Mara, Boivin, Michel, Vitaro, Frank, Bukowski, William M., Dionne, Ginette, Tremlay, Richard E., & Perusse, Daniel. 2008. Linkages between children's and their friends' social and physical aggression: Evidence for a gene-environment interaction? *Child Development,* Vol. 79, No. 1, pp. 13–29.

Brickman, Philip, Coates, Dan, & Janoff-Bulman, Ronnie. 1978. Lottery winners and accident victims: Is happiness relative? *Journal of Personality and Social Psychology,* Vol. 36, pp. 918–27.

Bruer, John T. *The Myth of the First Three Years: A New Understanding of Early Brain Development and Lifelong Learning.* New York: The Free Press, 1999.

Buehlman, Kim Therese, Gottman, John Mordechai, & Katz, Lynn Fainsilber. 1992. How a couple views their past predicts their future: Predicting divorce from an oral history interview. *Journal of Family Psychology,* Vol. 5, pp. 295–318.

Bukowski, William M., Newcomb, Andrew F., & Hartup, Willard W. *The Company They Keep: Friendship in Childhood and Adolescence.* New York: Cambridge University Press, 1996.

Buss, David M. The evolution of love. In *The New Psychology of*

Love, Sternberg, Robert J., & Karen Weis, eds. New Haven & London: Yale University Press, 2006, pp. 65–86.

Carey, Benedict. Bad behavior does not doom pupils, studies say. *New York Times.* November 13, 2007.

Caspi, Avshalom. 2000. The child is the father of the man: Personality continuities from childhood to adulthood. *Journal of Personality and Social Psychology,* Vol. 78, pp. 158–72.

Caspi, Avshalom, & Silva, Phil A. 1995. Temperamental qualities at age three predict personality traits in young adulthood: Longitudinal evidence from a birth cohort. *Child Development,* Vol. 66, pp. 486–98.

Caspi, Avshalom, Moffitt, Terrie E., Morgan, Julia, Rutter, Michael, Taylor, Alan, Arseneault, Louise, Tully, Lucy, Jacobs, Catherine, Kim-Cohen, Julia, & Polo-Tomas, Monica. 2004. Maternal expressed emotion predicts children's antisocial behavior problems: Using monozygotic-twin differences to identify environmental effects on behavioral development. *Developmental Psychology,* Vol. 40, pp. 149–61.

Ceci, Stephen J. *On Intelligence: A Bioecological Treatise on Intellectual Development.* Cambridge, MA: Harvard University Press, 1996.

Clark, David A., Beck, Aaron T., & Alford, Brad A. *Cognitive Theory and Therapy of Depression.* U.S.A.: John Wiley & Sons, 1999.

Coie, John D. Toward a theory of peer rejection. In *Peer Rejection in Childhood,* Asher, Steven R., & Coie, John D., New York: Cambridge University Press, 1990, pp. 365–401.

Coie, John D., & Kupersmidt, Janis B. 1983. Behavioral analysis of emerging social status in boys' groups. *Child Development,* Vol. 54, pp. 1400–1416.

Cole, Michael, Cole, Sheila R., & Lightfoot, Cynthia. *The Development of Children,* 5th ed. Worth Publishers, 2005.

Coles, Robert. *The Moral Intelligence of Children.* New York: Random House, 1997.

Collins, Nancy L., & Read, Stephen J. 1990. Adult attachment, working models, and relationship quality in dating couples. *Journal of Personality and Social Psychology,* Vol. 58, pp. 644–63.

Coplan, Robert J., Rubin, Kenneth H., Fox, Nathan A., Calkins, Susan D., & Stewart, Shannon L. 1994. Being alone, playing alone, and acting alone: Distinguishing among reticence and passive and active solitude in young children. *Child Development,* Vol. 65, pp. 129–37.

Corsaro, William A. *The Sociology of Childhood,* 2nd ed. Newbury Park, CA: Pine Forge Press, 2005.

Cramer, Phebe, & Tracy, Allison. 2005. The pathway from child personality to adult adjustment: The road is not straight. *Journal of Research in Personality,* Vol. 39, pp. 369–94.

Creswell, Julie, & Thomas, Landon, Jr., "The Talented Mr. Madoff," *New York Times,* January 24, 2009, p. B1.

Cui, Ming, Fincham, Frank D., & Pasley, Kay B. 2008. Young adult romantic relationships: The role of parents' marital problems and relationship efficacy. *Personality and Social Psychology Bulletin,* Vol. 34, pp. 1226–35.

Cytryn, Leon, & McKnew, Donald. "What is childhood depression?" In *Growing Up Sad: Childhood Depression and Its Treatment.* U.S.A.: W. W. Norton & Company, 1996.

Damon, William. *The Moral Child: Nurturing Children's Natural Moral Growth.* New York: The Free Press, 1988.

Damon, William. *Greater Expectations: Overcoming the Culture of Indulgence in Our Homes and Schools.* New York: Free Press Paperbacks, 1995.

DeLoache, Judy S., Simcock, Gabrielle, & Macari, Suzanne. 2007. Planes, trains, automobiles, and tea sets: Extremely intense interests in very young children. *Developmental Psychology,* Vol. 43, No. 6, pp. 1579–86.

De Waal, Frans. *Good Natured: The Origins of Right and Wrong in Humans and Other Animals.* Cambridge, MA: Harvard University Press, 1996.

Diamond, Adele, & Amso, Dima. 2008. Contributions of neuroscience to our understanding of cognitive development. *Current Directions in Psychological Science,* Vol. 17, pp. 136–41.

Diamond, Lisa M. 2003. What does sexual orientation orient? A biobehavioral model distinguishing romantic love and sexual desire. *Psychological Review,* Vol. 110, pp. 173–92.

Diener, Carol I., & Dweck, Carol S. 1978. An analysis of learned helplessness: Continuous changes in performance, strategy, and achievement cognitions following failure. *Journal of Personality and Social Psychology,* Vol. 36, No. 5, pp. 451–62.

Doherty, William R., Hatfield, Elaine, Thompson, Kari, & Choo, Patricia. 1994. Cultural and ethnic influences on love and attachment. *Personal Relationships,* Vol. 1, pp. 391–98.

Dovidio, John F., Piliavin, Jane Allyn, Schroeder, David A., & Penner, Louis A. *The Social Psychology of Prosocial Behavior.* Mahwah, N.J.: Lawrence Erlbaum Publishers, 2006.

Driscoll, Richard, Davis, Keith E., & Lipetz, Milton E. 1972. Parental interference and romantic love: The Romeo and Juliet effect. *Journal of Personality and Social Psychology,* Vol. 24, pp. 1–10.

Dubow, E.F., et al. 2006. Middle childhood and adolescent contextual and personal predictors of adult educational and occupational outcomes: A mediational model of two countries. *Developmental Psychology,* Vol 42., No. 5, pp. 937–49.

Duckworth, Angela L. (Over and) Beyond high-stakes testing. *American Psychologist,* Vol. 64, No. 4, pp. 279–80.

Duncan, Greg J., Dowsett, Chantelle J., Claessens, Amy, Magnuson, Katherine, Huston, Aletha C., Klebanov, Pamela, Pagani, Linda S., Feinstein, Leon, Engel, Mimi, Brooks-Gunn, Jeanne, Sexton, Holly, Duckworth, Kathryn, & Japel, Crista. 2007. School readiness and later achievement. *Developmental Psychology,* Vol. 43, pp. 1428–46.

Dunn, Judy. The beginnings of moral understanding: Development in the second year. In Jerome Kagan & Sharon Lamb, eds. *The Emergence of Morality in Young Children.* Chicago & London: The University of Chicago Press, 1987, pp. 91–112.

Dutton, Donald G., & Aron, Arthur P. 1974. Some evidence for heightened sexual attraction under conditions of high anxiety. *Journal of Personality and Social Psychology,* Vol. 4, pp. 510–17.

Dweck, Carol S. 1975. The role of expectations and attributions in the alleviation of learned helplessness. *Journal of Personality and Social Psychology,* Vol. 31, pp. 674–85.

Dweck, Carol S. 2008. Can personality be changed? The role of beliefs in personality and change. *Current Directions in Psychological Science,* Vol. 17, pp. 391–94.

Eisenberg, Nancy, Michalik, Nichole, Spinrad, Tracy L., Hofer, Claire, Kupfer, Anne, Valiente, Carlos, Liew, Jeffrey, Cumberland, Amanda, & Reiser, Mark. 2007. The relations of effortful control and impulsivity to children's sympathy: A longitudinal study. *Cognitive Development,* Vol. 22, pp. 544–67.

Elliott, Elaine S., & Dweck, Carol S. 1988. Goals: An approach to motivation and achievement. *Journal of Personality and Social Psychology,* Vol. 54, No. 1, pp. 5–12.

Emmons, Robert A., & Crumpler, Cheryl A. 2000. Gratitude as a human strength: Appraising the evidence. *Journal of Social and Clinical Psychology,* Vol. 19, p. 56.

Emmons, Robert A., & Michael E. McCullough, eds. *The Psychology of Gratitude.* New York: Oxford University Press, 2004.

Feshbach, Norma Deitch. Empathy training: A field study in affective education. In *Aggression and Behavior Change: Biological and Social Processes,* Seymour Feshbach & Adam Fraczek, eds. Praeger Publishers, 1979.

Feshbach, Norma Deitch. Sex differences in empathy and social behavior in children. In *The Development of Prosocial Behavior,* Nancy Eisenberg, ed. Academic Press, 1982.

Feshbach, Norma Deitch. 1983. Learning to care: A positive approach to child training and discipline. *Journal of Clinical Child Psychology,* Vol. 12, pp. 266–71.

Fox, Nathan A., Henderson, Heather A., Rubin, Kenneth H., Calkins, Susan D., & Schmidt, Louis A. 2001. Continuity and discontinuity of behavioral inhibition and exuberance: Psychophysiological and behavioral influences across the first four years of life. *Child Development,* Vol. 72, pp. 1–21.

Fox, Nathan A., Nichols, Kate E., Henderson, Heather A., Rubin, Kenneth, Schmidt, Louis, Hamer, Dean, Ernst, Monique, & Pine, Daniel S. 2005. Evidence for a gene-environment interaction in predicting behavioral inhibition in middle childhood. *Psychological Science,* Vol. 16, pp. 921–26.

Freeman, Leslie J., Templer, Donald I., & Hill, Curt. 1999. The relationship between adult happiness and self-appraised childhood happiness and events. *The Journal of Genetic Psychology,* Vol. 160, pp. 46–54.

Friend, Angela, DeFries, John C., & Olson, Richard K. 2008. Parental education moderates genetic influences on reading disability. *Psychological Science,* Vol. 19, pp. 1124–30.

Gardner, Howard, Csikszentmihalyi, Mihaly, & Damon, William. *Good Work: Where Excellence and Ethics Meet.* New York: Basic Books, 2001.

Gilbert, Daniel. *Stumbling on Happiness.* New York: Alfred A. Knopf, 2006.

Gillham, Jane E., Peivich, Karen J., Jaycox, Lisa H, & Seligman, Martin E.P. 1995. Prevention of depressive symptoms in schoolchildren: Two year follow-up. *Psychological Science,* Vol. 6, No. 6, pp. 343–51.

Gladwell, Malcolm. *Outliers.* New York: Little, Brown, and Company, 2008.

Gladwell, Malcolm. Late bloomers: Why do we equate genius with precocity? *The New Yorker,* October 20, 2008.

Gladwell, Malcolm. Most likely to succeed. *The New Yorker,* December 15, 2008.

Golombok, Susan. *Parenting: What Really Counts?* London & New York: Routledge, 2000.

Greene, Joshua D., Sommerville, R. Brian, Nystrom, Leigh E., Darley, John M., & Cohen, Jonathan D. 2001. An fMRI investigation of emotional engagement in moral judgment. *Science,* Vol. 293, pp. 2105–8.

Greene, Joshua D., Cushman, Fiery A., Stewart, Lisa E., Lowenberg, Kelly, Nystrom, Leigh E., & Cohen, Jonathan D. 2009. Pushing moral buttons: The interaction between personal force and intention in moral judgment. *Cognition,* in press.

Grevan, Corina U., Harlaar, Nicole, Kovas, Yulia, Chamorro-Premuzic, Tomas, & Plomin, Robert. 2009. More than just IQ: School achievement is predicted by self-perceived abilities—but for genetic rather than environmental reasons. *Psychological Science,* Vol. 20, pp. 753–62.

Grusec, Joan E., & Redler, Erica. 1980. Attribution, reinforcement, and altruism: A developmental analysis. *Developmental Psychology,* Vol. 16, No. 5, pp. 525–34.

Hallowell, Edward M. *The Childhood Roots of Adult Happiness: Five Steps to Help Kids Create and Sustain Lifelong Joy.* New York: Ballantine Books, 2002.

Hampson, Sarah E. *The Construction of Personality: An Introduction.* New York: Routledge & Kegan Paul, 1982.

Hampson, Sarah E. 2008. Mechanisms by which childhood personality traits influence adult well-being. *Current Directions in Psychological Science,* Vol. 14, No. 4, pp. 264–68.

Hampson, Sarah E., & Goldberg, Lewis R. 2006. A first large cohort study of personality trait stability over the 40 years between elementary school and midlife. *Journal of Personality and Social Psychology,* Vol. 91, pp. 763–79.

Hane, Amie Ashley, Cheah, Charissa, Rubin, Kenneth H., & Fox, Nathan A. 2008. The role of maternal behavior in the relation between shyness and social reticence in early childhood and social withdrawal in middle childhood. *Social Development,* Vol. 17, pp. 795–811.

Hane, Amie Ashley, Fox, Nathan A., Henderson, Heather A., & Marshall, Peter J. 2008. Behavioral reactivity and approach-withdrawal bias in infancy. *Developmental Psychology,* Vol. 44, pp. 1491–96.

Harris, Paul. Testimony and moral judgment. Personal correspondence.

Hart, Betty, & Risley, Todd R. *Meaningful Differences in the Everyday Experience of Young American Children.* Baltimore: Paul H. Brookes Publishing Co., 1995.

Hatfield, Elaine, Schmitz, Earle, Cornelius, Jeffrey, & Rapson, Richard L. 1988. Passionate love: How early does it begin? *Journal of Psychology and Human Sexuality,* Vol. 1, pp. 35–51.

Hatfield, Elaine, & Rapson, Richard L. *Love, Sex, and Intimacy: Their Psychology, Biology, and History.* New York: Harper Collins College Publishers, 1993.

Hatfield, Elaine, & Rapson, Richard L. 1994. Historical and cross-cultural perspectives on passionate love and sexual desire. *Annual Review of Sex Research,* Vol. 4, pp. 67–97.

Haworth, Claire M.A., Dale, Phillip S., & Plomin, Robert. 2009. The etiology of science performance: Decreasing heritability and increasing importance of the shared environment from 9 to 12 years of age. *Child Development,* Vol. 80, No. 3, pp. 662–73.

Hazan, Cindy, & Shaver, Phillip. 1987. Romantic love conceptualized as an attachment process. *Journal of Personality and Social Psychology,* Vol. 52, pp. 511–24.

Hoffman, Martin L. *Empathy and Moral Development: Implications for Caring and Justice.* New York: Cambridge University Press, 2000.

Hussar, Karen, & Harris, Paul L. Children who choose not to eat meat: A demonstration of early moral decision-making. *Social Development.* In press.

Iyer, Pico. The doctor is within. The Opinionater, *New York Times,* July 22, 2009.

Jaffee, Sara R., Caspi, Avshalom, Moffitt, Terrie E., Polo-Tomas, Monica, & Taylor, Alan. 2007. Individual, family, and neighborhood factors distinguish resilient from non-resilient maltreated children: A cumulative stressors model. *Child Abuse & Neglect,* Vol. 31, pp. 231–53.

Jaycox, Lisa H., Reivich, Karen J., Gillham, Jane, & Seligman, Martin E.P. 1994. Prevention of depressive symptoms in school children. *Behavior Research Therapy,* Vol. 32, No. 8, pp. 801–16.

Judge, Timothy A., & Hurst, Charlice. How the rich (and happy) get richer (and happier): Relationship of core self-evaluations to trajectories in attaining work success. *Journal of Applied Psychology,* Vol. 93:4, pp. 849–63.

Kagan, Jerome. *The Second Year.* U.S.A.: Harvard University Press, 1981.

Kagan, Jerome. *The Nature of the Child.* New York: Basic Books, 1984.

Kagan, Jerome. 2008. In defense of qualitative changes in development. *Child Development,* Vol. 79, pp. 1606–24.

Kagan, Jerome, & Nancy Snidman. *The Long Shadow of Temperament.* Cambridge, Massachusetts, and London, England, Belknap Press of Harvard University Press: 2004.

Kaufman, James C., & Agars, Mark D. 2009. Being creative with the predictors and criteria for success. *American Psychologist,* Vol. 64, No. 4, pp. 280–81.

Kazdin, Alan E. *Parent Management Training: Treatment for Oppositional, Aggressive, and Antisocial Behavior in Children and Adolescents.* New York: Oxford University Press, 2005.

Knee, C. Raymond, Canevello, Amy, Bush, Amber L., & Cook, Astrid. 2008. Relationship contingent self-esteem and the ups and downs of romantic relationships. *Journal of Personality and Social Psychology,* Vol. 95, pp. 608–27.

Kochanska, Grazyna. 1997. Multiple pathways to conscience for children with different temperaments: From toddlerhood to age 5. *Developmental Psychology,* Vol. 33, No. 2, pp. 228–40.

Kochanska, Grazyna, Askan, Nazan, & Nicholas, Kate E. 2003. Maternal power assertion in discipline and moral discourse contexts: Commonalities, differences, and implications for children's moral conduct and cognition. *Developmental Psychology,* Vol. 39, pp. 949–63.

Kochanska, Grazyna, Askan, Nazan, Prisco, Theresa R., & Adams, Erin E. 2008. Mother-child and father-child mutually responsive orientation in the first 2 years and children's outcomes at preschool age: Mechanisms of influence. *Child Development,* Vol. 79, pp. 30–44.

Kohlberg, Lawrence. *The Psychology of Moral Development.* New York: Harper & Row Publishers, 1984.

Kohnstamm, Geldolph A., Slotboom, Anne Marie, & Elphick, Eric. 1994. Conscientiousness in children. *Psychologica Belgica,* Vol. 34, pp. 207–29.

Kovacs, Maria, Joorman, Jutta, & Gotlib, Ian H. 2008. Emotion (dys)regulation and links to depressive disorders. *Child Development Perspectives,* Vol. 2, pp. 149–55.

Kovas, Yulia, Haworth, Claire M.A., Dale, Philip, & Plomin, Robert. 2007. The genetic and environmental origins of learning abilities and disabilities in the school years. *Monographs of the Society for Research in Child Development,* Vol. 72, No. 3.

Labile, Deborah, Panfile, Tia, & Makariev, Drika. 2008. The quality and frequency of mother toddler conflict: Links with attachment and temperament. *Child Development,* Vol. 79, pp. 426–43.

Lareau, Annette. *Unequal Childhoods: Class, Race, and Family Life.* Berkeley: University of California Press, 2003.

LaVoie, Joseph C. 1974. Cognitive determinants of resistance to deviation in seven-, nine-, and eleven-year-old children of low and high maturity of moral judgment. *Developmental Psychology,* Vol. 10, pp. 393–403.

Leadbeater, Bonnie J., & Hoglund, Wendy L.G. 2009. The effects of peer victimization and physical aggression on changes in internalizing from first to third grade. *Child Development,* Vol. 80, No. 3, pp. 843–59.

Lee, John Alan. 1977. A typology of styles of loving. *Personality and Social Psychology Bulletin,* Vol. 3, pp. 173–82.

Lee, John Alan. 1988. Love styles. In *The Psychology of Love,* Robert J. Sternberg & Michael L. Barnes, eds. New Haven and London: Yale University Press, 1988, pp. 38–67.

Lemelin, Jean-Pascal, Boivin, Michel, Forget-Dubois, Nadine, Dionne, Ginette, Seguin, Jean R., Brendgen, Mara, Vitaro, Frank, Tremblay, Richard E., & Peiusse, Daniel. 2007. The genetic environmental etiology of cognitive school readiness and later academic achievement in early childhood. *Child Development,* Vol, 78, No. 6, pp. 1855–69.

Lepper, Mark R., Greene, David, & Nisbett, Richard E. 1973. Undermining children's intrinsic interest with extrinsic reward: A test of the "overjustification" hypothesis. *Journal of Personality and Social Psychology,* Vol. 28, No. 1, pp. 129–37.

Lerner, Richard M. 1991. Changing organism-context relations as the basic process of development: A developmental contextual perspective. *Developmental Psychology,* Vol. 27, No. 1, pp. 27–32.

Lewis, Michael. 2005. The child and its family: The social network model. *Human Development,* Vol. 48, pp. 8–27.

Liben, Lynn S. 2008. Reflections on child development: The journal and the field. *Child Development,* Vol. 79, pp. 1597–99.

Liben, Lynn. 2008. Continuities and discontinuities in children and scholarship. *Child Development,* Vol. 79, pp. 1600–1605.

Lockhart, Kristi L., Nakashima, Nobuko, Inagaki, Kayoko, & Keil, Frank C. 2008. From ugly duckling to swan? Japanese and

American beliefs about the stability and origins of traits. *Cognitive Development,* Vol. 23, pp. 155–79.

Lyubomirsky, Sonja. *The How of Happiness: A Scientific Approach to Getting the Life You Want.* New York: The Penguin Press, 2008.

Lyubomirsky, Sonja, & Lepper, Heidi S. 1999. A measure of subjective happiness: Preliminary reliability and construct validation. *Social Indicators Research,* Vol. 46, p. 137.

Ma, Xin. 2000. A longitudinal assessment of antecedent course work in mathematics and subsequent mathematical attainment. *Journal of Educational Research,* Vol. 94, pp. 16–28.

Ma, Xin. 2005. Growth in mathematics achievement: Analysis with classification and regression trees. *Journal of Educational Research,* Vol. 99, pp. 78–86.

Malti, Tina, Gummerum, Michaela, Keller, Monika, & Buchmann, Marlis. 2009. Children's moral motivation, sympathy, and prosocial behavior. *Child Development,* Vol. 80, pp. 442–60.

Maron, Bradley A., Fein, Steven, Maron, Barry J., Hillel, Alexander T., El Baghdadi, Mariam M., & Rodenhauser, Paul. 2007. Ability of prospective assessment of personality profiles to predict the practice specialty of medical students. *Baylor University Medical Center Proceedings,* Vol. 20, pp. 22–26.

Miner, Jennifer L., & Clarke-Stewart, K., Alison. 2008. Trajectories of externalizing behavior from age 2 to age 9: Relations with gender, temperament, ethnicity, parenting, and rater. *Developmental Psychology,* Vol. 44, pp. 771–86.

Moffitt, Terrie E., & Caspi, Avshalom. 2001. Childhood predictors differentiate life-course persistent and adolescence-limited antisocial pathways among males and females. *Development and Psychopatholoy,* Vol. 13, pp. 355–75.

Nangle, Douglas W., & Erdley, Cynthia A., eds. *The Role of Friendship in Psychological Adjustment.* U.S.A.: Jossey-Bass, 2001.

Nangle, Douglas W., Erdley, Cynthia A., Newman, Julie E., Mason,

Craig A., & Carpenter, Erika M. 2003. Popularity, friendship quantity, and friendship quality: Interactive influences on children's loneliness and depression. *Journal of Clinical Child and Adolescent Psychology,* Vol. 32, pp. 546–55.

Nolen-Hoeksema, Susan, Girgus, Joan S., & Seligman, Martin E.P. 1986. Learned helplessness in children: A longitudinal study of depression, achievement, and explanatory style. *Journal of Personality and Social Psychology,* Vol. 51, pp. 435–42.

Nolen-Hoeksema, Susan, Girgus, Joan S., & Seligman, Martin E.P. 1992. Predictors and consequences of childhood depressive symptoms: A 5-year longitudinal study. *Journal of Abnormal Psychology,* Vol. 101, pp. 405–22.

Odgers, Candice L., Caspi, Avshalom, Nagin, Daniel S., Piquero, Alex R., Slutske, Wendy S., Milne, Barry J., Dickson, Nigel, Poulton, Richie, & Moffitt, Terrie E. 2008. Is it important to prevent early exposure to drugs and alcohol among adolescents? *Psychological Science,* Vol. 19, pp. 1037–44.

Olson, Kristina R., & Dweck, Carol S. 2009. Social cognitive development: A new look. *Child Development Perspectives,* Vol. 3, pp. 60–65.

Ozer, Daniel J., & Benet-Martinez, Veronica. 2006. Personality and the prediction of consequential outcomes. *Annual Review of Psychology,* Vol. 57, pp. 401–21.

Paciello, Marinella, Fida, Robert, Tramontano, Carlo, Lupinetti, Catia, & Caprara, Gian Vittorio. 2008. Stability and change of moral disengagement and its impact on aggression and violence in late adolescence. *Child Development,* Vol. 79, pp. 1288–1309.

Parker, Jeffrey G., & Asher, Steven R. 1993. Friendship and friendship quality in middle childhood: Links with peer groups acceptance and feelings of loneliness and social dissatisfaction. *Developmental Psychology,* Vol. 29, No. 4, pp. 611–21.

Parker, Jeffrey G., Rubin, Kenneth H., Price, Joseph, M., &

DeRosier, Melissa E. Peer relationships, child development, and adjustment: A developmental psychopathology perspective. *Developmental Psychopathology,* Vol. 2. Cicchetti, Dante, & Cohen, Donald J., eds. Oxford, England: John Wiley & Sons, 1995, pp. 96–161.

Pennebaker, James W., Dyer, Mary Anne, Caulkins, R. Scott, Litowitz, Debra Lynn, Ackreman, Phillip L., Anderson, Douglas B., & McGraw, Kevin M. 1979. Don't the girls get prettier at closing time: A country and western application to psychology. *Personality and Social Psychology Bulletin,* Vol. 5, pp. 122–25.

Pepler, Debra J., & Craig, Wendy M. 1995. A peek behind the fence: Naturalistic observations of aggressive children with remote audiovisual recording. *Developmental Psychology,* Vol. 31, No. 4, pp. 548–53.

Pollak, Seth D. 2008. Mechanisms linking early experience and the emergence of emotions: Illustrations from the study of maltreated children. *Current Directions in Psychological Science,* Vol. 17, pp. 370–76.

Pulkkinen, Lea, & Caspi, Avshalom, eds. *Paths to Successful Development: Personality in the Life Course.* Cambridge: Cambridge University Press, 2002.

Quinn, Paul C. 2008. In defense of core competencies, quantitative change, and continuity. *Child Development,* Vol. 79, pp. 1633–38.

Regents of the University of Minnesota, Institute of Childhood Development. 2000. Minnesota Longitudinal Study of Parents and Children: Overview. University of Minnesota. October 9, 2008. http://cehd.umn.edu/ICD/Parent-Child/PCPOverview.html.

Roberts, Brent W., Harms, Peter D., Caspi, Avshalom, & Moffitt, Terrie E. 2007. Predicting the counterproductive employee in a child-to-adult prospective study. *Journal of Applied Psychology,* Vol. 92, pp. 1427–36.

Roberts, Brent W., Kuncel, Nathan R., Shiner, Rebecca, Caspi, Avshalom, & Goldberg, Lewis R. 2007. The power of personality: The comparative validity of personality traits, socioeconomic status, and cognitive ability for predicting important life outcomes. *Perspectives on Psychological Science,* Vol. 2, No. 4, pp. 313–45.

Robins, Lee N., & Rutter, Michael. *Straight and Devious Pathways from Childhood to Adulthood.* Cambridge: Cambridge University Press, 1990.

Rubin, Kenneth H. *The Friendship Factor.* New York: Penguin Books, 2002.

Rubin, Zick. 1970. Measurement of romantic love. *Journal of Personality and Social Psychology,* Vol. 16, pp. 265–73.

Ruston, J. Phillipe, Fulker, David W., Neale, Michael C, Nias, David K.B., & Eysenck, Hans J. 1986. Altruism and aggression: The heritability of individual differences. *Journal of Personality and Social Psychology,* Vol. 50, pp. 1192–98.

Rutter, Michael. *Genes and Behavior: Nature-Nurture Interplay Explained.* Malden, MA: Blackwell Publishing, 2006.

Rutter, Michael, & Rutter, Marjorie. *Developing Minds: Challenge and Continuity Across the Life Span.* New York: Basic Books, 1993.

Sackett, Paul R., Borneman, Matthew J., & Connelley, Brian S. 2008. High-stakes testing in higher education and employment: Appraising the evidence for validity and fairness. *American Psychologist,* Vol. 53, No. 4, pp. 215–27.

Sackett, Paul R., Zedeck, Sheldon, & Fogli, Larry. 1988. Relations between measures of typical and maximum job performance. *Journal of Applied Psychology,* Vol. 73, No. 3, pp. 482–86.

Saegert, Susan, Swap, Walter, & Zajonc, R.B. 1973. Exposure, context, and interpersonal attraction. *Journal of Personality and Social Psychology,* Vol. 25, pp. 234–42.

Schweinhart, Lawrence J. How the High/Scope Perry Preschool Study Grew: A Researcher's Tale. High/Scope.http://www.highscope.org/Content.asp?ContentId=232.

Schweinhart, Lawrence J., Montie, Jeanne, Xiang, Zongping, Barnett, W. Steven, Belfield, Clive R., & Nores, Milagros. *Lifetime Effects: The High/Scope Perry Preschool Study Through Age 40.* U.S.A.: High/Scope Press, 2005.

Seligman, Martin E.P. *The Optimistic Child: A Proven Program to Safeguard Children Against Depression and Build Lifelong Resilience.* Boston & New York: Houghton Mifflin Company, 1995.

Seligman, Martin, et al. 1984. Attributional style and depressive symptoms among children. *Journal of Abnormal Psychology,* Vol. 93, pp. 235–38.

Shaver, Phillip R., & Mikulincer, Mario. A behavioral systems approach to romantic love relationships: Attachment, caregiving, and sex. In *The New Psychology of Love,* Robert J. Sternberg & Karen Weis, eds. New Haven & London: Yale University Press, 2006, pp. 35–64.

Shaw, Brian F. 1977. Comparison of cognitive therapy and behavior therapy in the treatment of depression. *Journal of Consulting and Clinical Psychology,* Vol. 45, No. 4, pp. 543–51.

Shiner, Rebecca L., Masten, Ann S., & Roberts, Jennifer M. 2003. Childhood personality foreshadows adult personality and life outcomes two decades later. *Journal of Personality,* Vol. 71:6, pp. 1145–70.

Shiner, Rebecca L., Masten, Ann S., & Tellegen, Auke. 2002. A developmental perspective on personality in emerging adulthood: Childhood antecedents and concurrent adaptation. *Journal of Personality and Social Psychology,* Vol. 83, No. 5, pp. 1165–77.

Shonkoff, Jack P., & Phillips, Deborah A., eds. *From Neurons to Neighborhoods: The Science of Early Development.* Washington, D.C.: National Academy Press, 2000.

Shure, Myrna B., & Aberson, Bonnie. Enhancing the process of resilience through effective thinking. In *Handbook of Resilience in Children,* Sam Goldstein & Robert B. Brooks, ed. U.S.A.: Springer, 2005, pp. 373–94.

Shurkin, Joel N. *Terman's Kids: The Groundbreaking Study of How the Gifted Grow Up*. New York: Little, Brown, and Company, 1992.

Sigelman, Carol, & Rider, Elizabeth. *Life-Span Human Development*, 5th ed. Florence, Ky.: Wadsworth Publishing, 2006, p. 361.

Silva, Phil A., & Stanton, Warren R., eds. *From Child to Adult: The Dunedin Multidisciplinary Health and Development Study*. New York: Oxford University Press, 1996.

Simonton, Dean Keith, & Song, Anna V. 2009. Eminence, IQ, physical and mental health and achievement domain: Cox's 282 geniuses revisited. *Psychological Science*, Vol. 20, pp. 429–34.

Simpson, Jeffry A. 1990. Influence of attachment styles on romantic relationships. *Journal of Personality and Social Psychology*, Vol. 59, pp. 971–80.

Smiley, Patricia A., & Dweck, Carol S. 1994. Individual differences in achievement goals among young children. *Child Development*, Vol. 65, pp. 1723–43.

Snyder, Mark, Tanke, Elizabeth D., & Berscheid, Ellen. 1977. Social perception and interpersonal behavior: On the self-fulfilling nature of social stereotypes. *Journal of Personality and Social Psychology*, Vol. 35, pp. 656–66.

Spencer, John. P., & Perone, Sammy. 2008. Defending qualitative change: The view from dynamic systems theory. *Child Development*, Vol. 79, pp. 1639–47.

Spencer, Steven J., & Walton, Gregory M. Identity safe environments: How positive environments can unlock latent ability. Presentation, Williams College, Williamstown, Mass., 2009.

St. Petersburg-USA Orphanage Research Team. 2008. The effects of early social-emotional and relationship experience on the development of young orphanage children. *Monographs of the Society for Research in Child Development*, Vol. 73, No. 3.

Sternberg, Robert J. *The Triangle of Love*. New York: Basic Books, Inc., 1987.

Stevenson, Leslie, & Haberman, David L. *Ten Theories of Human Nature,* 3rd ed. New York: Oxford University Press, 1998.

Stipek, D., Recchia, S., & McClintic, S. 1992. Self evaluation in young children. *Monographs of the Society for Research in Child Development,* Vol. 57, pp. 1–95.

Subbotsky, Eugene V. *The Birth of Personality.* New York: Harvester Wheatsheaf, 1993.

Sulloway, Frank J. *Born to Rebel: Birth Order, Family Dynamics, and Creative Lives.* New York: Pantheon Books, 1996.

Swensen, Clifford H., Jr. 1961. Love: A self-report analysis with college students. *Journal of Individual Psychology,* Vol. 17, p. 167.

Swensen, C.H. 1972. The behavior of love. In *Love Today,* H.A. Otto, ed. New York: Association Press, pp. 86–101.

Taumoepeau, Mele, & Ruffman, Ted. 2008. Stepping stones to others' minds: Maternal talk relates to child mental state language and emotion understanding at 15, 24, and 33 months. *Child Development,* Vol. 79, pp. 284–302.

Tremblay, Richard E., Hartup, Willard W., & Archer, John. *Developmental Origins of Aggression.* New York: The Guilford Press, 2005.

Ullman, Ellen. My secret life. *New York Times.* January 2, 2009.

Underwood, Bill, & Moore, Bert S. The generality of altruism in children. In *The Development of Prosocial Behavior,* Nancy Eisenberg, ed. Academic Press, 1982.

Wachs, Theodore D., Black, Maureen M., & Engle, Patrice L. 2009. Maternal depression: A global threat to children's health, development, and behavior and to human rights. *Child Development Perspectives,* Vol. 3, pp. 51–59.

Walton, Gregory M., & Spencer, Steven J. Latent ability: Grades and test scores systematically underestimate the intellectual ability of negatively stereotyped students. *Psychological Science,* in press.

Warneken, Felix, & Tomasello, Michael. 2008. Extrinsic rewards undermine altruistic tendencies in 20-month-olds. *Developmental Psychology,* Vol. 44, pp. 1785–88.

Werner, Emmy E., Bierman, Jessie M., & French, Fern E. *The Children of Kauai: A Longitudinal Study from the Prenatal Period to Age 10.* Honolulu: University of Hawaii Press, 1971.

Werner, Emmy E., & Smith, Ruth S. *Overcoming the Odds: High Risk Children from Birth to Adulthood.* Ithaca, N.Y.: Cornell University Press, 1992.

Werner, Emmy E., & Smith, Ruth S. *Journeys from Childhood to Midlife: Risk, Resilience, and Recovery.* Ithaca, N.Y., and London: Cornell University Press, 2001.

Wigfield, Alan, & Eccles, Jacquelynne, S., eds. *Development of Achievement Motivation.* Academic Press, 2002.

Wright, Margaret O'Dougherty, & Masten, Ann S. Resilience processes in development. In Sam Goldstein & Robert B. Brooks, eds. *Handbook of Resilience in Children.* U.S.A.: Springer, 2005.

Zahn-Wexler, Carolyn, Cummings, E. Mark, & Iaonnotti, Ronald. *Altruism and Aggression: Biological and Social Origins.* New York: Cambridge University Press, 1986.

Zernike, Kate. The cool factor: Never let them see you sweat. *New York Times.* November 30, 2008.

Zins, Joseph E., & Elias, Maurice J. Social and emotional learning. In *Children's Needs III.* National Association of School Psychologists, 2006.

Acknowledgments

Many smart and generous people shared their experiences and thoughts with me as I worked on this book. In particular, I want to thank Chris Moore, Margery Franklin, Lucy Prashker, Susanne King, Katherine Bouton, Bill Damon, Judy Deloache, and Paul Harris. Once again, Betty Prashker gave me just the right advice at just the right time.

Marlene Sandstrom and I talk about children and development all the time. Where my ideas are good, no doubt, she had something to do with it. Where they fall short, it's probably because she finally had to kick me out of her office and do something else.

I thank my wonderful agent, Neeti Madan. She's provided terrific support and guidance and seems to know exactly when I should say yes and when I should say no. Now I understand why people feel they cannot get on without their agents.

I thank my smart and delightful editor at Simon & Schuster,

Sarah Durand. She's been a complete pleasure to work with and made the difficult process of writing much smoother. I know this book is better because of her.

I adore my students at Williams. I am grateful to three in particular who helped me find material, read portions of the manuscript, and gave me feedback before anyone else. They are Kristen Baldiga, Laura Corona, and Kate Anderson.

My husband, Tom Levin, is part of everything I do and think. He's part of this book as well, and I thank him for that.

Watching my sons, Jake, Will, and Sam, grow up to be such strong, smart, funny, courageous, accomplished, and loving men has been the greatest pleasure of my life. It has also provided me with many insights about childhood.

From the bottom of my heart, I thank all of the mothers and fathers, brothers and sisters, sons and daughters, grandparents, uncles, and aunts whose life stories fill these pages. If the book is any good, it's because their lives offered such riches.

I dedicate this book to my mother, Tinka, and my sisters, Kathy and Jenno. Luckily for me, our lives are intertwined. I wouldn't be me without them, and neither would *Red Flags or Red Herrings?*

Index

The Future of Evangelical Christianity

A CALL FOR UNITY AMID DIVERSITY

By Donald G. Bloesch

DOUBLEDAY & COMPANY, INC.
GARDEN CITY, NEW YORK
1983

Printed in the United States of America

Library of Congress Cataloging in Publication Data

Bloesch, Donald G., 1928–
The future of evangelical Christianity.

Bibliography.
Includes indexes.
1. Evangelicalism. I. Title.
BR1640.B56 1983 270.8'2
ISBN 0-385-18356-9
Library of Congress Catalog Card Number 82-45519

To Brenda,
My Partner in Ministry

Acknowledgments

I WISH TO ACKNOWLEDGE the substantial help that I have received from my wife Brenda, particularly in her role as a copy editor of this book. I am grateful to Joseph Mihelic and Donald McKim, my colleagues at the University of Dubuque Theological Seminary, and to Roger Nicole, Clark Pinnock, Gerald Sanders and Kenneth Kantzer for providing important information and advice. As usual, Edith Baule of our seminary library staff has given invaluable assistance in obtaining books and checking publishing data. James Gingery, our newly appointed seminary reference librarian, Mary Anne Knefel and Duane Cavins have also been immensely helpful in this area. Finally, I want to thank Peg Saunders, our faculty secretary, for her painstaking typing of this and many other manuscripts in the past.

Some of the material in this book has been presented in the form of lectures at a Presbyterian Pastors' Conference at Hope Presbyterian Church in Spicer, Minnesota; a workshop at the First Covenant Church in Omaha, Nebraska; a Reformed Pastors' Conference at Trinity Reformed Church in Fulton, Illinois; the Board of Directors' National Meeting of the National Association of Evangelicals in Chicago; and at the following schools: Gordon-Conwell Theological Seminary, Winebrenner Theological Seminary, Wheaton College, Asbury Theological Seminary, Rockford College, Central Baptist Theological Seminary and Northern Baptist Theological Seminary.

Contents

Foreword

I HAVE BEEN LED to write this book for several reasons. First, I wish to defend the thesis that evangelicalism today exists as a cohesive, growing movement and must therefore be taken seriously by the church at large, both Catholic and Protestant. Despite its tensions and schisms, it has an inner theological unity in the midst of external theological and cultural diversity. Those who claim to be evangelical today generally have a solid historical basis for doing so. At the same time, they tend to exclude some who also have biblical credentials and to include some whose fidelity to the faith of the Scriptures and the Reformation is suspect.

Most people who stand in the heritage of the Reformation have at least one foot in evangelicalism. Yet many of these people are unwilling to associate themselves with the evangelical renewal movement. Some are undoubtedly reluctant because any show of support for the evangelical cause might result in the loss of academic or social respectability. Others, who have a genuine fear of sectarianism, see the evangelical movement as promoting divisiveness in the churches.

I identify myself as an evangelical because I definitely share in the vision of the Reformers, Pietists and Puritans of a church under the banner of the gospel seeking to convert a world under the spell of the powers of darkness to the kingdom of our Lord and Savior, Jesus Christ. I have moved in this direction from an earlier fascination with existentialism, for I believe that the rediscovery of the gospel is the key to the renewal of the church in our day. Though painfully aware of the current heterodoxies which give a distorted picture of evangelicalism, I am happy to note that the greatest theologians of Protestantism in the twentieth century have identified themselves as evangelical: P. T. Forsyth, Benjamin Warfield, Karl Barth, Helmut Thielicke, G. C. Berkouwer and Emil Brunner. The obvious disagreements among these giants of modern evangelicalism are overshadowed by what they have in common: an unswerving commitment to the biblical message of salvation through the grace of God revealed and fulfilled in Jesus Christ, in his sacrificial life and death and in his glorious resurrection.

It is possible to speak, as does Clark Pinnock, of a growing divide in theology today between a reborn evangelicalism and a chastened liberalism, paralleling the conflict between fundamentalism and modernism in the earlier part of this century.[1] We certainly need to remember that not all theology accepts the gospel as a revelation of God; instead, it is often understood as the product of human faith and experience. I do not agree with some of my neoevangelical friends, however, when they argue that the gospel needs to be shored up or validated by external evidence. The Word of God is self-authenticating, though its claims can be made more clear and intelligible by an enlightened reason in the service of faith.

The common distinction today between "mainline" and "evangelical" is sociological, not theological. I myself stand in a mainline Protestant denomination, but I am committed to evangelical theology.

A growing number of Roman Catholics wish to be known as evangelical, theologically speaking, but culturally and sociologically they belong in another camp. I agree with Howard Snyder: "Evangelical Christianity today is more than a group of theologically conservative churches. It is decreasingly a specific branch of Western Protestantism and increasingly a transconfessional movement for biblical Christianity within the worldwide Church of Jesus Christ."[2] In this book, I try to show that the evangelical movement has a distinctive theological thrust and undergirding.

A second reason for writing this book is to warn my fellow evangelicals of dangers that could disrupt and splinter this renewal movement. I explore the openness of a growing number of Protestant evangelicals to Catholicism,* seeing in this reason for hope as well as for uneasiness. I have no compunction in referring to myself as a catholic evangelical, because I recognize the need for cultus, liturgy and sacraments in addition to personal piety and a love for the Scriptures. The current fascination with Catholicism among many evangelicals is an understandable reaction against individualism and rational empiricism. Yet there is the everpresent danger of a new heteronomy, of viewing the church as a mediator of salvation, of making church tradition equal to Scripture. We would be wise to maintain a certain critical stance toward catholicizing tendencies within Protestantism; at the same time, we are called to discover anew the catholicity of Protestantism.

I also address myself to the other kind of heteronomy, which is more germane to Protestantism than Catholicism—the tendency to absolutize the Bible as a book. When an absolute equation is made between the words of the Bible and divine revelation, the Word of God is placed in the power of man, since words and propositions can be mastered by reason. I do not wish to deny the propositional dimension of revelation; the divine meaning shines through the propositions set forth in Scripture, but it is not encased in these propositions nor in any human formulas. Many evangelicals, in their antipathy to mysticism and existentialism, are hardening into a new rationalism and biblicism. A. W. Tozer has ventured to predict that the conflict in the future will be between evangelical rationalism and evangelical mysticism.

I am not among those who wish to give up inerrancy and infallibility when applied to Scripture, but I believe that we need to be much more circumspect in our use of these and related terms. Scripture is without error in a fundamental sense, but we need to explore what this sense is. Evangelicalism must not be confused with an obscurantist fundamentalism, though all evangelicals should be fundamental in the sense of holding to the fundamentals of the historic faith of the church.

Finally, I try in this book to build bridges between the various strands of evangelicalism and also between evangelical Protestantism and the Catholic churches. At the same time, I point out where

* Whenever the word Catholicism is used, it refers to the beliefs and practices shared by the Roman, Eastern Orthodox, and Anglo-Catholic churches, unless the context indicates otherwise.

bridges cannot be built, where compromise is out of the question. I write with the firm conviction that evangelicalism can have a bright future if it seeks to be a unifying rather than a divisive force within world Christianity. Yet I recognize the fact that real unity entails an accord on doctrinal essentials as well as fellowship in the spirit. Love and truth need to be united, and we should not rest until we reach this goal.

Abbreviations for Scriptural References

RSV	Revised Standard Version
NEB	New English Bible
GNB	Good News Bible
NKJ	New King James Version
KJV	King James Version
NIV	New International Version

There is an unfortunate tendency among some of us to "look down" upon theology and theologians! . . . I have heard some young people say: "I don't need *any theology!" How ridiculous! They don't need to study about God?*

George Verwer

Evangelicals are to be known in the world as the bearers of good news in message and life—the good news that God offers new life on the ground of Christ's death and resurrection. . . . The apostles did not go out into the world preaching . . . scriptural inerrancy, or a premillennial kingdom, or some of the other things that are made the foremost issues today.

Carl Henry

There is hardly a Church that has not suffered from its success. And when I say suffered, I mean it has suffered in its power of witnessing [to] the Gospel. It has gained comfort, affluence, and influence, but it has lost its prophetic soul, it has fallen from its apostolic insight and succession.

P. T. Forsyth

There can only be a church as a Confessing Church, i.e. as a church which confesses itself to be for its Lord and against its enemies. A church without a confession or free from one is not a church, but a sect, and makes itself master of the Bible and the Word of God.

Dietrich Bonhoeffer

I

Introduction

For I am not ashamed of the Gospel. It is the saving power of God for everyone who has faith . . . because here is revealed God's way of righting wrong, a way that starts from faith and ends in faith; as Scripture says, "he shall gain life who is justified through faith."

Romans 1:16, 17 NEB

Every true progress in theology is conditioned by a deeper study and understanding of the Word of God, which is ever . . . renewing the Church, and will ever remain the infallible and inexhaustible fountain of revealed truth.

Philip Schaff

Some even talk of being saved by Christianity, instead of by the only thing that could possibly save us, the anguish and love of God.

Wilfred Cantwell Smith

Christianity can endure, not by surrendering itself to the modern mind and modern culture, but rather by a break with it: the condition of a long future both for culture and the soul is the Christianity which antagonizes culture without denying its place.

P. T. Forsyth

IT IS COMMONPLACE, especially in establishment circles, to label any resurgence of biblical Christianity as "fundamentalist." Fundamentalism is a clearly defined movement within the church, and it is on the uprise today. Yet what is occurring as well is a reemergence of classical evangelicalism, and this poses a definite threat not only to fundamentalism but also and even more to liberalism.

Liberal religion is on the defensive today, despite the fact that its hold on the divinity schools of the great universities and the seminaries of most mainline denominations remains virtually intact. Even in these bastions of higher theological education, there is unquestionably a mounting interest in orthodoxy, particularly among the students. As a spiritual movement within the churches, liberalism is slowly but surely giving way to both classical evangelicalism and fundamentalism. The spell that it casts over the secular culture is still significant, though that too is eroding.

Evangelicalism is making a dramatic comeback in the mainline churches, but shadows loom on the horizon. A backlash against the evangelical boom is painfully evident. Among Lutherans, there is an increasing emphasis on baptismal regeneration, thus downplaying the need for personal decision. Among Reformed and Presbyterians, being born into the covenant community is often accorded greater value than either baptism or conversion. A bias against evangelicalism is also apparent in the new interpretation of mission as the self-development of deprived peoples or simply as the announcement of unconditional grace rather than the conversion of the spiritually lost. Reformed Christianity stresses *ecclesia semper reformanda* (the church always being reformed), but unless this is constantly seen in the light of the gospel, it invariably leads to latitudinarianism. Other ominous signs are the retreat into liturgy, the emphasis on the experiential over the cognitive in Christian education and the elevation of community consensus over biblical authority.[1]

Such developments only serve to intensify the growing reaction in lay circles against creeping formalism in church life and worship as well as against narrow denominationalism. The attraction for the electronic church among laity in the mainline churches is due in part to a thirst for biblical truth and even more for the spiritual reality that underlies this truth. Unfortunately, the hopes of many have been disappointed by the abysmal lack of solid biblical teaching on the part of the media preachers.

Evangelicalism as a spiritual renewal movement in the churches today cannot be adequately understood apart from its uneasy relationship to liberal Christianity. Religious liberalism, with its roots in the Renaissance and the Enlightenment, stresses the infinite possibilities of man. It sees the Christian life as a process of growth into salvation, which is redefined as spiritual maturity. Evangelical Christianity, on the contrary, which is anchored in Paul, Augustine and the Reformation, underlines the total depravity of man, his utter helplessness to save himself in the face of the vitiating power of sin. It regards salvation as a crisis by which one is transported from spiritual death into spiritual life.

One of the chief spiritual mentors of modern liberalism in its American guise is Ralph Waldo Emerson, with his romantic, optimistic view of human potentiality. A leading figure in the modern age who reflects the concerns of historical evangelical religion is Søren Kierkegaard, with his emphasis on Christ as both Savior from sin and Pattern for righteous living.[2] There is no doubt that Emerson's influence far exceeds that of Kierkegaard in popular American religion and culture, even among many of those who call themselves evangelical. Yet this may be changing, as the children of the evangelical revival are beginning to dig into the historical sources of their faith and rediscover the saints of biblical Christianity—Athanasius, Augustine, Calvin, Luther and Wesley.

In my opinion, the movement that presently bears the name *evangelical* stands in unmistakable continuity with the classical tradition of evangelicalism. At the same time, this is a broken continuity, for some are included as evangelical who are really Pelagian or semi-Pelagian, and some are excluded simply because they doubt the appropriateness of the term "inerrancy" when applied to Scripture. The word "evangelical" needs to be deepened and expanded if we are to do justice to the rich heritage it represents.

Evangelical, as used in this book, signifies an emphasis within Christendom or historic Christianity, one that intends to include as well as exclude. Its specific reference is to the doctrinal content of the gospel itself, with the focus on the vicarious, atoning sacrifice of Christ, on the unsurpassable grace of God revealed in Christ, which is laid hold of not by works of the law but by faith alone (Rom.

3:21–28; Col. 2:11–14; Eph. 2:4–8).[3] All Christianity will contain an evangelical element; otherwise the very claim to be Christian would be suspect. At the same time, the word "evangelical" is best reserved for that segment of Christianity that makes the proclamation of the biblical gospel its chief concern, that appeals to this gospel in its biblical setting as the final arbiter for faith and practice. Only the kind of preaching that celebrates the victory of Christ over sin and death and calls people to repentance and decision in the light of this victory can appropriately be designated as evangelical.

Today the battle is over biblical authority. Because Holy Scripture in all its parts witnesses to God's self-revelation in Jesus Christ, because the gospel of what God has done in Christ comprises the divine content of Scripture, evangelicals stress Scripture in its unity with the Spirit as the ruling norm (cf. John 5:46; 10:35; Rom. 16:25, 26; I Cor. 15:3, 4; I Pet. 1:10–12; II Pet. 1:20, 21; II Tim. 3:15, 16). All other norms—church councils, papal decrees, confessions, conscience and religious experience—are derivative from this higher norm. All are subordinate to the living Word of God attested to and revealed in Scripture.

Liberal Christianity, on the other hand, tends to read Scripture in the light of the wisdom and experience of modern culture. The truth of Scripture is judged on how it accords with the spirit of modernity. As a result, attention is focused no longer on the remission of sins through the atoning death and glorious resurrection of Christ but on any number of other things—character development, the cultivation of God-consciousness, salvation through education, psychological wholeness, existential commitment, social revolution, etc. The question is: Can this in any way be included under the rubric of evangelical religion, the faith of the apostles and Reformers? I am convinced that religious liberalism is basically incompatible with evangelical Christianity, though this is not to deny that it contains Christian elements. I also do not wish to preclude the very real possibility that some liberals who entertain a philosophy that stands at variance with biblical Christianity may still have an evangelical heart, i.e., they still may be in inward communion with the Christ whom they misunderstand. It is well to note that a growing number of revisionist theologians, including David Tracy[4] and Rosemary Ruether, readily acknowledge the tensions between their positions and historical evangelical religion.

I prefer the term "Evangelical Christianity" over "Evangelical Protestantism," because the evangelical thrust cuts across all denominational and confessional lines. Evangelical Christianity is not the only form of Christianity, but it is the truest and purest form. Yet it cannot stand by itself. The evangelical emphasis is not complete apart from structure and cultus. The evangelical message cannot maintain itself apart from the catholic concern with tradition and the means of grace. This is why the most authentic kind of evangelicalism is a catholic evangelicalism, and the purest form of catholicism is an evangelical catholicism.

An attempt is made in this book to differentiate the transcendent content of evangelical Christianity from its ideological form. Just as the gospel transcends and negates every formulation and witness to it,[5] so the true evangelicalism transcends and negates evangelicalism as a movement or party within the church. The gospel stands in judgment over all human ideologies, including the ideology of cultural evangelicalism.

In its ideal form, evangelicalism is a movement that points beyond itself to the gospel, a movement whose primary concern is to glorify not itself, its forms of worship, its doctrinal platform, its leading personalities but instead the message of the cross. The apostle Paul expresses what should be the sentiments of all evangelicals: "God forbid that I should glory except in the cross of our Lord Jesus Christ, by whom the world has been crucified to me, and I to the world" (Gal. 6:14 NKJ).

Evangelical Christianity is the true orthodoxy. Yet it is not an orthodoxy bent on preserving its own sacred traditions but one that uses these traditions to advance the cause of the gospel in the world today. Evangelical Christianity, in contrast to formalistic orthodoxy, seeks to lose itself for the sake of the salvation of the world.

Evangelicalism today presents the paradoxical picture of an emerging alliance of born-again Christians drawn from all communions and a movement rent by growing schism. Yet although there are centrifugal forces pulling evangelicals apart, there is also a unifying power bringing them back together. The key to evangelical unity lies in a common commitment to Jesus Christ as the divine Savior from sin, a common purpose to fulfill the great commission and a common acknowledgment of the absolute normativeness of Holy Scripture. Evangelicals of all stripes confess to an underlying affinity with their fellow believers no matter what their ethnic, denominational or confessional background. Evangelicalism may indeed be the ecumenical movement of the future because of this capacity to transcend age-old denominational and creedal barriers.

In the area of ethics, there is a developing consensus among evangelicals concerning the critical moral issues of our time. From the far right to the left, evangelicals find themselves in an unforeseen unity in their opposition to abortion on demand, pornography, euthanasia, and homosexuality as a valid alternative life-style. They are also increasingly acknowledging the sinfulness of divorce, a malady that has penetrated the evangelical as well as the secular world, though not to the same degree. Moreover, there is a growing agreement on the evils of nuclear and biochemical warfare. Billy Graham has become one of the leading voices on behalf of world peace.

A persistent temptation of modern evangelicalism is to rely on human strategy and technique in carrying out the great commission to make disciples of all nations (Matt. 28:18–20). Evangelicalism needs to break out of its ideological bondage to technological materialism and affirm once again the freedom of the gospel. The Word of God makes its own way in the world. It calls for our acclamation and honor but not for any undergirding to insure its success.

Jesus Christ does not need our aid, but he wishes to enlist us in his service. He does not need to be bolstered by our feeble efforts, but he invites us to share in his victory. He alone procures the victory over sin and death, but we can proclaim and celebrate what he has done. We can also cooperate with the Spirit of God in manifesting and extending this victory. We are the beneficiaries, not the causes, of this victory; at the same time, we can be instruments of the Spirit as he carries the impact of the reconciling and redemptive work of Christ into the world.

Even more dangerous than the desire to accommodate to worldly patterns of success is the pretension to possess the treasure of the gospel. The evangelical church has been as guilty of this as the Roman Catholic Church. We need to recover the biblical truth that we as Christians can never be masters but only servants of the Word. We can prepare the way, but we cannot force God to yield the treasure of salvation (neither through importunate prayer nor meritorious works). God will act in his own time and way, and sometimes he will act despite, even against, all our efforts and strategies.

Evangelicals today can best serve the cause of the gospel by refusing to join their liberal colleagues in trying to make the Christian religion credible or palatable to the "man come of age." Instead, they should try to regain the robust confidence of Calvin, Wesley and Whitefield, a confidence in the gospel itself to convert and renew. This does not mean that the gospel should be thrown at the world like a stone (an accusation leveled at the early Barth), but it does mean that the gospel should not be converted into a bridge that rests partly on worldly wisdom. The message of the cross will always confound the wisdom of the philosophers. As Paul so dramatically put it: "Jews demand signs and Greeks seek wisdom, but we preach Christ crucified, a stumbling block to Jews and folly to Gentiles, but to those who are called, both Jews and Greeks, Christ the power of God and the wisdom of God" (I Cor. 1:22–24 RSV; cf. 17, 18).

Rather than a bridge, the gospel is more appropriately likened to a battering ram that breaks down the defenses of the city of the world. It employs, moreover, a definite strategy and has a specific aim. Those whom the Word commissions do not hesitate to make use of the prevailing thought forms and symbols of a culture in order to challenge its pretensions. There cannot be theological points of contact between the gospel and the world, but there must be sociological and cultural points of contact. We must speak the language of our age even while seeking to overthrow its follies and superstitions.

The question today is what branch of Christendom can best survive in the uncertain future before us. Much conflicting advice is being given. Some counsel that we as Christians must learn to bend with the times. Others advise a retreat to a confessional stance of the past. Still others advocate a minimizing of doctrine and an elevation of liturgy and priestly ministrations.

It is my position that the future belongs to that branch of Christendom that is willing to make itself expendable for the sake of the evangelization of the world to the greater glory of God. This may well involve the death of denominations, even of mission boards and agencies, for the life of the paganized masses in the West and East.

II

The Problem of Evangelical Identity

Between the man who is bound to a God in heaven, and another who knows nothing of this bond, there is a contrast deeper than all other contrasts which separate men from men.

Karl Heim

Christianity is not the sacrifice we make, but the sacrifice we trust; not the victory we win, but the victory we inherit. That is the evangelical principle.

P. T. Forsyth

What disturbs me most about modern fundamentalism is its lack of spirituality, its utter carnality.

D. Martyn Lloyd-Jones

Fundamentalism and orthodoxy in general are a petrification of Christianity; and modernism and all doctrines of immanence are its dissolution.

Emil Brunner

EVANGELICALISM IN CRISIS

THE EVANGELICAL RESURGENCE forges ahead as conservative Protestant bodies gain in membership while the mainline denominations, including Roman Catholicism, barely hold their own in the light of the population increase or actually suffer losses in membership. Evangelicalism had one of its own in the White House in the person of Jimmy Carter, and its influence is also discernible in the Reagan administration.

While the evangelical renaissance continues, the term "evangelical" remains fluid. Even in the ranks of the far right, there is an amazing lack of consensus on what "evangelical" really implies.

In some strands of evangelicalism, there is an emphasis on experience over doctrine. We hear much of the "born-again experience" or the "experience of Pentecost," but very little of the need for correct theology and sacramental integrity. Evangelicals associated with the "New Pietism" frequently denigrate scholarship, especially in the area of theological and biblical studies. What they value is "relational theology," which focuses on cultivating a personal awareness of God and growing toward psychological and spiritual maturity.

Quite common in experientialist religion is a stress on extraordinary signs of having received the Holy Spirit. Miracles of healing, speaking in tongues, and prophecy are considered integral aspects of the life of a church based on the "full gospel." Where these extraordinary gifts are lacking, it is said, there is no fullness of the Spirit.

In other branches of evangelicalism, the focus is on biblical inerrancy and the need for rational corroboration of the claims of faith. Thus epistemology, not soteriology, becomes the watershed of evangelical faith.[1] Such a position betrays its distance from the Protestant Reformation, from early Protestant orthodoxy, and also from Pietism and Puritanism.

Modern evangelicalism is confronted with the embarrassing fact that its special emphases reveal considerable theological immaturity and even theological heterodoxy rather than dynamic, vibrant orthodoxy. Many of the cults and sects claim the signs, the special experiences, even inerrancy, yet their doctrines are manifestly unbiblical. The United Pentecostals, the Way, the Jehovah's Witnesses, the Moonies, and the Christadelphians are obvious examples. Several of these groups are avowedly anti-Trinitarian. A further cause for embarrassment is the number of celebrities who claim the so-called evangelical experience and yet whose lives testify against the truth of their experience.

Although evangelicalism constantly warns against the encroachment of worldliness, its accommodation to cultural norms and values is almost as noticeable as in liberalism. While it has been eager to maintain sharp lines of distinction from liberal theology, it has been too ready to come to terms with the technocratic mentality of our age. Busyness is considered more important than being in the truth, activism more commendable than contemplation. Evangelism is regarded as a technique to be mastered, not as a surprising movement of the Spirit into which one is caught. Teachers in evangelical colleges and seminaries are esteemed more as transmitters than as thinkers. Original, creative scholarship meets with suspicion in many of these circles. Significantly, many evangelical institutions of higher learning do not even grant sabbaticals to their faculties.

The electronic church, which is consciously evangelical, generally features those who are seen as successful according to the standards of a consumerist, technological culture. Sin is often portrayed as failure to make something of oneself rather than as revolt against God. With their emphasis on happiness and prosperity through faith in God, the electronic preachers tend to confirm the bourgeoisie in their complacency rather than convert people to a new way of thinking and living that calls into question the commonly accepted values of the technological society.[2]

The alliance of a major segment of evangelicalism with the political right is likewise a cause for concern on the part of those who affirm biblical Christianity.[3] Here the principal enemy is secular humanism, but there is no comparable prophetic indictment of technological materialism or nationalism. Far-right evangelicals often assail humanism as antifamily and propornography, but they tend to overlook the fact that at least some so-called secular humanists are actively engaged in combating evils of this kind.[4] Because of its stress on the autonomy and infinite possibilities of mankind, secular humanism (a life- and world-view having its roots in the Renaissance and the Enlightenment) does pose a serious challenge to the Christian understanding of life and traditional Christian values.[5] But secular humanism is not the only enemy, and it may not always be the principal enemy.[6]

Those who are sometimes known as "young evangelicals" often display a similar imbalance in their uncritical fascination with left-wing ideologies. For them the enemy is big business and capitalism; the shortcomings of socialism remain virtually unheeded. Their tirades against Anglo-American imperialism, without any comparable indictments of international Communist subversion, can only give comfort to the Soviet Union and its allies. This one-sided approach can also destroy the impact of their sometimes valid critiques of Western society.

Evangelicalism is in crisis not only because of its theological immaturity and isolation and its ideological coloration but also because of its marked sectarian propensity. It is inclined to function as a party within the church that promotes its own particular interests rather than as a genuine movement of renewal that is ready to sacrifice itself for the good of the wider church. A sectarian mentality exacerbates the tensions within the church by elevating nonessentials, whereas a catholic mentality binds the wounds of the church by focusing attention on essentials. Ideally, evangelicalism should be a spiritual movement of purification and renewal that breaks down ideological polarization, party division and class distinction within the church universal. In practice, evangelicalism has too often been an ideological movement of reaction which polarizes rather than unites and which fortifies rather than overcomes ethnic and class loyalties and biases. It should be recognized that in some periods of history evangelicalism has indeed approached the ideal of being a unifying and renewing force within world Christianity. If it could disengage itself from those forces that pull it in an ideological and sectarian direction, it might yet become the spiritually revolutionary and dynamic movement that it essentially was and is.

CURRENT MISUNDERSTANDINGS

Today, some of the definitions of what it means to be evangelical are too narrow. To equate evangelicalism with a belief in biblical inerrancy is to leave out many in the past and present who staunchly affirm the gospel in all its breadth and depth and yet who recoil from applying the term "inerrancy" to Scripture. "Inerrancy" can indeed be used to describe Scripture, but even many of its supporters acknowledge that it is an ambiguous term capable of lending itself to various interpretations. The term "infallibility" is stronger, in my estimation, but it, too, is not without ambiguity, since it can be used to denote quite different understandings of biblical authority. This does not mean that neither term should ever be employed, but it does mean that the essence of being evangelical must not be tied to any one symbol or slogan.

The experiential criterion is also too narrow in determining the substance of evangelical faith, particularly where this means a datable, rapturous experience. Even Philip Spener and Count Nikolaus von Zinzendorf, two of the luminaries of German Pietism, did not claim this kind of experience as integral to their faith.

Some scholars limit the term "evangelical" to eighteenth- and nineteenth-century revivalism and its descendants. But this disregards the awakening movements within Reformed and Lutheran churches in the late sixteenth and seventeenth centuries. It overlooks the resolute evangelical witness that has continued within Anglicanism from the sixteenth century on. Worse still, it leaves out the Protestant Reformation of the sixteenth century, which can only be rightly understood as a rediscovery of the biblical gospel in an age dominated by formalism, scholasticism and superstition.

Even if we included the whole of the evangelical tradition within Protestantism, this would still be too limiting. An evangelical thrust has not been entirely lacking in the Catholic and Orthodox churches. Cyril Lucaris, Orthodox Patriarch of Constantinople in the seventeenth century, vigorously affirmed the priority and sovereignty of grace, though his teachings were condemned by synods held at Constantinople (1638, 1642), Jassy (1642) and Jerusalem (1672). Russian Orthodox bishop Tikhon in the eighteenth century based his spirituality almost exclusively on the Scriptures and had a warm sympathy for German Pietists and English Evangelicals. A number of Roman Catholic theologians, notably Augustine, Ambrose, Ambrosiaster, Pascal[7] and in our own day Hans Urs von Balthasar and Ida Friederike Görres, are identified with such evangelical themes as divine election, the radical pervasiveness of sin, the sovereignty of grace, the cruciality of faith for salvation, and the substitutionary atonement. One could also make a case that there is a definite evangelical strand in Thomas Aquinas[8] and in some of the Catholic mystics (though not in all).[9]

In some circles today, evangelicalism is virtually equivalent to premillennialism and even to dispensationalism. One of the key issues is whether the rapture of the saints will occur before or after the great tribulation at the end of the age. Such a position connotes a sectarian mentality, for it reduces evangelicalism to a sect or party within the church, sadly out of contact with the broader stream of Christian tradition.

At the opposite extreme, we find those who conceive of evangelicalism in too broad or inclusive a way. Some argue that anyone can be called evangelical who acknowledges Jesus as Savior and Lord. But this would include many Unitarians and Arians, who clearly stand outside the mainstream of evangelical, catholic faith. Others contend that anyone who experiences forgiveness or inner peace must be an evangelical Christian. This would then open the door to any number of cults that deny the basic precepts of historic Christian faith. A similar problem arises with those who base the case for evangelicalism on the reality of a personal communion or personal relationship with Jesus Christ. To make evangelicalism roughly tantamount to Christian supernaturalism or classical theism is to risk confusing evangelical theology with a philosophy of religion in which the saving work of Christ plays no crucial role.

There are many who define "evangelical" on the basis of a particular approach to Holy Scripture. Some hold that the hallmark of evangelical Christianity is an affirmation of the divine authority and inspiration of the Bible. Yet this could include sacramentalist Roman Catholics, Moonies, Mormons, the Local Church of Witness Lee, the more tradition-bound Eastern Orthodox, and many others who would find it difficult if not impossible to accept the basic message of the Protestant Reformation.

In an illuminating and provocative article in *The Christian Century,* Peter Schmiechen maintains that all Christian theology is by definition evangelical and that it is wrong for any particular theological movement to claim the word "evangelical" for itself.[10] Yet this is to overlook the fact that many theologians, though speaking out of a Christian orientation, tacitly if not explicitly deny the motifs that have characterized evangelical Christianity in the past—*sola gratia* (salvation only by the grace of God), *sola fide* (justification by faith alone), *sola scriptura* (Scripture as the final arbiter for faith and practice).[11] We can certainly consider a theology that does not incorporate these themes as deficiently Christian, but can we condemn it as non-Christian? Pelagius in his battle with Augustine surely cannot be described as evangelical, but he can still be regarded as representative of a continuing theological position in the church.[12] Similarly, Erasmus, who was drawn into a conflict with Luther on the sovereignty of grace and the bondage of the will, was still writing Christian theology, albeit not evangelical theology. Albert Schweitzer could accept neither the deity of Christ nor his vicarious, substitutionary atonement; it was the mystical Christ that was the focus of his concern. His admirers claim that he was a model Christian, but he certainly stood outside the circle of evangelical faith.[13] There are theologians in the contemporary period who underline the need for an existential encounter with Christ and yet view the Bible as a basically unreliable witness. Can they in all honesty be included under the rubric of evangelical?

Dietrich Bonhoeffer is instructive in this connection. Though acutely aware of the dangers of religious triumphalism, he nonetheless held that some communions are closer to the truth of the gospel than others. In his view, the Evangelical church, the church that stands in the tradition of the Reformation, is "the true one," even though it cannot claim to be in and of itself "the essential church."[14] It can claim, however, to be "the church of the Gospel," for, despite its faults, it can be deemed a more fitting instrument of the grace of God than the church that rejected the Reformation. Yet Bonhoeffer readily acknowledged that the fellowship of the saints (*sanctorum communio*) was also present in the Roman Catholic Church and in various sects.

For Bonhoeffer, the Evangelical church exists in tension not only with Catholicism but with liberal Protestantism as well. He contrasted "the church of the Gospel" with the hodgepodge of voices in the ecumenical movement:

> The churches included in the World Alliance have no common recognition of the truth. It is precisely here that they are most deeply divided. When they say "Christ" or "Gospel," they mean something different.[15]

REDEFINING "EVANGELICAL"

Before redefining "evangelical," it is necessary to explore the historical background of this word. It was not used in a partisan or polemical sense until the sixteenth century when the Reformers increasingly designated themselves as Evangelical as opposed to Roman Catholic.[16] As early as 1520 Luther referred to "those who boldly call themselves Evangelicals" and in 1522 to "this common Evangelical cause." Several years later Erasmus acknowledged the common usage by describing "some who falsely boast they are Evangelicals." When the Reformers called themselves Evangelicals, they did not think of themselves as a schismatic group within the church but as representatives of the true church—the church founded by Jesus Christ and based on the biblical gospel.[17]

In the spiritual movements of purification subsequent to the Reformation, Pietism and Puritanism, the term "evangelical" became further refined to include the necessity for the personal appropriation of the gospel. The so-called Evangelical movement in eighteenth-century England, Scotland and Wales associated with the names of George Whitefield, John and Charles Wesley, Daniel Rowlands and Howel Harris gave special emphasis to the new birth without intending to minimize or downplay justification (though the dialectic between justification and regeneration was not always maintained).[18]

"Evangelical" is derived from the Greek word *evangelion,* meaning the gospel or message of good news concerning what God has done for us in Jesus Christ. Because this message is the dominant theme of the New Testament and is indeed present in anticipatory form even in the Old Testament, evangelicals maintain a high view of Scripture as well as fidelity to the gospel. Because the gospel focuses upon God's free, unconditional grace rather than on human achievement or merit, evangelicals steadfastly affirm *sola gratia* (salvation by grace alone).

"Evangelical" can therefore be said to indicate a particular thrust or emphasis within the church, namely, that which upholds the gospel of free grace as we see this in Jesus Christ. An evangelical will consequently be Christocentric and not merely theocentric (as are the deists and a great many mystics). Yet it is not the teachings of Jesus Christ that are considered of paramount importance but his sacrificial life and death on the cross of Calvary. The evangel is none other than the meaning of the cross.

Evangelicalism may take the form of a particular party within the church, but its intention is not to remain a mere party but instead to serve as a catalyst that unifies the whole church under the gospel.[19] Today, as in the time of the Reformers, the Pietists and the Puritans, evangelicalism is best understood as a movement of spiritual renewal within the wider church. Its purpose is not simply to enhance the spiritual life, moreover, but to renew the church by calling it back to its theological and biblical foundations. It is a movement based on and reformed by the gospel as attested in Holy Scripture. It seeks not to advance itself but to serve the cause of Jesus Christ and his kingdom. Though ready and willing to challenge heresy, its basic orientation is positive, since it focuses on the glad tidings of God's act of reconciliation and redemption in Jesus Christ. Unlike ideological movements, it is willing to sacrifice or lose itself for the truth of the gospel and the well-being of the church. It seeks to confess not a party line (a characteristic of sects) but the holy catholic faith, the faith shared by the entire church.

The substitutionary atoning work of Christ on the cross has special significance for evangelicals. This is not the whole of the gospel, but it is the essence of the gospel. A key verse is I Cor. 15:3: "Christ died for our sins according to the scriptures" (KJV). What is at stake in the battle that evangelicals wage is not only the significance of Christ and the meaning of his salvation but also the integrity of Holy Scripture. Scripture's account of Christ's life, passion, death and resurrection must be seen as trustworthy and reliable.

In stressing the vicarious atoning death of Christ for our sins, evangelicals see this as an act performed not simply by Christ as man but by Christ as God. Various cults incorporate theories of penal redemption and substitutionary atonement but deny the deity of Jesus Christ. The Jehovah's Witnesses are a contemporary example of this aberration.

In evangelical theology, Scripture is the source; the atonement or message of the cross is the central content. Later Protestant orthodoxy referred to the first as the formal norm and the second as the material norm of faith. The incarnation of Christ is, of course, also vigorously affirmed, but always the incarnation seen in the light of the cross. As opposed to the mystical tradition in Catholicism, evangelicalism subordinates the incarnation to the cross, not vice versa. Christ came into the world to save humankind through his dying and rising again. It is not simply the event of the incarnation but the purpose of the incarnation that is decisive for our salvation.

From the evangelical perspective, true Christianity entails *doctrine, experience* and *life*. Whenever any one of these elements is underplayed or denied, something crucial to the faith of the church is lost. The great luminaries of evangelical Christianity—Irenaeus, Augustine, Luther, Calvin, Pascal, Forsyth and Karl Barth—sought to do justice to all these elements, though some assigned more importance to one than to another. It can be said that we are deficiently evangelical if we emphasize the *person* and *work* of Christ and treat lightly the *effect* of Christ in the lives of his people. Evangelicals, particularly in the tradition of Pietism and Puritanism, have underlined the need for regenerate theologians as well as correct theology. Here we see the difference between a formalistic orthodoxy and a vital, biblical faith.

At this point it is appropriate to define *evangelical* more precisely: An evangelical is one who affirms the centrality and cruciality of Christ's work of reconciliation and redemption as declared in the Scriptures; the necessity to appropriate the fruits of this work in one's own life and experience; and the urgency to bring the good news of this act of unmerited grace to a lost and dying world. It is not enough to believe in the cross and resurrection of Christ. We must personally be crucified and buried with Christ and rise with Christ to new life in the Spirit.[20] Yet even this is not all that is required of us. We must also be fired by a burning zeal to share this salvation with others.[21] To be evangelical therefore means to be evangelistic. We are not to hide our light under a bushel but manifest this light so that God might be glorified in the world (Matt. 5:15, 16).

If asked to list the key elements in a vital Christian faith, an evangelical in the classical sense might well reply: biblical fidelity, apostolic doctrine, the experience of salvation, the imperative of discipleship, and the urgency of mission. Holding firm to the doctrine taught by the prophets and apostles in Holy Scripture, evangelicals stress the need for personal experience of the reality of Christ's salvation as well as the need to carry out the great commission to teach all people to be his disciples and to call all nations to repentance.

Undergirding this whole pattern of discipleship and mission is a further element in the evangelical vision: the eschatological hope.

Evangelicals affirm as belonging to the essence of faith not only belief in the first advent of Christ but also hope for his second advent. While the messianic kingdom is already present in the community of faith, this kingdom is yet to be consummated and fulfilled in the kingdom of glory. Evangelicals look forward not to a gradual evolution of humanity into a kingdom of freedom (the Enlightenment position) but to a cataclysmic intervention of the Son of God into human history at his second coming. Yet this eschatological vision not only has an apocalyptic dimension (dualism, supernatural intervention) but also includes elements of the prophetic hope—an earth transfigured by the glory of God.

Evangelical theology not only entails the explication of the message of Scripture, but it is done by those who have experienced the Holy Spirit as the interpreter of Scripture. This means that theology is not only the language about faith but also the language of faith. It cannot be stressed too often that true theology presupposes converted or regenerate theologians.

Evangelicals maintain a high view of Scripture. They affirm its divine authority and its full inspiration by the Holy Spirit. They do not hesitate to speak of the inspiration of words as well as of authors, though this does not commit them to any theory of mechanical inspiration or dictation. They acknowledge Scripture as the medium by which those who earnestly seek hear the voice of the living God (cf. Rom. 16:25, 26). With St. Paul they regard Scripture as "the sword of the Spirit" (Eph. 6:17), the sword by which the powers of sin and death are routed and lives are renewed. Scripture is more than edifying religious literature: It is the divinely chosen vehicle of redeeming grace.

Furthermore, evangelicals have a high view of God. They affirm his sovereignty over the world he created. In contrast to many immanentalist theologians today, they have no difficulty in addressing God as "Lord" and "Master," even though they also see him as Savior and Friend, but he is Lord before he is Savior, Master before he is Friend. What Kierkegaard called the infinite qualitative distinction between God and humanity, eternity and time, is integral to evangelical faith. Even when they speak of the mystical union between Christ and the believer, they are acutely aware that this union does not obliterate but instead more fully reveals the abysmal gulf between deity and humanity. In upholding the sovereignty of God, evangelicals also affirm the sovereignty and sufficiency of his grace. The word of God goes forth from him mightily and does not return to him void (Isa. 55:11).

Similarly, evangelicalism emphasizes the sovereign love of God, the love that conquers and does not simply accept. This love, moreover, is a holy love, since God is infinite majesty and holiness as well as boundless compassion. These attributes are inseparable, yet distinct. They were fully reconciled in the incarnation and cross of Jesus Christ where God both satisfied the demands of his holy law and demonstrated his incomparable self-giving love that goes beyond the law.

Despite a profound sense of absolute dependence on God, evangelicals are reluctant to speak of God's absolute power, since this connotes arbitrariness or lawlessness. They prefer to speak of God's sovereign will and to understand this as a will to love. Instead of focusing on the power of God's eternal decree, they dwell on the power of his suffering yet conquering love. In contrast, theologies that concentrate on the unrestricted, absolute power of God as well as those that posit a secret will of God at variance with his revealed will are in philosophical rather than biblical territory. To be evangelical means to affirm both the invincibility and the universal outreach of God's love. Indeed, the heart of the gospel message is that God loved the whole world, that he justified the ungodly even while they were yet in their sins (cf. John 3:16; Rom. 4:5; 5:6).

Finally, evangelicals have a high view of man. We were given dominion over the animals and made a little lower than the angels (Ps. 8:5–8 KJV). We were created in the image of God and elected for salvation by God. We were even chosen to be covenant partners with God. Yet evangelical theology does not have an exaggerated view of humanity. There is no identity with God even in the exalted state of mystical union. Nor is there deification if this means being transformed into divinity.

Evangelicals are pessimistic with regard to what human beings can do on their own but optimistic about what God can accomplish in and through them. Grace does not reduce man to nothingness but instead raises him to fellowship with his Creator. Irenaeus put it succinctly: "The glory of God is man fully alive." Amandus Polanus, sixteenth-century Basel professor and Reformer, stated the complementary truth: "The glory of man is the living God." In other words, the glory of man lies outside himself in Jesus Christ.

While recognizing the myriad possibilities given to humanity in creation and the new powers of faith, hope and love given in redemption, evangelical theology is agonizingly aware of the lostness and despair of humanity as well. It fully accepts the biblical testimony that sin has penetrated into every area of human existence, thereby distorting and corrupting the creative accomplishments of humankind (Ps. 14:1–3; 36:1–4; 53:1–3; Isa. 64:6; Jer. 17:9; Rom. 3:9–12, 23; 7:18; Eph. 2:3; 4:18). It is not averse to speaking of the bondage of the will, the incapacity of sinful human beings to come to God or to do the good that God demands. Although fallen humanity is still free in the things below, it is not free in the things above—in the area of morality and salvation. As sinners we still have free choice, the freedom to do what we please, but it is only by grace that we receive the liberty of the children of God, the freedom to do what pleases God.

EVANGELICALISM, ORTHODOXY AND FUNDAMENTALISM

From this list of theological distinctives, it might be inferred that evangelicalism is merely a form of traditionalism or what might be called orthodoxism. Such is far from the case. Evangelicalism seeks to be orthodox, but it places its orthodoxy under the judgment of the Word of God. The ruling norm for faith is not the creeds and confessions of the church, nor the consensus of the church fathers, nor the affirmations of the Reformers (though all of these may function as subordinate norms). Instead, the infallible standard is the biblical Christ whose word is communicated through and attested in Holy Scripture. Church tradition also serves as a vehicle and witness of the living Word of God, but as a secondary, not a primary witness (unlike Holy Scripture).

Evangelical theology holds that what Christ says today does not contradict what his witnesses say in Scripture but may go beyond it, as the Spirit of Christ clarifies and makes explicit what may be only implicit in the text. Against an orthodoxy that is content to live in the past and does not seek a fresh word from God in Scripture, evangelical theology shares the confidence of the Puritan divine John

Robinson that "the Lord has more light and truth yet to break forth out of his holy Word."

At the same time, evangelicals vigorously object to the current tendency in neo-Protestantism to draw a cleavage between God's self-revelation in Christ and the biblical testimony. We have this revelation only in the earthen vessel of the prophetic and apostolic witness in the Bible. To bypass this witness or to seek a Word that in effect supersedes this witness is to veer either toward rationalism, in which we interpret the Bible through the eyes of a secular philosophy, or toward mysticism, in which we try to get beyond words and concepts altogether. Neo-Protestants following Schleiermacher and Hegel often appeal to the Spirit over the Bible. But the Spirit does not overthrow God's inspired Word, but instead enables us to hear it anew, to understand it rightly, and to apply it to our lives.

Doctrinal orthodoxy will always rank high on the agenda in authentic evangelicalism, but orthodoxy in thought is never enough: We must also have orthodoxy in life, orthopractice. Christian practice is as necessary as Christian doctrine, though in some periods of history one of these will probably have to be stressed more than the other. The evangelical seeks to be not only a herald of the true gospel but also a servant of the One who has embodied this truth.

Just as evangelicalism is not to be identified with an orthodoxy oriented to the past or divorced from life, so it must not be confused with fundamentalism. Fundamentalism as a folk religion elevates human traditions to practically the same level as God's self-revelation in Christ, attaching inordinate importance to such things as the pre-tribulation rapture, the seven dispensations, Sabbatarianism, and the various taboos on liquor, tobacco, dancing, the theater, etc.

The preaching of the gospel, it might be supposed, would be central in worship services of fundamentalist churches. The sad but irrefutable fact is that in many cases the sermons consist largely of reductionist Bible studies (in which the biblical passage is reduced to a topic of current interest) instead of the proclamation of the good news of God's act of reconciliation in Jesus Christ.[22] In some of these so-called biblical sermons, the grace of Christ is barely mentioned, and what we then have is the preaching of law rather than gospel. Equally disturbing is the frequency with which sectarian themes form the content of the sermonic witness rather than God's saving work in Jesus Christ. Or the preacher begins sharing his own personal experiences, and the gospel is then in danger of being confused with an interior state of subjective illumination.[23] Still another temptation is to politicize the gospel, to show how faith in God undergirds the American Way of Life. Here as elsewhere an affinity can be discerned between cultural fundamentalism and an accommodationist religious liberalism.[24]

Evangelicalism unashamedly stands for the fundamentals of the historic faith, but as a movement it transcends and corrects the defensive, sectarian mentality commonly associated with fundamentalism. Though many, perhaps most, fundamentalists are evangelicals, evangelical Christianity is wider and deeper than fundamentalism, which is basically a movement of reaction in the churches in this period of history. Evangelicalism in the classical sense fulfills the basic goals and aspirations of fundamentalism but rejects the ways in which these goals are realized.

III

The New Conservatism

We do not belong to our Lord Jesus Christ, nor can we be of God's church, except it be by following the pure doctrine of the law and the gospel.

JOHN CALVIN

Orthodoxy is a willingness to fight and, if necessary, die for the continuity and authenticity of the tradition.

THOMAS ODEN

So carnal is the body of Christians which composes the conservative wing of the Church, so shockingly irreverent are our public services in some quarters, so degraded are our religious tastes in still others, that the need for [sanctifying] power could scarcely have been greater at any time in history.

A. W. TOZER

He who boasts of orthodoxy . . . sins against Justification by Christ alone, for he justifies himself by appeal to his own beliefs or his own formulations of belief and thereby does despite to the Truth and Grace of Christ. Once a Church begins to boast of its "orthodoxy" it begins to fall from Grace.

THOMAS TORRANCE

THEOLOGICALLY CONSIDERED, the new conservatism is by no means a monolithic movement. It includes a wide variety of people from the far right to the right of center on the theological spectrum. Depending on one's perspective, it even embraces some who could properly be classified as centrist and yet who are especially intent on preserving the abiding values and essential doctrines of the historic faith. All of the various strands in the new conservatism would gladly accept the term "evangelical" with very few exceptions (mainly on the far right). Even pastors and theologians who stand in the theological tradition of Karl Barth and Emil Brunner have no compunction in identifying themselves as evangelical, though the left wing of the neo-orthodox movement might feel uncomfortable with this designation.[1]

In this chapter I shall delineate the various movements that are part of the new theological conservatism and name persons and churches associated with each one. I shall be frank in stating my own allegiance and showing where the future of a vital evangelical Christianity lies.

FUNDAMENTALISM

Fundamentalism represents the right wing of the evangelical movement, though it contains thrusts and ideas that signify a divergence from classical Protestant orthodoxy. Essentially, fundamentalism is a phenomenon of the late nineteenth century and the twentieth century. It arose specifically to counter the growing modernism in the churches, evidenced in the often uncritical acceptance of the theory of evolution and the historical-critical method in biblical interpretation. Fundamentalism has thus for the most part been a defensive movement designed to safeguard the supernatural elements in the faith.

The movement derived its name from twelve pamphlets entitled *The Fundamentals: A Testimony to the Truth,* published from 1910 to 1915.[2] It took on a more organized form in May of 1919, which saw the convening of the World Conference on Christian Fundamentals in Philadelphia. Among the doctrines affirmed were the divine inspiration of Scripture, the deity of Christ, the substitutionary atonement, the creation and fall of man and the personal and imminent return of Christ. On the whole, fundamentalism has stressed the plenary, verbal inspiration of Scripture, and only in its later development has special emphasis been placed on biblical inerrancy.[3]

One of the hallmarks of fundamentalism is the inordinate attention given to eschatology. Besides the visible, imminent return of Christ, it has generally upheld the millennial reign of Christ on earth before the final consummation of all things in the kingdom of God. This premillennial doctrine differentiates fundamentalism from the theology of the Reformation (which was basically amillennial) and from the Puritans and Pietists (who were generally postmillennial).[4] One strand of fundamentalism has adopted the dispensational form of premillennialism in which history is said to be divided into seven dispensations, the last of which will be the millennial reign of Christ from an earthly Jerusalem. Dispensationalism makes a sharp distinction between the church and the messianic kingdom of Christ and speaks of the rapture of the saints into glory before the great tribulation that immediately precedes the premillennial coming of Christ. Dispensationalism was given special promotion in the widely circulated *Scofield Reference Bible.*

Another hallmark of fundamentalism is its separatism. This is most prominent among the dispensationalists, who dwell on the twilight of the church in the end times and the need to separate from the apostate (mainline) churches. Fundamentalists like to appeal to Paul's warning against fellowship between the children of light and the children of darkness (II Cor. 6:14). The hard core of the fundamentalist movement has expressed its displeasure with Billy Graham because of his willingness to cooperate with nonfundamentalist Christians in his evangelistic crusades. Graham's participation in a Russian Orthodox-sponsored peace conference in Moscow (May, 1982), in which he acknowledged a certain degree of religious freedom in the Soviet Union, has further riled the evangelical right wing.

In the area of epistemology, fundamentalism represents a kind of evangelical rationalism, since it identifies the revelation of God with the propositions of Scripture. Its approach is either deductive, by which we deduce logical conclusions from metaphysical first principles (as with Gordon Clark) or inductive, by which we reason from particular facts to general conclusions (as with Charles Hodge). Being a defensive movement, fundamentalism gravitates toward an apologetic theology which seeks to justify the tenets of the faith at the bar of reason. Any conflict between reason and revelation is due either to faulty logic or to a misleading use of Scripture. One of their critics contends that for fundamentalists "saving faith" is indistinguishable from "warranted belief," belief validated by the canons of scientific rationality.[5] Not all fundamentalists elevate reason over faith, but even a theologian like Cornelius Van Til, who argues that one must begin with faith presuppositions, calls Christianity "an absolute rationalism."

Fundamentalism is also noted for its emphasis on individual salvation and the church's spiritual mission. Needless to say, it has been conspicuously deficient in the areas of ecclesiology and social ethics. This is not to suggest, however, that it is without a social vision. The early fundamentalists were one of the main forces behind the prohibition movement, and their spiritual descendants are active in the right-to-life and antipornography movements. Yet its social message can be criticized for focusing on curtailing wayward human passions while neglecting the plight of the economically deprived and the politically oppressed (including racial and ethnic minorities).

What has prevented fundamentalism from being in the foreground in the battle against social injustice is its tacit and sometimes open alliance with capitalism.[6] It is common in these circles to identify Christian values and the American Way of Life, and to regard economic prosperity as a providential sign of sanctity.

Fundamentalism as a religious movement is a complex phenomenon, and there is some disagreement in scholarly circles on how it should be defined. Ernest Sandeen sees the roots of fundamentalism in the coalescing of the eschatological views of the Plymouth Brethren and the late scholastic orthodoxy of the so-called Princeton School of Theology (Charles Hodge, A. A. Hodge, Benjamin Warfield).[7] George Marsden regards fundamentalism as a broader movement, including a large part of the revival tradition, and argues that it is the direct heir of nineteenth-century evangelicalism.[8] In my estimation, fundamentalism is a distinctly modern expression of historic evangelicalism, reflecting as well as obscuring significant motifs and emphases of the evangelical heritage.

One strand of fundamentalism has its roots in evangelical Pietism. The spirituality of this group is manifested in the Bible and missionary conferences that still continue across the nation and in other countries. The other strand is closer to confessional or scholastic orthodoxy. Its conferences are inclined to be of a more intellectual nature, with an emphasis on points of doctrinal precision. The Philadelphia Conference on Reformed Theology is an heir to this particular tradition, though the sponsors of the conference have moved from a rigid fundamentalist posture and are better classified as neofundamentalist or neoevangelical.[9]

Fundamentalism has made special inroads in the Presbyterian and Baptist churches. Pockets of fundamentalism remain in the Presbyterian Church (U.S.A.), the Reformed Church in America, the American Lutheran Church, the Lutheran Church in America, the American Baptist Churches in the U.S.A., and the Southern Baptist Convention.

Churches today that stand more or less in the tradition of separatistic fundamentalism are the following: the General Association of Regular Baptist Churches, the Conservative Baptist Association of America, the Independent Fundamental Churches of America, the Independent Fundamental Bible Churches, the Baptist Bible Fellowship, the Fundamental Baptist Fellowship, the Bible Presbyterian Church, the Missionary Church, the Christian (Plymouth) Brethren, the Fellowship of Grace Brethren Churches, the Fellowship of Independent Evangelical Churches and Grace Gospel Fellowship. There are some other denominations that have been noticeably influenced by fundamentalism, but their ethnic or confessional particularity differentiates them from the wider fundamentalist movement. They include the Lutheran Church–Missouri Synod; the Wisconsin Evangelical Lutheran Synod; the Churches of Christ; and the Reformed Episcopal Church. Parachurch movements that can be categorized as fundamentalist are the American Council of Churches, the International Council of Churches, the World Fundamentalist Fellowship, Word of Life, Youth for Christ, Operation Mobilization and Campus Crusade for Christ.

Theological schools reflecting the fundamentalist mentality include Dallas Theological Seminary, School of Religion of Bob Jones University, Grace Theological Seminary, Capital Bible Seminary, Western Conservative Baptist Seminary, Liberty Baptist College and Seminary, Luther Rice Theological Seminary, and Faith Evangelical Lutheran Seminary. One could add to this list a large number of Bible schools, for example the Criswell Bible Institute, the Moody Bible Institute, Northeastern Bible College, the Multnomah School of the Bible, Washington Bible College, the Philadelphia College of the Bible and the Prairie Bible Institute. Some of these institutions (such as Dallas Seminary and the Moody Bible Institute) represent a more open fundamentalism, not averse to cooperating with other evangelical Christians. Others (such as Bob Jones University) typify a closed fundamentalism, which anathematizes those who engage in fellowship with Christians regarded as heterodox.

A number of publishing houses are committed to advancing the fundamentalist cause: the Moody Press, Vision House, Victor Books (Scripture Press), Regal Books, and Loizeaux Brothers. Some of these also publish books from authors whose spiritual affinities are closer to neofundamentalism and neoevangelicalism.

Magazines that mirror the fundamentalist ethos are the *Fundamentalist Journal*, publishing arm of Jerry Falwell's ministry; the *Southern Baptist Journal;* the *Baptist Bible Tribune; Christian News; Sword of the Lord; Christian Beacon; Bibliotheca Sacra,* a high-powered theological journal based at Dallas Seminary; *Voice,* published by the Independent Fundamental Churches of America; *Moody Monthly;* and *Lutherans Alert.*

Among the spiritual leaders and philosophical lights of the fundamentalist movement in its early days were William B. Riley, Arthur T. Pierson, Charles R. Erdman, J. Frank Norris, Clarence E. Macartney, Arno C. Gaebelein, T. T. Shields and R. A. Torrey. More recent on the scene are John R. Rice, Carl McIntire, Ian Paisley, J. Oliver Buswell, Cornelius Van Til, Gordon Clark, John F. Walvoord, Robert Lightner,[10] René Pache, Hal Lindsey, James Robison and Jerry Falwell.[11] Princeton Theological Seminary professors Benjamin Warfield and A. A. Hodge, whose roots lay in the older scholastic Calvinist orthodoxy, prepared the way for fundamentalism by contending that Scripture is without error in matters of science and history as well as faith and morals.[12] Norman Geisler, professor of systematic theology at Dallas Seminary seeks to combine Thomism and dispensationalism. His empathies are with an open fundamentalism that is willing to engage in dialogue with opposing views.[13] J. Gresham Machen, one of the founders of Westminster Theological Seminary, rejected the fundamentalist label and preferred to be known simply as "orthodox."

In recent years political movements such as Jerry Falwell's Moral Majority, Christian Voice and Religious Roundtable indicate that a resurgent fundamentalism is breaking away from privatism and individualism. Among characteristic themes of these movements are the right to life, a strong military defense, the integrity of the family, the evil of forced busing, prayer in the public schools and free enterprise. Their strength belies the ever recurring rumor that fundamentalism is in eclipse.[14]

Fundamentalism at its best has preserved the supernatural dimension of the faith in an age when the mainline churches and seminaries have too readily accepted the naturalistic presuppositions of the higher critics. It has also maintained a needed critical stance toward the theory of evolution, whose scientific basis is still very much in question.[15] Again, it has fostered personal fellowships of faith where the innermost needs and concerns of its people are satisfied, where the koinonia (fellowship of love) is very much in evidence. The recent involvement of fundamentalism in politics is not altogether to be deplored. Though it is inclined to oversimplify and take an absolutist position against abortion, its advocacy of the rights of the unborn child is consistent with the historic Christian witness on this question. Fundamentalism, moreover, has continued the strong missionary emphasis that certainly belongs to a vital evangelical Christianity.

At its worst, fundamentalism has promoted divisiveness in the church by elevating sectarian tenets (such as the pretribulation rapture) into doctrinal essentials. It has also been guilty of maintaining a docetic view of Scripture which in fact denies the true humanity of Scripture. By refusing to deal with the question of historical and cultural conditioning in the writing of Scripture and by insisting on the literal facticity of practically everything reported in Scripture, it encourages obscurantism and thereby sets up false stumbling blocks to faith. Finally, in the area of interpersonal relationships, fundamentalism can be justly accused of promoting a rigid patriarchalism which has denied to women their rightful role in the ministry of the church.

NEOEVANGELICALISM

Since the end of the Second World War, there has been a significant shift in the attitudes and concerns of many of those who have come out of fundamentalism. While the doctrinal basis is still more or less intact, the emphasis has changed, and it is therefore appropriate to speak of a "neoevangelical" movement. This is one of the principal strands in the emerging new evangelicalism, which is broader and deeper than any one movement or school. Neoevangelicalism seeks to relate the historic evangelical faith to current needs and problems in the church and in the wider society.

Within neoevangelicalism, moreover, two distinct strands can be detected. The first signifies a cautious opening to modern trends which might best be described as neofundamentalism. The second is a more progressive evangelicalism which seeks to move beyond a rigid position on biblical inerrancy. Both these movements wish to be known as evangelical rather than fundamentalist, but only the second is inclined to reject the fundamentalist label.

While the right wing of the neoevangelical movement is particularly insistent on the inerrancy of Scripture, the moderate and left wings prefer to speak of the infallibility of Scripture.[16] Following Hodge and Warfield, the right-wing evangelicals nonetheless qualify inerrancy, claiming that only the original manuscripts or autographs (which are no longer available) are without error. This allows for critical textual work on the various copies and translations. When moderate neoevangelicals employ the term "inerrancy" in reference to Scripture, they generally have in mind its teaching or doctrine.

A rationalistic apologetics is still very much in evidence among neoevangelicals; at the same time, there is an attempt to dialogue with antirationalistic modern philosophies and learn from them. As in the older fundamentalism, there is a special interest in the rise of the cults and the need to meet this challenge. The task of reconciling the conflicting claims of science and religion is also a major preoccupation.[17] Among the moderate and left-wing evangelicals, there is a marked openness to theistic evolution, the idea that God is at work in the process of evolution.[18] C. S. Lewis is held in high esteem by almost all neoevangelicals and is considered a model in the apologetic task.

In contrast to the older fundamentalism, neoevangelicals have not hesitated to speak out on the problems of race, poverty and war. Carl Henry's *The Uneasy Conscience of Modern Fundamentalism* was a harbinger of an awakened evangelical social consciousness.[19] Neoevangelicals have also become involved in the right-to-life movement, but they generally maintain a critical stance toward the political new right.

An openness to Christians of other traditions is another salient feature of neoevangelicalism, marking a definite break with the separatistic mentality of the older fundamentalism. The emphasis is no longer on *separation* from the mainline denominations but rather on the *infiltration* of these denominations. Many people who can be categorized as neoevangelical cooperated in the ecumenical evangelistic campaign known as Key '73, and nearly all identify with the Billy Graham crusades, which sometimes even have Catholic sponsorship. The anti-Catholicism that has so often tainted fundamentalism is not nearly so evident in neoevangelicalism; yet there is a continued resistance to many of the emphases and practices within Catholicism.

Among neoevangelicals, premillennialism recedes into the background, though this is still the dominant position of those on the right. Many moderate and left-wing evangelicals are moving toward amillennialism and some even toward postmillennialism.[20] All neoevangelicals are united with their fundamentalist brethren in affirming the second advent of Christ and seeing it as a cataclysmic intervention into human history.

Whereas fundamentalists of the dispensational variety look to late nineteenth-century revivalism and those of the Reformed variety appeal to the Calvinistic Reformation and Protestant orthodoxy, neoevangelicals are ready to include among their spiritual forbears not only the Reformers and their orthodox interpreters but also the Pietists and Puritans. The Puritans in particular are being increasingly appreciated, especially in the neo-Reformed strand of neoevangelicalism.

In the area of biblical interpretation, we find a growing diversity in the ranks of neoevangelicalism. In the right wing, there is a general acceptance of textual or lower criticism but still a profound distrust of higher or historical-literary criticism. The moderate and left-wing neoevangelicals have no difficulty in accepting historical investigation of Scripture, including even form and redaction criticism, but they are emphatic that such investigation must be separated from the naturalistic presuppositions that have dominated this kind of study in the past.[21] Moderate evangelicals now stress the need to discover the intention of the author in the hermeneutical task. Those in the neofundamentalist camp continue to hold to the Mosaic authorship of the Pentateuch, the single authorship of Isaiah, the early date for Daniel, and the first eleven chapters of Genesis as literal history. A growing number of evangelical scholars, however, are willing to entertain other positions.

Neoevangelicals generally hold to propositional revelation, but not all are willing to equate revelation with the very words of Scripture. While recognizing that revelation may take propositional form, they are acutely aware that it contains a personal and historical dimension as well. Bernard Ramm prefers "conceptual revelation" to "propositional revelation," since the latter term tends to reduce faith to mental assent and pictures God as "dictating Euclidean theological statements to the prophets and apostles."[22] For Carl Henry, on the other hand, revelation, even though mediated through history and personality, is essentially ideational and propositional.[23]

The left wing of the new evangelical movement sees as the main theological issue not the inerrancy of Scripture (as in the right wing) nor biblical hermeneutics (as in the moderate wing) but the authenticity of a gospel existence. It is not right doctrine nor methods of biblical interpretation but faithfulness in vocation that should be given top priority. Some of the new breed of evangelicals sense an affinity to liberation theology, but they generally eschew violence as a means of accomplishing social justice, and they are not hesitant to subject the Marxist analysis of society to the scrutiny of Scripture. One part of the evangelical left is also involved in the feminist movement, though it repudiates the call of radical feminists for a new religion. Paul Jewett takes issue with many evangelical feminists in resisting their demand for a new inclusive gender language regarding God and Christ.[24]

Evangelical theologians who still move within the thought patterns of fundamentalism but try to engage in dialogue with the modern world include Francis Schaeffer, R. C. Sproul, James Boice, James Packer, Harold O. J. Brown, John Gerstner, John Warwick Montgomery and Harold Lindsell. Scholars noted for their ecumenical openness and innovative spirit but who generally remain within the framework of the Hodge-Warfield position on biblical authority and inerrancy are Carl Henry, Roger Nicole, John R. W. Stott, Morris Inch, Vernon Grounds, Ronald Nash and Kenneth Kantzer. Other scholars have questioned the emphasis on inerrancy but still see the Bible as the infallible standard for faith and practice. Among these are Clark Pinnock, F. F. Bruce, Bernard Ramm, H. M. Kuitert, Ray S. Anderson, Stephen Davis, Bruce Metzger, George Eldon Ladd, Kenneth Grider, Robert Johnston, Richard Coleman, Jack Rogers, Richard Mouw, James Daane, Ward Gasque, Paul Jewett, Lewis Smedes, M. Eugene Osterhaven and Timothy L. Smith. Not all these theologians would jettison the term "inerrancy," but they would reinterpret it in order to do justice to the true humanity of Scripture. The Lausanne Covenant, which declares that the Bible is "without error in all that it affirms," reflects the viewpoint of the dominant stream in neoevangelicalism today.[25]

Magazines that mirror the new mood in evangelicalism include *Eternity, Christian Scholar's Review, United Evangelical Action, Crux, The Evangelical Quarterly, Evangel* and *Evangelical Newsletter*. Concerns of the evangelical right find expression in the *Journal of the Evangelical Theological Society, The Westminster Theological Journal* and *Trinity Journal*. The influential *Christianity Today,* which reaches a wide and ever-growing audience, seeks to speak for both the evangelical right and center. *The Presbyterian Journal* has a similar orientation except that its clientele is mainly Reformed and Presbyterian. More avant-garde are *TSF Bulletin* (edited by Mark Branson) and *Themelios,* both reflecting concerns of the Theological Students Fellowship (the seminary branch of Inter-Varsity Christian Fellowship). Representing the evangelical left are *Sojourners, The Other Side, Radix, Katallagete* and the *Wittenburg Door*. The first freely acknowledges its indebtedness to the Anabaptists.

Neoevangelicalism has also made an impact among publishing companies. Those addressing themselves to neoevangelical concerns but still seeking to retain their fundamentalist constituency include Zondervan Publishing House, Thomas Nelson, Baker Book House, Tyndale House Publishers and Banner of Truth Publishing Company. More receptive to new trends in theology and the church but still unreservedly evangelical are the William B. Eerdmans Publishing Company, InterVarsity Press, Fleming H. Revell, Word Books and Paternoster Press.

Seminaries that are open to the new mood but retain distinctives associated with fundamentalism (such as premillennialism and biblical inerrancy) are Trinity Evangelical Divinity School, Denver

Theological Seminary, Covenant Theological Seminary and Talbot Theological Seminary (the last can also be placed in the category of open fundamentalism). Some other schools have moved further from fundamentalism but still preserve the evangelical heritage: Fuller Theological Seminary, Gordon-Conwell Seminary, Anderson School of Theology, Bethel Theological Seminary, Regent College, Eastern Mennonite Seminary, Eastern Baptist Theological Seminary, North Park Theological Seminary, Southwestern Baptist Theological Seminary at Fort Worth, Asbury Theological Seminary, Nazarene Theological Seminary and Trinity Episcopal School for Ministry in Ambridge, Pennsylvania.

Churches where neoevangelicalism has made a significant impact include the Evangelical Free Church, the General Conference Baptists, the Conservative Baptist Association of America, the Evangelical Covenant Church, the Salvation Army, the Evangelical Church of North America, the Wesleyan Church, the Church of the Nazarene, the Church of God (Anderson, Indiana), the Christian and Missionary Alliance, the American Baptist Churches in the U.S.A., the Southern Baptist Convention and nearly all the Presbyterian communions.

In the mainline denominations, various evangelical renewal fellowships seek to reform the church from within: the Lutheran Evangelical Movement (in the American Lutheran Church), Presbyterians United for Biblical Concerns (in the Presbyterian Church [U.S.A.]), the Presbyterian Lay Committee (in the PCUSA), the Covenant Fellowship of Presbyterians (in the PCUSA), the Fellowship of Witness (in the Episcopal Church), United Church People for Biblical Witness (in the United Church of Christ), the American Baptist Fellowship (in the American Baptist Church), the Brethren Revival Fellowship (in the Church of the Brethren), the National Evangelistic Association (in the Disciples of Christ), the United Church Renewal Fellowship (in the United Church of Canada) and the Good News movement (in the United Methodist Church).

Other parachurch movements reflecting an ecumenical kind of evangelicalism are the National Association of Evangelicals, the Evangelical Theological Society, World Vision, the Inter-Varsity Christian Fellowship, the International Fellowship of Evangelical Students, Young Life and the World Evangelical Fellowship.

What is important to recognize is that every person and fellowship mentioned in this section, as in the rest of the chapter, is moving. While some may be neoevangelical or neofundamentalist in this period, in another few years they may belong more properly in another category. Some neoevangelicals are returning to fundamentalism, whereas others are breaking through to a catholic vision of the church.

It should also be borne in mind that the various persons and groups mentioned have more in common than might be supposed. Evangelicals of all varieties sense an affinity to one another that simply does not exist, for example, between evangelicals and ideological liberals. Evangelicals, unlike Catholics and liberals, steadfastly affirm the divine authority and primacy of Holy Scripture over the church and religious experience. The tragedy is that they have frequently given more attention to those things that divide rather than unite them.

CONFESSIONALIST EVANGELICALISM

Besides the evangelicals coming out of Protestant fundamentalism, where the revival tradition plays a major role, many of those who call themselves both conservative and evangelical stand in the tradition of Protestant confessionalism. All evangelicals are confessional in the sense of confessing Christ as Lord and Savior, but I am thinking here of statements of faith that function together with the Bible as standards for faith and conduct. While the confession of faith is never placed on the same level as Scripture, it frequently carries the force of a divine mandate. Those who are confessional in this sense include the old Lutherans and the old Reformed, those who pride themselves on being Lutheran or Calvinist.

Confessionalist evangelicals seek to preserve continuity with the Protestant Reformation, and especially with the confessions of the Reformation or those that are in accord with Reformation faith. Conservative Lutherans are inclined to uphold both the Augsburg Confession and the Formula of Concord. Reformed Christians of continental lineage are particularly fond of the Heidelberg Catechism, the Belgic Confession and the Canons of the Synod of Dort. Anglo-Saxon Reformed Christians generally adhere to the Westminster Confession of Faith.

Confessionalist evangelicals distinguish themselves from fundamentalists by the important role they assign to the teaching authority of the church. While the church is always under Scripture, the Spirit of God, they believe, guides the church in its interpretation of Scripture. The church's interpretation must itself be subjected to the scrutiny of Scripture, but in fact they often read Scripture through the eyes of the confession rather than vice versa.

Among confessionalist evangelicals there is a growing social awareness as well as an increasing openness to critical biblical study. Horace Hummel's *The Word Becoming Flesh* demonstrates how a respected Missouri Synod Lutheran scholar using the tools of historical-literary investigation understands the formation of the Pentateuch and other Old Testament writings.[26] While adhering to the tradition of Mosaic authorship, he contends that much of the original material was amplified and supplemented by redactors.

Theologians in recent times who would identify themselves as confessionalist evangelicals include Fred Klooster, Horace Hummel, Anthony Hoekema, Cornelius Van Til, Martin Scharlemann, Edmund Schlink, Robert Preus, David Scaer, Paul Althaus, Ford Lewis Battles, G. C. Berkouwer, Peter Beyerhaus, Gerhard Maier and Walter Künneth. The last three have been active in the No Other Gospel movement (*Kein Anderes Evangelium*) in Germany. A much more irenic spirit is present in G. C. Berkouwer, who has been a source of inspiration to many neoevangelicals, especially to those of Presbyterian and Reformed backgrounds.

Theological schools that seek to be evangelical within a confessionalist context are Concordia Seminary (St. Louis), Concordia Theological Seminary (Fort Wayne, Indiana), Calvin Theological Seminary, Wisconsin Lutheran Seminary and Reformed Theological Seminary (Jackson, Mississippi). The last school, as well as Westminster Theological Seminary, contains both confessionalist and neoevangelical strands. Western Theological Seminary in Holland, Michigan, an institution of the Reformed Church in America, is confessionalist in its background, but it now has a neo-orthodox slant.

In the publishing world Concordia Publishing House, Northwestern Publishing House, Presbyterian & Reformed Publishing Company and Verdict Publications tend to maintain a confessionalist evangelical stance. The last is perhaps more neo-Reformational than confessionalist, but it has had a high regard for such confessions as the Lutheran Formula of Concord.

Verdict Ministries is of special significance, since it was founded by ex-Seventh-Day Adventists who rediscovered the message of the Reformation, particularly salvation by the righteousness of God apprehended by faith alone. Like the old Lutherans, Robert Brinsmead, editor of *Verdict* magazine, contends for a forensic, extrinsic justification, the kind portrayed in the Formula of Concord. At the same time, Brinsmead is adamant that the gospel alone is the final criterion and that it takes priority over every creedal or doctrinal formula. Verdict Ministries is steadily becoming more critical of classical Protestantism.

A number of magazines consciously promote a confessionalist evangelicalism: *Concordia Monthly; The Banner; Calvin Theological Journal; The Journal of Theology*, representing the Church of the Lutheran Confession; and the *Wisconsin Lutheran Quarterly*. *Lutherans Alert* is both confessionalist and neofundamentalist. *The Reformed Journal* brings together motifs drawn from both confessional Reformed theology and neo-orthodoxy.

Churches that can be called confessionalist evangelical are the American Lutheran Church; the Lutheran Church–Missouri Synod; Association of Evangelical Lutheran Congregations; the Wisconsin Evangelical Lutheran Synod; the Christian Reformed Church; the Reformed Church in America; the Protestant Reformed Churches in America; the Church of the Lutheran Confession; the Orthodox Presbyterian Church; and the Presbyterian Church in America. The new Presbyterian Church (U.S.A.) does not have any one guiding confession of faith but a book of confessions, which provides some kind of normativeness in the area of doctrine and conduct but which is frequently treated historically rather than juridically, as comprising statements that command allegiance. The confessional basis of the old United Presbyterian Church (now part of the PCUSA) was strengthened at its General Assembly in 1981 in that ordinands were required to "sincerely adhere" to the Book of Confessions. Not surprisingly, there was massive resistance to this proposed change.

The strength of confessionalist evangelicalism lies in its recognition that God is at work in the history of the church as well as in the history of biblical times, that the message of the gospel has been rediscovered and interpreted anew in certain periods of ecclesiastical history. Its weakness is that by emphasizing the merits of the creeds and confessions of the Reformation, it tends to underplay the working of the Spirit in the ecclesiastical history prior to the Reformation. There is also the temptation to absolutize the position of the Reformation so that confessional statements are seen no longer as broken symbols needing to be fulfilled in new interpretations but as sacrosanct symbols having eternal validity. The way is then open to a creedal idolatry, which confessionalist evangelicalism at its best rightly abhors.

CHARISMATIC RELIGION

Still another branch of the new conservatism is the movement of the charismatic or latter rain revival. I am here including traditional Pentecostalism as well as neo-Pentecostalism, the charismatic renewal within the mainline churches. Pentecostalism began at the turn of the century with the manifestation of glossolalia in a Holiness prayer meeting at Bethel Bible College in Topeka, Kansas. Charles Parham, founder of the college, and William Seymour, a black Holiness preacher and pastor of the famed Azusa Street Mission in Los Angeles, were the two men most prominent in the beginnings of modern Pentecostalism. Neo-Pentecostalism dates back to 1960, when a rediscovery of the charismatic gifts (especially the charism of tongues) described in I Corinthians 12–14 took place at St. Mark's Episcopal Church in Van Nuys, California, under the ministry of Dennis Bennett. The Catholic charismatic movement was born in Duquesne University in Pittsburgh in 1966.

Out of Pentecostalism and neo-Pentecostalism have emerged various charismatic theologies which seek to articulate the experience of the baptism of the Holy Spirit with its accompanying gifts, notably speaking in tongues. Originally the gift of tongues was thought to be the empirical evidence of having received the Holy Spirit, but in Pentecostal and neo-Pentecostal bodies today there is great diversity in this as in other areas. Some charismatic theologians regard speaking in tongues as only one of the evidences of the baptism of the Spirit.[27] Others virtually equate the baptism of the Spirit and the new birth, though most view Spirit baptism as an experience subsequent to conversion.

Where charismatic theology differs from mainstream evangelical theology is in its emphasis on the gifts of the Spirit and the present work of the Spirit in addition to biblical fidelity. Special attention is given to healing, the discernment of spirits, miracles, the word of knowledge, prophecy, speaking in tongues and the interpretation of tongues.

While classical evangelicalism has underscored the need to walk by faith alone, charismatic theologians contend that signs and wonders will follow the preaching of the Word. Frequently appealing to Hebrews 2:4 and Mark 16:17, 18, they believe that these signs are given to induce faith and confirm faith.

Whereas church tradition, both Catholic and Protestant, has generally perceived the Holy Spirit as an invisible and transcendent reality, charismatics regard the Holy Spirit as a demonstrable, empirical reality. God is not the Wholly Other of Barthianism nor is he the undifferentiated unity of mysticism. Instead, he is the power of creative transformation that revitalizes the believer from within, and this power can be felt and experienced.

A dualistic perspective is another hallmark of charismatic theology. In historic evangelicalism, the human predicament is believed to be rooted in an inherited spiritual affliction (original sin); for charismatic evangelicalism, on the other hand, the key to human misery is being held captive by a foreign power (the devil). While traditional faith stresses human bondage to sin, charismatic religion speaks of being victimized by the devil. Though not denying that sin and death are also major problems confronting the human race, it focuses primarily on the need to combat the demonic adversary to God and man called Satan, Lucifer or the devil.

In addition to the devil, charismatic theology also warns against demons which are sometimes but not always connected with the devil.[28] For the most part, demons are conceived in animistic terms, as disembodied spirits coming out of the nether world of darkness in search of bodies to inhabit. Demon possession is often regarded as a result of misfortune rather than of sin.

With such a strong emphasis on the devil and demons, it is not surprising that charismatics give much attention to the deliverance ministry. The exorcism of unclean spirits, which has only survived as a little-practiced ritual in the Catholic branches of mainline Christianity, is a major ingredient in the ministry of the charismatic or Pentecostal churches.

Where Pentecostalism (both classical and new) deserves special acclaim from the mainline churches is in its remarkable success in giving tangible expression to the priesthood of all believers. In stark contrast to the prevailing pattern in Reformed and Lutheran churches, where the pastor alone is seen as the minister in a congregation, Pentecostalism makes a place for many types of ministry including evangelism, prophecy, healing, deliverance and spiritual counsel. Moreover, it has given due recognition to the role of women in ministry. Half the staff of the Azusa Street Mission in 1906 were women. Aimee Semple McPherson was the celebrated founder and leader of the International Church of the Foursquare Gospel. Women leaders in the neo-Pentecostal movement include Agnes Sanford; Jean Stone, founder of the now defunct Blessed Trinity Society; Kathryn Kuhlman, whose ministry of healing extended throughout the world; Jean Darnall in England; and Catherine Marshall, Presbyterian laywoman and novelist.

Another area where charismatics have pioneered is in their surmounting of age-old barriers between churches. The ecumenical dimension is much more noticeable in neo-Pentecostalism than in classical Pentecostalism. The former movement is for the most part reformist, not separatist. At many charismatic gatherings, Catholics and Protestants have come together in a display of ecumenical fellowship that is rarely equaled in establishment Christianity. On some occasions there has even been sacramental intercommunion. Michael Harper, an Anglican charismatic, asserts that "this movement is the most unifying in Christendom today . . . *for only in this movement are all streams uniting, and all ministries being accepted and practiced.*"[29] Even Pentecostals who have been influenced by the separatism of dispensational fundamentalism often display an ecumenical openness not found in non-Pentecostal dispensationalism.

Less commendable, however, is the way in which many Pentecostals have embraced the prosperity doctrine, originating in New Thought and other varieties of neotranscendentalism. According to this doctrine, a sure indication of being in the favor of God is good health and financial prosperity. When we place our trust in God, it is said, we shall be given the desires of our heart (an appeal is often made to Psalm 37:4). We need only ask in faith, and we shall then receive. Indeed, we should claim what we ask for, since faith entails such bold presumption. Also fostered in these circles is the closely related idea of "seed faith," which means that to get wealth one must give wealth. Therefore, financial sacrifice may be viewed as a means to prosperity or as a test of obedience and faith. Not surprisingly, the prosperity doctrine is being repudiated by an increasing number of theologians in both Pentecostalism and neo-Pentecostalism.[30]

Pentecostalism in its widest sense has affinities to Montanism, radical Pietism and Christian mysticism. Its immediate precursor was the Holiness movement, in which Wesleyan theology was united with a kind of biblicistic fundamentalism. Most Pentecostals of the classical type are premillennial and some are dispensational. Neo-Pentecostalism is characterized by a deeper appreciation of the tradition of the whole church, including the church fathers.

Among the thriving Pentecostal churches in this country are the Assemblies of God;[31] the Church of God in Christ; the United Pentecostal Church International (which holds to a unitarianism of the second person); the Pentecostal Holiness Church; the Pentecostal Assemblies of the World; the Apostolic Faith Mission; the Elim Fellowship; the International Church of the Foursquare Gospel; the Open Bible Standard Churches; and the Church of God of Prophecy. Communions somewhat different from historical Pentecostalism in their general orientation but nonetheless making a real place for the gifts of the Spirit and various other Pentecostal emphases include the Catholic Apostolic Church and the New Apostolic Church.

Paraparochial movements associated with either classical or neo-Pentecostalism are Fountain Trust in England, the Full Gospel Business Men's Fellowship, the PTL Club, the 700 Club, Teen Challenge and the Blessed Trinity Society (now defunct). Religious communities where Catholic and Protestant charismatics have come together for the purpose of fellowship and mission include the Word of God community in Ann Arbor, Michigan; the People of Joy community in Phoenix, Arizona; the People of Praise community in South Bend, Indiana; and the People of Hope community in Newark, New Jersey.

Seminaries and Bible colleges that promulgate charismatic theology are the following: Melodyland School of Theology in Anaheim, California; Whole Word Theological Seminary in Oakton, Virginia;

Oral Roberts School of Theology in Tulsa, Oklahoma; Evangel College in Springfield, Missouri; Assemblies of God Graduate School, also in Springfield, Missouri; Faith Bible Institute in Oklahoma City, Oklahoma; Liberty Bible College in Pensacola, Florida; Berea Bible Institute in E. Montreal, Quebec; and Eastern Pentecostal Bible College in Peterborough, Ontario.

Magazines that carry the Pentecostal message should also be noted: *New Wine; New Covenant,* the voice of Catholic Pentecostalism; *The Logos* (Eastern Orthodox); *Theosis* (Eastern Orthodox); *Logos Journal; Renewal,* the magazine of Fountain Trust; *Full Gospel Business Men's Voice; Pastoral Renewal; Charisma; Charisma Digest;* the *Pentecostal Evangel;* and *Agora,* with roots in classical Pentecostalism and a reputation for the avant-garde. Some of these journals have in recent years become more consciously evangelical and less distinctively Pentecostal.

Among theologians who can be called Pentecostal or neo-Pentecostal are J. Rodman Williams;[32] Gordon Fee; Robert E. Cooley, president of Gordon-Conwell Seminary; Pat Robertson, founder of the 700 Club; Larry Christenson, a spark plug in the charismatic revival movement in the American Lutheran Church; Thomas Smail;[33] Michael Harper; Derek Prince; Arnold Bittlinger, prominent in renewal circles in German Protestantism; and Tormod Engelsviken, a pioneer in the charismatic renewal in Norwegian Lutheranism. Various Roman Catholic scholars, too, have been active in the charismatic movement: Edward O'Connor, Simon Tugwell, Donald Gelpi, Cardinal Léon Suenens, Josephine Massingberd Ford, Kevin Ranaghan, Stephen Clark and Ralph Martin (the last two from the Word of God community). Eusebius Stephanou, Gregory Gavrilides, Gerrald Munk and Angelo Hoty are representative of the charismatic renewal in Eastern Orthodoxy.

Pentecostalism and neo-Pentecostalism are to be included as part of the new conservatism, because their emphasis is on the restoration of biblical faith in all of its purity and power. In Catholic Pentecostalism this is united with an appreciation of Catholic tradition and a reaffirmation of the Marian doctrines and the papacy. Yet evangelical motifs are prominent among Catholic Pentecostals, and a few are even willing to critique church practice and doctrine in the light of Holy Scripture.[34]

NEO-ORTHODOXY

Some may question whether neo-orthodoxy really forms a part of the new conservatism, but any serious reading of the writings of Karl Barth and Emil Brunner, for example, will show that their aim was the recovery of true orthodoxy. Their attack was leveled at both liberal theology and a dead or scholastic orthodoxy. Their hope was for the emergence of a living, dynamic orthodoxy that would be related to the contemporary situation. Their concern, moreover, was not only the renewal of theology but also the renewal of the church.

Neo-orthodoxy has been in partial eclipse in the past decade and a half. In 1974 Diogenes Allen of Princeton Seminary commented that the "most significant event [in recent years] has been the collapse of the middle ground between liberalism and fundamentalism." By the middle ground he had in mind the neo-orthodoxy of Barth, Brunner, the Niebuhrs and Tillich.[35]

Neo-orthodoxy emerged in the 1920s after the First World War and was sparked by Barth's *The Epistle to the Romans* (1918), which went into six editions. Originally known as the dialectical theology and in this country as the theology of crisis,[36] the new movement enlisted the support of many disillusioned liberals whose faith in the natural goodness of man and the dogma of progress had been irrevocably shattered. It also attracted some of those who had been identified with the old orthodoxy, such as John Mackay and Frederick Bronkema.

In its earlier phase neo-orthodox theology was largely shaped by Karl Barth, Emil Brunner, Eduard Thurneysen, Friedrich Gogarten and Rudolf Bultmann, though the last two began moving in another direction in the later 1920s. Hendrik Kraemer in the Netherlands; Dietrich Bonhoeffer, Otto Weber and Wilhelm Vischer in Germany; Daniel Jenkins in England; and Thomas Torrance in Scotland were also attracted to this movement. In Sweden Gustaf Aulén and Anders Nygren spearheaded a parallel movement, which might be considered a type of neo-Lutheranism.[37] The American contingent was best represented by Reinhold Niebuhr, who increasingly moved from an existentialist orientation toward classical orthodoxy.[38]

Conservative evangelicals have generally not been happy with neo-orthodoxy, mainly because of its openness to historical and literary criticism in biblical studies and its candid recognition of the element of myth in the Scriptures. Cornelius Van Til has denounced the neo-orthodox movement as a "new modernism," regarding it as a greater threat than the old liberalism. Charles Ryrie contends that "neo-orthodoxy is a theological hoax. It attempts to preserve the message of the Bible while denying the facts of the Bible."[39] On the other hand, Bernard Ramm believes that liberalism was not successfully countered until the rise of neo-orthodoxy.[40]

A particular distinctive of neo-orthodoxy is its stress on the uniqueness of the biblical revelation. This was already evident in the early writings of Karl Barth, where revelation was depicted in Kierkegaardian terms as "the Moment" when Eternity entered into time. The Bible itself was not seen as the revelation but as the original witness to the one and final revelation, Jesus Christ. God revealed himself fully and definitively once for all times (*Einmaligkeit*) in the person and work of his only begotten Son, Jesus Christ.

Revelation was said to have a dynamic character. It was not simply propositional truth but the reality of the living presence of God that could only faintly be grasped through propositions and concepts. Revelation was described in terms of "events" rather than "ideas," though the cognitive quality of revelation was never seriously disputed. Barth has been accused by some of his critics of "actualism," imposing a philosophical principle of truth as act upon the Scriptures.

A disjunction was also drawn between revelation and religion. Barth described revelation as the abolition of religion, and yet he acknowledged the possibility of a true religion, a religion purified of egocentricity, one that could serve as a vehicle of revelation. Just as revelation has its source in God's search for man, so religion is rooted in man's quest for God. Even empirical Christianity, it was said, must be judged in the light of God's self-revelation in Jesus Christ attested to in the Bible.

Neo-orthodox theologians have also been noted for their strictures on natural theology. Even Emil Brunner, who consistently affirmed the reality of a natural knowledge of God, nonetheless held that this knowledge always results in a misunderstanding because of human sin. Theology therefore cannot be built on an erroneous understanding of God but can only be based on the revelation of God in Jesus Christ, which brings people a true understanding of God's will and purpose for the world. Conservative evangelicals have been quick to fault neo-orthodoxy for downplaying or ignoring the general revelation of God in nature.[41]

An emphasis on the utter transcendence of God has also been characteristic of neo-orthodoxy. Barth in his earlier phase frequently referred to God as the Wholly Other (*totaliter aliter*), steadfastly affirming Kierkegaard's principle of the "infinite qualitative difference between God and man." In the early and later (as opposed to the middle) phases of his theology, Barth regarded the Bible and the church as only pointers to the Word of God, not as means by which we come to receive the Word of God. Here we see a disjunction or separation between the divine Word and the human words of the Bible. A continuing theme in neo-orthodoxy has been the "Word behind the words" in contradistinction to the "Word within the words" or the "Word becoming words." Unlike neo-evangelicalism, neo-orthodoxy has difficulty with the historic Christian affirmation that the Bible *is* the Word of God.[42]

The historic Christian conception of the sacraments is also called into question. No longer means of grace or salvific signs by which we receive the remission of sins and the power of the new life in Christ, they are often reduced to "vivid illustrations of the Word." Barth came to view baptism and the Lord's Supper as ethical ordinances affording us an opportunity to dedicate ourselves to the way of the cross. In his mind, only Jesus Christ can legitimately be referred to as a sacrament, a visible sign of an invisible grace. Joseph Haroutunian saw the means of grace as neither the sermon nor the sacraments as such but as interpersonal relations.[43]

Having inherited the Ritschlian suspicion of metaphysics, neo-orthodoxy placed the emphasis on ethics. The gospel was seen as a report of the saving deeds of God rather than a view of life and the world that competed with secular world views. This was more true of Barth than of either Brunner or Reinhold Niebuhr.

In the area of apologetics, neo-orthodox theologians unanimously criticized efforts to harmonize biblical and philosophical themes. The biblical-classical synthesis of the early church in which biblical doctrines were virtually Hellenized was laid at the door of apologetics. Yet neo-orthodox scholars have generally made a place for "eristics," the attack upon the cultural and philosophical presuppositions of secular man. Barth, as opposed to Brunner and Niebuhr, questioned the validity of the whole apologetic enterprise because of the almost irresistible temptation to compromise with secular thought. According to Tillich, Barth's theology is kerygmatic rather than apologetic, based on the conviction that the only way to reach secular man is through the power of the proclamation of the gospel itself. There nevertheless persists an apologetic element in Barth's *Church Dogmatics* in that he gives a biblical critique of non-Christian systems of thought. At the same time, he seeks to speak to the church and not to the world as such, though always with the hope that the world, too, might listen.

Finally, we should take note of the downplaying of sanctification by neo-orthodox theologians. Niebuhr concentrated on the sin of man rather than on the renovation of man through grace. He could even say that we are saved "in principle, but not in fact." Humility in the face of the awesome presence of God was more important for him than the victorious life in Jesus Christ. Barth made a real place for sanctification in his later writing, but even then he remained suspicious of human virtue. His emphasis was on the call to discipleship, never on the call to sainthood. His concern was not so much purity of life as ethical obedience to the social imperatives of the faith. The focus of neo-orthodoxy remained on God's invasion into history rather than on man's ascent to God. This explains in part neo-orthodoxy's aversion to Pietism and mysticism (here again we see an affinity with Ritschlian theology).

Additional neo-orthodox themes include the portrayal of sin as willful revolt against God and idolatrous pride (as opposed to ignorance and weakness);[44] a fascination with messianic socialism but stopping short of confusing a socialist utopia with the kingdom of God; a futuristic over a realized eschatology; and a tendency to see the kingdom of Christ as more inclusive than the empirical church.

The following theologians have continued to maintain the salient emphases of neo-orthodoxy: Helmut Gollwitzer, Rudolf Ehrlich, Jacques Ellul, Markus Barth, William Hordern, Arthur Cochrane, Werner Koch, Joseph Haroutunian, Ronald Goetz, David Demson, Paul Lehmann, W. A. Whitehouse, John Leith, Paul and Elizabeth Achtemeier and to a lesser extent Paul Holmer. Donald Dayton seeks to unite both a Wesleyan holiness tradition and an Evangelical Left orientation with Barthian theology. Philip Watson has tried to forge a synthesis between classical Wesleyanism and the Lundensian theology. Neo-orthodoxy has also proved to be a formative influence on Brevard Childs, Yale Old Testament scholar.

Churches in this country that have been heavily influenced by neo-orthodoxy are the old Evangelical and Reformed Church (now part of the United Church of Christ), the Reformed Church in America, the Lutheran Church in America, the former United Presbyterian Church in the U.S.A. and the former Presbyterian Church in the U.S. These last two denominations have recently merged to form the Presbyterian Church (U.S.A.). Among seminaries where neo-orthodoxy has made an impact are Princeton Theological Seminary, Lancaster Theological Seminary, Eden Theological Seminary, Union Theological Seminary (New York), McCormick Theological Seminary, Western Theological Seminary and the University of Dubuque Theological Seminary. Only the last two schools continue to reflect, at least in part, motifs associated with neo-orthodoxy.[45]

Periodicals that generally maintain a neo-orthodox slant are *Scottish Journal of Theology, Reformed Review, Interpretation* and to a lesser degree *The Reformed Journal.* The now defunct *Theology and Life* was neo-orthodox, with a pronounced ecumenical orientation. *Theology Today,* though at one time predominantly neo-orthodox, has become more pluralistic. The William B. Eerdmans Company is one of the few publishing concerns today that tend to promote neo-orthodox (especially Barthian) theology. The Westminster Press, an organ of the Presbyterian Church (U.S.A.), though once known as the voice of neo-orthodoxy, now stands closer to neoliberalism.

The question has been raised: Can one be evangelical and neo-orthodox at the same time? It is well to remember in this connection that Karl Barth attacked Emil Brunner for compromising the doctrine of *sola gratia,* which is probably the principal evangelical distinctive. Markus Barth has criticized both the sermons and the theology of Reinhold Niebuhr for taking as their point of departure not the gospel but the human predicament. Karl Barth himself has been indicted by conservative evangelicals for a universalistic thrust and for underplaying the decision of faith.

Yet it should be borne in mind that the leading spokesmen of neo-orthodoxy in both the recent past and the present definitely regard themselves as evangelical.[46] It can be shown, moreover, that neo-orthodoxy has generally reaffirmed the basic affirmations of the Reformation including *sola scriptura, sola gratia* and *sola fide*. Its view of revelation has much more in common with the original Reformers than its conservative critics care to acknowledge. Where neo-orthodoxy can be described as deficiently evangelical is in its tendency to speak of the inspiration only of the writers of Scripture and not also of the words, its emphasis on the objective atonement to the detriment of subjective decision (this is not true of either Brunner or Niebuhr), its stress on justification over sanctification (the later Barth is here more balanced than either Brunner or Niebuhr) and its reluctance to see the mission of the church in terms of the conversion of souls.

What are the prospects for neo-orthodoxy? While it is true that both Emil Brunner and Reinhold Niebuhr are in partial eclipse, it is also true that the 1980s are experiencing a Barthian renaissance (in both America and Germany). The Karl Barth Society of North America has been holding well-attended meetings for several years, and books on Karl Barth are beginning to appear once again, especially in evangelical circles.[47] Barth is also being rediscovered by some liberation theologians, who can identify with his call to ethical obedience. It is interesting to note that while the political right (Michael Novak and Jeffrey Hart) is beginning to draw upon Reinhold Niebuhr, so the political left sees in Barth a source of support.

In my opinion, neo-orthodoxy can be faulted not only for its neglect of the call to sainthood and the life of holiness but also for not giving sufficient attention to the doctrine of the church and the sacraments. It sparked a renewal in theology but not a renewal of the church, though this was its intention.[48] Neo-orthodoxy failed to realize that the Protestant principle needs to be united with catholic substance if the church is to be revitalized and restored as the vehicle of the kingdom of Christ.

CATHOLIC EVANGELICALISM

The last category that I shall deal with is catholic evangelicalism, a movement embracing not only mainliners who are seeking renewal within their respective denominations but also many who have come out of a restrictive fundamentalism and have grown weary of battles over nonessentials. Unlike restorationists, who simply wish to return to New Testament Christianity,[49] they are concerned to maintain continuity with the tradition of the whole church. At the same time, they generally see the Bible as having priority over tradition. There is in this camp a stress on evangelical essentials but within the context of catholic faith. A serious attempt is made to uphold the inspiration and infallibility of Scripture but without getting bogged down in interminable warfare over inerrancy or the millennium.

Catholic evangelicals not only draw on the Reformation and the post-Reformation purification movements of Pietism and Puritanism, but they also encourage a renewed appreciation for pre-Reformation evangelicalism. In striving for a revitalized church in our time, they seek to enlist the support not only of the Reformers but also of the church fathers and doctors of the medieval church. Whereas fundamentalists and many Pentecostals look to separatist, nonconformist groups like the Donatists, the Montanists, the Novatians and the Waldensians,[50] catholic evangelicals appeal to the mainstream of the church, particularly to the early fathers.

In marked contrast to popular evangelical conservatism today, catholic evangelicalism is profoundly disturbed by the mindless activism that pervades the evangelical and indeed the wider Christian community. It sees the fascination with communication skills over sound theology and the concentration on church growth techniques over purity of worship as a sign of capitulation to the technological materialism of our age. Acutely aware of the need for training in discipleship, catholic evangelicals emphasize evangelism *and* nurture. While acknowledging the crucial role of evangelism in any vital Christianity, they are insistent that evangelism can never take the place of worship. Nor can social service preempt our obligations to draw near to God in prayer and adoration. In line with the catholic tradition at its best, catholic evangelicals stress being before doing, faith before works, contemplation before action.

At the same time, works whether of mercy or piety are by no means neglected. Indeed, a hallmark of the movement for catholic evangelical renewal is the attempt to hold justification and sanctification in balance. The Reformation emphasis on the justification of the ungodly must be united with the Catholic and Wesleyan concern for the sanctification of the godly. The call to repentance must be supplemented by the call to sainthood. Growth in faith is almost as important as the decision of faith.

Like classical Calvinism, this new kind of evangelicalism sees the church as always being reformed (*ecclesia semper reformanda*). The Reformation must continue, and this means that theological formulations as well as confessional statements need always to be further refined, amplified and even corrected.

A catholic evangelical church will be confessional in the sense that it will seek to confess the historic faith anew but in the language of our own age. Such a confession may well take the form of a confessional statement of faith, but this statement will always be seen as a broken symbol that allows for further amplification and even reformulation. The confession, moreover, will never have equal validity with the Bible but will always be under the Bible.

In contrast to the sectarianism that afflicts the ideological right wing of the evangelical movement, catholic evangelicals desire church unity. They are not content with spiritual unity but press on to the ideal of visible unity. This does not necessarily mean a superchurch, but it does surely entail altar and pulpit fellowship between all the branches of Christendom. These people are also not satisfied with a panevangelicalism but entertain the hope of Evangelical-Catholic unity. At the same time, with confessionalist evangelicals, they have serious reservations about "unionism," the attempt to merge denominations for the purpose of greater efficiency. In unionism truth is invariably sacrificed to "love."

At the Chicago Call conference in 1977, two divisions became readily apparent in the catholic evangelical movement.[51] First, there were those who sought to underline Catholic concerns and subordinate Reformation emphases to a more inclusive thrust. The appeal was not to the Protestant Reformation of the sixteenth century but to the undivided church of the first five centuries. Persons identified with the New Covenant Apostolic Order (now the Evangelical Orthodox Church) and the new Oxford movement within Anglicanism could be included in this first strand within catholic evangelicalism.

The second strand was composed of persons who did not wish to bypass the Reformation but who believed that the coming great church must incorporate the valid and enduring contributions of the Reformation. For them, the path to renewal lies not in returning to a pre-Reformation golden age of the church but in identifying with the battle that the Reformation waged on behalf of purity in worship and doctrine. At the same time, unlike many confessionalist evangelicals, this segment of catholic evangelicalism does not accept the Reformation uncritically. With Jaroslav Pelikan, it regards the Reformation as a tragic necessity.[52] It was tragic because it sundered the unity of the Western church. It was necessary because the Church of Rome was not open to basic reform in doctrine, though it was amenable to various reforms in practice.

A third branch of catholic evangelicalism was also evident at the Chicago Call conference, and since then it has become more visible. This position, with which I identify, appeals not only to the Reform but also to the Revival. It sees the evangelical awakenings for all their excesses as something positive, and here the differences from neo-orthodoxy, the new Oxford movement and liberal Christianity become apparent. It believes that it is better to err on the side of enthusiasm than on the side of formalism. At the same time, it acknowledges the need for cultus as well as charism, for sacraments as well as inward spiritual experience. It shares the concern in the wider catholic evangelical movement for appreciation of the church fathers and medieval reformers, but it insists that the Roman and Eastern Orthodox traditions (as well as the Reformation tradition) must be purified of unbiblical practices and ideas before any kind of church unity can become a practical reality.

The catholic evangelicalism that I uphold seeks always to distinguish a vital Christianity from formalistic orthodoxy or ecclesiasticism. Even though it makes an important place for sacraments and an ordained ministry, it eschews sacramentalism and sacerdotalism. Like the Puritans, it also objects to unnecessary or overelaborate symbolism in the church and to a concern for vestments and liturgy over inward faith and experience. Nonetheless, with Calvin and other mainline Reformers, it also regards with disapproval an unstructured or totally free service of worship. It favors a liturgy of the Word and the sacrament, but with the sacrament subordinated to the Word.[53] Its objections to Roman Catholicism arise, at least partly, out of the conviction that catholicity is unnecessarily confined to one particular tradition in the church; therefore, the Church of Rome is not catholic enough. This criticism is shared by other strands of catholic evangelicalism, though the new Oxford movement, for example, is anxious to maintain a conciliatory stance toward Rome.

Among the luminaries in the past with whom I can identify in this connection are Richard Sibbes,[54] Philip Spener, Count Nikolaus von Zinzendorf, P. T. Forsyth, Philip Schaff,[55] Friedrich Heiler and Nathan Söderblom.[56] It was Söderblom who brought the term "evangelical catholicity" into prominence in the twentieth century.

People in our day who might be included in the catholic evangelical movement in its wider sense are Daniel Jenkins, Michael Green, Thomas Torrance, G. W. Bromiley, J. J. Von Allmen, J. L. Leuba, Max Thurian,[57] A. W. Tozer,[58] Klara Schlink,[59] Max Lackmann,[60] Howard Hageman, Richard Lovelace,[61] John Hesselink, Robert Webber,[62] Bela Vassady,[63] John Weborg, Robert Paul, Peter Gillquist[64] and Thomas Howard. Roman Catholic scholars who are striving for an Evangelical-Catholic rapprochement include Kevin Perrotta, Stephen Clark, Ralph Martin[65] and Kerry Koller (all related to ecumenical charismatic communities).

Publications that reflect this new mood are *Living Faith* and *"No Other Foundation,"* renewal magazines in the United Church of Christ; *New Oxford Review*, which seeks to bring together evangelicals and Anglo-Catholics; *Christian Challenge; New Heaven/New Earth; Again*, the voice of the Evangelical Orthodox Church; *Common Life;*[66] and *Pastoral Renewal.* Publishing companies supportive of this kind of orientation include the Augsburg Publishing House, William B. Eerdmans Publishing Company, Servant Publications and Crossway Books (a branch of Good News Publishers). The last, whose editors are Jan and Lane Dennis, both conveners of the Chicago Call conference, seeks to voice the concerns of that brand of conservative evangelicalism associated with Francis Schaeffer and the L'Abri Fellowship and that kind of catholic evangelicalism associated with the new Oxford movement.

THE ROAD AHEAD

It should be kept in mind that the categories presented in this chapter are ideal types. No one theologian or spiritual leader fits completely into any one type, and most have associations with various types.[67] Both Luther and Calvin, for example, can be claimed by fundamentalists, neoevangelicals, confessionalist evangelicals and catholic evangelicals.[68] At the same time, because modern evangelicalism is so diverse, it is important to make distinctions for the purpose of showing who we are and where we are going.

Evangelicalism today is open and fluid, and this accounts for its strengths as well as its weaknesses (e.g., its surprising susceptibility to heterodoxy). A growing number of fundamentalists are moving toward neofundamentalism and neoevangelicalism. Pentecostals, even those in sectarian churches, are increasingly willing to identify with the larger evangelical community. Many neoevangelicals are moving toward what I have called a catholic evangelicalism. Some of the new evangelicals are discovering that they have much more in common with liberalism than was first supposed (e.g., various evangelical feminists). Others are finding the key to evangelical renewal in the theology of Karl Barth.[69] Still others are moving back into neofundamentalism and fundamentalism. We are witnessing today signs of growing retrenchment as well as new openness.

Richard Quebedeaux, always an astute observer of the evangelical scene, sees the principal cleavage today as between establishment evangelicals and young evangelicals. Without denying what is valid in his perception, I regard the new cleavage as between a sectarian evangelicalism united with the new right and an ecumenical evangelicalism that is concerned to bind the wounds that divide the churches today.

The new stirrings of evangelical sentiment within the mainline denominations[70] are a sign that all is not lost and that many evangelicals are splitting from their parent bodies prematurely. My advice is for evangelicals to remain within their respective denominations as long as they can, indeed, until they are practically forced to leave. Both Calvin and Luther, it should be remembered, did not wish to leave the Roman Catholic Church but were thrown out because they persisted in adhering to Reformation doctrine. Dispensationalists call their fellow evangelicals out of churches that they regard as apostate. But we should bear in mind that there are heresies on the right as well as the left, and dispensationalism itself is already a kind of heterodoxy.

It is important that the new conservatism not become allied with any ideology—either of the right or the left. Ron Sider, head of Evangelicals for Social Action, has tried to break through the ideological cleavage, as can be seen in his forthright stand against both abortion on demand and militarism.[71]

While there is much diversity in the evangelical fold, I believe that evangelicals of all varieties have more in common with each other than with liberalism or modernism. J. Gresham Machen was not far from the truth when he contended that evangelical Christianity and Protestant liberalism represent two different religions.[72] Yet this does not mean that many of our liberal colleagues and friends are necessarily non-Christian. While their interpretations of the faith can be questioned, it is undeniable that many of them continue to maintain a personal relationship with the living Christ that often conflicts with their theological formulations. Karl Barth kept a portrait of Schleiermacher near his desk and would sometimes point some of his ultraorthodox friends and students to this portrait with the words, "He too is a Christian." Evangelicals need to be charitable without being compromising. We, too, stand under the judgment of the Word of God, and if we persist in living in the past and closing our eyes to the real spiritual and moral issues of our time, then we will be judged more severely than the others (cf. James 3:1).

IV

Evangelical Disunity

Have nothing to do with stupid, senseless controversies; you know that they breed quarrels.

II Timothy 2:23 RSV

He will also judge those who cause divisions. Void of the love of God, they look to their own advantage and not to the unity of the church: for small and trifling reasons they rend the great and glorious body of Christ into pieces.

IRENAEUS

Union among Christians is becoming more and more an imperative necessity if they are to conquer in the great conflict with infidelity and anti-Christ.

PHILIP SCHAFF

You Christians must show me that you are redeemed before I will believe in your Redeemer.

FRIEDRICH NIETZSCHE

THE PRESENT SITUATION

WITH SUCH A DIVERSITY OF STRANDS, it is scarcely surprising that the evangelical fabric is showing signs of strain. Membership is growing and giving increases; yet there are widening cracks in the citadel of evangelicalism. Carl Henry voices the new mood of uneasiness: "Despite its far-reaching theological agreement, the evangelical body lacks a sense of comprehensive family identity and loyalty."[1] Even this supposed theological agreement is open to question: there is ample reason to believe that the growing dissension in evangelical ranks has a theological as well as a sociological or cultural basis. To be sure, an inner bond of unity persists in the evangelical community, but how long this can be maintained in the midst of polemical strife is debatable.

Old divisions in the evangelical family are reappearing. One of these is Calvinism versus Arminianism. While Calvinists or Reformed Christians champion predestination, those whose theological heritage goes back to Arminius and Wesley stress the need for personal decision and obedience. Calvinists complain that Arminians sacrifice the sovereignty of grace for human potentiality. Arminians retort that Calvinists compromise human responsibility by an exaggerated emphasis on divine grace, which finally leads to philosophical determinism. It is becoming commonplace today to hear both Reformed and Lutheran theologians criticize "decisionism," which, in their view, is the latest variety of Pelagianism.

Another relatively ancient schism that is resurfacing is that between Calvinism and Lutheranism. Many neo-Lutherans are noted for their questioning of the third use of the law, the law as a guide for the Christian life, whereas Calvinists faithful to their tradition insist that the third use is the principal one. Calvinists accuse Lutherans of downplaying sanctification; Lutherans express an ever-recurring and sometimes justified fear that a rigid Calvinism ends in legalism.

Then there is the perennial battle between Baptists and those in the mainstream Reformation tradition over the meaning and mode of baptism. Baptists vigorously contend that the practice of infant baptism smacks of magic, especially where baptismal regeneration is affirmed. Reformed theologians argue that the promises of the covenant extend to the children as well as to the parents (cf. Acts 2:39), and therefore baptism as the sign and seal of these promises can legitimately be offered to infants.[2]

Lutherans generally hold that grace is imparted through the sacramental signs irrespective of whether the recipient has faith. The hope is that the infant when reaching the age of reason will discover and dedicate himself to the faith into which he was baptized. Whatever the case, regeneration has already occurred if there has been a valid baptism. One must struggle to remain true to one's baptism, but, Lutherans insist, to suppose that regeneration is withheld until one makes a personal commitment of faith smacks of the decisionist heresy.

Karl Barth has added fuel to the fire by withdrawing his support from infant baptism and concluding that believer baptism is the only practice that has biblical and theological sanction.[3] He sees baptism as an ethical ordinance of the church whereby the believer pledges to follow Christ in a daily walk of obedience. At the same time, it is a sign of God's incomparable grace poured out in Jesus Christ for all people. This grace is for us and with us before our decision, but not until we take up the cross and follow Christ in daily obedience is it manifested to the world.

Finally, it should come as no surprise that the conflict between amillennialists, postmillennialists and premillennialists is becoming more acrimonious after a decade of relative peace on this issue. What is surprising is that evangelical adherents of postmillennialism are beginning to express themselves. Support of what had seemed to be a discredited theory is coming from such Reformed bastions as Westminster Theological Seminary and the Christian Reconstructionist movement.[4] Within the ranks of premillennialism, debate is sharpening between the classical premillennialists, represented by George Eldon Ladd, and the dispensationalists, who hold that the church will be raptured into heaven seven years before the inbreaking of the millennial kingdom.[5]

In addition to these simmering historical conflicts, new divisions are beginning to appear in the evangelical movement. One of these concerns the charismatic renewal within the churches, which is welcomed by some evangelicals but castigated by others. This controversy corresponds in part to that between the New Lights and the Old Lights in eighteenth-century Congregationalism and in nineteenth-century Presbyterianism in America. It also has parallels to the dispute between the Pietists and the Established churches in Norway and Sweden in the late nineteenth and early twentieth centuries.

Charismatics urge their fellow Christians to seek a still higher experience, the baptism of the Holy Spirit, which brings power for witnessing and a deeper degree of holiness. They insist, moreover, that speaking in tongues is *the* sign or one of the principal signs of having received this baptism of fire. Traditional evangelicals assert that there is only one work of grace but with a twofold aspect—justification and sanctification. To seek for a higher salvation detracts not only from justification but also from faith and baptism.

Another salient indication of growing polarization in evangelical ranks is the conflict between the so-called pietists and social activists.[6] Salvation, the pietists say, is an inward experience, with outward manifestations to be sure, but basically a matter of one's personal relationship with God. The social activists argue that salvation is realized in the ongoing struggle on behalf of the poor and the oppressed. Thus, the evangelical left tends to be politically activist, whereas the evangelical right focuses much more attention on cultivating personal piety.[7]

There is also mounting tension between rationalists and fideists. On the evangelical right, it is fashionable to express this dichotomy in terms of confessionalists versus evidentialists.[8] Not all rationalists, however, are evidentialists (Gordon Clark certainly is not), though most, but not all, confessionalists tend toward fideism. The rationalists accuse the fideists of portraying faith as a blind leap in the dark and thus disregarding the confirmatory evidence which history and archaeology provide concerning the extraordinary events in biblical history. The fideists charge the rationalists with underplaying, even ignoring the noetic effects of sin and making faith conditional on historical and rational proofs for God's self-revelation in Christ and the full reliability of Scripture. While the first position sees a creative role for reason in preparing the way for faith, the second stresses understanding proceeding out of faith.

Those closer to fideism generally appeal to the Pietist tradition and the Reformation; those assigning a greater role to reason are likely to hold Augustine and, even more, Thomas Aquinas in high esteem.[9] The second group is also at home in the thought world of Protestant orthodoxy (both Lutheran and Reformed), which brought back Aristotle in the elucidation and defense of the faith.[10] Fideists find some support in the Dutch theological tradition emanating from Abraham Kuyper.[11]

Francis Schaeffer reveals his affinity to the scholastic tradition of Protestant orthodoxy in his well-known and ground-breaking work *Escape From Reason*.[12] For Schaeffer, the malady of modern civilization is a flight from reason into the irrational. He cites various existentialist writers to illustrate the modern contempt for logic and reason. While presenting some substantiation for his thesis, Schaeffer does not fully consider that behind the flight from reason there is a flight from faith itself and that the former is only a symptom of the latter. He also tends to ignore the other side of the flight from faith—the enthronement of reason, which is present in educational and analytic philosophies as well as conservative theology.

Among those in the evangelical camp who seek to retain a determinative role for reason in preparing the way for faith are Carl Henry, Gordon Clark, Bruce Demarest, Paul Feinberg, Francis Schaeffer, Kenneth Kantzer, Gordon Lewis, Norman Geisler and Clark Pinnock. Those who stress the priority of faith over reason include G. W. Berkouwer, Jack Rogers, Mark Noll, David Wells, Donald McKim, Lewis Smedes, James Daane, Arthur Cochrane and this author.

The sacraments also signify an area of recurring tension within evangelicalism. I have already touched on the conflict over baptism, but the whole question of sacraments is becoming an issue today. A large part of the evangelical community does not even regard baptism and the Lord's Supper as sacraments, i.e., means of grace; instead, they are reduced to mere ordinances whereby we pledge ourselves to the service of the kingdom. Two of the most influential Reformed theologians, Charles Hodge and Karl Barth, declared themselves against a sacramental view. Hodge went so far as to argue that Calvin was wrong in his interpretation of the Eucharist.[13] It should be borne in mind that having a high view of the sacraments (as the Reformers did) does not mean sacramentalism, in which the outward rite is regarded as efficacious for salvation simply by virtue of being performed (*ex opere operato*).[14] Significantly, even Baptist theologians are beginning to recognize the sacramental character of baptism and the Lord's Supper, though they are always careful to relate this to faith in Jesus Christ.[15]

Then we come to the debate between the inerrantists and infallibilists. The former, represented by the International Council on Biblical Inerrancy, hold that the Bible is without error in matters of science and history as well as faith and morals. They sometimes speak of total inerrancy, meaning that whatever Scripture "touches upon" is immune from error. Because God, the primary author of Scripture, is wholly truthful, Scripture itself cannot lie. For the infallibilists, who constitute the great majority of moderate evangelicals, Scripture is infallible in the sense that it unfailingly communicates the will and purpose of God for our salvation, but this does not mean that the writers were lifted out of their cultural and historical environments and exempted from cultural and historical limitations. The infallibilists, following Calvin, often speak of the accommodation of the Spirit to the world-view of the times, thereby acknowledging the element of historical and cultural contingency in Scripture. The Toronto Conference on Biblical Authority (June 1981), sponsored by Fuller Theological Seminary and the Institute for Christian Studies in Toronto, reflected the moderate evangelical consensus on this question. Among those who follow Warfield and A. A. Hodge in contending for total inerrancy[16] are R. C. Sproul, Harold Lindsell, James Boice, Norman Geisler and Carl Henry. Those who are prepared to qualify inerrancy in order to make room for cultural and historical factors in the writing of Scripture include Clark Pinnock, Jack Rogers, Daniel Fuller and James Daane.

No less heated than the inerrancy debate is the currently accelerating conflict between the solifidians (those who defend justification by faith alone) and the Holiness and Pentecostal movements, which insist that maintaining a Christian life is necessary for final salvation. This tension was already evident in the eighteenth century between John Wesley on the one hand and the Moravians and the hyper-Calvinists on the other. For Lutherans, Calvinists and Barthians, we do not procure our sanctification, though we can manifest and demonstrate it in a Christian life. But our final salvation is already assured because of our justification in Jesus Christ apprehended by faith, which is a completed act.

Verdict magazine, which celebrates the Protestant Reformation and regards the Holiness movement as a dangerous aberration,[17] argues that works of faith and love are necessary fruits of salvation but in no way contribute to the gaining of our salvation. Geoffrey Paxton, an Episcopal theologian from Australia and a longtime contributor to *Verdict,* is quick to attack the current emphasis on being born again as a perversion of the gospel.[18] In his view, the new birth is only an effect, not an integral part of the gospel. The gospel is an announcement of what has happened fully and definitively in the past history of Jesus Christ. Those who stand closer to the Pietist and Wesleyan traditions rightly object that this position underplays the outpouring of the Holy Spirit and indeed tends to separate the work of the Spirit from that of Christ.

In my lecture tours, the one issue that is almost invariably brought up is the running battle that has developed between feminists and patriarchalists. It is an issue with far-reaching practical consequences, which we are only beginning to see. Evangelical feminists object to the biblical principle of subordination on the grounds that it reflects the patriarchal ethos of the times and is in no way a part of revelation. From their perspective man and woman are equal at work and at home, and both should be granted positions of spiritual leadership in the church. Patriarchalists argue that the biblical teaching is that though men and women are equal heirs to salvation, only men are called to assume positions of leadership in church and family.[19] Some feminists seek an inclusive gender language in worship. Instead of addressing God as Father or Lord (symbols associated with a patriarchal culture), they prefer such substitutes as Father-Mother, Heavenly Parent, or even better, Spirit. Many of the recent splits in the Anglican and Presbyterian churches have been over the question of women's ordination to the ministry. In the Christian Reformed Church one of the burning issues is whether women should even be admitted as deacons, since that, too, is an office of spiritual leadership. Many conservatives see the traditional position on this question as the distinguishing mark between the true and the false church.

One of the promising signs in the evangelical renaissance today is the rebirth of social concern. This is true for the evangelical right as well as the left. Yet even in this area, and perhaps especially in this area, we see signs of disunity. *Sojourners* magazine upholds the Anabaptist ideal of renouncing coercive power in favor of the violence of love to bring in the new world order. *The Reformed Journal,* on the other hand, following Calvin, advocates the right use of power to fashion a holy community.

A large part of the evangelical community is involved in the right-to-life movement. Even *Sojourners* has taken an uncompromising stand against abortion on demand. Opposed to this movement are many of those evangelicals involved in women's liberation, who hold that abortion is a matter to be decided between the woman and her physician. While evangelical feminists generally repudiate pornography, they often tend to support gay liberation.[20] The evangelical right and center, on the contrary, are adamantly opposed to homosexual practices and are stout defenders of family solidarity.

A more recent issue which is beginning to split the evangelical world as well as the wider Christian community is that of nuclear weapons. There has always been a pacifist contingent in evangelical Protestantism, such as the Mennonites and Quakers, but now many of those who come out of the mainstream Reformation question whether the just-war theory can ever apply to a war that involves the use of weapons of mass extermination (nuclear and biochemical).[21] Ironically, many in the right-to-life movement are nonetheless hawkish concerning the need to maintain a strong military defense, and this includes for them a formidable nuclear deterrent. I am thinking here of such persons as Pat Robertson, Francis Schaeffer, Jerry Falwell and Harold O. J. Brown.[22]

Vernon Grounds of Denver Theological Seminary (Conservative Baptist) is one evangelical who is raising his voice against the enigmatic mind-set of many of his colleagues who decry abortion and yet remain silent in the face of the horrendous evil of nuclear war:

> What about the schizophrenia of people who cry out against the murder of embryonic babies yet refuse to cry out against wholesale murder by atomic bombs? For the use of nuclear weapons will indiscriminately kill millions of incalculably precious persons including, no doubt, at least a few million babies! In my judgment, consequently, the same logic which motivates the evangelical battle against abortion as an evil that destroys human life ought to motivate an impassioned anti-nuclear crusade. To denounce one evil while condoning the other is surely schizophrenic.[23]

Billy Graham, too, has become disturbed, if not alarmed, by the accelerating nuclear armaments race.[24] Graham does not call for unilateral disarmament, but he has urged the nation's leaders to take a few risks in curtailing our nuclear arsenal, advocating a freeze on the manufacture of nuclear weapons.

Matters such as these are of momentous significance, entailing grave and difficult ethical decisions. Much of the dissension in the evangelical world today, however, is to be attributed to the elevation of marginal matters into essentials. One of the divisive issues among conservative Baptists is whether the church will have to go through the tribulation before the millennium. In the Restoration movement a pivotal cause of schism has been the use of musical instruments in worship. The current debate on how inconsistencies in dates and numbers in the Bible can be reconciled also appears to be an example of majoring in minors. I think, too, of the preoccupation with behavioral requirements for evangelical clergy and faculty, such as total abstinence from liquor and the taboos on social dancing and card playing.[25]

On the other hand, the great questions of doctrine, including the authority and inspiration of Scripture, the sovereignty of divine grace, the centrality of the atonement, the necessity of a holy life, the meaning of the sacraments and the reality of the second advent of Christ, are indeed issues that the church of today (both liberal and conservative) must grapple with if it is to maintain its identity as the church of Jesus Christ. The role of women in ministry is also of major theological and social significance, and deserves the serious attention of evangelical scholars and leaders. Similarly, the pressing moral issues of our day—abortion, the population explosion, world-wide hunger, the growing disparity between rich and poor, persisting racial discrimination, and nuclear and chemical warfare—have to be included in any evangelical agenda that bears on the Christian life.

Division or polarization is not always a bad thing, because it is often only through vigorous debate that we can arrive at the truth that God wants us to hear. On the other hand, divisiveness or party spirit (Rom. 13:13; 14:19; Gal. 5:20; I Cor. 1:10–15) is always detrimental to the cause of Christ, for it signifies an unwillingness to listen to what our fellow believers are saying and a stubborn refusal to change, even when this may be the will of God. We should not hide from the great issues out of fear of causing a split in the church, but we should resolutely face these issues out of a real concern for the unity of the church. We should enter the debates of our time in a spirit of love and out of fidelity to the truth of the gospel. We should be strong in the confidence that the Spirit of God himself will lead us into all truth if we remain open to his guidance as given through the shared experiences of the believing community and preeminently through the Bible.

THE SCANDAL OF DISUNITY

The disunity of the Christian church today in the face of a resurgent paganism is indeed deplorable. But even more scandalous is the disunity that plagues the evangelical family, the very group within the wider church that stresses fidelity to the gospel and to the Bible. Christian disunity is a contradiction of Christ's prayer that his people be one (John 17:20–23). It also conflicts with Paul's declaration that there is only "one body and one Spirit . . . one Lord, one faith, one baptism" (Eph. 4:4, 5). Disunity on theological and even sociological grounds betrays an appalling ignorance of the nature of the church. Indeed, the classical marks of the church of Jesus Christ are oneness, holiness, apostolicity and catholicity. The last term denotes universal outreach and continuity with the tradition of the whole church.

It is incontestable that the church, and especially the evangelical church, has lost much of its credibility on the mission field because of the bitter infighting between missionary boards and churches. Some have conjectured that China's capitulation to Communism was due, at least to some extent, to the spiritual vacuum in China fostered partly by intra-Christian warfare which prevented the church from giving a consistent and united witness to the truth of the gospel. Some observers are of the opinion that evangelical Protestantism has not advanced in Peru because of "painful historic divisions."[26] The well-known missiologist Pierce Beaver has declared: "More and more I am convinced that exported divisiveness is the greatest hindrance to the spread of the gospel in the non-Christian world."[27]

The ecumenical ideal is not a deadening uniformity but a diversity within unity. The evangelical coat should be a coat of many colors. Yet it is not a coat in which the colors do not harmonize. There can be only one faith and one dogma, but much room for variation in liturgical practices, theological systems and modes of evangelism.

We need to ask: What is the nature of the unity that we should seek? Some evangelicals define this unity in terms of a particular approach to the Bible. The problem with this position is that it is possible to have a high view of Scripture and yet be off-center in both theology and spirituality. At the same time, the pathway to Christian unity certainly involves an acknowledgment of the Bible as the inspired Word of God, the infallible rule for faith and practice. Some contend that the key to unity lies in a common confession of Jesus as Lord. But we already have that, at least outwardly, and disunity is still a glaring reality in our midst.

In my view, there will never be real evangelical unity, let alone Christian unity, until there is an awakening to the reality of the oneness and catholicity of the church, and this will surely entail a confessional agreement on the essentials of the faith as well as an acceptance of the Reformation principle of the church always reforming itself in the light of the higher norm of the gospel as declared in Holy Scripture. With our technocratic mentality, it is painful for us to have to acknowledge that such an awakening will depend not on us (with our multifarious strategies and skills) but on a new outpouring of the Holy Spirit; this means that real unity, both visible and spiritual, will only come in God's own time and way. Yet we can pray and seek for this. We can prepare the way, but unity itself must finally come as a gift from God.

The growing worldliness of the church today perhaps accounts for the fact that so little progress toward church unity is being made. It is disconcerting to reflect that the early evangelicals were forces of *dissent*, but now, by and large, they have become forces of *consent*. Whereas once they were known as nonconformists, they are now for the most part defenders of the status quo, both political and religious.

The values of the technological society have penetrated the enclave of evangelicalism as much or nearly as much as they have the liberal establishment. Prayer is now seen as a technique for satisfying the desires of the heart. Salvation is interpreted as the fulfillment of the self in terms that society can understand and respect. God is portrayed as the unlimited possibility which we can tap into in order to gain security and happiness. Success is measured in terms of productive achievement. The Bible is evaluated according to how it functions in bringing people their desired goals in life.

The blight of modern liberalism since the Enlightenment has been latitudinarianism, the attitude that allows for a variety of ways to come to God. Today this is known as pluralism, which is considered an ideal in many liberal churches, such as the Disciples of Christ, the United Church of Christ, and the United Methodist Church. What liberals do not sufficiently grasp is that while there can be a certain pluralism in doctrinal formulation, there can never be a pluralism in dogma. For then the church ceases to be the church.

Paul Holmer astutely points to the baneful effects of the latitudinarian mentality:

> It certainly was one thing to have Lutherans, Calvinists, and Catholics contending; but at least there was a semblance of argument amid the acrimony. . . . But now there is seldom either acrimony or argument. Much of what we thought was standard and minimal, a kind of point of departure, is no longer quite that. There is hardly anything but the sight of theologians talking past one another.[28]

What evangelicals need to realize is that there is a creeping latitudinarianism in their own circles, especially among the so-called young evangelicals who are understandably trying to break loose from the theological and cultural rigidity and provincialism of their backgrounds. With the ebbing of confessionalism, the growth in mysticism and ethicism comes as no surprise. Mysticism connotes the spiritualizing of religion; ethicism signifies the moralizing of religion. The latter may also involve politicizing religion, a tendency discernible not only in liberal circles but also among some fundamentalists and evangelicals.

If evangelicalism abandons the quest for Christian unity and theological and social relevance, it is liable to become, in Carl Henry's words, "a wilderness sect." On the other hand, if it responds creatively to the challenges of the day by acknowledging its own deficiencies and by being willing to use contemporary rather than archaic philosophical tools to carry on the battle for the faith in our time, it may become the vanguard of a reborn Christianity. The great danger today is that evangelicalism may retreat into a religious ghetto characterized by biblical obscurantism and cultural isolationism. Evangelicalism must neither withdraw from the culture nor capitulate to it but confront it with the biblical gospel which alone can heal the wounds of division in both church and society by opening up a new horizon of meaning to an age afflicted by the anxiety of meaninglessness.

THE IDEOLOGICAL TEMPTATION

Nowhere is the church's capitulation to the culture more apparent than in ideological entanglements. One of the startling facts of the present time is the often tacit and sometimes open alliance of religion with economic and political interests. Perhaps this has always been the case in the history of religion, but we are more aware of this now, thanks to the rise of the science of the sociology of religion. The historical and cultural conditioning of religion is acknowledged not only by sociologists and historians of religion but by theologians as well, including Reinhold Niebuhr and Karl Barth.

Both evangelicals and liberals need to come to grips with the phenomenon of ideology, which has distorted the perception of both Christians and non-Christians and which in no small way accounts for the ruptures and schisms in the Christian world today. Drawing upon the insights of Karl Marx, Karl Mannheim[29] and Reinhold Niebuhr, we might define an ideology as a vision of society that serves to justify or rationalize the interests of a particular class or power structure in the social order. According to Langdon Gilkey, "Ideologies are views of the whole of reality, especially of historical and social reality, which are believed by a community, which claim to be the truth about the whole, but which actually represent a particular point of view or bias, and . . . which in that bias represent and further the interests of a certain class or group."[30] With Hans Küng, we need to recognize that an ideology "produces a distorted picture of the reality of the world, disguises real abuses and replaces rational arguments by an appeal to emotion."[31]

An ideology entails in addition to a theoretical system a definite sociopolitical program. Ideas are no longer abstract models of truth (as in pure philosophy) but now become tools in a program of social restructuring. Ideologies rely not on rational argument but on propaganda, which is truth twisted for political ends.

As Niebuhr astutely observes, there is an ideological taint to all human reasoning, but it is possible to transcend ideology by the humility which rises out of prophetic religion; such humility acknowledges that truth is both a matter of having and not having, that the final synthesis lies beyond the reach of human perception and conception.[32] Ideologists claim a premature possession of the truth and for the purpose of furthering vested interests. Theologians ideally see the truth as a possession of God and consider themselves servants rather than masters of the truth.

It is possible to be conservative or liberal, in both the theological and political sense, without necessarily being ideological. An ideologist regards politics as a matter of ultimate concern, whereas Christian faith relegates politics to the area of preliminary or penultimate concerns.

Evangelicalism is especially vulnerable to the lure of ideologies, because it is generally naive regarding the influences of historical and cultural factors on religious commitment. With disturbing frequency, it falls under the delusion that it is possible to arrive at a system of truth that is valid for all ages (à la Hegel). It sometimes makes the claim that the believer can attain a univocal (and not merely an analogical) knowledge of God that is exempt from the relativity of history (Gordon Clark, Carl Henry).

The impact of ideology can definitely be discerned on both the evangelical right and left. When Carl McIntire ventures to suggest that the New Testament church is being called today "to be a right-wing political organization,"[33] there is reason to believe that he has succumbed to the ideological temptation. Examples of sacrilege in Jerry Falwell's eyes are busing for racial integration, environmental protection laws, and social welfare and deficit spending. One can only conclude that he has not effectively resisted the ideology of conservatism (or classical liberalism). Similarly, Joseph Jackson, then president of the National Baptist Convention, reveals a not so subtle accommodation to conservative ideology: "We must support law and order, for there are no problems in American life that cannot be solved through commitment to the highest laws of our land and in obedience to the American philosophy and way of life."[34]

The shadow of ideology has also penetrated into Southern Baptist churches. Already in the spring of 1969 at a Christian Life Commission seminar at the University of Chicago, John Nichol, pastor of an integrated Southern Baptist church in Decatur, Georgia, lamented the ideological character of so many Southern Baptist churches reflected in "the absence of the cross in the call to discipleship" and "a commitment to secular standards of institutional success."[35]

Ideological coloration is present in the evangelical left as well. Vehement attacks on the injustices spawned by capitalism but the relative silence concerning the destruction of human liberties under socialism and communism are commonplace in left-wing circles, including parts of the evangelical left. A case can be made that as many younger evangelicals gravitate out of the lower middle class into the middle and upper middle classes, they often assume the cultural and political values of their peers. Hence their support for careerism for women, abortion rights and gay rights.[36]

Peter Berger has advanced the thesis that the principal ideological conflict today is between the business and farming communities that can only thrive apart from state regulation and control and the new class, the managerial and professional interests that depend upon state aid for carrying out their programs (such as ecological planning, the distribution of welfare benefits, the supervision of day-care centers, education for the underprivileged).[37] The evangelical right tends to be allied with the first, and the evangelical left with the second.

TYPES OF IDEOLOGY

In order to ascertain the extent of ideological bias in modern evangelicalism and how much it contributes to evangelical disunity, it is necessary to explore the various types of ideology that present particular threats on the American scene today. Much of what will be said here has relevance for the church in all countries forming part of Western civilization.

First, I shall consider what is commonly called conservative ideology, though in fact it represents the values and thought world of classical liberalism. This is the ideology that upholds private initiative and industry, what we have come to call free enterprise.[38] It sees a centralized government as the main threat to individual liberties and consequently supports governmental decentralization. Reflecting continuity with the liberal ideology of the Enlightenment, it regards property rights as practically on a par with human rights. In its rhetoric it champions individualism over statism, though its support of corporate expansion and its insistence on a strong national defense often serve to sacrifice individual freedom to the collective welfare. When H. Richard Niebuhr described the church in bondage to capitalism,[39] he was referring to an ideological, not strictly a political bondage. Conservative ideology fosters a spirit of nationalism by its appeal to the American Way of Life and its preoccupation with national security.

Reinhold Niebuhr was particularly sensitive to the hold of this ideology over American Protestantism, both liberal and conservative. An observation made many years ago has remarkable relevance to the religious and political situation today: "The effort to make voluntary charity solve the problems of a major social crisis, on the score that it represents a higher type of spirituality than coerced giving through taxation, results merely in monumental hypocrisies and tempts selfish people to regard themselves as unselfish."[40]

Whereas classical liberalism or conservatism celebrates free enterprise and private initiative, the emerging ideology of welfare liberalism accentuates the need for social planning and controls within a democratic context. This ideology stresses the safeguarding of human rights and human equality, but at the same time it places an almost inordinate trust in social planners, who are generally drawn from the disciplines of sociology and psychology, since it is assumed that these experts in human behavior will choose what is good for all.[41] While classical liberalism esteems the entrepreneur, welfare liberalism favors the functionary or "organization man" who will carry out the mandate of the corporation or government bureau. The team worker is prized over the rugged individualist. While the prime virtues in the older liberalism (what is now called conservatism) were thrift and industry, the prime virtues in this new ideology are utility, efficiency and loyalty. Welfare liberalism stresses the mastery of nature by technique; therefore, it may legitimately be regarded as the ideology of the technological society.[42]

Closely related is the ideology of socialism, which has made significant inroads throughout the world and which has cast a spell over various neo-orthodox, liberal and evangelical left theologians.[43] Socialism represents not only an economic philosophy but an ideology that seeks to convert the world into a utopia in which everyone will receive an equal portion of available goods. As the ideology of the revolutionary left, socialism purports to speak not for the aristocracy or the bourgeoisie but for the working masses. It champions a radical egalitarianism and interprets social conflict in terms of the class struggle. With Karl Marx and Friedrich Engels, its first two philosophers, it looks forward to a classless society when capitalism will be replaced by communism. In contrast to classical liberalism, it defends human rights over property rights; in contrast to welfare liberalism, it advocates state control of the means of production, not simply state regulation. Personal freedoms are subordinated to the cause of social justice. Socialism seeks to place technology in the service of the class struggle rather than in the service of business expansion (as in classical liberalism) or social stability (as in welfare liberalism).

Like conservatism and welfare liberalism, socialism is also a product of the Enlightenment. It emphasizes the last two of the Enlightenment values: liberty, *equality and fraternity*. David Beckmann has observed that the rich tend to support the liberty and efficiency of the market; the poor, on the other hand, favor a planned economy where equality and fraternity are fostered.[44] Ideological commitment is inseparable from the desire for economic gain and security, and this is why it will always be a part of the human condition.

Modern evangelicalism has been more successful in resisting the allurements of socialism than have neo-orthodoxy and liberalism. Yet this is in no small part because evangelicalism now represents the interests of the moneyed class. In Europe it has become largely removed from the concerns and expectations of the working masses, with the result that many of the working people are aligning themselves with the Socialist or Communist parties. The danger is not that evangelicalism will succumb to socialism but that it will become allied with the interest of the big property owners and corporations.

Another ideology that has infiltrated the church and become a significant factor in much of the inner turmoil within evangelicalism today is feminism. This is the ideology of women's liberation, which strives for a new social order characterized by unisex and the egalitarian family. Feminism generally tries to blur the distinctions between the sexes and consequently promotes the ideal of androgyny, in which men and women are urged to integrate within themselves the masculine and feminine attributes present in all human beings.[45] Divorced from marriage and reproduction, sex becomes a purely private experience contributing to the self-fulfillment of autonomous individuals. Rosemary Ruether, a moderate feminist, declares, "In androgynously developed persons it is not possible to rule out sex/love relations between women or between men."[46] Radical feminists generally support gay liberation, and some, such as Mary Daly, uphold the ideal of lesbianism for women. Ideological feminism also throws its weight behind abortion on demand, no-fault divorce and value-free sex education.

Among the conflicts precipitated by feminists in evangelical circles are women's ordination and desexing the language of worship. It is possible to argue on the grounds of faith itself that women as well as men may be called to the ministry of the Word and sacraments and that gender-inclusive language in worship may have a place, depending on the context. Feminists, however, make women's ordination (to the office of deacon, elder or pastor) a matter of human rights. They contend that it is the *right* of women to be ordained, whereas faith insists that the ministry of the Word is a special calling from God, a *privilege* extended only to some, and not to others, men or women.

On the matter of the language about God, feminists reject such symbols as Father, Lord and Son in reference to the deity on the grounds that these reflect an outmoded patriarchal culture. Most evangelicals retort that we cannot alter the language of revelation without ending in a new religion. To address God as Divine Providence, World Spirit or Source of Sustenance instead of Father (as some feminists recommend) is to depersonalize God. To refer to God as Father-Mother, another feminist substitute, is to make God androgynous.[47]

Many feminists sense an affinity to socialism, having come to the conclusion that women's rights are ultimately dependent on laws rigorously enforced by a federal agency with coercive power. They also generally support day-care centers and abortion clinics run by the state, as well as state-funded sex education programs.

Other feminists feel much closer to libertarianism and anarchism, which relegate decision making to local communities. Many of these people are attracted to neopaganism, where God and the world are practically equated. Communitarianism and nature mysticism form a part of this radical feminist vision, in which witchcraft is readily endorsed. The monotheistic religion of the creator God is replaced by the pantheistic religion of the Goddess.[48]

Another distinctly modern ideology which nevertheless draws upon the past is fascism.[49] Here the principal concern is with national rights over both human rights (as in socialism) and property rights (as in classical liberalism). Fascism champions the rights of the majority over the rights of minorities. It places national honor and security above all else and sees the state in the service of these ideals. It is also intent on preserving the racial or ethnic heritage of a nation. While profamily in its rhetoric, it ends by subordinating the family to the state. Fascism is often allied with a repressive patriarchalism in which marriage is seen as a vocation to fertility. It can also be regarded as a form of elitism, since it pins its hope on the privileged few whom destiny chooses to be leaders.

Fascism, like one part of feminism, is to be associated with neopaganism. It looks back before the Enlightenment, even before the rise of Christianity, to the ancient myths of the old pagan civilizations and barbarian tribes, where the instinctual drives and heroism were celebrated. Unlike socialism and classical liberalism, fascism glories in the irrational. Again, in contrast to socialism, it harbors a distrust of bureaucracy and rational controls and is attracted instead to a voluntarist activism and adventurism. In its economic philosophy, fascism sees the corporations and unions allied with the state for the purpose of creating a homogenous racial and national unit. While Marxist socialism is hostile to religion and seeks ultimately to destroy it, fascism is often outwardly friendly to religion but seeks to contain it or even to transform it.

Fascism is often considered counterrevolutionary rather than genuinely revolutionary, since it promotes a nostalgia for the ideals and values of the past. Yet this kind of distinction can be deceptive, because even though making use of traditionalist rhetoric, it aspires to fashion a wholly new social order.

Many scholars mistakenly label any authoritarian or military regime as fascist, but fascism is something narrower and deeper than state authoritarianism. It is distinguished by charismatic leadership and the call to heroic sacrifice for the tribe (or *Volk*). National Socialism and Italian Fascism were the two principal expressions of fascist ideology in the twentieth century. Falangism in Spain, Peronism in Argentina and Christian Nationalism in South Africa represent incipient fascism. The same can be said for the present regime in Iran, where the masses are mesmerized by a charismatic leader and where fidelity to a particular religioethnic heritage is made the badge of acceptance. This regime also has an adventurist or expansionist foreign policy in that it is intent on exporting its revolution.[50]

Fascist ideology was responsible for the cleavage in the German church in the 1930s when the so-called "German Christians" sought to accommodate their religious heritage to the rising tide of National Socialism. An attempt was made to purge Christianity of its Jewish roots. The Old Testament was denigrated, and Jesus was hailed as cosmopolitan or Aryan rather than Jewish. Other revelations beyond the Bible were posited, such as revelations in nature and history. It was against this perversion of the faith that the Confessing Church came into being, and the Barmen Declaration, drawn up by Karl Barth, became the battle cry of this protest movement.[51] A segment of evangelical Christianity was beguiled by the ideology of National Socialism, but another segment, by standing firm, helped to preserve a genuine Christian witness in those dark days.

I have not given here an exhaustive list of ideologies. A number of others could indeed be mentioned: anarchism, populism,[52] pacifism, environmentalism and libertarianism. The ones I have discussed were chosen because in my opinion they pose peculiar temptations to the church in our day, especially the evangelical church.

Ideological polarization has immense significance for the tensions in evangelicalism today. I believe that it can be shown that the traditionalist evangelicals are tied to or at least sympathetic with classical liberalism or conservatism. The new evangelicals (in common with many academic religious liberals) are attracted to welfare liberalism and socialism. The radical evangelicals are more at home with anarchism and communitarianism, with what Charles Reich calls "Consciousness III."[53]

In the contemporary American context, one can perceive a certain convergence of ideologies. The ideology of the new left and that of the American Way of Life (conservatism) have this in common: an unwarranted trust in technology and an abiding faith in the democratic consensus. The late Huey Long commented that if fascism ever came to America, it would come in the guise of democracy. When the will of the people is equated with the voice of God, we are already under the shadow of a new totalitarianism. Furthermore, when it is said that the will of the people must be interpreted by a socially enlightened elite, whether they be welfare planners, aristocrats or patriots, then individual liberties are in jeopardy.

The overarching ideology of our time might be called secular humanism, the enthronement of cultural values and the mastery of nature by human reason.[54] Salvation is understood in terms of the quest for personal and social well-being. Sin is seen as ignorance, which can be overcome through education, or sickness, which can be dispelled by therapy. This foundational ideology might also be aptly referred to as technological materialism, since the goal in life is the accumulation of material goods and comforts.[55] It sometimes poses as the ideology of the center, which seeks to unite all groups under the umbrella of the general will.[56] It may use the rhetoric of conservatism, but its program is actually closer to that of welfare liberalism and socialism—expanding technology in the service of the corporate state. Because it makes class interest and party loyalty subservient to the good of the larger whole—the people or nation-state (*Volk*)—it has the enigmatic and paradoxical appearance of a democratic fascism.[57]

One cannot predict the future of ideological movements and alignments, but what can be safely said is that the taint of ideology colors our religious commitment and accounts in no small part for the way Christians treat one another and why they are so often at loggerheads with one another.

THE NEED TO RESIST IDEOLOGY

Ideology is spiritually beguiling because it offers those whose faith is eroding a substitute faith. Wherever there is a religious or metaphysical vacuum, bogus religion or ideology enters to fill the vacuum. Indeed:

> Ideological systems provide what Max Scheler called *redemptive knowledge* (*Heilswissen*)—that is, knowledge that not only provides intellectual understanding but also provides existential hope and moral guidance. This is particularly seductive in an age of secularization and relativity, where the traditional religious bodies of "redemptive knowledge" have become implausible to many (especially to intellectuals) and where morality is a very uncertain business.[58]

What we need to realize is that there is a qualitative difference between simple or genuine faith and ideological commitment. The marks of an ideology are intolerance and fanaticism; the marks of faith are humility and openness to the unconditional. Unlike ideology, faith does not claim a premature possession of the truth, but it does profess to know the One who is the truth. While ideology seeks to impose its distorted perception of truth on others, faith simply points others to the truth in the hope that they will come to know in their own way and time. While politics is the passion of ideology, prayer is the passion of faith. Faith cares even for those who spurn the truth of faith, whereas ideology regards with contempt those who resist its allurements. Faith views salvation as an unmerited gift from God; ideology, on the other hand, regards its own program as the way to salvation.

Evangelicals need to understand ideology so that they can better resist it. Marxists contend that all religious commitment is ideologically tainted, but Christians insist that ideology can be transcended at least in part. With Reinhold Niebuhr, I hold that it is possible to rise above ideology in moments of "prayerful transcendence," but nonetheless theological systems and church programs can never be ideologically free. Yet in the humble recognition that even our theologies are mixed with human error and therefore need to be justified by grace, we can begin the process of distinguishing the truth of faith from ideological untruth. Christians should try to detach themselves from ideologies in order to be free to work within ideological movements for greater social justice as genuinely free agents. Yet as Jacques Ellul has many times pointed out, Christians will always be thorns in the flesh in the social movements in which they work, since their ultimate loyalty is not to the movement but to the living God.

It is important for us to be aware of the sources of ideology in social upheavals and conflicts of the past. Both the ideology of the moderate right (classical liberalism) and that of the left (welfare liberalism and socialism) focus on the invincibility of the human spirit, a trademark of the Renaissance and the Enlightenment. Christian faith, on the other hand, upholds the sovereignty and irresistibility of divine grace. Whereas all ideology aggrandizes humanity or at least part of humanity, whether this be the masses, the racially pure minority, or the enlightened social engineers, Christianity seeks to give all the glory to God, though recognizing that through faith we can have a share in this glory as humble recipients and servants of the Most High.

Ideology sees the source of hope in human reason or the instinctual life of man. Christian faith, on the contrary, regards humanity as ensnared in the web of sin, and this means that hope must lie outside humanity in God. Emil Brunner has perceptively remarked, "Religion does not merely criticize one form of civilization or another but casts doubt upon civilization itself and upon humanity, because it casts doubt upon man."[59]

This is not to suggest that the church should withdraw from social conflict. Its role is to inject a salutary word of caution and hope into this conflict. It must seek to remain above ideology, even while it works with the left or right in trying to bring about a greater degree of justice and freedom for all.

The best contribution that evangelicals can make to our pluralistic society today is to emphasize the uniqueness and disparateness of the Christian faith, to point people to a transcendent hope when they see this world as their only hope. Evangelicals should acknowledge and respect the pluralism in American life today without succumbing to the secular dogma that there are many ways to salvation or that no truth is absolute.

Our role as evangelicals is to sound a discordant note that calls into question the universal assumptions of our age. Evolution, for example, when elevated into a dogma that embraces even the moral and spiritual areas of life needs to be unmasked as woefully inadequate and palpably unchristian. Evangelicals have an obligation to stand against the utopianism which is characteristic of the ideological left even while they make common cause with socialists and others in the struggle for justice in our time. The holy community, which has traditionally been part of the Calvinistic and Puritan vision, always needs to be seen as a sign and parable of the kingdom of God, but not as the realization of this kingdom on earth.

Conscious as they are that power in the hands of sinful humanity corrupts, evangelicals are obliged to resist the growing centralization of power in all areas of national and social life. Yet their protest against the unwarranted accumulation of power should be aimed not only at the nation-state but also at the multinational corporations, the labor unions and even the churches.

Another strategy that evangelicals might well consider is the promotion of genuinely Christian schools as an alternative to the public school system, which is deeply penetrated by the values of secular humanism.[60] But so many Christian schools today prove to be the refuge of people who are resisting racial and class integration, and these schools thus end in promoting another kind of humanism or ideology—that of the right. The answer to secular ideology is not a chauvinistic American or even a Christian ideology but a genuinely religious attitude toward life and the world that points beyond ideological polarization.

Living as we do in a technological society, where the emphasis is on productivity, utility and efficiency, evangelicals need to stress the values of faith—integrity, piety, humility and love. In a church that has succumbed to the activist mentality, evangelicals need to emphasize that being in Christ takes precedence over busyness in the name of Christ.

It is important, however, that we oppose the demands of the ideological and religious right for prayer in the public schools. The kind of prayer that would be sanctioned by the state would be innocuous at best and blasphemous at worst. Christian prayer cannot be imposed upon non-Christians nor even upon believers, and even though pending legislation calls for voluntary prayer, it would not remain voluntary once zealots gained control of the particular schools in question.[61] Prayers stemming from coercion or from the desire to give no offense to others are surely not pleasing sacrifices to God.

Karl Barth has wisely seen that the church must always stand against the stream of the culture if it is to make its witness known.[62] When the culture becomes dominated by the ideological or religious right, then the church must tilt toward the left. When the ideological left gains control, the church must lend its support to the valid concerns of the right. It must always champion the oppressed, but when the oppressed become the new oppressors, it must then be ready to pronounce God's judgment upon them. It should seek to comfort the afflicted, but when the afflicted gain the comforts and peace that were withheld from them, then its task is to afflict the newly comfortable.

Finally, evangelicals should come to realize that one of the salient marks of the true church is racial and class inclusiveness. Too many evangelicals enamored with church growth have sought to build culturally homogeneous congregations. Such homogeneity is conducive to stability and expansion but often at the cost of obedience to the prayer of Christ that his people be one (John 17:20–22).

H. Richard Niebuhr has documented in his careful study *The Social Sources of Denominationalism* that it is not so much doctrinal disagreement as class conflict that lies behind the proliferation of denominations and sects in our time.[63] We need to recognize that classism is as much a sin as nationalism, racism and sexism and that the gospel will break down the barriers that divide the classes, races and nations if we will only take the risk of letting the gospel do its work (cf. Eph. 2:14–16). A case could be made that the movement from fundamentalism to evangelicalism and neoevangelicalism is motivated partly by a change in class status. The reason why so many young evangelicals are feminists is surely in part because they are moving from the patriarchal culture of the lower and lower middle classes into the more egalitarian culture of the upper middle class, where autonomy and independence are prized.[64]

One of the lasting contributions that evangelicals could make to the wider church and even to the secular culture is to demonstrate that racial, class and ethnic divisions can be surmounted in a fellowship of faith and love which the New Testament calls the koinonia. The best way to counter ideology is to prepare the way for a society where ideology is not a real temptation. The most powerful answer to Marxism would be for the church itself to become the classless society that socialists dream about but never seem to find.

THE GROWING CHURCH CONFLICT

As the values of our secularized society increasingly penetrate the church, the church is placed in the position of being obliged to strive to maintain its identity and the integrity of its message. On the left, Christian faith is threatened by an ever bolder secular humanism, and on the right by an emerging nationalism.

The evangelical community itself has proved to be vulnerable to ideological and cultural infiltration despite its claim that it has remained separate from the world and has thereby preserved the gospel in its pure form. The evangelical right is tempted to align itself with the political and ideological right, whereas the evangelical left is increasingly enchanted with the ideological left.

Liberal Protestantism, having severed itself from the historical and theological heritage of the church, is even more open to ideological seduction. Some segments of liberalism have been caught up in the ideology of the right. I am thinking here of Moral Re-Armament, Up With People, and Spiritual Mobilization (now defunct). Others have embraced the ideological left, with its uncritical support of radical feminism, abortion on demand and the revolutionary struggles of the third world. The magazine *Christianity and Crisis*, which at one time maintained a genuinely prophetic stance, seems in danger of succumbing to the ideological temptation on the left. The *National Catholic Reporter*, by so closely identifying with left-wing causes, including gay liberation, furnishes still another example of how ideology undermines a genuinely prophetic critique of society.[65] Susceptibility to Marxist ideology is becoming ever more apparent in the boards and agencies of the World Council of Churches and National Council of Churches.[66]

The growing church conflict (*Kirchenkampf*) crosses all denominational and ideological lines.[67] The life of the church is not at stake (Christ will always maintain his church), but the ability of the church to speak a sure word from God to the present cultural situation is seriously impaired. In the industrial nations of the West, the church is not threatened by persecution (as is the case behind the Iron Curtain and in many parts of the third world), but it is threatened by seduction by the principalities and powers of the world that sometimes appear in the guise of angels of light.

Where does the pivotal issue lie? Some argue that the church will become relevant again only when it identifies with the poor and the homeless of the world, only when it throws its weight behind the struggle of the dispossessed peoples of the world for liberation. They contend that the church, to maintain itself as the church, must take a firm stand in support of socialism, feminism and pacifism.

Others see the overriding issue as the safeguarding of the transcendent vision of the church. They fear that the church is succumbing to an idealistic or naturalistic monism in its encounter with current philosophies and other world religions. This is the concern of those who drew up the Hartford Appeal in 1975.[68]

Still others hold that the church will not free itself from heterodoxy until it reaffirms the infallibility and inerrancy of the Bible, its ruling standard for life and conduct. The issue is fidelity to the

Bible, and only when this fidelity is restored will we see a growing sensitivity to the world's needs and the rediscovery of transcendence. This view is represented by the International Council on Biblical Inerrancy and the recent books in defense of biblical inerrancy by Harold Lindsell, Norman Geisler, John Warwick Montgomery, R. C. Sproul and others.

My position is that the crucial issue today is the battle for the gospel. It is not simply the authority of the Bible but the integrity of the gospel that is at stake. This includes the ethical imperatives of the gospel as well as the doctrinal distinctives integral to the gospel.

We need to reaffirm what Paul Tillich calls "the Protestant principle," the protest against absolutizing the relative.[69] Both church and culture today are guilty of creating idols, of absolutizing ideas and values that supposedly serve the cause of human advancement. When either the state or the church, the Bible or the creeds, are invested with divinity, they become obstacles to worship that is done in spirit and in truth; indeed, they become substitutes for the true faith. As evangelicals, we believe that the Bible, the church and the creeds can become the channels or vessels of the Word of God, which alone is absolute; they can render an authentic and binding witness to the Word of God, but in and of themselves they are not to be confused with the very voice of God.[70] We cannot have the Word of God in our pockets, as is the case with the Bible or a church decree, but the Word can have us in his possession. We cannot possess or control the Word of God, but the Word of God can possess and control us. The Word can make us his fitting servants and instruments.

Today, our task is to emphasize the freedom of the gospel in the face of growing centralization of power and authority in the hands of the nation-state or the giant corporations. In America, it seems, the main enemy is the corporate state, the multinational corporations allied with a strong national government. A highly centralized state is not itself the main problem, though it is a contributing factor to the present malady. The real problem is the state in the service of secular humanism (the ideology of democratic socialism) or nationalism (the ideology of the right). It is not the state but state idolatry, it is not secular culture, but culture idolatry, that prove to be adversaries of the church and its gospel. I agree with Dorothy Sayers that

> people who say that this is a war of economics or of power-politics, are only dabbling about on the surface of things. . . . At bottom it is a violent and irreconcilable quarrel about the nature of God and the nature of man and the ultimate nature of the universe; it is a war of dogma.[71]

The time is approaching when the church in America, like the church in Germany in the 1930s, may be compelled to become a confessing church, one that confesses its faith out of fidelity to the divine commandment in the face of certain hostility and even persecution. A confessing church will invariably have a confessional statement of faith, though it is not the statement of faith but the gospel that is the real object of its confession. Abraham Kuyper gives this sound advice:

> When principles that run against your deepest convictions begin to win the day, then battle is your calling, and peace has become sin; you must, at the price of dearest peace, lay your convictions bare before friend and enemy, with all the fire of your faith.[72]

It may well be that the present divisions within evangelicalism will be overshadowed by future divisions. The authentic heirs of the evangelical heritage—those whose ultimate trust is in Jesus Christ alone and whose only message is the gospel that he gives us—may find themselves allied with fellow believers who happen to be in liberal churches and even in the Catholic and Eastern Orthodox churches. They may also find themselves opposed by their kinsmen in the faith, those who pride themselves on being evangelical or orthodox.

Before it brings about unity at a deeper level, the gospel creates division among people. The disunity that has its source in personal or denominational pride or in ideological or sociological alignments is an abomination to God. But the disunity that is brought about by the sword of the gospel may indeed be a blessing, since the true church then becomes distinguished from the false church, and people know where the real battle lines are (cf. II Cor. 2:15, 16; Heb. 4:12, 13).

The church today is called to speak a sure word from God concerning the critical social issues of our time: abortion, the population explosion, nuclear war, the poisoning of the environment, the breakdown of the family and the growing disparity between rich and poor. It is also imperative that it address itself to the crucial theological issues of today: the authority of the Bible, the uniqueness of Jesus Christ, the meaning of the cross of Christ, the decisive role of the sacraments and the mission of the church.

A church that claims to be evangelical, catholic and reformed will have to speak to these and other pressing issues. But what it speaks must be the Word of God and not the word of the "new demons," the harbingers of ideology, for then the church would in fact be the false, not the true church. The test of true prophecy is whether the church will recognize and successfully meet the challenges that the Spirit of God has placed upon it for our day.

V

Pathways to Evangelical Oblivion

Let us remember here that on the whole subject of religion one rule is to be observed, and it is this—in obscure matters not to speak or think, or even long to know, more than the Word of God has delivered.

JOHN CALVIN

To mingle in politics, before all else, is today to kill hope and to turn back God's gift.

JACQUES ELLUL

The intention should be not to justify Christianity in this present age, but to justify the present age before the Christian message.

DIETRICH BONHOEFFER

Are we to be primarily and almost exclusively concerned with evangelistic campaigns and with the attempt to make them more efficient by new methods and techniques? Or, should we not concentrate more . . . upon praying for, and laying the basis of Christian instruction for, revival as it is described in the Bible?

D. MARTYN LLOYD-JONES

RESTORATIONISM

OF ALL THE STRATEGIES that could insure the eclipse of evangelicalism as a movement of renewal in the church today, none is more dangerous than the way of repristination. This is the temptation to romanticize past periods in the history of the church or creeds and confessions associated with particular traditions in the church. It signifies a flight from responsibilities in facing the challenges of the present and future and a retreat into a supposedly safe enclave of the past. Every vital theological movement will seek to learn from the past; but it is another thing to enthrone the past. The latter is antiquarianism; the former is true conservatism. Evangelicals should not be reactionary in the sense of clinging to the past, but they should be conservative in the sense of drawing upon the past.

Repristination in the area of biblical studies is remarkably evident in evangelical circles. There is often a return to a precritical approach even while lip service is given to the proper place for historical and literary criticism. The reticence of evangelicals to question publicly the Pauline authorship of the pastoral epistles is deplorable so long as it is motivated by political instead of scholarly considerations. Many of those in the scientific creationist movement bring evangelicalism into disrepute by treating the first chapters of Genesis as literal rather than sacred history and then trying to reconcile the details of what is written with the latest findings of science.[1] John R. W. Stott wisely espouses the ideal of being a fundamentalist and a higher critic at the same time.[2] It is possible to hold to the fundamentals of the faith and yet be thoroughly critical in the examination of the materials in which the fundamental truth of the faith is given to us.

Restorationism is also apparent in the area of ecclesiology. A growing number of evangelicals are seeking to return to the undivided church of the first five centuries and make subscription to the so-called ecumenical creeds mandatory for all clergy and even for laity.[3] Some wish to revive the office of bishop (this in itself is not objectionable), and a few are even giving serious consideration to apostolic succession as the guarantee for a valid ministry.[4]

In a similar spirit, there is a movement to invest the priest or pastor with sacerdotal authority; as a result, the ministry acquires a supernatural aura. One evangelical minister serving in the United Church of Christ has described the body of Christ in his church paper in the following way: Christ is the head, the pastor is the neck and the laypeople comprise the lower members of the body. The conclusion is that one can reach Christ only through the mediation of the pastor.[5] Many Catholics in the post-Vatican II tradition would argue that this represents not authentic Catholic teaching but an exaggeration of certain valid emphases in Catholic thought in the High Middle Ages when the juridical model of the priesthood reigned supreme.[6] Most catholic restorationists in the evangelical churches do not go to this extreme, but it shows the dangers inherent in this kind of orientation.

Significantly, many of those in the new Oxford movement display uncritical admiration for Pope John Paul II, often depicting him as the model of Christian piety.[7] He is without doubt a man of courage and vision, but is his vision sufficiently biblical and fully ecumenical? His statements on moral issues today frequently reveal a biblical and pastoral orientation that is sorely lacking in both Protestant ecumenical and evangelical circles. At the same time, he closes his eyes to the implacable reality of the population explosion, refusing even to reconsider the traditional Catholic ban on all forms of artificial birth control. His stubborn resistance to the growing demand for clergy marriages in the face of declining vocations to the priesthood indicates a person who is fixated on the past rather than alive to the myriad possibilities that God brings to the church in the here and now.

Through their nostalgia for the early church, restorationists of the catholic type often end in making antiquity rather than divine revelation the norm for truth. By regarding church tradition or the consensus of the whole church as the criterion for judging and interpreting Holy Scripture, they succumb to one of the endemic errors of historical Roman Catholicism. Of course, the Catholic churches (Roman Catholicism, Eastern Orthodoxy, Anglo-Catholicism) are not alone in misunderstanding the respective roles of Scripture and tradition. Many of the cults (Mormonism, the Jehovah's Witnesses, the sectarian Church of Christ in the Philippines) are no less guilty in this respect. Authentic evangelical theology, by contrast, contends that the church is servant rather than master of the Word of God, that its task is to witness to and proclaim rather than contribute or add to the truth of Christian faith.

Those who call themselves catholic evangelicals, in the sense in which I use this phrase, wish to maintain continuity with the tradition of the whole church, but they nevertheless see the Word of God revealed in the Bible as having priority over the decrees and councils of the church. The church recognized but did not create the canon. It acknowledged the divine authority of the canonical books which they already possessed by virtue of their inspiration by the Holy Spirit. A church that is truly catholic is a church based on the apostolic doctrine contained in the New Testament, not a church supervised by bishops who supposedly stand in an unbroken succession to the original apostles. It is the doctrine that validates the ministry and not vice versa. I heartily concur with the Puritan father Richard Sibbes: "Beloved, that *that makes a church to be a catholic church . . . is the catholic faith.*"[8]

Antiquarianism is by no means confined to those who are attracted to the undivided church of the first five centuries. Others exalt the Protestant Reformation and its confessions to an excessive degree. The sixteenth century is no more sacrosanct than any other; to be sure, it heralded the rediscovery of the biblical message concerning salvation by the unmerited grace of God, but at the same time it precipitated a nearly fatal rupture in the ranks of believers that continues to this day.

The Reformation recovered the forensic or juridical meaning of the doctrine of justification, hitherto sorely neglected or virtually ignored in the Catholic theological tradition. Yet because of the polemics of the time, it failed to do justice to the mystical and eschatological dimensions of justification.

In Lutheranism, justification was emphasized to such an extent that sanctification was underplayed. Whereas justification was practically absorbed into sanctification in Catholic mystical theology, sanctification faded into insignificance in some strands of Reformation biblical theology. In his battle against the antinomians, Luther sought to correct this one-sided emphasis on justification: "They may be fine Easter preachers, but they are very poor Pentecost preachers, for they do not preach . . . 'about the sanctification by the Holy Spirit,' but solely about the redemption of Jesus Christ."[9]

We need to draw upon the abiding insights of the great Reformers without idolizing the Reformation. We must build upon the enduring truths of the Reformation without simply returning to that age. Similar advice can be given to those in conservative Methodism and the Holiness movement whose goal is to restore the pristine truths of Wesleyanism.

There is a place for a distinctly Lutheran, Calvinist, Wesleyan or Roman Catholic witness, but whatever the form, it should always point beyond itself to Jesus Christ, the one Lord of the church to whom all of us are subject. Calvinists should always ask where they can learn from their Arminian opponents. Instead of condemning the Reformation outright, Catholics should investigate the deficiencies in their own church that gave rise to the Reformation.[10] Those who champion the Reformed tradition should inquire why so many of its children are disavowing their heritage and embracing Pentecostalism. Until the church attains visible unity, we need to keep alive the distinctive hallmarks of our respective traditions, but this must be done in a spirit of self-criticism and humility. We should always remember that our foremost loyalty is to Jesus Christ and that when anything in our tradition becomes more of an obstacle than an aid to the proclamation of the gospel of Christ, we must then be willing to give up what had been previously cherished.

The lure of repristination is a problem, too, in the Roman Catholic Church, where many in reaction against the excesses resulting from Vatican Council II yearn for the triumphalist church of Vatican I. Charismatic Catholics (who sometimes identify themselves as evangelical Catholics) seem drawn to a restorationist posture, though it would be a mistake to characterize the mainstream of the Catholic charismatic movement in this way. Doctrines and practices dear to restorationist Catholics include papal infallibility, the Latin mass, novenas, the veneration and invocation of the saints (especially Mary), the veneration of the relics of saints, pilgrimages to shrines and the meritoriousness of monastic vocations. The great Marian doctrines, such as the Immaculate Conception and the Assumption of Mary, are also highly prized by these Catholics. One of their mottoes is "To Jesus through Mary."

Regrettable though these tendencies are, the growing reaction against creeping liberalism in the Catholic Church is understandable. For it is not only traditional formulas and practices but the gospel itself that is being called into question by some of those in the avant-garde. Karl Barth had serious reservations about various thrusts of Vatican II and warned against any rapprochement with the Enlightenment.[11] At the same time, evangelicals can appreciate Vatican II for its willingness to rethink traditional doctrine and practice in the light of the gospel and for its readiness to enter into dialogue with the "separated brethren" for the purpose of furthering the cause of Christian unity.

Those who are attracted to the spirit of repristination need to remember that some of the great saints of the church have called bishops and even popes to repentance, that the giants of Catholic tradition were nearly always involved in movements of radical church reform and were more often than not suspected of heresy. Catholics, particularly those who consider themselves evangelical, should bear in mind that a flight into the past is not the only alternative to a capitulation to the *Zeitgeist* of the present. The great saints of Catholic tradition displayed a readiness to follow Christ into the darkness of their age, fortified in the knowledge that he is already the victor against the prince of darkness. Both Protestant and Catholic evangelicals would do well to emulate these enduring models of holiness in the world.

Finally, we need to give attention to a restorationism in theological method. Right-wing evangelicals in particular are fascinated by the empirical rationalism of the later Enlightenment, especially as it came to America in the form of Scottish realism.[12] When John Warwick Montgomery maintains that "the sole ground" for judging the truth-claims of faith is "empirical probability,"[13] he is manifesting a philosophical bias endemic to the evangelical world. In these circles, the inductive method is prized over the deductive, and the Bible is treated as "a storehouse of facts" (Charles Hodge). Some in this camp, e.g., Norman Geisler, are also attracted to the philosophical method of Thomas Aquinas, since Thomas was more empirically oriented than many of his contemporaries, who stood in the tradition of Platonism and Neoplatonism. Among these same evangelicals, there is a concerted attempt to revive the cosmological proofs for the existence of God, which had supposedly been demolished by Hume and Kant in the eighteenth century.

Another strand in modern evangelicalism tends to maintain continuity with the idealistic rationalism of the early Enlightenment and the seventeenth-century Age of Reason. Rational clarity and logical consistency are valued more highly than empirical verification, the norm for truth in the later Enlightenment. Deduction is defended over induction, though the latter is not wholly discounted. Some who gravitate toward rationalism, e.g., Gordon Clark and Ronald Nash seek to rehabilitate the theory of innate ideas,[14] which ultimately goes back to Plato but which reappears in Augustine, Descartes and Leibniz, among others. Needless to say, deduction from metaphysical first principles is the method that has the approbation of these evangelicals. Gordon Payne's contention that biblical inerrancy "is established by logical reasoning from premises stated in the Bible" reflects this same kind of orientation.[15]

When theological method is so closely tied to philosophical method, theology is transmuted into philosophy of religion. A concomitant danger is that philosophical presuppositions are imposed upon Scripture, with the result that the real meaning and impact of the scriptural revelation are lost. The mystery and paradox in revelation are reduced to logical axioms capable of being understood by unbelievers as well as believers. The Word of God becomes a rational formula wholly in the control of the theologian, and theology becomes the systematic harmonizing of rational truths rather than an incomplete and open-ended explication of revelational meaning that always stands in need of revision and further elucidation.

Too often in the past history of the church, theologians have confused the living God of the Bible with the God of philosophical theism. It is possible to speak of a biblical theism (cf. Heb. 11:6), which is rooted, however, not in abstract speculation but in the event of the incarnation of the Word of God. The God of biblical faith is not a construct of the mind but a supramundane reality beyond the reach of human conception and perception. "Philosophical theism," Paul Holmer reminds us, "despite its long and hallowed history, is not the essence of Christian and Jewish religion; neither is the denial of that theism invariably and necessarily the denial of God Almighty."[16]

We can learn from the partial understandings and misunderstandings of the theology of the past, but our final criterion must always be the self-revelation of Jesus Christ attested in Holy Scripture. We can even learn from the methodologies of the philosophical theologians, but these must constantly be measured by the revealed wisdom in the Scriptures.

I agree with Paul Tillich that theology is neither an empirical-inductive nor a metaphysical-deductive science.[17] Nor is it a combination of induction and deduction, as some contemporary evangelicals would have it.[18] Yet I am reluctant to endorse the Tillichian understanding of theology as an elucidation of the symbols of church tradition correlated with the creative questions of the culture. For Tillich, the object of faith is the mystery of the New Being which transcends the subject-object cleavage and therefore can only be grasped in moments of ecstatic self-transcendence; this mystery, moreover, can be communicated only by ciphers or symbols which give a true awareness but not conceptual knowledge.

I see theology as a faith-responsive investigation which rests fundamentally neither on induction nor deduction nor even on intuition but on a receptivity to revelation, a receptivity created by the Holy Spirit and itself forming a part of revelation. God can be an object of knowledge but only because he makes himself so in the event of his self-revelation in Jesus Christ. Induction and deduction are employed in the service of faith, but faith gains its fundamental understanding from neither of these, indeed from no cognitive capacity within man but only from the Word itself.

We shall be immeasurably richer if we draw upon the wisdom of the fathers, the Reformers, the Pietists and Puritans, and even from the luminaries of Protestant orthodoxy, but let us take care that we do not simply repeat their errors. We need to take into consideration the modern philosophical critiques of the philosophies of the Enlightenment (given by Hume, Kant, Kierkegaard, Wittgenstein) as well as the theological critiques of the whole philosophical enterprise (Barth, Brunner, Reinhold Niebuhr). Instead of trying to restore the biblical-classical synthesis in which biblical meanings are united with the secular philosophical wisdom of Hellenism (a temptation of Renaissance and Enlightenment thinkers), we need to forge a new theological method that will be true to the Scriptures but also cognizant of the theological and philosophical revolutions in the past two centuries.

SEPARATISM

If many evangelicals have sought refuge in the allurements of restorationism, even more are tantalized by the appeal of separatism, a perennial temptation for earnest believers throughout the history of the church. Evangelicals especially are attracted to the ideal of a pure church in which the wheat has been separated from the tares, despite the fact that our Lord regarded this ideal as not realizable in earthly history (Matt. 13:24–30). Separatism leads to sectarianism (the delusion that we are the only true church) and ghettoism, in which the church becomes isolated from the theological and moral debates of the age. Carl Henry has rightly warned against the perils of "social isolationism" and "spiritual individualism" which so often afflict evangelicalism.[19]

It is disturbing but true that most current evangelical thought is not on the cutting edge of theology. It is characterized by a preoccupation with issues that no longer trouble the church at large. Some of these issues should be left buried in the past.

Many evangelicals appeal to II Corinthians 6:17, 18, where Paul gives salutary advice designed to keep believers from going astray: "Come out from them, and be separate from them, says the Lord" (v. 17 a RSV). Yet the apostle is not encouraging either corporate or individual withdrawal from society; instead, he is trying to steer believers away from marriage and intimate companionship with unbelievers. His admonition is similar to the warning in I John against love of the world, "the lust of the flesh and the lust of the eyes and the pride of life" (2:15, 16 RSV). Paul's concern is that believers maintain the values and goals of their faith which will invariably set them in opposition to the world; yet it is precisely in this opposition that believers can penetrate the bastions of the world and bring them into subjection to Jesus Christ.

Nothing is said in II Corinthians 6 about separation from other believers. While we are called to break fellowship with those in the community of faith who become immoral or apostate (I Cor. 5:9–13),[20] we are obliged to retain our ties with believers who hold to a slightly different understanding of the mission and goal of the church. Paul entered into dialogue with Peter and the other apostles at Jerusalem, but by no means was he contemplating the possibility of a new church (Acts 15).

The counterfeit religion of separatism has a long and checkered history in the life of the church. We see it in Tertullian, who finally broke with the Catholic Church and joined the Montanist sect, which elevated virginity over marriage and enjoined on its members all kinds of ascetic disciplines. Augustine was caught up in the struggle against the Donatists, who refused to readmit as members of the church those who had fallen away under persecution. "If you love the Head," declared Augustine, "you love the members." The Donatists manifestly failed this test, thereby proving that they were themselves a false church.

A sectarian mentality is evident in modern fundamentalism which is adamantly opposed to fellowship with persons and churches whose theologies are suspect. Dispensational fundamentalists speak of the "twilight of the Church" and urge regenerate Christians to withdraw from the established churches into enclaves of holiness in a hostile world. The Exclusive Plymouth Brethren have no compunction in terminating fellowship even with those in their own church who fraternize with other Christians. The disowning of apostates, which is supported by Scripture, is quite different from breaking dialogue and fellowship with Christians whose life-style reflects spiritual immaturity or who verge toward heterodoxy. The community of faith includes a vast array of people who still hold to the core of the faith but whose theological understanding is deficient or unbalanced. We should remember that Jesus himself continued to attend the temple and the synagogue even after he announced the message of his kingdom.

Many sincere but misguided Christians seek an ideal church and therefore give up on the local church because they regard themselves as superior morally and religiously to their brothers and sisters in the faith. But our commitment is not to a romantic idealism but to the evangelical faith, which sees the ideal as always ahead of us, something for which we should strive but never claim to possess. Evangelical Christianity holds that the true church is a church of sinners, that the church without spot or wrinkle (Eph. 5:27) is an eschatological goal, never a present achievement. Augustine on one occasion compared the church of Jesus Christ to Noah's ark: If it were not for the storm outside no one could stand the stench inside. Luther often likened the church to a hospital for sick souls. Instead of being already well, we as Christians are convalescents on the road to recovery. We still require the medicine of the Word and sacraments as well as the support of the koinonia. Once we suppose, however, that we can stand on our own apart from the life-support system of the church, then we shall suffer a relapse and our condition will be worse than it was previously.

Jesus' battle with the Pharisees was directed against the idea that the community of faith is a holy club in which only those who qualify morally and religiously are admitted. Our Lord expressly said that he had come to call not the righteous but sinners to repentance (Mark 2:17). The Pharisees, obsessed as they were with the moral and religious taboos of rabbinic Judaism, felt threatened by both the words and life-style of Jesus, whose goal was to break down the walls that divide people from one another (cf. Eph. 2:14–16). Jesus condemned the Pharisees for trusting in themselves and despising others (Luke 18:9).

Against John Nelson Darby and Ellen White, who in the nineteenth century called people out of the institutional churches, I side with Richard Sibbes, sixteenth- and seventeenth-century Puritan, who remained within the Anglican church; Philip Spener and Count Nikolaus von Zinzendorf, German Pietists who sought to reform the church from within; and Gerhard Tersteegen, the eighteenth-century German Reformed mystic, who continued to be loyal to a church that opposed him and even persecuted him.

Tersteegen, a layman and ribbon weaver by trade, was careful to hold his meetings for renewal at times that did not conflict with church services. Yet pastors in the area of Mülheim, Germany, were still alarmed enough to pressure the authorities to forbid Tersteegen from holding public meetings. For ten years Tersteegen was prohibited from preaching the gospel in Protestant Germany, but he sought to combat his accusers by prayer and goodwill, instead of setting up a new church. Eventually he was able to begin his meetings again after winning at least a modicum of respect from church and state authorities. Tersteegen declared, "A true mystic does not easily become a separatist, he has more important things to do."[21]

Despite their wide theological differences on matters of grace and free will, John Wesley and George Whitefield frequently exchanged pulpits and preserved an affectionate respect for one another. Even though they eventually had to maintain separate congregations and separate meeting places, they did not see these as separate churches. When Whitefield preached for Wesley, he tactfully avoided commending predestination or disparaging perfection. Whitefield's tabernacles were always open to Wesley, as were the chapels of the Countess of Huntingdon, a convinced Calvinist. When a censorious Calvinist asked Whitefield whether they would ever see Wesley in heaven, he received this retort: "I fear not, he will be so near the throne, and we shall be at such a distance, that we shall hardly get a sight of him."[22] Wesley and Whitefield were enabled to make an enduring and socially revolutionary witness in eighteenth-century English Protestantism, because their faith had, to a considerable degree, been perfected in love.

J. Gresham Machen felt constrained to break with Princeton Theological Seminary, because what he regarded as the true biblical witness was scarcely tolerated. At the same time, he strove to remain within the Presbyterian Church in the U.S.A., though he could not maintain that position. He was finally defrocked for trying to start a mission order within the denomination closely adhering to the tenets of the Westminster Confession. John Gerstner, retired professor of church history at Pittsburgh Theological Seminary, has more than once threatened to withdraw from the United Presbyterian Church, U.S.A. because of the inroads of secularism in that denomination. Yet he decided to maintain his affiliation in order to work for reforms as best he can.[23]

The great Reformers, Luther and Calvin, also had to decide whether to continue to work for reform within the Catholic Church or to carry on their work outside. Actually the decision was forced upon them when the church in its defensiveness expelled both of them, even though they remained adamantly opposed to all forms of separatism and sectarianism. Luther was compelled to leave both his Augustinian order and the Catholic Church, because his doctrine was not tolerated. Far from being a radical or liberal, he was basically a conservative anxious to maintain continuity with the church's tradition but also eager to revivify this tradition in the light of the gospel of Jesus Christ. Luther was one of the last of the monks who embraced the Reformation doctrine to give up his monastic cowl, and he did so with sadness.[24]

The debate today on the charismatic renewal in the church revolves around whether the new wine of the Spirit can be poured into the old wineskins of churches that have fallen under the spell of a stultifying formalism. Some charismatics have elected to stay in their respective churches and have proved to be a salutary leavening influence. Others have chosen separation, contending that the churches are controlled by spiritless rather than Spirit-filled Christians.[25]

Karl Barth has called for a thorough reformation in the life and thought of the church today. Yet he saw reformation not as the overthrow of existing practices and attitudes (though sometimes it would entail this) but rather as the renewal of what has become moribund or inert but which is not destitute of saving grace. He contrasted reformation with restoration as well as with revolution, both of which are often associated with separatism:

> Reformation is not the restoration and conservation of the old and sacrosanct. Nor is it revolution. Fundamental crises are the last thing that the church needs or that is good for it. Reformation is provisional renewal, a modest transforming of the church in the light of its origin.[26]

At the same time, Barth recognized that when the church becomes the false church, as in the case of a significant segment of the German church under the Nazis, then the only pathway is restitution, not reformation. Restitution means cutting away the cultural and philosophical baggage that has subverted the church's message and mission and returning to the beginnings. Such radical surgery, Barth held, is necessary only in extreme situations. As a general rule, one should not lightly discard those things that have for so many years been employed in the service of the church's message, even the philosophical concepts of Hellenism. Barth lent his support to the ecumenical movement but always with reservations. Likewise, he was favorably disposed toward the Second Vatican Council, but again maintained a critical stance.

Like Barth and the Reformers, we must recoil from separatism not only because it fosters unnecessary discord and divisiveness in the church but also because it subverts the understanding of the truth of faith. Right doctrine and the right attitude toward our neighbor are inextricably intertwined, and when we break off relations with our neighbor, this means that our perception of the mysteries of revelation is seriously impaired (cf. I John 2:5, 6; 3:6; 4:8). Without love, Augustine maintained, one cannot properly understand the truths of Scripture. According to the eminent church historian and theologian of the Mercersburg movement, Philip Schaff, "Heresy is always latent schism, and schism is always latent heresy." When we separate from those we consider heretical, he suggests, we shall probably fall into heresy ourselves. Indeed, the implication is that the very desire to separate may be born out of a heretical distrust of the dogmas of the faith.

Robert Brinsmead, an ex-Seventh-Day Adventist, who has learned from bitter experience the virulent fruits of sectarianism,[27] makes an important distinction between the sectarian and catholic spirits: "Whereas the sectarian spirit is anxious to draw a line which identifies the spiritual elite, the gospel is accompanied by the catholic spirit, which is anxious to draw a circle that makes the Christian fellowship as wide as Christ intended."[28] The sectarian spirit not only subordinates the gospel to its distinctive doctrine but may actually present this doctrine as the gospel. Yet Brinsmead is keenly aware that sectarianism is not the greatest evil: "We would gain nothing if, after fleeing from the bear of sectarianism, we were bitten by the viper of compromise. The agony of divisions is better than the complacency of indifference."[29]

We may sometimes have to separate from the parent body (as Brinsmead did),[30] but we must never be separatists. If we separate we should do so for the purpose of a new church alignment that will be even more inclusive than the old. We should not so much will to separate from the church that has nurtured us, but we should be driven out and then only for the sole reason of standing firm for the truth of the gospel. Troublemakers are expelled or forced to leave a church because they persistently place their own interests above the common good. Saints are forced to leave because they willingly sacrifice their own interests for the sake of the gospel.

ACCOMMODATIONISM

Among all the factors that are causing evangelicals to leave mainline denominations today, none is more frequently cited than the capitulation to worldly mores and goals. What those who opt to leave do not always realize is that this problem afflicts the whole theological spectrum, from the far left to the far right. The peril of accommodationism often takes the form of revising or updating the thought and practice of the faith in order to bring them into harmony or at least correlation with the highest values of the culture. Richard Quebedeaux has aptly coined the phrase "worldly evangelicals" to denote those evangelicals who have succumbed to worldly standards in order to establish the credibility and relevance of their faith.[31]

Accommodationism is apparent in modernist attempts to rethink theology in order to make it meaningful to contemporary man.[32] On the left, we see feminist, political, third-world, relational, liberation and socialist theologies, all trying to show that their particular emphases are in tune with modern times. On the right, Christianity is depicted as a superior philosophy or the highest of the world religions, to which every earnest seeker after truth must surely give a serious hearing. Or the Christian faith is presented as the crown and fulfillment of the cultural values of peace, success and happiness.

Another form of accommodationism is aestheticism. Here the idea is to update worship and the communication of the gospel by means of the arts—music, drama, sculpture, etc. Some of the avant-garde, who concentrate on making worship contemporary, try to reach the world, especially modern youth, through gospel rock or liturgical jazz. The emphasis is on putting people into the proper frame of mind or creating the right kind of impression. It is said, for example, that people are more prone to worship God if they are in a worshipful mood.

The profound danger in such an approach was perceived by the eminent Congregational theologian P. T. Forsyth (d. 1921). His admonition against the culture-religion of his time has perhaps even more relevance today:

> This is the bane of much popular religion, and the source of its wide collapse. People are hypnotised rather than converted. They are acted on by suggestion rather than authority, which lowers their personality rather than rallies it, and moves them by man's will rather than God's.[33]

Aestheticism lies behind the current fascination with creative spirituality. It is instructive to observe that as the interest in spirituality rises, the concern about justification and the remission of sins correspondingly diminishes. Forsyth, who wrote at length on true spirituality, issued this prophetic warning:

> To put spirituality in the place of justification is to vaporise the Church. It is to detach the soul from the one decisive, final, and eternal act whereby it is placed within the eternal will of a God whose holy love founded our destiny and our peace before all worlds.[34]

Evangelicals as well as liberals have joined the cultural quest for spiritual fulfillment. As a result, their focus is on the journey *inward* to the ground and depth of all being rather than *outward* to God's redemptive act in Jesus Christ in history. Forsyth's cogent critique of this narcissistic kind of religion needs to be pondered anew:

> We can really develop our spiritual personality at last only by thinking about it less, and by being preoccupied with the realisation and confession of God's holy personality. The object of ethics is the development of personality, but the object of religion is the kingdom and communion of a holy God, which is the only means of securing, through a new creation, a personality worth developing at last.[35]

If we eschew the journey inward, however, it must not be to succumb to the opposite danger of spurning contemplation for productivity and efficiency, values prized by the technological society. Here evangelicals are perhaps even more derelict than their liberal and Catholic kinsmen in the faith. Activism is indeed one of the banes of evangelical religion today, and it is integrally tied up with anti-intellectualism. Evangelicals, it seems, want people who are energetic, not thoughtful. Busyness in the name of Christ appears to take precedence over being in Christ.

The custom of counting conversions is a distinctly modern phenomenon and is associated with the liberal ideology of achievement. The evangelist George Whitefield wisely refused to speak of the number of conversions at his revival meetings. Referring to some who claimed to "know when persons are justified," he remarked: "It is a lesson I have not yet learnt. There are so many stony-ground hearers which receive the word with joy, that I have determined to suspend my judgment, till I know the tree by its fruits."[36]

With a buoyant optimism fortified by rapid increases in membership and expanding building programs, evangelicals like to believe that God is blessing their institutions. Bus ministries which augment the Sunday School rolls are often pointed to as evidence of a spiritual church. The nagging question arises: Is our reliance on church growth techniques or on the surprising work of the Holy Spirit?

Karl Barth has these instructive words for evangelicals who are mesmerized by worldly standards of success:

> It is comforting to think that the good God likes to be on the side of the big battalions, so that we have only to look to these to find traces of the true Church. Certainly great membership rolls and good attendance and full churches and halls . . . are facts which naturally impress us . . . but what do they really have to do with the truth?[37]

Before liberal critics of evangelicalism congratulate themselves, let me hasten to free them from the delusion that falling membership and attendance show that their churches are closer to the truth. The declining fortunes of the liberal establishment are sometimes attributed to its prophetic stance or to the sociological fact that middle- and upper-class women bear fewer children. There may be some truth in these claims, but this is not the core of the problem of the demise of liberal Christianity. What is not sufficiently perceived is that God withdraws his blessing from churches that substitute public lectures for gospel preaching and a concern for the development of personality for a passion for souls. A vital church will repel because of its prophetic witness, but it will also attract because of its evangelistic zeal, and I am afraid that most liberal churches today have neither.

Yet evangelicals dare not view the weaknesses and misfortunes of fellow-Christians with sanctimonious detachment. Their own religion has by no means escaped the corroding influences of a blatantly secular culture. The fascination of a considerable segment of the evangelical community with worldly success and celebrities is nothing less than scandalous. A. W. Tozer laments that while Christ calls people to holiness, too many contemporary representatives of the old-time religion "call them to a cheap and tawdry happiness that would have been rejected with scorn by the least of the Stoic philosophers."[38] This prophet from the Christian and Missionary Alliance presents a rather bleak picture of modern evangelicalism:

> Evangelical Christianity is fast becoming the religion of the bourgeoisie. The well-to-do, the upper middle classes, the politically

> prominent, the celebrities, are accepting our religion by the thousands . . . to the uncontrollable glee of our religious leaders who seem completely blind to the fact that the vast majority of these new patrons of the Lord of glory have not altered their moral habits in the slightest nor given any evidence of true conversion that would have been accepted by the saintly fathers who built the churches.[39]

The proper attitude for both evangelicals and liberals today is one of penitence and humility, born out of the knowledge that our supposed virtue and wisdom prove again and again to be a cloak for disobedience. When we begin boasting of our achievements, especially those of a moral and religious kind, this may well be a sign that we have forsaken our high and holy vocation. According to Barth, "The Church which does not ask itself whether it is not threatened by apostasy, and therefore in need of renewal, should beware lest it become a sleeping and a sick Church, even sick unto death."[40]

The same fascination with tangible success is present in unionism, the attempt to forge denominational mergers for the sake of greater efficiency in organization or a higher degree of cultural homogeneity rather than obedience to the will of God. Unionism places unity over truth, practice over doctrine. Its goal is denominational consolidation at the expense of dogmatic consensus. Unionism is a false ecumenism, since it controverts the ideal of the unity of truth and love.

Unionism has been one of the principal forces undermining the vitality of the liberal churches. Kierkegaard had this to say about this latest form of culture-Christianity:

> We are always hearing "Let us unite, in order to work for Christianity." And this is meant to be true Christian zeal. Christianity is of another view, it knows very well that this is trickery, for with union Christianity is not advanced, but weakened; and the more union there is, the weaker Christianity becomes.[41]

As might be expected, unionism is pervasive in the conciliar movement, since one of the aims of the great ecumenical bodies is to promote church union, even at the cost of blurring doctrinal distinctives. Christian unity is a biblical ideal, and much was said in the previous chapter on the need for making progress toward it. The question remains: Is the modern drive toward unity inspired by biblical fidelity or modern idealism? Forsyth uttered these prophetic words before the ecumenical dream became an organized movement: "A Christian optimism has grown up which had begun (like the social passion for brotherhood without righteousness, or with righteousness which was only fraternity) to dream of a speedy unity of the Churches without a prime regard to their belief."[42]

Unionism is endemic to liberalism, but the spirit of unionism is also beginning to penetrate the enclaves of evangelicalism. We hear much of the need to create a panevangelicalism that will present a united front against the liberal and modernist churches. But is this obedience to the prayer of Christ that his people be one in love and in truth? We also sometimes hear the call for a pan-Protestantism that will stand against a resurgent Roman Catholicism. Is this a true ecumenism motivated by the desire to convert the nations or a false ecumenism born out of a defensive mentality desirous of maintaining a particular tradition in the church?

Interchurch cooperation in the area of social services is indubitably a step toward the goal of Christian unity, but it can also be a device to avoid hastening toward this goal. I remember that when the ecumenical movement began to falter, the term "secular ecumenism" was increasingly used to denote the ecumenism of the future. Indeed, it seemed that the focus on overturning oppressive social structures and alleviating human suffering was more worthy than reaching agreement on the sacred mysteries of revelation, which for some appeared to be an impossible task and therefore no longer worth pursuing. Underlying this attitude was a disdain for doctrine and a distrust of biblical and ecclesiastical authority. Liberation theology today, which seeks to substitute praxis for logos, is a current manifestation of this same spirit which allows for latitude in doctrine but not in conduct.

A somewhat more subtle but no less pernicious form of accommodationism is psychologism, where the gospel is reduced to personal attitudes or interior experiences. We see this at least in part in the Faith at Work movement, which favors relational over doctrinal theology. It can also be discerned in the Clinical Pastoral Education movement, with its stress on psychic integration rather than eternal salvation. It is manifest, too, in the electronic church movement, where God is depicted as "an unlimited pool of power" that we need only to tap into in order to gain peace, health and prosperity.

The devotees of Clinical Pastoral Education promote what they call holistic salvation, where the accent is placed on the achievement or recovery of psychological wholeness. What is suspect in this emphasis is that the correlation between justification and regeneration on the one hand and normalcy as this is understood in the cultural sciences on the other is left unclear. It is an incontrovertible fact that not a few of the great saints in Christian history were considered mad or at least eccentric by cultural or psychological standards.

Bernard Ramm detects a distinct openness to psychologism among so-called young evangelicals. In reaction to the polemics of an earlier generation, they have come to believe that psychological wholeness is a more salutary goal than doctrinal correctness. The question is: Can we have an integrated personality apart from an integral vision of life? Are deep personal relations with others possible apart from a common faith and commitment?

It is disconcerting to realize that at so many evangelical conferences and retreats, group dynamics and small group discussion figure more prominently than scholarly lectures. Even prayer groups and Bible study groups are conducted in such a way that group process techniques tend to impede the free movement of the Holy Spirit. It is not an exaggeration to claim that John Dewey wields greater influence at many such meetings than either Karl Barth or John Calvin.

The fathers of the faith correctly perceived that the torments of the soul cannot be alleviated by therapeutic and medicinal techniques. "There is death," said Calvin, "even a spiritual death, which cannot be corrected by all the means and nostrums of the world. God has to put forth his hand, and that mightily."[43] Even Paul Tillich, who has pioneered in the dialogue between theology and psychotherapy, acknowledges that the latter, though helpful for mastering neurotic anxieties, is woefully incapable of overcoming the ontological anxiety of meaninglessness.[44]

Drawing on the insights of neo-orthodoxy and Tillichian theology, the modern pastoral care movement often stresses the unmerited forgiveness of God, indeed an integral part of the gospel, but at the expense of the demands of the gospel for personal holiness (cf. I Cor.

6:18–20; II Cor. 7:1; Heb. 12:14). The result is that people are soothed or tranquilized rather than challenged to live a godly and disciplined life. Kierkegaard foresaw that such an attitude could only lead to cheap grace and a hedonistic life-style:

> In *Christendom* Christianity has been employed as a stimulant oriented toward enjoying life. . . . Therefore Christendom is: refined life-enjoyment, dreadfully refined, for in paganism's enjoyment there was always a bad conscience. But in Christendom an attempt has been made to eliminate conscience by introducing atonement in the following manner: You have a God who has atoned—now you may really enjoy life. This is the greatest possible relapse.[45]

Accommodationism is also expressed in the politicizing of religion, in which the gospel is transmuted into a political-social program. This can be called the heresy of ideologism, and much has already been said about this in the last chapter. What is necessary to understand is that ideologism is as conspicuous in evangelical as in liberal circles. The Puritan vision of America as the new Israel destined to be a light to the nations is indeed pervasive in the evangelical right.[46] On the left, there is a fascination with messianic socialism, which has left its mark on the various liberation and third-world theologies. Both right- and left-oriented evangelicals are under the spell of utopianism, whose source is the millenarian tradition in Christian faith. We cannot afford to dismiss the millennial hope, but we must not confuse it with the blessed hope of the second advent of Christ, which will bring in the new heaven and the new earth (Isa. 65:17; Rev. 21:1). Evangelicals as well as liberals need to reflect on Forsyth's effort to disassociate himself from the social gospel of his day: "The largest and deepest reference to the Gospel is not to the world or its social problems, but to Eternity and its social obligations."[47]

Much of the accommodationism of today, as of yesterday, is rooted in the concern to make the faith palatable or desirable to its cultured despisers. Whenever apologetics preempts dogmatics as the central focus of the church, the slide toward an accommodation to the values and standards of the culture is almost inevitable. The apologetic thrust is highly visible not only among modernists but also among restorationists and separatists. Though claiming that Jerusalem has nothing in common with Athens, Tertullian was nonetheless a formidable apologist bent on demolishing the wisdom of Athens in order to insure the triumph of Jerusalem. Fundamentalists who call for a restoration of the old-time religion are as immersed in the apologetic enterprise as are the modernists. In seeking to combat rationalistic unbelief on its own ground, both parties betray the pitfalls of this kind of apologetic venture, which in the long run debilitates rather than strengthens the church.

An apologetic concern dominates the evangelical left almost as much as it does the right. Whereas the first tries to make the faith credible by the demonstration of a life-style of simplicity and caring, the second is intent on proving the superiority of the Christian world-view. The first often reduces Christianity to ethics; the second is in danger of confusing it with logic.

Kierkegaard, who did not abandon the apologetic task, claimed that so many apologists go wrong because they do not sufficiently perceive that the resistance to the Christian message is rooted in the sin in the human heart rather than in intellectual doubt:

> The arguments against Christianity arise out of insubordination, reluctance to obey, mutiny against all authority. Therefore, until now the battle against objections has been shadow-boxing, because it has been intellectual combat with doubt instead of being ethical combat against mutiny.[48]

Kierkegaard believed in witnessing indirectly by Christian presence but only as a preparation for the opportunity to witness directly by presenting the evangelical proclamation.

Karl Barth, who has been accused by evangelicals of giving up on apologetics, was acute enough to see that people need to be delivered before they can be persuaded. In his view, dogmatics must itself include the apologetic dimension, but the latter must not be construed as a foundation or stepping-stone to the former. He came to the conclusion that "even philosophers will not listen to a theologian who makes concessions, who is half-philosopher himself. But when you ring the bell of the Gospel, philosophers will listen!"[49] According to Barth, unbelief must not be taken too seriously, lest we imply that Jesus' victory over doubt, death and sin is incomplete. Such an attitude rests on the dubious assumption that the gospel is no match for the wisdom of the age, that the outpouring of God's grace is unable to break through the hardness of the human heart.

Barth can be criticized for ignoring the fact that an apologetic defense of the faith can awaken within the unbeliever a thirst for the Christian message, that apologetics can be a form of pre-evangelism. Yet we must not claim that apologetics can do anything more than silence criticisms and stir the conscience. In and of itself it is powerless to move the hardened sinner toward the grace of God unless grace is already present in the situation, working through the preaching of the Word of God. Harold J. Ockenga has rightly observed: "Christianity is intellectually defensible, but such intellectual apologetics do not make Christians. Christians are made by the Holy Spirit."[50]

The error of accommodationism is that it seeks to make the truth of faith contemporary whereas this truth is eternal and therefore always contemporary. The error of restorationism is that by seeing the truth encased in past formulations and practices handed down by the church, it invariably loses sight of the fact that this truth is living and therefore speaks anew to every age. Accommodationists can be accused of futurism, a desire to insure the revelance of the faith for future generations. Restorationists are guilty of archaism, the temptation to protect the faith against the allurements of the present and the future. An archaism that simply returns to the creeds and liturgies of the past can be as detrimental to the health and advancement of the churches as a futurism that in its passion to modernize the church fails to maintain continuity with its abiding tradition.

REVISIONIST VERSUS CONFESSIONAL THEOLOGY

The emerging conflict in theology today is between a revisionist and a confessional theology. The first is bent on revising or updating the life and thought of the church in the light of the new world consciousness. As David Tracy puts it, "a revisionist theology" seeks a "possible basic reconciliation between the principal values, cognitive claims, and existential faiths of both a reinterpreted post-modern consciousness and a reinterpreted Christianity."[51] For Langdon Gilkey, another revisionist theologian, the task of the church is to effect "a reinterpretation of our common Christian symbols of God, revelation, authority, salvation, law, and hope for the future—and their relation to historical change and becoming—in *non*supernaturalistic terms so that they can be means of grace to our time."[52] Confessional theology, on the other hand, has for its aim the overthrowing of the new world consciousness and its supplanting by fear and trust in the living, holy God revealed in the Scriptures. In this perspective, it is not the faith of the church but the ideologies of the world that need to be demythologized or reconceptualized.

Revisionist theology takes various forms. Feminist theologians are occupied in revising the language and content of faith on the basis of feminist experience. Liberation theology endeavors to reinterpret the faith in the light of the class struggle, the mythical vision of Marxism. In process theology, the aim is to rethink the classical doctrines of the faith, particularly the doctrine of God, in order to bring them into accord with the creative insights of Whiteheadian or Teilhardian philosophy.

Against the above approaches, evangelical theology is unashamedly confessional. It seeks to confess the great doctrines of Scripture and the church in a fresh language but with a continuity in meaning. This new language, moreover, is not a substitute for the language of Zion, the imagery of Holy Scripture, but instead a supplement to it. Evangelicals may also speak of revision, but what they have in mind is a revision not of Scripture or church dogma but of our present theological formulations in the light of Scripture and church tradition. A confessional theology does not simply seek to return to past times, nor does it try to accommodate to present times; instead, it heralds the fulfillment of all times in Jesus Christ.

A revisionist theology will necessarily be modernist in the sense that it represents an accommodation to the *Zeitgeist* (the spirit of the times). Though not accepting uncritically all the claims of modernity, revisionism does try to bring the faith into accord with the spirit of modernity. It often assumes the guises of latitudinarianism and universalism, both of which deny the absolute necessity of a personal commitment of faith in Jesus Christ for salvation.

Kierkegaard powerfully enunciated the evangelical reaction to the latitudinarian and universalist theology of his day:

> It is supposed that we shall all be saved, that we are Christians from birth—and instead of the fearful effort of having to make use of this

> life for an eternal decision it is supposed that everything is already settled, and at most it is a question of whether out of gratitude we live a reasonably decent life, which in any case from the purely earthly and worldly point of view is the most prudent thing to do.[53]

Confessional theology strives to be liberal in the sense of self-critical, but it is adamantly opposed to the ideology of liberalism with its naive belief in moral progress and its almost unreserved trust in human reason. Whereas revisionist theology seeks the radical revision of the values and concepts of Christian tradition, confessional theology is radical in the sense of returning to the roots of the faith. At the same time, confessional theology is conservative, for it strives always to maintain the truth of Scripture and tradition.

Confessional theology is not, however, restorationist. It does not simply wish to return to past theological formulations or cultural attitudes that belong to a bygone era. It is confessional without being confessionalist in the sense of the old orthodoxy. It seeks to confess the abiding doctrines of the faith in the language of our day. It is also intent on applying the scriptural message to the critical social and spiritual issues of our time.

An evangelical theology of this kind does not deny or underplay the role of experience in faith (as is sometimes the case in neo-orthodoxy). It sees experience, however, not as the source but as the medium of a transcendent revelation. It believes that the revelation of God must be received in experience, though it does not derive its criterion for truth from experience. The gospel does not nullify experience but instead redeems it. Forsyth ably expresses the equivocal and yet crucial role of experience in evangelical theology: "Christian experience is the experience of the authority of the Gospel; it is not an experience which becomes the authority for the Gospel; whose authority can be most mighty when every reason drawn from human experience is against it."[54]

Our confession is not simply an intellectual commitment but is born out of the agony and joy of a transforming experience, thus becoming an existential witness. We cannot inwardly know the truth of the gospel apart from the evangelical experience, but this experience always points beyond itself to the reconciling and redeeming work of God in Jesus Christ in the history attested to in Holy Scripture.

Finally, confessional theology confesses not only the faith once for all delivered to the saints (Jude 3) but also the insufficiency and weakness of its response to this faith, even its sin. The evangelical theologian recognizes that he will be judged more severely than the others because his vocation is to enunciate not his own opinions but the very Word of God (cf. James 3:1). While the revisionist theologian is concerned about the judgment that the world gives, the confessional theologian believes that opposition by the world may be an invincible sign of the truth of his witness (cf. Matt. 5:10–12; 10:22; John 15:18–20).

A confessional theology is anchored in the assurance that faith itself provides and not in the certainty of its own grasp of the faith. It will be a theology of the cross rather than a theology of glory, though it makes a place for the proleptic experience of coming glory as an illumination and partial confirmation of faith.

Karl Barth here manifests the humility and searching attitude that should characterize all bona fide evangelical theology:

> Are we quite sure that what we, with hasty decision, call the gospel of Jesus Christ is the gospel? Are we quite sure that a victory of a so-called Christian view of the world would be a victory of God? Are we quite sure that a prosperous church is evidence of the progress and coming of the kingdom of God?[55]

The differences between confessional and revisionist theology become clear when seen in the context of H. Richard Niebuhr's typology set forth in his provocative book *Christ and Culture.*[56] A revisionist theology corresponds to the Niebuhrian category of "Christ of culture," since it focuses upon an underlying identity between the highest values of the culture and the message of faith. A confessional theology, on the other hand, is closer to the position of "Christ transforming culture," for its aim is the conversion of the values and thought forms of the culture into the service of the kingdom of Christ. At the same time, a confessional theology will also incorporate motifs associated with "Christ against culture," since it acknowledges that only by standing against the world can it overcome the world.

Christian action in the world most nearly resembles neither an ambulance service nor a peace corps devoted to rebuilding a society in disarray. Instead, it is more like a sortie from a fortress, which by its very presence poses an unmistakable challenge to worldly authority. The Christian should neither seek a new fortress (the way of sectarianism), nor be content to remain within the walls of the fortress (the way of restorationism). Nor should he abandon the fortress for the sake of greater relevance and acceptance by the world (the way of modernism). Instead, he should venture out with boldness doing battle with the principalities and powers of the world, thereby extending the influence and authority of the fortress (the church). The fortress is indeed a signpost of a kingdom that is not of this world, but it should be something more: It should serve as a launching vehicle for an invasion of the world, for bringing the world into submission to the Lord of the fortress. This was the transformationist vision of John Calvin and the Puritans, and it is this vision that we sorely need to recover today.[57]

VI

Toward the Recovery of Evangelical Faith

Protestantism stands or falls with the Bible, Romanism stands or falls with the papacy. We cannot go back to Romanism; still less can we surrender ourselves to the icy embrace of Rationalism.

PHILIP SCHAFF

We refuse to bow to the spirit of the age, but we ought at least to speak the language of that age, and address it from the Cross in the tone of its too familiar sorrow.

P. T. FORSYTH

The whole church must become a mobile missionary force, ready for a wilderness life. It is a time for us to be thinking of campaign tents rather than of cathedrals.

JOHN MACKAY

The Church will win the world for Christ when—and only when —she works through living spirits steeped in prayer.

EVELYN UNDERHILL

EVANGELICAL CHRISTIANITY can only survive by discovering anew the meaning of the biblical gospel for our day. It must also be willing to subordinate itself to the gospel, to alter its own strategies and programs in the light of the gospel. Unfortunately, latter-day evangelicalism is marked by the tendency to seek mastery over the gospel in order to advance itself. The gospel is either converted into a creedal formula possessed by the church or reduced to a therapeutic product dispensed by the clerics of the church. Unless this tendency is reversed, evangelicalism will most certainly lose its spiritual dynamic and momentum. The evangelical church may then see the new wine of the gospel being placed in new wineskins.[1]

As an evangelical passionately concerned with the future of this renewal movement, I venture to offer some correctives which, it seems to me, are needed if evangelicalism is to become all it was meant to be.

RECLAIMING HISTORICAL ROOTS

The Chicago Call conference (1977) reminded us that the rediscovery of historical roots is vital to a renewed evangelical faith. Among our spiritual forbears are the great theologians of Protestant orthodoxy—Chemnitz, Hollaz, Flacius, Polanus, Heidegger, Cocceius, Wollebius and Voetius. Certainly not all of these men can be considered rationalists. For the most part, they eschewed the later fundamentalist error of making an absolute equation between the words of the Bible and the revealed Word of God.[2]

Evangelicals should also recognize what they owe to the spiritual movements of purification subsequent to the Reformation—Pietism and Puritanism.[3] The Pietists and Puritans were reacting against both a deadening formalism and a stultifying creedalism in the church. Many evangelicals today seem to be fearful of the free movement of the Spirit, wishing to confine him to the formulas and credos of their own particular traditions. What we can learn from Pietism and Puritanism as well as from eighteenth- and nineteenth-century Evangelicalism is that the Spirit constantly breaks through our creedal and liturgical forms, overturning our traditional modes of understanding and behavior. Out of these renewal movements new forms of ministry emerged—house gatherings for prayer and Bible study (*collegia pietatis*), deaconess sisterhoods, institutes for lay evangelism, epileptic homes, homes for unwed mothers, orphanages, rescue missions and, much later, lay witness missions. It should also be borne in mind that the great missionary outreach to foreign lands (in which women played a significant role) had its fundamental source in these movements of inward purification.[4]

Surely, a reappropriation of the abiding insights of the Protestant Reformation of the sixteenth century is indispensable for a revivified evangelicalism today. The Reformation can indeed be considered evangelical in the most fundamental sense of that word: its focus was on doctrines that are integral to the gospel itself—*sola gratia* (salvation by grace alone), *sola fide* (justification by faith alone), *sola scriptura* (the primacy of Scripture over the church), and *Soli Deo gloria* (glory to God alone). Certainly these were not original with the Reformers, but they had fallen into obscurity, especially in the later Middle Ages when semi-Pelagianism was dominant.[5] No Christian can claim to be evangelical who does not stand with the Reformers in insisting on the priority and sovereignty of the grace of God and the infallibility and absolute normativeness of Holy Scripture.

It is a matter of debate among scholars whether the Reformation signified a recovering of New Testament Christianity or simply a modification and corrective to Latin Christianity. Brian Gerrish reminds us that the Reformers, unlike the revolutionary Spiritualists, were intent not on overthrowing the values and institutions of their times but instead on renewing them in the light of the gospel.[6] Ernst Troeltsch once remarked that the Middle Ages are the maternal womb of us all, including Protestants. According to Philip Schaff, the Reformation was "the legitimate offspring" and "greatest act" of the Catholic Church—the unfolding of the "true catholic nature itself."[7]

Yet although it is true that the Reformation cannot be adequately understood apart from the cultural and historical context of medieval Catholicism, it should also be stressed that the Reformation introduced something radically new for that time—the idea of the church as a community of faith instead of a hierarchical institution.[8] All Christians, said Luther, are members of the royal priesthood rather than being under the direction of a special priesthood. This means that all believers have the privilege of being intercessors, all may hear confessions, all may share in the ministry of mutual consolation.

In its stress on the universal call to discipleship, the Reformation broke irrevocably with the double standard of Catholic spirituality, in which a demarcation was made between the religious, who were expected to live according to the counsels of perfection (celibacy, poverty, obedience) and the ordinary believers, whose mandate was to maintain life in society. For the Reformers, all believers are summoned to the high and holy vocation of being witnesses and ambassadors of Jesus Christ.[9] Most Christians realize this vocation precisely in their secular occupations, which are no less sacred in their motivation and goal than the pastoral ministry.[10]

It can also be argued that the Reformation distinction between justification, fundamentally a forensic act by which God declares us just through the merits of Christ, and sanctification, the interior renewal by the Holy Spirit, represented a reappropriation of Pauline theology, which was only anticipated but never developed in Catholic and Eastern Orthodox theology. For the most part, justification was considered by Catholic scholars as something intrinsic rather than extrinsic. The Reformation view that we remain sinners even while covered by the perfection of the holiness of Christ stood in precarious tension if not diametrical opposition to the Catholic and Eastern Orthodox emphasis on deification, the idea that the sinner is transformed into godlikeness through grace.

While the Reformers continued to maintain the Catholic emphasis on the divine authority of Scripture, they insisted on its primacy over church tradition as well as religious experience. Here they could appeal to some of the church fathers for support, but when they went on to contend for the self-authenticating character of Scripture, the break with the Catholic Church was irremediable. Holy Scripture does not need to be interpreted by the teaching authority of the church to the laity; instead, Scripture interprets itself by the action of the Spirit to the whole church. The church magisterium can amplify and clarify the Word of God in Scripture, but this Word is fundamentally perspicacious to all who come to the Scriptures in faith.

Certainly we who stand in the tradition of the Reformation must not proudly exult in our particular heritage. We must not be blind to the tragic fact that the Reformation fractured Christian unity, that it discarded not only cultural and philosophical accretions that obscured the gospel of free grace but also some of the treasures in Catholic tradition which have yet to be taken seriously by Protestants (including the intercessory and exemplary role of Mary and the saints in Christian devotion). In addition, we should be willing to consider that the Counter-Reformation also laid hold of some important aspects of biblical truth, that it, too, produced models of piety worthy of emulation.

By no means should we be ashamed of the Reformation or downplay its enduring contributions (as do liberals who verge toward humanism and evangelicals captivated by positive thinking).[11] At the same time, when we celebrate this great reforming movement in Christian history, we must be poignantly aware of its failings as well as its successes, of its disobedience as well as its faithfulness to the mandate of the holy God.

In recovering our indebtedness to the Reformation, we must, of course, include the Anabaptists, with their pronounced stress on the Christian life. The Reformation message of justification by the free grace of God becomes rationalization for sin and cheap grace unless it is united with the New Testament call to radical discipleship, the salient emphasis of the Anabaptists. Whereas the mainline Reformers held up the Word and the sacraments as the two practical signs of the true church, the Anabaptists contended that the true church must also be distinguished by the marks of suffering for the faith, the effects of persecution by the world. A truly evangelical and catholic church will seek to incorporate the Anabaptist vision but within the context of the great Pauline and Reformation doctrines of salvation by grace through faith (cf. Rom. 1:16, 17; Eph. 2:8).

Yet evangelicals should not be content to draw upon both the mainline and left-wing Reformations; they can be immensely enriched by rediscovering the genuinely evangelical motifs in many of the church fathers and medieval theologians. Protestants often point to John Huss, John Wycliffe and Savonarola[12] as precursors of the Reformation, with their emphasis on scriptural authority and their attack on corruption in the church. To our detriment, most of us forget those who stand in the mainstream of Catholic tradition and yet who enunciated doctrines that exalt rather than detract from the gospel. The fathers of the church who successfully defended the faith against the ancient heresies—Gnosticism, Arianism and Neoplatonic mysticism—should be included among the pioneers and perfecters of the faith (cf. Heb. 11). Long before the Reformation contended for grace alone and faith alone, these biblical principles were stoutly affirmed by Ambrose, Augustine and Ambrosiaster. It was the last who declared, "It is ordained of God that whoever believes in Christ shall be saved, and he shall have forgiveness of sins, not through works but through faith alone, without merit."[13]

The doctors of the medieval church should also be regarded as sources for evangelical renewal in our day, even though we must read these men and women with biblical discrimination (but this applies also to the church fathers and Reformers). In Protestant evangelical circles, Thomas Aquinas is often accused of trying to construct a natural road to faith in God that would in effect supplant the road marked out by the biblical revelation. Yet Thomas insisted that though rational argument can demonstrate the reasonableness of belief in a supreme being and in a moral law, only faith can lay hold of the revelation of God in Jesus Christ that alone saves from sin and death. Moreover, he steadfastly affirmed that free will is inadequate for the act of faith, since the truth of faith is beyond reason. In accord with the Augustinian tradition, he was emphatic that faith is given to us by God apart from the merit of our preceding actions. "The reason," he said, "why God saves man by faith without any preceding merits" is "that no man may glory in himself but refer all the glory to God."[14]

Evangelical motifs can even be discerned in the tradition of Christian mysticism, though here we need to be particularly cautious because of the indebtedness of this tradition to Platonism and Neoplatonism. Yet we should remember that Luther was influenced positively in his spiritual development by John Tauler and the *Theologia Germanica*.[15] Both Calvin and Luther often referred to Augustine and Bernard of Clairvaux in support of their positions. Catholics of a somewhat mystical bent after the Reformation whose piety has been decidedly more biblical than Platonic include Cornelius Jansen, Pascal, Thérèse of Lisieux and Hans Urs von Balthasar.

The catholic heritage of the past is being increasingly rediscovered by Protestant evangelical scholars. Robert Webber's *Common Roots*, Thomas Oden's *Agenda for Theology*, and the Chicago Call conference in 1977, out of which came the book *The Orthodox Evangelicals*,[16] are all evidence of this trend. I also point the reader to my own books *The Reform of the Church* and *Essentials of Evangelical Theology*, particularly the second volume.[17]

A word of warning is appropriate at this juncture. In our endeavor to recover continuity with the whole tradition of the faith, we must resist the temptation to interpret the Bible in the light of classical Christianity rather than vice versa. A nostalgia for the past may blind us to errors in the past that have crippled the Christian witness in various periods of church history. Catholics as well as Protestants would do well to keep in mind that the church must continually be reformed in the light of the revelation given once for all in the past through the inspired witness of Holy Scripture.

The more prevalent failing in modern evangelicalism is to ignore the past altogether, to emphasize communication skills over the commentary on Scripture in the history of the church, to downplay nurture in the faith of the church in favor of strategies for expanding the church. Some of the new evangelical schools advertise programs in church growth and electronic media studies but are strangely silent regarding their offerings in systematic theology or the history of Christian thought. Evangelicalism will be caught up and submerged in the mainstream of popular culture-religion unless it rediscovers its identity as a bona fide branch of the holy catholic church. It needs to reclaim its glorious heritage, which extends from the first century of the church onward but which was given special visibility in the Protestant Reformation of the sixteenth century and the evangelical revival movements of the seventeenth and eighteenth centuries.

NEW STATEMENTS ON BIBLICAL AUTHORITY

If the neglect of historical roots is not widely recognized in the evangelical world, the question of biblical authority is readily acknowledged as a crucial issue. That the battle for the gospel today will also be a battle for the Bible is becoming abundantly clear. The erosion of biblical authority has seriously undermined the preaching ministry in both Protestant and Catholic communions. It has also had deleterious consequences in the areas of personal and social ethics. The facile acceptance by clerical as well as secular leaders of abortion on demand and deviate forms of sexuality signifies that in many circles biblical norms are now passé; indeed, the social sciences increasingly occupy the position formerly held by Scripture in determining what is normative in the areas of sexuality and family life.

It is commonplace today to try to draw a wedge between the historical expression of the faith given in Scripture and the object of faith, which is Jesus Christ. Yet we must recognize that we cannot have the divine content apart from the cultural and historical form in which this content comes to us. We must be frank enough to acknowledge a certain degree of historical and cultural contingency in the biblical witness to God in Christ; at the same time, we must insist that there is also an unchanging truth.

As I see it, there are three basic approaches to scriptural authority: the sacramental, the scholastic and the liberal-modernist.[18] In the first, the Bible is a divinely appointed channel, a mirror, or a visible sign of divine revelation. This was the general position of the church fathers, the doctors of the medieval church, and the Reformers. In the second, the Bible is the written or verbal revelation of God, a transcript of the very thoughts of God. This has been the viewpoint of Protestant fundamentalism, though it was anticipated in both Catholic and Protestant scholastic orthodoxy. In the third, the Bible is a record of the religious experience of a particular people in history; this reflects the general stance of liberalism, both Catholic and Protestant. Only the first position does justice to the dual origin of Scripture—that it is both a product of divine inspiration and a human witness to divine truth. We need to recognize the full humanity of Scripture as well as its true divinity. Indeed, it should be impressed upon us that we can come to know its divinity only in and through its humanity. As Luther put it, the Scriptures are the swaddling clothes that contain the treasure of Jesus Christ.

A careful examination of early Protestant orthodoxy as well as of Puritanism and Pietism reveals that the distinction between the word of God and the words of the Bible was quite common. Our spiritual forebears referred to the form and the content of Scripture, the shell and the kernel, the meaning and the words. David Hollaz distinguished between what God has revealed (the absolute principle) and the scriptural witness to this (the relative principle). He spoke of a divine revelation which is "contained in the writings of the prophets and apostles."[19] The Puritan Richard Sibbes could assert: "The word of God is ancienter than the Scripture. . . . The Scripture is but that *modus,* that manner of conveying the word of God."[20] For Sibbes, the truth of faith is not a propositional formula that remains lifeless until it is perceived by the hearer; instead, "divine truth is holy, full of majesty and power in itself."[21]

Philip Schaff, in whom Protestant orthodoxy and Pietism coalesce, is helpful in this regard. Schaff drew a distinction between the "matter" of Scripture and its "peculiar form." He pointed to the need to do justice to both the divine side of Scripture and its "human and historical character."[22] Portraying the Bible as "a mirror which reflects Christ," he held that "we must not look *at* the mirror, but *through* the mirror to the glorious object which it reveals."[23] Schaff stood close to Calvin in viewing the Bible as the unerring rule for faith rather than contending for an errorless book in the modern sense of technical accuracy. He referred to "the sufficiency and unerring certainty of the holy Scriptures" and the "unerring" truth which the Scriptures contain.[24] At the same time, he rejected a mechanical theory of inspiration in favor of an organic one, in which the Holy Spirit enters into the thought forms and life history of the authors.

The difference between liberalism and orthodoxy is the way in which each applies the form-content distinction to Scripture. The liberals (à la Harnack) seek to extract the content from the form and treat it apart from the form. Evangelical Christianity wisely recognizes that the divine content is available to us only in the language of Zion, that is to say, in the inspired symbolism and imagery of Holy Scripture. I affirm a union but not a fusion between the divine content and its worldly form.

Today, we should insist that Scripture be interpreted by Scripture, not by the new world consciousness of living in a male-female world (as some feminists advocate) or the emerging class consciousness of being poor in a world of affluence (as in the case of the liberationists). We must steadfastly refrain from accommodating the message of Scripture to any cultural ideology, whether on the right or left. The Scriptures stand in judgment over every cultural ideology. To be sure, God is also speaking to us in the times; but unless we first hear the Word of God in Scripture, we shall never recognize the hand of God in the times.

Neo-orthodoxy has helped us to recover the dynamic character of divine revelation, but it lost sight of an inspired text as the earthen vessel of this revelation. It is important to understand that there are three components in God's Word: words, meaning and power. All three must be present if we are to hear and know the veritable Word of God. Fundamentalism has placed the accent on the words, whereas liberal and neo-orthodox theology emphasize the spirit. We need today a new statement on biblical authority that will stress the organic connection between words and meaning, external symbols, and spiritual truth and power. Revelation is not simply a witness frozen in past formulations but an event in which the truth of this witness is unveiled to the perceiver in the here and now. Certainly this is the understanding conveyed by the psalmist: "Open my eyes, so that I may see the wonderful truths in your law" (119:18 GNB cf. Eph. 1:17, 18 NIV).

On the intractable problem of whether Scripture contains errors, we need to recognize that this conflict is rooted in disparate notions of truth. Truth in the Bible means conformity to the will and purpose of God. Truth in today's empirical, scientific milieu means an exact correspondence between one's ideas or perceptions and the phenomena of nature and history. Error in the Bible means a deviation from the will and purpose of God, unfaithfulness to the dictates of his law. Error in the empirical mind-set of a technological culture means inaccuracy or inconsistency in what is reported as objectively occurring in nature or history. Technical precision is the measure of truth in empiricism. Fidelity to God's Word is the biblical criterion for truth. Empiricism narrows the field of investigation to objective sense data,[25] and therefore to speak of revelation as superhistorical or hidden in history is to remove it from what can legitimately be considered as knowledge. The difference between the rational-empirical and the biblical understanding of truth is the difference between transparency to Eternity and literal facticity.[26]

We also seek a statement on scriptural authority that will do justice to the integral relation between Scripture and the tradition of the church. Just as the trunk and branches of a tree are as necessary for the life of the tree as its roots (though the roots have priority), so the whole of the tree is dependent for its life on water (the living Word of God), which is conveyed through the roots (the Bible) to the other parts of the tree. It is fallacious to assume, as do some evangelicals, that we can neglect the branches that have sprung from the roots and begin over again with the roots alone (a false conception of *sola scriptura*). At the same time, we should recognize that some branches become crooked and others die. Those that die need to be pruned, but they do not negate the strength and validity of the life of all. Though some traditions may become worthless or even dangerous, tradition itself is necessary to convey the truth of the Bible to the world.

BREAKTHROUGHS IN THEOLOGICAL METHODOLOGY

One tradition that has served to impede the theological enterprise —the alliance with philosophy—can well be discarded. If there is to be authentic spiritual renewal in our churches today, evangelicals will have to divest themselves of dependence on current and past philosophical methodologies. We will be obliged to bring our philosophical and sociological presuppositions under the searchlight of Scripture. By no means dare we impose them on Scripture. Karl Barth has rightly observed that we should come to the Bible laying aside all overt philosophical presuppositions. He asserted this against both Bultmann and Tillich, for whom the insights of existentialist analysis were an invaluable aid in the study of the Bible.[27]

Within the church today (both Catholic and Protestant), there is a pressing need to transcend the cleavage between fideism and rationalism. We must realize that reason is involved in faith from the very beginning, because faith is a rational commitment as well as a decision of the will. At the same time, we should beware of seeking a rational or philosophical basis for faith. Reason is a useful instrument in explicating the truth of revelation, but it cannot prepare the way for the reception of this truth.

While affirming that the whole of creation reflects the light and glory of God (cf. Ps. 19:1–4; Rom. 1:19, 20), we must steer clear of any natural theology that supposes valid knowledge of God on the basis of this general light in creation. Indeed, the universal awareness of God made possible by the light in nature and conscience is the basis for the *misunderstanding*, not the *understanding* of God. Such knowledge of God as we can glean from nature gives us not a capacity but an incapacity for revelation. The light in nature can be a positive guide to the believer, since his eyes have been opened to the source of this light—Jesus Christ. Because of sin, our inward eyes are blinded to the objective glory of God reflected in nature, and yet we have enough intimation of this glory to render us inexcusable (Rom. 1:20; 2:1).[28] The natural knowledge of God is sufficient neither for a valid understanding nor for salvation but only for condemnation. Augustine confessed that before his conversion he did not really know God, that his ideas of God were only constructs of his mind.[29] The mixture of truth and untruth in pagan philosophy caused him to seek and resist God at the same time. In our era, Karl Barth has helped us to recover the truth that natural theology leads only to a dead end, which was fully recognized by Luther and Calvin and to a lesser extent by Augustine.

There is need today for a methodology that has its source of inspiration in Scripture, not in some philosophy extraneous to Scripture. In my opinion, Augustine and Anselm were true to the central thrust of the Bible when they propounded "faith seeking understanding" as the method of scientific theology. This must not be interpreted in a purely fideistic way as beginning with a leap of faith. Our point of departure is neither faith nor reason but divine revelation, which can be apprehended to be sure only with the eyes of faith. Yet the light of faith is a light that also illumines our reason, so that a reborn reason is capable of understanding the truth of revelation, not exhaustively but adequately. Christianity does not contradict rationality, for the Word of God is also the Logos or wisdom of God, but it does oppose rationalism, which seeks to bring revelation into accord with the canons of human logic.

The task of theology is not a systematic overview of God and the world but instead a true understanding of the will and purpose of God disclosed in Jesus Christ, an understanding that eventuates in obedience. The object is not to acquire observational knowledge about God (as in naturalistic empiricism) nor conceptual mastery of him (as in idealistic rationalism). Biblical theology is a more modest enterprise, for it seeks to know not the mystery of God in himself but the plan or purpose that God has for our lives, one that is revealed and exemplified in Jesus Christ. The goal of faith is not comprehension of the divine essence but conformity to the divine will. It is not so much transcendent wisdom (as in Gnosticism) as sacrificial discipleship under the cross. Our motto should be: "I believe and seek to understand in order to obey" (cf. Rom. 1:5; 16:26; II Cor. 10:5, 6; I Pet. 1:2).

It is also imperative that we begin to see the limitations of apologetics. Too often in the past, apologetics occupied the central role in Roman Catholic and Reformed theology. The evidence for the faith took precedence over the substance of the faith, and theology invariably became a philosophical justification for belief in God rather than a systematic explication of the revealed truth of God. Arguments and proofs for the gospel are hardly convincing to the man come of age, the liberated man of the world. Yet they can be useful as testimonies to the faith, which can make the outsider willing to listen to our gospel. Apologetics can also enable the insider to understand his faith better—in the light of attacks upon it.

Regrettably, in much current apologetics Christianity is recommended as a means to a higher end, such as personal integration or social harmony. Harry Blamires has some harsh words on this kind of defense of the faith:

> We must not *exploit* our Faith by advertising it as a technique for achieving earthly satisfactions. The Faith is not a recipe and not a program. It is a Way. Recipes and programs are made to help you to carry out earthly jobs successfully. But a Way is something you walk in.[30]

It is incumbent on us to recover dogmatics as the central task in theology, though not to the exclusion of apologetics. Apologetics will still have an important place in the theological enterprise, but it will now be seen as a branch of dogmatics, the branch that seeks to combat the attacks upon the faith from its cultured despisers. It is not to be construed, however, as a propaedeutic device that leads to faith; instead, it is a tool of discernment that enables believers to clarify their faith and answer objections to it. Apologetics can silence the criticisms of unbelievers, but it cannot move them to accept the truth claims of the faith. Those in the grip of unbelief are dead in sin and need not so much to be persuaded as to be resurrected. Only the Spirit of God can raise people from the dead, and he does this through the preaching and hearing of the gospel (Rom. 10:14–17; I Cor. 1:21).

It is significant that those who see apologetics as a stepping-stone to dogmatics or who contend that reason can gain some valid knowledge of God apart from revelation also allow a role for good works prior to faith. In his *Christian Commitment*, Edward John Carnell argues that the law of justice, available to everyone, leads to the law of consideration, which in turn leads to the law of love (salvation).[31] According to Norman Geisler, "If one follows the light he has, then God will give him the added (supernatural) light he needs to be saved."[32] Surely this represents the semi-Pelagianism against which the Reformers rallied. Many evangelicals today need to ask whether they really stand in the great heritage of the Reformation, Augustine and Paul.[33]

FRESH CONFESSIONS OF FAITH

Paradoxically, with the ebbing of confessionalism there is occurring a resurgence of denominationalism, where the focus is on parochial rather than universal concerns. The confessions, it should be remembered, despite their polemical thrust, have provided a platform for dialogue with other Christians. Moreover, they are generally addressed to the whole church, not just to a particular constituency. Not surprisingly, we are also witnessing today the rise of an uncritical experientialism. When the church moves away from its confessional standards, it is prone to demand absolute loyalty to its leadership, its program or even to its polity. The other alternative is to enthrone personal experience or the light of conscience, and the church thereby becomes another club, a society of like-minded individuals.

The Chicago Call statement put it very succinctly: "We deplore two opposite excesses: a creedal church that merely recites a faith inherited from the past, and a creedless church that languishes in a doctrinal vacuum."[34] The indisputable fact is that this is precisely what we have today—churches that are merely creedal or churches without any creed whatsoever.

A genuine confession of faith will be aimed at the heresies of the time in which the confession is written. It will arise out of a poignant realization that the church is being threatened by false teaching, that the very identity of the church is at stake. Karl Barth has said that a confession will come "when a man realizes that . . . the faith of the Christian community is confronted and questioned either from within or without by the phenomena of unbelief, superstition and heresy."[35] In Germany at the time of the Barmen Declaration, the threat to the church was the cultural ideology of racism. In Western democratic culture, the threat seems to be a radical egalitarianism allied with a technocratic liberalism. Because the exact nature of this threat is not yet clearly seen, it is premature to plan a new confession of faith at this time. The signs are nonetheless unmistakable that we are fast approaching a confessional situation in this country. In all likelihood, the needed confession of faith will arise not from the councils of the church but from prophets specially chosen by God. It is to be hoped that it will cross all denominational lines and bring biblically oriented Catholics and Protestant evangelicals, both in the mainline denominations and in the smaller sects, to a doctrinal and moral consensus for our day.

The object of a genuine confession of faith is not to reiterate the views already held by a particular constituency. It is instead to challenge the partial conceptions and misconceptions of our people in the light of a vision given to the church by the Holy Spirit. A true confession will say something definite on ethics as well as dogmatics. It will address itself to life in society as well as to doctrinal issues. The task of the church is not to solve the problems of society but to relate to them and challenge them.

Many evangelical Protestant churches hold to the "Bible alone," disdaining all confessions. They rightly see that confessions may usurp biblical authority, and indeed, a true confession will always be under Scripture, not alongside Scripture. A confession is a broken symbol and should therefore always be open to revision and correction in the light of the new truth that the Spirit reveals through Holy Scripture. The answer to the temptations of a false confessionalism is not a creedless church, however, since this can lead to self-deception. Every church is creedal to some degree, if only implicitly. Yet we must guard against the danger of making the confession into a new law. Ideally, it should be a guide and norm for Christian belief and action in a particular period of history.

Pietism is inclined to downplay the role of confessions because of its emphasis on practical obedience. Such an attitude too easily prepares the way for latitudinarianism, which tolerates misunderstandings of the faith. The University of Halle, founded by Pietists, became in an amazingly short time a bastion of rationalism. Pietism, if it is to continue to be biblically vital, must be anchored in a solid confession of faith and nurtured by a concern for orthodoxy.

Yet latitudinarianism is not the only peril confronting those who seek to maintain the true faith. There can be a misplaced zeal, aimed at hounding the heretic rather than countering the heresy. In combating heresy, we should focus our attack on the false doctrine, not the person. We should seek to restore the heretic even while killing the heresy. Calvin sagaciously observed, "We delight in a certain poisoned sweetness experienced in ferreting out and in disclosing the evils of others."[36]

We should also not be too quick in judging the opinions of others, remembering that some of the most brilliant minds in the history of the church have been accused of heresy. It is the better part of wisdom to tolerate rather than root out the misguided speculations of others if these only remain on the periphery of church life and do not constitute a serious threat to the church's mission. Such opinions may not even be heresy, flagrant untruth, but only heterodoxy, an unbalanced emphasis on one segment of the truth to the detriment or exclusion of others.

At the same time, we should not remain indifferent to the threat of real heresy in the life and thought of the church. When a heretical doctrine begins to usurp the gospel in the church's proclamation, then the church must act or else become a false church. Philip Schaff, himself for a time under surveillance for theological deviation, has stated: "There are, indeed, differences which can never be reconciled; of two contradictory propositions one must be false and resisted to the end. Between truth and error, between God and Belial, between Christ and Anti-Christ there can be no compromise."[37]

The real division in the church today is not political or sociological but theological. Behind the class and ethnic barriers separating Christians in our time are deep-seated theological divisions that simply will not go away. It is the task of the church in this situation to explore these differences and to redefine the true faith against the various distortions of the faith that are so rampant.

The key to church renewal does not lie in simply returning to confessions of past ages. Such documents have been and continue to be guidelines for correct belief, but they do not carry the same authority and power for our day as they once did. The Holy Spirit always speaks a new word to his people, a word that does not negate the words he has spoken in the past but clarifies and fulfills the partial illuminations already given. Evangelicals in both Protestant and Catholic communions need to be prepared for a new confessional controversy that will divide Christians before it unites them on a deeper level.

A VIABLE DOCTRINE OF THE CHURCH

Confessions of faith have not been given the attention they deserve because of the appalling neglect of ecclesiology in the circles of conservative evangelicalism. Perhaps one reason for this is the legacy of revivalism, with its emphasis on individual decision and commitment. The decision of faith was given priority over nurture in a Christian fellowship. The church, moreover, was generally regarded as a gathered fellowship of true believers where the accent was on community rather than on loyalty to a divine institution founded by Christ.

What we need today is to recover the classical marks of the church: catholicity, apostolicity, holiness and oneness. It is especially important for evangelicals, who are accustomed to elevate personal experience over church authority, to realize that the church, too, is a gift of God. It is well to remind ourselves, moreover, that the church is not many but one, that it is not parochial but universal, that it has apostolic foundation and therefore antedates the Reformation and the great revivals. The church is also holy, not because it is comprised of a people who have attained personal holiness, but because it is covered by the holiness of its Lord and head—Jesus Christ. The holiness of Christ must, of course, be reflected in all the members of his body, but we should recognize that our holiness is derivative and fragmentary. This is why the church is both sinful and righteous at the same time.

To these classical marks of the church, Luther and Calvin added the practical marks of the pure preaching of the Word and the right administration of the sacraments. Martin Bucer also argued for the inclusion of church discipline as a hallmark of the true church. In Pietism and Puritanism all of these were supplemented by two additional practical signs—fellowship and mission. It was rightly recognized that where the fellowship of love (koinonia) and the imperative to mission are absent, we do not have the church in its fullness. Today, Catholics and Protestants alike would do well to acknowledge that the church is indeed deficient apart from the fellowship of love, the urgency of evangelism and the practice of discipline.

A further salient mark of the holy catholic church, one that should perhaps be given special emphasis in our time, is racial and social inclusiveness. If a major source of division in the church is racial and class consciousness, then the church cannot be fully catholic or truly holy unless such barriers are overcome. Evangelicals who are attracted to church growth strategies often stress cultural and racial homogeneity as essential for a strong and vital church. This may be a valid sociological observation, but it is theological heresy, since the holy catholic church transcends and relativizes, without necessarily canceling out, those things that divide humankind (cf. Gal. 3:28). It is an incontestable fact that early Pentecostalism succeeded in overcoming racial and class antagonisms, but as Pentecostalism became steadily more institutionalized and ceased to be a free movement of the Spirit, it began to take on the restrictive patterns of the surrounding society, where racial, class and ethnic distinctions block significant human communication.

Mindful of the importance of each of these marks, we must strive for a renewed appreciation of the church in the plan of salvation. The church is not simply the herald or witness to Christ's salvation (as Barthianism envisages it) but is indeed a divinely chosen instrument and means of salvation. Calvin, who was not averse to referring to the church as "our holy mother," declared: "It is not enough to know that Jesus Christ has made amends for us, and even that all things necessary for our salvation were fully accomplished and performed by his death and passion, but we must also at the same time receive the benefit of it in such way as it is ministered to us."[38]

Neo-orthodoxy renewed theology, but it was not able to renew the life of the church. Yet the renewal of the church will entail theological renewal. Emil Brunner saw authentic community as nonstructural, and this accounts for his interest in the Oxford Group movement and the nonchurch movement in Japan.[39] Karl Barth conceived of the true church as a church in mission, which to him meant a church involved in the suffering of the world. Continuity with the tradition was not of great importance in their theologies, and this is perhaps one reason why they lost sight of the divinity of the church.

Evangelicals should also earnestly seek to recover the crucial place of the sacraments in the life of the church. For Zwingli, the sacrament augments faith but cannot give it. For Barth, Jesus Christ is the only sacrament, baptism and the Lord's Supper being ordinances concerned with the ethical mandate of the church. According to Calvin, by contrast, "The sacraments . . . are treasures which we can not esteem and prize too highly."[40] Calvin and Luther both insisted that the sacrament should be celebrated in the context of the Word and that it is effectual only where it is received in faith. Nonetheless, they recognized that God deigns to meet us in visible signs instituted by Christ and that intimate communion with Christ is nowhere more powerfully present than in holy baptism and the holy Eucharist.[41]

A viable doctrine of the church for our time will involve us in a passionate concern for church unity. If the church is one, holy and apostolic, we need to discover and demonstrate the unity that we already have as brothers and sisters in Christ. Too often in the evangelical world with which I am acquainted, the ideal is a pan-Protestantism or pan-Evangelicalism, but unity with our fellow believers in the Catholic and Eastern Orthodox churches is not in the picture. The charismatic movement has bridged some of these barriers, but its vision of a renewed church is on the basis of a common experience rather than doctrinal consensus. Doctrine, life and experience need to be held together in a catholic balance, and if any one of these is neglected we are on the slippery slope to heresy.

Because of the encroaching secularism of our time, it is incumbent on us to seek not only evangelical but catholic unity, not only spiritual but visible unity. Yet visible unity should not be conceived in terms of a monolithic, hierarchical institution; this would betray an accommodation to the values of the technological society with its penchant for centralization and consolidation for the purpose of greater efficiency and productivity. In my opinion, the Consultation on Church Union (COCU) has not escaped the spell of the technocratic culture in which we live, because the practical consequences of union seem to be given more prominence than biblical fidelity or doctrinal loyalty.

In Catholicism the conception of a monolithic and hierarchical church is based on a juridical understanding of authority, which did not become dominant in the church until the controversies in the Middle Ages and the Counter-Reformation. Avery Dulles gives a timely warning against the tendency in Catholicism to define the church primarily in terms of its visible structures, to see authority in the church as essentially hierarchical and juridical.[42] In this understanding, the clergy, especially the higher clergy, are viewed as the source of all power and initiative. The church becomes virtually identical with the kingdom of Christ, and the gospel becomes a new law.

The unity we should aim for is a pulpit and altar fellowship among all churches that is based on biblical, evangelical truth. We should allow for a certain diversity within this unity. There can be a pluralism of witness, though not a pluralism of dogma in the holy catholic church. Pluralism in theological matters should never be a goal in the life of the church; instead, it should be regarded as a means to the desired end of confessional unity or doctrinal harmony, which is not the same as theological uniformity. There can exist in a vital united church various liturgical rites and differing theological formulations but not doctrinal positions that are in open conflict with one another.

I can, for the most part, identify with this prophetic vision of Philip Schaff, who wrote before the ecumenical movement came into full bloom:

> Union is no monotonous uniformity, but implies variety and full development of all the various types of Christian doctrine and discipline as far as they are founded on constitutional differences, made and intended by God himself, and as far as they are supplementary rather than contradictory. True union is essentially inward and spiritual. It does not require an external amalgamation of existing organizations into one, but may exist with their perfect independence in their own spheres of labor.[43]

As Protestant evangelicals, we should endeavor to appreciate the catholic heritage of the church as well as the Reformation witness. My reservations concerning Roman Catholicism are that it is not sufficiently catholic, since it has not included the Reformation witness in its doctrinal and confessional stance. At the same time, there are promising signs that today the contribution of the Protestant Reformers is being re-evaluated and appreciated by Catholic scholars, and there may yet be an ecumenical breakthrough in this area. It should be borne in mind that the mainline Reformers never wished to found a new church, only to reform and purify the old one. Bullinger spoke for many when he declared, "We never departed from the catholic church of Christ."[44]

In our concern for church unity, we must avoid the pitfall of restorationism, which was examined at length in the preceding chapter. I take issue with the renowned Anglo-Catholic theologian Edward Pusey, who wrote, "We dare not go outside the first six centuries."[45] Nor do I empathize with John Nevin, who contended that Protestantism "must in the end fall back into the old Catholic stream in order to fulfil its own mission."[46] Instead, our vision should be fixed on the coming great church which stands in continuity with the church of the past but which represents a new work of the Holy Spirit in the latter days when the true church will be separated from the false church.

The quest for church unity must never supplant zeal for the truth. This is what divided Luther from Erasmus. Luther rightly recognized that the true church will be characterized by unswerving devotion to the truth of Holy Scripture, that compromise can be considered in the area of nonessentials but not of essentials. Erasmus, on the other hand, sought a church that would be informed by the latest scholarship, that would be open to the spirit of enlightenment and therefore closed to any firm dogmatic stance.

Church unity is especially urgent today on the mission field, as already noted in an earlier chapter. As the church confronts the great world religions and the new political religions, it needs to speak with an undivided voice. It is also obliged to demonstrate to the pagan world the love that Jesus taught and embodied. Christians at war with each other undermine the very gospel they proclaim.

A BIBLICAL, EVANGELICAL SPIRITUALITY

The Pietists rightly remind us that a reformation in doctrine is not enough. We also stand in need of a "reformation unto holiness." This is why Pietism, with its emphasis on practical holiness, claimed to be the fulfillment of the Reformation. At its best, this renewal movement kept alive the concern for spirituality within the churches of the Reformation.

Spirituality basically refers to the style or mode of life that emanates from faith in the living God. It concerns the practical appropriation of the truth of faith by the believer. In the Christian sense, its goal is conformity to the image of Christ.

True spirituality must always be on guard against misconceptions of the spiritual life. The legacy of Neoplatonism has given rise to many such misconceptions, which have reappeared with disturbing frequency in the history of Christian mysticism. A common understanding in these circles is that the goal in life is to transcend the material and to escape into the spiritual. The Eros philosophy of Hellenism has portrayed the spiritual quest as the reunion of the soul with the Eternal. But such a conception stands opposed to the biblical vision of Agape, the love that goes out to the despised and forsaken.[47] It is not the love that ascends to the highest but the love that descends to the lowest that is the biblical ideal. Self-sacrifice, not self-realization, is the hallmark of evangelical spirituality.

Catholic and Eastern Orthodox theologians have generally been aware of the danger of accommodating the faith to classical philosophy, though they have not always been able to avoid compromises that dilute or undercut the biblical motifs. In Catholic spirituality, it is common to hear warnings against "angelism," trying to be superhuman through heroic feats of asceticism. The biblical ideal indeed is not a superhumanity but a restored humanity. At the same time, as our Catholic brothers and sisters remind us, this will be a transfigured humanity, one that is transformed by the grace of God.

Besides Neoplatonic mystical spirituality, we must equally beware of modern, secular spirituality where the accent is on immersion in the world. Here we see a naturalistic mysticism, which celebrates the instinctual drives of man and the will to power and success.[48] The spiritual is seen as an aspect of the material, just as the supernatural is regarded as a dimension of the natural. The only transcendence is a transcendence within immanence. Prayer is regarded not as the elevation of the mind to God (as in classical mysticism) nor as supplication before a holy, all-powerful God (as in biblical prophetic religion); instead, it is viewed as the penetration through the world to God. Among scholars associated with this kind of outlook are J. A. T. Robinson, Thomas Altizer, Albert Schweitzer, Nikos Kazantzakis, Dorothee Sölle and Matthew Fox.[49]

The biblical view sharply contradicts both the classical and modern versions. In the biblical perspective, the spiritual embraces the material but at the same time transcends it. The spiritual enters into the material rather than calls us away from it (as in the classical view). At the same time, the goal of the material is to be taken up into the spiritual (in opposition to the modern view). The material is neither an obstacle to the spiritual (as in the classical view) nor the other side of the spiritual (as in the modern view). Instead, it is the vessel of the spiritual.

The atoning work of Christ is the basis of a biblical, evangelical spirituality. Here Christ is seen not simply as the representative of fallen humanity nor as the model of the new humanity but as Mediator, Expiator and Sin Bearer. Before he can be our example, he must be acknowledged as our Savior and Lord. True spirituality views the Christian life as primarily a sign and witness to the atoning work of Christ. The imitation of Christ is a token of our gratitude for his incomparable work of reconciliation and redemption on Calvary. It is not to be seen as a means to gain additional merits, insuring us a place in heaven.

Certainly true spirituality will also emphasize the outpouring of the Holy Spirit, for there can be no Christian life that is not inspired by the Spirit. In our theology of the Holy Spirit, we should strive for a balance between the gifts and the fruits of the Spirit. The gifts are necessary for the upbuilding of the church; the fruits are necessary as the evidence before the world of our incorporation into the body of Christ.

Spirituality will entail ethical action, but it must not be reduced to ethicism. Similarly, it will involve mystical communion with God, but it must not be dissolved into mysticism. We must seek in our time to recover the mystical dimension of the faith without succumbing to what Aldous Huxley calls "the perennial philosophy"—monistic mysticism.

Finally, as evangelicals who stand in the tradition of Reformation Protestantism, we should learn to appreciate Catholic spirituality without imitating Catholic forms of devotion. We likewise urge our brothers and sisters in the Catholic churches to draw upon the abiding values of evangelical devotion, including the spirituality of the Reformation, without jettisoning their own rich spiritual heritage. We need to be faithful to our own traditions but at the same time open to broadening our perspective and even having it corrected.

The Reformation, in its reaction to perversions and misunderstandings of biblical truth in the popular Catholic piety of the time, regrettably discarded much in the catholic heritage that is of enduring value. I have in mind such things as religious orders within the church,[50] celibacy, retreats and spiritual disciplines, including meditation and silence. In the evangelical perspective, the purpose of such disciplines is not to merit God's favor but to prepare ourselves to hear God's Word. It is not to insure a place for us in eternity but to make us more available for service in the world.

The doctrine of the saints was another casualty of a reforming zeal that understandably could not tolerate the idea, nurtured in Catholic popular devotion, of saints as mediators alongside of Christ. Some of the confessional documents of the Reformation sought to make a place for the role of the departed saints as intercessors, but for the most part even the idea of the communion of saints fell more and more into the background. The overriding concern of the Reformation was the holy gospel, not holy people. The role of Mary in the plan of salvation and in the life of the church was likewise neglected, though Luther at one time in his life was willing to make a place for a Christocentric form of Marian devotion.

An interest in spiritual formation presently engrosses a large part of both the liberal and evangelical communities. This can be a promising sign provided that the development of spiritual life is always based on the decisive act of God in Jesus Christ in biblical history. But when spirituality becomes divorced from its objective historical foundation, then we are engulfed in the peril of subjectivism. This is an omnipresent danger in the popular religion of our culture, whether it carries a conservative or liberal label.

Forsyth, a spiritual theologian of the first order, has this timely word of warning:

> To make the development of man the supreme interest of God, as popular Christianity sometimes tends to do, instead of making the glory of God the supreme interest of man, is a moral error which invites the only treatment that can cure a civilisation whose religion has become so false—public judgment.[51]

REDISCOVERING ETHICAL IMPERATIVES

What is missing in so much current spirituality is the ethical or prophetic note. Certainly the time is ripe to rediscover the ethical imperatives of the faith, for today there is an accelerated erosion of moral values. I am convinced that the current moral decay is associated with the rise of a moral relativism that denies a universal moral law or an absolute, binding moral norm.

We need to remember that faith not only has a kerygmatic but also a prophetic dimension. Our mandate as ambassadors of Christ is to bring the law of God to bear on the critical moral issues of the time. As concerned citizens of the state, we are then under the imperative to implement the divine commandment through legal measures that will insure a greater measure of justice in the land.

Among the burning social issues of our time is abortion on demand. Abortion has been condemned with a rare degree of consensus through Christian history from the first century onward. Both Karl Barth and Dietrich Bonhoeffer have described it as an undeniable evil. Although not explicitly condemning abortion, Scripture is quite clear that human personhood already begins at conception and that the unborn child is infinitely precious in the sight of God (Ps. 139:13–16; Isa. 49:1; Jer. 1:5; Luke 1:44; Gal. 1:15).[52] To countenance the wanton killing of innocent life on the grounds of freedom of choice is to abandon Christian norms in favor of a pagan, radical egalitarian ideology. In my opinion, the church should press for legislation that would put an end to the abortion traffic, which is creating a climate of opinion that regards human life as expendable if the common good demands it.

Yet while supporting laws that would severely restrict abortions, I do not share the absolutist position of some of my evangelical colleagues, who contend that the taking of a fetal life is always tantamount to murder.[53] The divine commandment cannot be frozen into a moral code that allows for absolutely no exceptions.[54] When the mother's life is at stake or when evidence indicates that genetic deformity or structural abnormality is so severe that the unborn child faces a life of agonizing pain or untold misery, we may hear God's permission for an abortion, but this is a possibility granted only by God; it is not ours to claim.[55] After birth, a distinction should be made between the deliberate taking of life and the withholding of medicinal aids or artificial supports necessary for the continuation of life.[56] The church needs to reach some consensus on this whole problem, but it should draw its main source of guidance from Holy Scripture, not from the biological and social sciences (though the latter should not be discounted).

Another intolerable social evil that casts a pall over the modern world is the nuclear armaments race. The church must certainly address itself to this spiritual issue if it is to maintain the relevance of the gospel for our age. The mainstream of Christian thought has never embraced an absolutist pacifism, but it has maintained that only some wars can be deemed just. Christian leaders, including the present pope, are fast coming to the conclusion that the concept of a just war is now passé in light of the emergence of weapons of mass extermination, which makes it impossible to discriminate between combatants and noncombatants and which eliminates any possibility of proportionality between the means used in warfare and the results effected. It is justifiable for a nation to defend itself against attack, but in responding to attack it is never justifiable for a nation to demolish civilian populations and to deform millions yet unborn, which would be the case in nuclear and biochemical warfare. The saturation bombing of Dresden was already a sign of a creeping callousness in warfare that can only be attributed to the triumph of nihilism over historic Christian values in the modern world.

Christians today are divided on what their response should be to the war strategies of the superpowers, which can only result in mass murder. Certainly the church should throw its weight behind an arms control program leading to a drastic reduction in biochemical and nuclear weapons and a verifiable ban on nuclear testing. It should also press for selective conscientious objection, so that nuclear pacifism is given legal recognition by the state. Withholding of income tax payments or refusal to register for the draft are actions that probably have to be left to the individual conscience. The call for a bilateral freeze on the manufacture of nuclear weapons would seem to be in accord with the divine commandment for our time. The policy of total obliteration and the building and deployment of first strike nuclear weapons should be unequivocally rejected.[57]

Whether the church should urge the unilateral dismantling of the nuclear arsenal of the West is quite another question, however, since such an action could well invite open aggression, even precipitating a nuclear attack, either against us or against weaker nations. Yet the church must not permit the state to rest content in the illusion that nuclear weapons can be an adequate deterrent to war, for even the possession of such weapons fosters a climate of fear and violence.

War takes on the character of a fateful tragedy when nations can no longer free themselves from their idolatrous dependence on weapons of terror and destruction (cf. Ps. 9:15, 16; Isa. 31:1–3). War could be avoidable if nations would turn to God in repentance and forsake their trust in military might (cf. Ps. 33:13–22). It becomes unavoidable when nations in their folly persist in their feverish war preparations, thereby reaping the retribution that follows from disobedience (cf. Matt. 26:52; Gal. 6:7, 8). A nation has the right and obligation to maintain the security of its people, but the lines between a legitimate military defense and an acceleration in military expenditures that is no longer subject to rational controls is very thin indeed.

Christians, even pacifist Christians, cannot escape involvement in the tragedy of war, when discord between nations erupts into violence, but they can make their protest known in both words and deeds. If they embark on a program of civil disobedience, they must be ready to accept the penalty for their transgression—fines or imprisonment (as Martin Luther King was wise enough to discern). In this way, they will still give honor to the state as an authority set over us by God, even while taking issue with its policies. The Christian who seeks to make his witness within the power structures of government cannot necessarily be considered a greater sinner than the Christian who repudiates the social system that fosters the war mentality and withdraws into a communitarian enclave dedicated to nonviolence. It may be that the commandment of God will become ever more clear to the church as a whole in the dark days ahead, and Christians must be willing to follow the divine mandate wherever it might lead us.

The trouble with the "Ban the Bomb" movement today is that it is basically motivated by the desire for self-preservation rather than by obedience to the commandment of God. Whenever self-preservation is made into an absolute principle, we are no longer under grace but under law. We are also placing human survival over both fidelity to God's Word and a concern for the total welfare of our neighbor (including his or her eternal salvation). Especially disconcerting is the fact that many church groups today which align themselves with the peace movement in decrying the horrors of nuclear war are strangely silent on the mass murder of millions of unborn children through abortion. The credibility of their witness is thus seriously impaired, particularly among lower middle class and poorer people.

Where the Christian witness on peace differs most radically from the secular peace movement is in its focus on Jesus Christ as the key to real peace in the world. Only when people have been converted by the Spirit of Christ do they gain the motivation and power to be authentic peacemakers. This is why the Christian strategy for peace entails not only peacemaking, not only announcing the divine commandment against nuclear war but also, and above all, preaching the gospel of regeneration. This does not preclude Christians from working with secular people in the promotion of peace, but it does mean that we will try to stay clear of both utopianism and unrestrained pessimism (the secular temptations).

Even while disagreeing with the absolute pacifist and semianarchist position of the Sojourners fellowship, I fully concur with these words of Jim Wallis:

> His victory is the basis for our hope. I am convinced that the nuclear arms race will not be overcome by an appeal to fear. Its own basis is fear, and more fear will not finally prevail against it. Rather, nuclear violence will be overcome with hope. Christian hope sees the nuclear situation realistically, with no false optimism. But Christian hope knows that the victory of Christ is stronger than the nuclear powers. Prayer helps us to continue to believe that. Our actions must show the world that we believe.[58]

Among other critical social and moral issues which the church needs to come to grips with today are the growing use of torture as a means of human intimidation, euthanasia, the widening disparity between rich and poor, the virtually unchecked population explosion, the rape of the environment in the name of technological progress and the breakdown of the family, brought about partly by the sexual revolution.

This is not the place to delve into all of these critical moral issues, but a word should be said about moral decay in the area of sexual ethics and family life. The new permissive morality, which countenances any kind of sexual activity so long as it does not directly injure another person, is diametrically opposed to the Christian ethic, which calls men and women to live responsibly in a relationship either of holy virginity or holy marriage. In either case chastity, the channeling or sublimation of sexual desire, is the mode of life that has divine sanction. Christians today who justify fornication, extramarital relations, homosexuality or pornography on the grounds that these can all be stepping-stones to self-fulfillment reveal their distance from the thought world of the Bible.

This is not to argue for a return to Victorian morality, with its double standard and its suspicion of sex as something degrading. Pornography should be opposed not because it focuses upon nudity (which in itself is morally neutral) but because it portrays human beings not as persons but only as objects to be used for sexual gratification. Yet in opposition to the new religious and political right, I do not see any justification for opposing sex education in principle. Where the moral values of the Judeo-Christian tradition are shelved in favor of the value-free orientation of modern nihilism, then of course we must register a vigorous protest. But sexual ignorance is not a Christian solution to the growing problem of illegitimacy, venereal disease and abortions, and the sad fact is that most homes fail to provide the necessary information.

In contradistinction to new class liberalism today, I see no reason for not cooperating with Moral Majority and kindred groups in combating pornography, the abortion mills, no-fault divorce, incest, homosexuality, etc., because a society cannot long endure without a foundational moral code. I agree with Jacques Ellul that the common morality of a society is in most cases more salutary than destructive and therefore deserves the relative support of all people of goodwill.[59] On the other hand, this common morality or civil righteousness must not be confused with the higher righteousness of the kingdom, which calls us to works of mercy and sanctity beyond our obligations to society. While we should be generally supportive of the mores of a society, we must always look beyond these codes to the divine commandment, which stands in judgment over our morality as well as our immorality.

It is commonplace to hold that Christians live under grace, not a moral code, and yet the implications of this can be devastating for a society if it is supposed that grace annuls morality. To affirm *sola gratia* does not mean that we may therefore live in flagrant disregard of the moral codes that society sets up to protect itself. These codes comprise the dike that secures society from moral and social chaos.

Yet the moral codes and taboos of a society must not be accepted as absolute or unalterable. They should always be weighed in the light of the one norm that is absolute—God's self-revelation in Jesus Christ, which is both promise and command. Reinhold Niebuhr has urged that society's quest for order and justice be constantly judged and measured by the higher standard of sacrificial love; otherwise, this very quest may itself become an obstacle to the kingdom of God.[60]

I do not agree with Flo Conway and Jim Siegelman in their wholesale condemnation of modern fundamentalism, since I believe that it is prompted in part by a commitment to secular humanism.[61] When they can see only a right-wing conspiracy in the fundamentalist opposition to abortion on demand, pornography, the portrayal of homosexuality as a valid alternative life-style and the teaching of evolution as a metaphysical dogma, then they have failed to appreciate the genuine and often valid concerns of lower and lower-middle-class America regarding the intrusion of a humanistic and nihilistic mentality that threatens the values and freedoms of all religious people. The authors argue that the United States cannot long survive "as two nations—one fundamentalist, one secular."[62] But the alternative they propose to fundamentalist totalism is a secular pluralism, which in reality is a humanistic totalism that tolerates religion only insofar as it remains confined to charitable service or spiritual worship. Moral Majority, Religious Roundtable and other fundamentalist groups need to be critiqued and in some areas even opposed, but the only critique that will be convincing to evangelicals as well as many other Christians is one that arises out of a deep-seated commitment to biblical faith.[63]

In its ethical witness, the church should be conscious that if it is truly being faithful to the divine commandment, its word will always go against the values and ideals embraced by society, both right and left. Indeed, one of the tests of authentic prophecy is whether it calls into radical question the mythologies and idolatries dominating the culture of its time. True prophecy means speaking a word from God that judges speaker and hearer alike. The object of a genuine prophecy is liberation from ideological and religious bondage.

Finally, we as Christians need to keep in mind that our efforts to carry out our ethical responsibility are not a means to our salvation but a concrete sign and testimony of a salvation already won for us. We are summoned not to meritorious works but to an obedient life with the sole motivation of glorifying Christ and serving our neighbor for whom Christ died. The ethical goal is neither self-realization (eudaemonia) nor eternal security but the extension of the kingdom of God by upholding Jesus Christ before the world.

OVERCOMING POLARIZATION ON THE WOMEN'S ISSUE

The ethical seriousness of the faith is also put to the test in the drive for equal rights and working opportunities for women. When this drive tends to blur or disregard the very real differences between the sexes, then we have a theological issue of momentous import.

Women's liberation has precipitated at least two crises in the church: the first pertains to the issue of women in positions of spiritual leadership (elder, pastor) and the second to desexing the language about God. Of all the issues that threaten schism in the American church today, this is perhaps the most volatile. Indeed, some schisms have already resulted (especially in the Anglican and Presbyterian churches). The blame cannot be placed only on those who seek to cling to a waning patriarchalism. The strident demands of some feminists have contributed in no small measure to the widening splits in many local churches as well as denominational bodies.

Behind the current dissension in the churches and in society at large over the role of women lies the all-pervasive sin of sexism. Many evangelicals, to their shame, have difficulty even in recognizing sexism as a sin. Yet treating women as inferiors, which is basically what sexism is, reveals the arrogance of power, the urge to dominate and control—one of the more ugly manifestations of sin. We also need to realize that sexism contravenes the faith affirmations that *all* people are created in the image of God, *all* are called to be witnesses and ambassadors of Jesus Christ.

Sexism is rampant in nearly every area of society. It is most blatant in the traffic in prostitution and pornography, where women are reduced to nothing more than sex objects serving male gratification. It is also apparent in the still appreciable disparity in the salaries of men and women who perform the same services and in a host of other ways.

Sexism is indissolubly linked to the often harsh patriarchalism inherited from both Hebraic and Hellenic cultural traditions. In the patriarchal ethos, woman is not so much the helpmate of man as his servant, always there to do his bidding. Marriage is seen in the service of biological fertility, and a childless marriage or even a marriage without male heirs is considered a signal misfortune. In most patriarchal societies of the past and many in the present, women are even denied the right to vote.

Modern feminism signifies a vehement, almost violent, reaction against the sexism and patriarchalism that have been part of the heritage of virtually all of Western civilization (as well as most other cultures). Whereas in patriarchalism woman is the property of man, in feminism woman is the equal, even the rival of man. The independence of woman from man is one of its cardinal principles. Mutual responsibility is seen to be in the service of the Enlightenment ideal of autonomy. Career development is championed over the often humdrum service in home and family, which is for the most part considered demeaning.

Feminist ideology generally favors the mythical vision of androgyny over complementarity, which supposes that male and female are incomplete apart from the other. In androgyny man and woman seek to discover the masculine and feminine elements present within all human beings and to integrate these within themselves.[64]

Just as patriarchalism, where the male is seen as dominant over the female, is associated with an ideology of restoration, so feminism represents an ideology of accommodation. Its motto is not a return to the past but an openness to the future. In Christian circles feminism takes the form of a revisionist theology in which the Spirit of God is identified with the new consciousness of a world free from exploitation and oppression.

The biblical alternative to both patriarchalism and feminism is the covenant of grace in which marriage is patterned after the covenant that God made with Israel. Marriage is now seen as a partnership in kingdom service in which man and woman realize a common vocation under the cross. Even in the single state, it is contended, man and woman cannot live unto themselves alone but must live in interdependence, not independence. Against both heteronomy (subjection to external authority—the patriarchal model) and autonomy (freedom from all outward authority—the feminist ideal), biblical faith upholds theonomy, in which man and woman are joined together in service to the living God. Faithfulness to God means not servile subjection to the will of a tyrant but following the lead of a loving Father. No longer servants, men and women are now sons and daughters, brothers and sisters, members of a community characterized by loving fellowship rather than an authoritarian chain of command.

The concept of subordination is not abrogated in biblical faith but instead drastically transformed. Just as Christ demonstrated his lordship by laying down his life for his church, so the husband is called to exercise his headship in the role of a servant.[65] It is still his task to provide protection and guidance for his family, but as much as possible he should do this indirectly. He should seldom if ever arbitrarily impose his will on his family but instead endeavor with them to discover the will of Jesus Christ, the one Lord of both church and family. Similarly, a wife must still subordinate herself to her husband and the children to their parents, but this subordination now takes the form not of servile submission but of loving assistance.[66] The church as the bride of Christ responds to her bridegroom in love and gratitude; the wife responds in a like manner to the love of her husband (cf. Song of Solomon 7:10–13).

In the biblical scheme, man and woman are essentially equals by virtue of their creation in the image of God and a common calling to the service of the kingdom (cf. Gen. 1:27; 5:1, 2; Gal. 3:28, 29). They are equal heirs to a salvation already secured through faith in Christ (I Pet. 3:7). Yet biblical equality does not eradicate biological differentiation, but instead seeks to harness the unique capabilities and talents of each sex for the purpose of creating community. Biblical faith affirms both biological and psychic differences between the sexes,[67] but this does not necessarily relegate woman to a background role. The Bible allows for the fact that women, too, may be called to leadership positions, both civil and spiritual, but that in assuming such responsibilities, they must do so as women and not try to imitate men.[68]

The move to obliterate the ineradicable differences between the sexes today is detrimental to both sexes and renders genuine community between them impossible. The search for a unisex utopia can only end in the masculinization of women and the feminization of men. Dietrich Bonhoeffer has some timely words on this subject:

> There is something wrong with a world in which the woman's ambition is to be like a man, and in which the man regards the woman as the toy of his lust for power and freedom. It is a sign of social disintegration when the woman's service is thought to be degrading, and when the man who is faithful to his wife is looked upon as a weakling or a fool.[69]

Regarding the debate on the language about God, evangelicals must hold firm to the biblical principle that form and content are inextricably bound together, that the personal and mainly masculine metaphors pertaining to God given in Holy Scripture cannot be jettisoned without turning Christianity into an immanentalistic or naturalistic religion. The biblical terms "Father, Son and Holy Spirit" are not merely symbols that point to an undifferentiated ground of being (as in monistic mysticism) but instead analogies revealed by God himself concerning his own person and activity. When Jesus himself taught his disciples to pray addressing God as Father, we are bound to do likewise if we wish to identify ourselves with the same community of faith.

To substitute an inclusive language in reference to God for the personal metaphors of Scripture signifies a move away from Trinitarianism. To think of God as Father-Mother rather than heavenly Father is binitarian. To envision God primarily or exclusively as Spirit or heavenly Parent or Divine Providence is to end in unitarianism.

Feminists seek to do away with not only masculine but also hierarchical metaphors, thus contradicting the biblical principle of the infinite qualitative difference between God and man. God is not the creative depth of being but the Sovereign Creator who brought us into the world out of nothing. He is not simply Friend or Companion but Lord and Master, and he is the latter before he is the former.

When feminists attack the biblical symbol "Lord" in reference to both God and Christ, they are robbing the church of a politically revolutionary symbol, for to confess Jesus as Lord calls into question all worldly claims to absolute power. The confession of Jesus as Lord is a challenge not only to fascist and communist dictatorships but also to the totalitarianism of the democratic consensus, the idea that the will of the people is sovereign. The ancient Roman Empire was not alarmed by the various mystical cults of its time, because they did not pose a challenge to civil authority; yet it did feel immensely threatened by the confession of Jesus as Lord, which dethroned the gods of the pantheon and effectively undermined the idolatry of the emperor. Pagan Rome felt compelled to stamp out the Christian "heresy" in order to survive as a cultural entity.

Although sacred Scripture generally envisions God in masculine terms, this is not always the case. There are also metaphors pointing to the divine motherhood.[70] In the Wisdom literature, the Wisdom of God (practically equivalent to the Word of God) is always portrayed as feminine—as mother and sister (cf. Prov. 7:4; 8:32–36; Sirach 24:18; Wisd. of Sol. 7:12 RSV; Matt. 11:19). Moreover, the Spirit of God in the Hebrew Scriptures and the glory of God (*Shekinah*) in later rabbinical literature are likewise represented as feminine, not masculine.

W. A. Visser't Hooft rightly argues that to try to overcome personal metaphors for an inclusive language in which God is portrayed as neuter is ultimately to depersonalize God.[71] This was the way of the deists and many Neoplatonic mystics, and the end result was the impersonal Absolute of philosophical speculation, far removed from the living, personal God of biblical faith.

Yet Visser't Hooft is ready to acknowledge that the fatherhood of God is not a closed or exclusive symbolism: "It is open to correction, enrichment, and completion from other forms of symbol, such as 'mother,' 'brother,' 'sister' and 'friend.' "[72] He is willing to allow for describing or even addressing God in certain contexts by feminine symbols so long as these are subordinated to the masculine symbols of faith, which in the Bible are dominant.[73] In his view, we need to make room for a certain amount of spiritual imagination in describing God by metaphors other than masculine and hierarchical, but we do not transgress the limits of biblical faith provided that "Father, Son and Spirit" remain central.[74]

The threat to the church today lies in a neo-Gnosticism and naturalistic mysticism in which the boundaries between the infinite and the finite, the supernatural and the natural, are overcome, and the sovereignty and transcendence of God are then called into question. It is crucial in this age of immanentalistic mysticism to preserve the metaphors and symbols of transcendence if the church is to maintain its identity and integrity. It is also imperative that we oppose the feminist appeal to new revelations in nature and inward experience and affirm the uniqueness and decisiveness of the one final revelation of God in the biblical history culminating in Jesus Christ.[75]

RENEWAL THROUGH BIBLICAL PREACHING

There can be no biblical renewal in our churches today (Catholic or Protestant) without a renewal of biblical preaching. If the problems associated with naturalistic mysticism and radical feminism are fairly recent arrivals on the religious scene, the crisis in preaching has been looming for decades. The anecdotal nature of much preaching today has led Daniel Jenkins, a pastor and theologian in the United Reformed Church in England, to predict that within one or two generations people will begin turning away from the churches out of a depressing awareness that they have not been spiritually fed. Many factors have precipitated the present disarray in Roman Catholicism, evident in the loss of vocations and decreasing attendance at mass, but certainly we should not discount the slow but irrefragable erosion of biblical, kerygmatic preaching in that communion through the centuries.

The demise of biblical preaching has both sociological and theological roots. Part of the legacy of revivalism was the turning of the focus from an objective message to personal experience. Individual conversion rather than the conversion of the world in Jesus Christ became the paramount concern. Both, of course, are important, but the loss of an objective, historical content seems the greater peril today. Romanticism also played a significant role in undermining biblical, evangelical preaching. For Schleiermacher, who regarded himself as a Pietist of a higher order, the purpose of preaching is not to herald a definite message but to evoke a sense of the mystery of God.[76] The transcendentalist movement in America posed a similar threat, placing the emphasis on internal experience rather than external authority, on the perfecting of the self rather than the deliverance of the world through the redemptive work of God in biblical history.[77] Most sermons today are constructed with an eye on the impression they will make on the subject, not the glory they will give to the object of faith—the living God.

Growing ritualism in worship is also responsible for undermining evangelical preaching. Sermons are reduced to moral homilies, and the main action is what goes on in the Mass or Eucharist. The retreat into liturgy can be observed not only in Roman Catholic, Anglo-Catholic and Lutheran churches but also in mainstream evangelical Protestantism.

Biblical preaching consists in the diligent and faithful exposition of the biblical text, taking into consideration its literary and historical background as well as assessing its theological significance for the present age. An effort will always be made to examine the text in the light of the law and the gospel, which are either implicit or explicit in the whole of Scripture. Preaching that is true to the scriptural imperative entails more than fidelity to the text and to the central message of the Bible: it also presupposes a personal encounter between the preacher and the Holy. Biblical preaching includes not only *soundness* in exposition but also spiritual *fervor* and *power*. What is at stake is not only the viability of the message but also the credibility of the messenger.

In an age when the average sermon has degenerated into an after-dinner speech, random thoughts on the contemporary scene, or a soothing pep talk to carry us through the week, we need to rediscover the sacramental character of gospel preaching. James Hastings Nichols has trenchantly observed that the Reformation made preaching into a third sacrament, one that effectively took the place of absolution.[78] Indeed, it was through the renewed preaching of the gospel that people of that time received deliverance from guilt and inner torment. Puritan preachers were commonly referred to as "physicians of the soul." Such a designation can help to remind us all, preachers and congregations alike, of the seriousness and cruciality of the homiletic task.

Biblical preaching at its best will be expositional, evangelical and prophetic. It will seek not only to expound the text but to relate the text to the gospel, the central content of Scripture. It will also take care to apply the imperatives of the gospel to the society in which we live as well as to our personal lives. It will therefore include the note of divine judgment as well as divine grace.

Preaching will be in the context of worship. Indeed, preaching serves the worship of God and not vice versa. Calvin said that the purpose of worship is to glorify God and lead people to Christ. This is also the purpose of preaching.[79]

We are living in an age where the focus of ministry is upon counseling and group manipulation rather than upon preaching. Expertise in psychology and in church management are deemed more important than immersion in the Word of God. If there is to be a genuine revival of biblical preaching, the spiritual hunger of people for the Word of God will have to be rekindled.

A BIBLICAL AND RELEVANT ESCHATOLOGY

Paradoxically, in popular evangelical circles, while there is a ready acceptance of the modern virtues of psychological maturity and efficiency, indicating a preoccupation with the immanent at the expense of the transcendent, in the area of eschatology the thrust is otherworldly and escapist. Nonetheless, the selfist mentality persists, for in this kind of eschatology people are led away from concern for social justice to an egocentric obsession with personal security. We need an eschatology that will give hope and significance to this present age without denying that this-worldly hopes can only be provisional and that the blessed hope signifies the end of this age. We need to perceive Pentecost as the second stage of the advent of Christ and the latter-day Pentecost before his second advent as the dawn of the glory of the millennium.

In constructing an eschatology capable of bringing hope to a spiritually destitute humanity, we have to keep in mind that what God has done in the past is not to be subordinated to what God will do in the future. What he will do in the future is the outcome of what he has done in the past and what he is doing in the present. He has already set up his kingdom in our midst, Pentecost has already occurred, though, to be sure, his kingdom has yet to be consummated. Though mindful that the full realization of the kingdom lies in the eternal future, we must include in our message that the kingdom has already come, the new age is already here, even though the old has not yet passed away. This means that we can even now proclaim liberty to the captives (cf. Luke 4:18), for the devil was dethroned when Jesus rose from the dead.

In forging a new eschatological vision, we should not minimize the role of the church. Evangelicals of the dispensationalist variety often refer to the "twilight of the church" and issue a call to separation from the institutional church, which they regard as apostate. We should remember Christ's promise that the gates of hell will not prevail against his church (Matt. 16:18 KJV). We should consider that the church is not condemned to be an ever dwindling minority but is destined to include a vast multitude of people of all races and nations (Col. 1:6; Rev. 7:9). The New Testament vision of the church is that it will withstand and overcome the principalities and powers, that it will finally inherit the world (Matt. 5:5).

We should, of course, be alert to the opposite error of unduly exalting the church, of seeing the eschatological victory already finalized in the church. This imbalance is present in both Reformation and Catholic traditions, stemming partly from Augustine, who practically identified the church with the kingdom of Christ. The church is the vessel of the kingdom, the herald of the kingdom, but it will not become the kingdom until the wheat is separated from the tares on the last day. The kingdom, which might be regarded as the invisible church, is hidden in the church as a historical institution. It is both more narrow and more extensive than the visible church, since the latter contains some who are faithless and does not yet include on its membership rolls many who are faithful. Already partially realized in the fellowship of love, the kingdom is still coming as the messianic rule of Christ over the whole of creation. The church as well as the world looks forward to the coming of the kingdom (Rom. 8:19–22), though only the former is granted the right understanding of this.

Our eschatology will not be sufficiently realistic or fully biblical unless it does justice to the ineradicable and persistent dualistic motif in Scripture—the idea of two kingdoms arrayed against one another. The kingdom of Christ is not the only one in this world; there is also the kingdom of evil, the kingdom of the devil which continues to hold the world in subjection. Even though the principalities and powers have been overthrown by the cross and resurrection victory of Christ, they continue to exert real power by virtue of the spell that they cast over those who have not truly awakened to the full dimensions of Christ's victory. Jesus Christ is already Lord over all earthly powers (Rev. 17:14; 19:16), but the salvific fruits of his victory extend only to the community of faith, where his Lordship is acknowledged and his will obeyed.[80] His rule continues to be challenged even by a devil who is in his death throes, whose power is more psychological than ontological, whose time is already practically at an end. Yet just as a mortally wounded beast can be all the more dangerous in its desperation, so the devil presents a still greater peril as he struggles to rebound from defeat. Evangelical theology must indeed take this into consideration if it is to avoid the utopianism and spurious idealism of neoliberal and neo-Barthian theology.[81]

Finally, we should strive for a new statement on the millennium that will do justice to the total biblical vision. The millennium signifies the end-time age, but this age is already here in part, because Christ's reign has already begun. The millennial age overlaps the present age, for Christ's messianic kingdom has already been established, though it does not yet extend throughout the entire earth.

The universal revelation of its power and glory will not take place until Christ comes again, but partial revelations of the millennial triumph within worldly history are apparent wherever there is a marked breakthrough in Christian mission. We must do justice to the millennial hope without abandoning the present world to the devil.

We are challenged today to avoid both a crippling pessimism and an unrealistic optimism. The end times will be marked by growing persecution and tribulation for Christians, but they will also witness wholesale conversions to the gospel. The rapture of the church will be manifest in the way it emerges triumphant over the anti-God powers in the last days. The millennium means the victory of the church, not its defeat at the hands of worldly power.

PROMISE OF RENEWAL

The impending collapse of Western civilization does not mean the defeat of the holy catholic church. Nor does the decline of the mainline denominations signify the end of Christianity. Never before have so many missionaries gone out from the churches of Western nations to the third world and other mission areas. Christianity may be declining in Europe, but it is on the march in Africa and southeast Asia. The church is even advancing behind the Iron and Bamboo curtains, despite periodic and often severe persecution. We have reason to hope even amid the encroaching desert of secularism and nihilism, because Pentecost is a continuing reality in the life of the people of God, a reality that the world is powerless to extinguish. The transforming power of Pentecost is currently manifest in the burgeoning evangelical movement in this country and other countries throughout the world.

The growing cleavage in the church could be a signal opportunity for the church to redefine itself against the beguiling forces of secular humanism and modernism. Heresy has always been the catalyst which orthodoxy has needed to put its house in order and rediscover the abiding relevance of the gospel. When a false church emerges on the horizon, the true church will also become more visible.

We should recognize that the evangelical movement could itself fall into heresy if it continues its slide into sectarianism. It is imperative that the evangelical church reappropriate those elements that belong to the church in its fullness—catholicity, apostolicity, holiness and love.

The true church, the church of Jesus Christ, will be centered in the gospel, anchored in church tradition and imbued with the fire of Pentecost. It will be evangelical in the sense that it will be devoted to the proclamation of the gospel as attested in Holy Scripture. It will also be catholic, for it will strive both to maintain continuity with the tradition of the whole church and to include the whole world under the banner of the gospel. It will be Reformed in that it will commit itself to continual reformation in the light of the criterion of God's self-revelation in Jesus Christ. It will be inclined to view the Protestant Reformation as the model of a church striving for biblical reform.[82] It will also be Pentecostal (but not in the sectarian sense), since it will live on the basis of the outpouring of the Holy Spirit upon the community of faith, bearing in mind that it is the Spirit who "will convince the world of sin and of righteousness and of judgment" (John 16:8 RSV).

A church that is truly catholic, evangelical and Reformed will make room for the liberal spirit—the spirit of inquiry and openness. Indeed, such a church will eschew all obscurantism and maintain a self-critical stance concerning its own formulations of the truth of faith.[83] At the same time, it will vigorously oppose liberalism as a theological movement that seeks to bring the faith into accord with modernity, that strives for a biblical-cultural synthesis in which the claims of faith are justified at the bar of reason. It will concur in the judgment of P. T. Forsyth: "What is called liberal theology . . . works on the whole against the preaching of the Gospel, and becomes little more than an enlightened Judaism."[84]

Liberal theology in the sense of modernism identifies the Spirit of God with the interior spirit of the age and holds that the life of the time appoints the creed of the time. Evangelical theology, on the contrary, maintains that there is an infinite qualitative distinction between the Spirit of God and the spirit of the time and that the creed of the church must be based on the light of the Word of God, even though it is addressed to the age in which we live. We do not draw our agenda from the world, but we bring God's agenda, as delineated in the Scriptures, to the world.

An evangelical catholic church will also be committed to the ideal of church unity. Revivification by the Holy Spirit is nowhere more evident than in love for our brothers and sisters in the faith. Indeed, such love is a sign that spiritual renewal has already begun to take place. Philip Schaff declares, "If we love Christians of other creeds only as far as they agree with us, we do no more than the heathen do who love their own."[85] The key to renewal in the church lies not only in love, however, but also in humility. "We look hopefully for a reunion of Christendom and a feast of reconciliation of churches," Schaff continues, "but it will be preceded by an act of general humiliation. All must confess: We have sinned and erred; Christ alone is pure and perfect."[86]

In our striving for church unity, we must not lose sight of our mandate to counter doctrinal error, for nothing subverts the cause of unity more than a latitudinarianism which signifies giving up on real church unity in favor of mutual tolerance. Yet in our ongoing battle with heresy, we should be poignantly aware of the fact that there are heresies on the right as well as on the left. Luther reminds us that the Christian must always be fighting on two fronts. Today, the two enemies are an obscurantist biblicism on the right and modernism on the left. If we focus on only one of these threats, the overwhelming temptation will be to forge an alliance with the opposite heresy and thus begin to compromise the faith unwittingly.

I have discussed at length the centrifugal forces threatening the unity of the evangelical catholic church: restorationism, separatism and accommodationism. But there is also a centripetal power drawing evangelical Christians from all communions into a deeper unity —namely, the movement of the Holy Spirit in these last days, the awakening to evangelism and mission. We can face the future with confidence because of the irreversible victory of Jesus Christ and the continuing life-transforming reality of Pentecost, which confirms this victory in the hearts of all who believe. Just as the devil is making his final stand against a church emboldened and renewed by the Holy Spirit, so Jesus Christ is preparing to bring down the curtain on the history of the old aeon and complete his mission—the salvation of a lost and despairing humanity and the creation of a new heaven and a new earth.

Notes

Notes to the Foreword

1. Clark Pinnock, "God Made in the Image of Man," in *Christianity Today,* Vol. 26, No. 14 (September 3, 1982), p. 35.

2. Howard A. Snyder, *The Community of the King* (Downers Grove, Ill.: InterVarsity Press, 1978), p. 180.

Notes to Chapter I—Introduction

1. The subordination of Scripture to tradition is evident in James Barr. He rejects the traditional model "God → revelation → scripture → church" and substitutes "God → people → tradition → scripture." In his view, revelation is derived from all these sources. See James Barr, *The Scope and Authority of the Bible* (Philadelphia: Westminster Press, 1980), p. 60.

2. That Kierkegaard was a theologian of grace as well as of Christian discipleship is made abundantly clear by Vernard Eller in his brilliant work *Kierkegaard and Radical Discipleship: A New Perspective* (Princeton, N.J.: Princeton University Press, 1968). See especially pp. 172 ff.

3. Cf. Forsyth: "The great dividing issue for the soul is neither the Bethlehem cradle nor the empty grave, nor the Bible, nor the social question. For the Church at least . . . it is the question of a redeeming atonement. It is here that the evangelical issue lies." P. T. Forsyth, *The Cruciality of the Cross* (London: Independent Press, 1948), p. 39.

4. While revealing his distance from "theologians of the word" such as Calvin, Barth, Brunner and Nygren, David Tracy acknowledges the deep similarities between Catholic and liberal Protestant theologians both

in structure and in spirit. See David Tracy, *The Analogical Imagination* (New York: Crossroad Publishing Co., 1981), pp. 180, 213, 214, 217, 220, 379, 444. Tracy seeks to bring together motifs from Thomist and process thought, but he displays a distinct preference for the latter (see pp. 439, 440, 443, 444).

5. Our words are nevertheless accepted and justified by God if they are born out of a sincere faith in Jesus Christ and are in accordance with the New Testament witness to God's redemptive act in Christ. Despite the lack of perfect correlation, they may be accepted as the vehicle or instrument of God's Word. Yet a qualitative distinction will always remain between God's eternal Word and the earthen vessel of the human witness (II Cor. 4:7). What saves is not our broken testimony but the divine blessing upon our testimony.

Notes to Chapter II—The Problem of Evangelical Identity

1. This appears to be the stance of many of those associated with the International Council on Biblical Inerrancy. This doctrine, which even its supporters acknowledge is not specifically stated in Scripture, can never be the foundation for faith but only an inference from faith, and even then it needs to be qualified.

2. It would be a mistake to regard these preachers as charlatans. For the most part, they are sincere and God-fearing people. Moreover, I acknowledge that through their ministries there are genuine healings and conversions. But their overall impact is to reinforce traditional values and mores rather than to bring a prophetic word to bear on what the culture holds most dear. By shoring up the moral codes by which society lives, the media preachers perform a distinct service, but they dismally fail to move society toward a new social vision which calls for drastic changes in our mode of life.

An illuminating critique of the electronic church and modern popular religion is given in Richard Quebedeaux, *By What Authority* (San Francisco: Harper & Row, 1982). While much of what the author says rings true, he can be faulted for being at times too negative, for not giving adequate recognition to the evangelistic concern of the electronic church movement and the genuinely Christian motivations of many of its leaders. He is nonetheless accurate in perceiving the impact of New Thought on a significant part of this movement.

3. For a judicious assessment of the new religious right by an evangelically oriented scholar, see Gabriel Fackre, *The Religious Right and Christian Faith* (Grand Rapids, Mich.: Eerdmans, 1982).

4. One of the most devastating exposés of pornography was published in *The Humanist,* an antireligious journal. See Sarah J. McCarthy,

"Pornography, Rape, and the Cult of Macho," in *The Humanist,* Vol. 40, No. 5 (October 1980), pp. 11–20. Similarly, one of the most telling indictments of abortion is to be found in the leftist *Progressive,* which is humanist in its value orientation but not necessarily antireligious. See Mary Meehan, "Abortion: The Left Has Betrayed the Sanctity of Life," in *The Progressive,* Vol. 44, No. 9 (September 1980), pp. 32–34. This does not alter the fact that secular humanism on the whole is militantly supportive of the right to abortion.

5. For a penetrating critique of secular humanism in American society, see John X. Evans, "Definition as Dr. Jekyll and Mr. Hyde," in *Center Journal,* Vol. 1, No. 2 (Spring 1982), pp. 53–83. The author states the case for a Christian humanism against secularist inhumanism.

6. Hans Küng argues with some cogency that the principal threat today is nihilism, the dissolution of all values and norms. See his *Does God Exist?,* trans. Edward Quinn (Garden City, N.Y.: Doubleday, 1980), pp. 341–477.

7. Pascal was associated with the Jansenist movement within the Roman Catholic Church. Jansenism sought to recover the Augustinian emphases on the sovereignty of grace and unconditional election, but it was condemned by Pope Urban VIII in 1642 and again by Pope Clement XI in 1713.

8. G. W. Bromiley, professor emeritus of church history and historical theology at Fuller Theological Seminary, tries to establish that Thomas Aquinas is really a theologian of grace, not of works, and of revelation, not of revelation *and* reason. While some of his interpretations are debatable, it nonetheless shows how one evangelical theologian in our day is able to appreciate the contribution of one of the foremost thinkers in Roman Catholicism. See G. W. Bromiley, *Historical Theology: An Introduction* (Grand Rapids, Mich.: Eerdmans, 1978), pp. 208–209.

9. An evangelical note can be detected in the spirituality of the nineteenth century French Carmelite nun Thérèse of Lisieux, who upheld the "little way" over the heroic way and who spoke of a lift or elevator to heaven, the lift of free grace, rather than the mystical ladder to heaven. See Thérèse of Lisieux, *Story of a Soul: the Autobiography of St. Thérèse of Lisieux,* trans. John Clarke (Washington, D.C.: Institute of Carmelite Studies, 1975); and Ida Friederike Görres, *The Hidden Face,* trans. Richard and Clara Winston (New York: Pantheon Books, 1959).

10. Peter M. Schmiechen, "The Challenge of Conservative Theology," in *The Christian Century,* Vol. 97, No. 13 (April 9, 1980), pp. 402–406. For my reply to Schmiechen, see Donald G. Bloesch, "To Rec-

oncile the Biblically Oriented," in *The Christian Century*, Vol. 97, No. 24 (July 16–23, 1980), pp. 733–735.

11. I would argue that these motifs are integral to the evangel or gospel itself. Even if they are not explicitly affirmed, they are definitely implied. A theologian or church that questions these motifs is surely on the way to heterodoxy if not outright heresy. Yet it would be wrong to condemn any person or group as apostate so long as the confession was made that Jesus is Lord and Savior.

12. Pelagius' position is intellectually viable but not theologically legitimate, since a Christian can hold to it only by ignoring or misinterpreting certain biblical passages that bear on the matter of human bondage and freedom.

13. Albert Schweitzer is reported to have said to Karl Barth at a historic meeting between the two in Münster, Germany: "You and I started from the same problem, the disintegration of modern thought; but whereas you went back to the Reformation, I went back to the Enlightenment." George Seaver, *Christian Revolutionary* (New York: Harper & Bros., 1944), pp. 42–43.

14. Dietrich Bonhoeffer, *Sanctorum Communio*, trans. R. Gregor Smith (London: Collins, 1963), p. 187.

15. Dietrich Bonhoeffer, *No Rusty Swords*, trans. Edwin H. Robertson and John Bowden (New York: Harper & Row, 1965), p. 172.

16. See Kenneth S. Kantzer, "The Future of the Church and Evangelicalism," in Donald E. Hoke, ed., *Evangelicals Face the Future* (South Pasadena, Calif.: William Carey Library, 1978), [pp. 127–146], pp. 127–129. Kantzer points out that the word "Evangelical" was in use by the adherents of the Reformation before "Protestant," which did not enter the vocabulary of western European languages until after 1529.

17. The term *evangelisch* now applies in German-speaking Europe to the state-supported Lutheran, Reformed and United churches and has a sociological more than a theological meaning. The term *pietistisch* (pietist) generally is the German equivalent of the Anglo-American *evangelical*. But in recent years *evangelikal* has come into use in German-speaking lands to indicate the resurgence of a conservative orthodoxy that is united with Pietism.

18. For a graphic account of the Evangelical revival in England, Scotland and Wales in the eighteenth century, see A. Skevington Wood, *The Inextinguishable Blaze* (Grand Rapids, Mich.: Eerdmans, 1960).

19. The reference here is to evangelicalism in its ideal form, in what it seeks to be, in what it is at its best. Most of the evangelical leadership

today, particularly the academic leadership, would understand evangelicalism in the way it is here delineated.

20. The gulf between vital evangelical Christianity and formalistic orthodoxy or ecclesiasticism is evident in this confession of George Whitefield: "God showed me that I must be born again, or be damned! I learned that a man may go to church, say his prayers, receive the sacrament, and yet not be a Christian. How did my heart rise and shudder. . . . With what joy . . . was my soul filled, when the weight of sin went off, and an abiding sense of the pardoning love of God . . . broke in upon my disconsolate soul!" Arnold Dallimore, *George Whitefield,* Vol. I (London: Banner of Truth, 1970), pp. 73, 77.

21. In other words, it is not only *what* we believe but *how* we believe that is important for evangelicals. It is not simply the *truth* of faith but the *conviction* of faith that is decisive in this perspective.

22. Jerry Falwell and his associates candidly admit: "It is possible to attend a fundamentalist church and hear a great deal of preaching about and against all sorts of things and almost never hear the Gospel." *The Fundamentalist Phenomenon,* ed. Jerry Falwell with Ed Dobson and Ed Hindson (Garden City, N.Y.: Doubleday, 1981), p. 181.

23. This is not to deny the place for personal testimonies in the context of a biblical sermon, but the testimony of our experience must always point beyond itself to God's great act of deliverance in Jesus Christ. Paul reminds us that we are to "preach not ourselves, but Christ Jesus the Lord" (II Cor. 4:5 KJV; cf. I Thes. 2:4–6).

24. Neo-orthodox theologians have often been fond of saying that liberalism and fundamentalism are two sides of the same coin—trust in reason over revelation. While there is some truth in this allegation, it must nonetheless be recognized that most people who follow fundamentalist teachings are still basically evangelical, whereas most liberals have jettisoned apostolic doctrine altogether.

NOTES TO CHAPTER III—The New Conservatism

1. Evangelicalism has a greater range and depth than many of its adherents have been willing to acknowledge. An evangelical contingent is even present in the Unitarian-Universalist Association, the Seventh-Day Adventist Church and the United Pentecostal Church. My two-volume work *Essentials of Evangelical Theology* (San Francisco: Harper & Row, 1982, 3rd printing) has been used as a text at the United Pentecostal Seminary in Jackson, Mississippi, though the professor responsible, Dan Lewis, has since left because of his growing reservations with the doctrinal stance of that denomination. An evangelical surge has also been

evident in the Coptic Church of Egypt. See Edward E. Plowman, "Egypt: A Crisis in the Coptic Church," in *Christianity Today*, Vol. 22, No. 19 (July 21, 1978), p. 50. Evangelical stirrings can even be detected among the Jehovah's Witnesses. See "Witness Under Prosecution," in *Time* (February 22, 1982), p. 66; and "The Watchtower Cracks Again," in *Christianity Today*, Vol. 26, No. 4 (February 19, 1982), pp. 27, 32.

2. See *The Fundamentals: A Testimony to the Truth*, ed. by R. A. Torrey and others (reprint ed., Grand Rapids, Mich.: Baker Book House, 1980).

3. This point is made by Ramsey Michaels in Roger Nicole and J. Ramsey Michaels, eds., *Inerrancy and Common Sense* (Grand Rapids, Mich.: Baker Book House, 1980), pp. 49–70; and James Barr, *The Scope and Authority of the Bible* (Philadelphia: Westminster Press, 1980), pp. 81, 82.

4. Whereas premillennialism teaches that Jesus' second coming inaugurates the thousand-year period of peace on earth referred to in Revelation 20, amillennialism sees this as symbolic of the age of the church (between the first and second coming), and postmillennialism regards it as a period within world history before the second advent. On the postmillennialism of the Puritans see Iain Murray, *The Puritan Hope* (London: Banner of Truth, 1971). That a premillennial strain was also apparent among the Puritans is documented by Richard Lovelace in his *The American Pietism of Cotton Mather* (Grand Rapids, Mich.: Eerdmans, 1979), pp. 64–72.

5. John Opie, Jr., "The Modernity of Fundamentalism," in *The Christian Century*, Vol. 82, No. 19 (May 12, 1965), pp. 608–611.

6. Harold Lindsell seeks to show the affinity between Christianity and capitalism in his *Free Enterprise: Judeo-Christian Defense* (Wheaton, Ill.: Tyndale House, 1982). Robert Webber, on the other hand, contends that true Christianity will always be in conflict with free-enterprise capitalism. See his *The Moral Majority: Right or Wrong?* (Westchester, Ill.: Cornerstone Books, 1981).

7. Ernest R. Sandeen, *The Origins of Fundamentalism* (Philadelphia: Fortress Press, 1968).

8. George Marsden, *Fundamentalism and American Culture* (New York: Oxford University Press, 1980).

9. Among these are James Boice, pastor of the Tenth Presbyterian Church, Philadelphia (which has withdrawn from the United Presbyterian Church in the U.S.A.) and R. C. Sproul of the Ligonier Valley Study Center near Pittsburgh.

10. In his *Neo-Evangelicalism* (Des Plaines, Ill.: Regular Baptist Press, 1965), Robert P. Lightner distinguishes neoevangelicalism from true evangelicalism or fundamentalism.

11. See Jerry Falwell, *Listen, America!* (Garden City, N.Y.: Doubleday, 1980); and *The Fundamentalist Phenomenon*, ed. Jerry Falwell with Ed Dobson and Ed Hindson (New York: Doubleday, 1981).

12. See their article "Inspiration," in *The Presbyterian Review*, Vol. 2, No. 6 (April 1881), pp. 225–260. For the reprint see Archibald A. Hodge and Benjamin B. Warfield, *Inspiration*, Introduction by Roger R. Nicole (Grand Rapids, Mich.: Baker Book House, 1979).

13. Geisler identifies himself as orthodox as opposed to both neoevangelical and fundamentalist in his *Decide for Yourself* (Grand Rapids, Mich.: Zondervan, 1982). Yet his acceptance of dispensationalism marks him as closer to historical fundamentalism.

14. On the resurgence of fundamentalism, see George W. Dollar, *A History of Fundamentalism in America* (Greenville, S.C.: Bob Jones University Press, 1973).

15. For a penetrating introduction to the debate on evolution today, see Huston Smith, "Evolution and Evolutionism," *The Christian Century*, Vol. 99, No. 23 (July 7, 1982), pp. 755–757. A perceptive critique of evolutionary dogma is given by Magnus Verbrugge in his "Animism in Science," *The Journal of Christian Reconstruction*, Vol. VIII, No. 2 (Winter 1982), pp. 79–107. Also see L. Duane Thurman, *How to Think About Evolution and Other Bible-Science Controversies* (Downers Grove, Ill.: InterVarsity Press, 1978). For a hard-hitting attack on the theory of evolution from a non-Christian source, see Fred Hoyle and C. Wickramasinghe, *Evolution from Space* (London: Dent, 1981).

16. Jack Rogers and Donald McKim try to show that inerrancy in its modern sense has little solid support in the history of theology. See their *The Authority and Interpretation of the Bible* (San Francisco: Harper & Row, 1981). John Woodbridge of Trinity Seminary seeks to refute their position in his *Biblical Authority: A Critique of the Rogers/McKim Proposal* (Grand Rapids, Mich.: Zondervan, 1982). In polemical debates of this kind, the temptation is to disregard evidence contrary to one's own position. Part of the problem lies in whether there is a common understanding of truth and error that has remained unchanged through the centuries.

17. Karl Heim, whose affinities are with German Pietism, is widely respected among Anglo-Saxon evangelicals for his work in defense of a supernatural world-view. See his *The Transformation of the Scientific*

World View, trans. W. A. Whitehouse (London: SCM Press, 1953); and *Christian Faith and Natural Science,* trans. N. Horton Smith (New York: Harper & Row, 1953).

18. Even Benjamin Warfield, much to the chagrin of many of his orthodox colleagues, was willing to affirm theistic evolution. Bernard Ramm states the case for a progressive creationism in his *The Christian View of Science and Scripture* (Grand Rapids, Mich.: Eerdmans, 1954).

19. Carl Henry, *The Uneasy Conscience of Modern Fundamentalism* (Grand Rapids, Mich.: Eerdmans, 1947).

20. Even some right-wing and confessionalist evangelicals have aligned themselves with postmillennialism. The Christian Reconstructionist movement headed by Rousas J. Rushdoony is emphatically postmillennial and looks forward to the building of a holy community before the second coming of Christ. Its magazine is *The Journal of Christian Reconstruction,* and its seminary is the Geneva Divinity School in Tyler, Texas.

21. George Eldon Ladd offers an evangelical alternative to the historical-critical method in his *The New Testament and Criticism* (Grand Rapids, Mich.: Eerdmans, 1967). Also see Gerhard Maier, *The End of the Historical-Critical Method* (St. Louis: Concordia Publishing House, 1977); and his "Concrete Alternatives to the Historical-Critical Method," in *Evangelical Review of Theology,* Vol. 6, No. 1 (April 1982), pp. 23–36.

22. Bernard Ramm, *Special Revelation and the Word of God* (Grand Rapids, Mich.: Eerdmans, 1961), pp. 154–160.

23. Carl Henry, *God, Revelation and Authority,* 6 vols. (Waco, Tex.: Word Books, 1976–83).

24. Paul K. Jewett, *The Ordination of Women* (Grand Rapids, Mich.: Eerdmans, 1980), pp. 44–47, 122, 127.

25. See J. D. Douglas, ed., *Let the Earth Hear His Voice* (Minneapolis: World Wide Publications, 1975), p. 3.

26. Horace Hummel, *The Word Becoming Flesh* (St. Louis: Concordia Publishing House, 1979).

27. Donald Gelpi contends that "it is dangerous and misleading to demand that the divine response be the gift of tongues, just as it is dangerous and misleading to call the gift of tongues, which is the least of the gifts, the 'fullness of the Spirit.'" In his *Pentecostalism: A Theological Viewpoint* (New York: Paulist Press, 1971), p. 185.

28. Don Basham explores conflicting views on demons in his *Deliver Us From Evil* (Washington Depot, Conn.: Chosen Books, 1972), pp.

219–220. Basham is open to the view of Derek Prince that demons are disembodied spirits of a pre-Adamic race of beings corrupted by Satan and his angels.

29. Michael Harper, *None Can Guess* (Plainfield, N.J.: Logos International, 1971), pp. 149, 153.

30. See James S. Tinney, "The Prosperity Doctrine: An Accretion to Black Pentecostalism," in *Evangelical Review of Theology,* Vol. 4, No. 1 (April 1980), pp. 84–92.

31. The Assemblies of God and the Church of God in Christ, which ministers to the black community, are the two largest Pentecostal denominations in this country. The former had a growth rate of 70 percent from 1970 to 1980. See Dean Merrill, "The Fastest-growing American Denomination," *Christianity Today,* Vol. 27, No. 1 (January 7, 1983), pp. 28–34.

32. Key books by J. Rodman Williams include *The Era of the Spirit* (Plainfield, N.J.: Logos International, 1971); *Pentecostal Reality* (Logos International, 1972); and *The Gift of the Holy Spirit Today* (Logos International, 1980).

33. In his *Reflected Glory* (Grand Rapids, Mich.: Eerdmans, 1976), Thomas Smail, active in the charismatic movement in the Church of Scotland, makes a good case that the church of Jesus Christ is charismatic as well as evangelical and catholic. See also his attempt to restore a Trinitarian balance to current Pentecostalism in his *The Forgotten Father* (Grand Rapids, Mich.: Eerdmans, 1981).

34. Books by Catholic charismatics in which evangelical themes are in evidence include Simon Tugwell, *Did You Receive the Spirit?* (New York: Paulist Press, 1972); and Ralph Martin, *A Crisis of Truth* (Ann Arbor, Mich.: Servant Books, 1982).

35. See *Theology Today,* Vol. XXX, No. 4 (January 1974), p. 333. Both Tillich and Bultmann belong in the category of neoliberalism. Reinhold Niebuhr and his brother H. Richard Niebuhr can be placed on the extreme left of neo-orthodoxy.

36. Other names by which it was known even in its early stages were neo-Reformation theology, neo-Calvinism and neo-orthodoxy.

37. Helmut Thielicke in Germany also belongs in the tradition of progressive or neo-Lutheranism. Thielicke, however, is more open to the contribution of Reformed theology than the Lundensian school and is even willing to give a prominent place to the third use of the law, the law as a guide for the Christian life. See Helmut Thielicke, *Theological Ethics,* Vol. I, ed. William H. Lazareth (Philadelphia: Fortress Press, 1966), pp. 123–139.

38. Paul Lehmann maintains that Niebuhr makes contemporary sense of the basic insights of classical orthodoxy. Paul Lehmann, "The Christology of Reinhold Niebuhr," in Charles W. Kegley and Robert W. Bretall, eds., *Reinhold Niebuhr: His Religious, Social, and Political Thought* (New York: Macmillan, 1956), pp. 252–280. Edward J. Carnell, on the other hand, sees Niebuhr at variance with historical orthodoxy at many points. See his *The Theology of Reinhold Niebuhr* (Grand Rapids, Mich.: Eerdmans, 1951).

39. C. C. Ryrie, *Neo-orthodoxy: An Evangelical Evaluation of Barthianism* (Chicago: Moody Press, 1956), pp. 14, 15.

40. Bernard Ramm, *The Evangelical Heritage* (Waco, Tex.: Word Books, 1973), pp. 103, 104, 111.

41. See Bruce Demarest, *General Revelation* (Grand Rapids, Mich.: Zondervan, 1982).

42. Neo-orthodox theologians have at times described the Bible as the medium of the Word. Or they say that the Bible contains the Word of God, or that it becomes the Word by the action of the Spirit. The most common designation, especially among Barthians, is that the Bible is a witness to the Word.

43. Joseph Haroutunian, *God With Us: A Theology of Transpersonal Life* (Philadelphia: Westminster Press, 1965).

44. Neo-orthodox theologians can be criticized for not doing justice to another dimension of sin—self-loathing. For significant works on the subject of sin by neo-orthodox scholars see Emil Brunner, *Man in Revolt*, trans. Olive Wyon (New York: Scribner, 1939); Reinhold Niebuhr, *Moral Man and Immoral Society* (New York: Scribner, 1932); Reinhold Niebuhr, *The Nature and Destiny of Man*, Vol. 1 (New York: Scribner, 1951); Joseph Haroutunian, *Lust for Power* (New York: Scribner, 1949); and E. La B. Cherbonnier, *Hardness of Heart* (Garden City, N.Y.: Doubleday, 1955). This last work sees pride and self-contempt as two sides of the same coin—hardness of heart.

45. Theologians who presently teach at Dubuque include Donald Bloesch, Donald McKim and Arthur Cochrane. All are active members of the Karl Barth Society of North America.

46. Whereas Barth's first attempt at systematizing theology was entitled *Christian Dogmatics* and his second *Church Dogmatics*, his final work was significantly called *Evangelical Theology*. See Karl Barth, *Evangelical Theology: An Introduction*, trans. Grover Foley (Garden City, N.Y.: Doubleday Anchor Books, 1964).

47. See Gregory G. Bolich, *Karl Barth & Evangelicalism* (Downers

Grove, Ill.: InterVarsity Press, 1980); and Donald G. Bloesch, *Jesus Is Victor!* (Nashville: Abingdon Press, 1976).

48. Barth's theology was the main force behind the Confessing Church movement in Germany, but this renewal was short-lived.

49. Only those restorationists who ignore history and simply wish to return to the ideal church of the past, i.e., the New Testament church, fall under my stricture. I believe in a restoration of New Testament doctrine but not of all practices in the New Testament church.

50. See Jerry Falwell, ed., *The Fundamentalist Phenomenon*, pp. 28 ff.

51. See Robert Webber and Donald Bloesch, eds., *The Orthodox Evangelicals* (Nashville: Nelson, 1978).

52. Jaroslav Pelikan, *The Riddle of Roman Catholicism* (Nashville: Abingdon Press, 1959), pp. 45–57.

53. The catholic evangelicalism that I espouse concurs with the Puritans and the Reformed tradition generally that every Communion must be preceded by rigorous self-examination and that therefore it is not appropriate for Communion to be offered every Lord's Day, though this is the ideal. In contrast to the Puritans, however, catholic evangelicalism sees the usefulness of the church year in guiding the pastor in the selection of the text, but does not regard this as a law that must be rigidly obeyed.

54. Both Richard Sibbes, the Puritan, and Philip Spener, the Pietist, remained in their own churches to bring renewal from within. Their approach is to be contrasted with that of the radical Pietists and Separatists, who urged withdrawal from the established churches. John Wesley also sought to work for reform within his own Church of England, but the Methodist movement could not be contained within the parent body.

55. Schaff, who was associated with the Mercersburg movement, still maintained his earlier connections with the Evangelical Alliance. Unlike his colleague John Nevin, he had only kind words for John Wesley, regarding him as a preacher in the apostolic tradition. See Philip Schaff, *History of the Christian Church*, Vol. VIII (Grand Rapids, Mich.: Eerdmans, 1958), p. 815.

56. Others in the past who approached this ideal of catholic evangelicalism include John Nevin and Wilhelm Loehe. Both Nevin and Schaff were identified with the Mercersburg movement within the German Reformed Church in this country, which sought a restoration of emphases and practices associated with the pre-Reformation Catholic tradition. The Mercersburg movement is best understood as a reaction against

the rampant individualism and subjectivism in American Protestantism. It has been criticized for its neglect of the area of preaching in favor of a more sacramental orientation. See Howard G. Hageman, *Pulpit and Table* (Richmond, Va.: John Knox Press, 1962), p. 97. The newly formed Mercersburg Society is seeking to keep this tradition alive in the United Church of Christ.

57. Max Thurian is the theologian of the Taizé Community, a Protestant monastery in Burgundy, France.

58. A. W. Tozer, famed preacher and spiritual writer in the Christian and Missionary Alliance, sought to draw from the wellsprings of the Catholic mystics, whom he credits with leading him to the gospel.

59. Klara (Mother Basilea) Schlink, sister of the noted Lutheran theologian Edmund Schlink, is cofounder of the Evangelical Sisterhood of Mary in Darmstadt, Germany, an evangelical convent, which brings together Reformation theology and the fervor and concerns of evangelical revivalism, including Pentecostalism. For a report on this as well as other current religious communities, see Donald G. Bloesch, *Wellsprings of Renewal* (Grand Rapids, Mich.: Eerdmans, 1974).

60. Max Lackmann, German Lutheran pastor, was the former head of the League of Evangelical-Catholic Reunion. For many years he maintained a close association with The Gathering (*Die Sammlung*). See Max Lackmann, *The Augsburg Confession and Catholic Unity,* ed. and trans. W. R. Bouman (New York: Herder & Herder, 1963).

61. See Richard Lovelace, *Dynamics of Spiritual Life: An Evangelical Theology of Renewal* (Downers Grove, Ill.: InterVarsity Press, 1979).

62. See Robert E. Webber, *Common Roots: A Call to Evangelical Maturity* (Grand Rapids, Mich.: Zondervan, 1978).

63. See Bela Vassady, *Christ's Church: Evangelical, Catholic and Reformed* (Grand Rapids, Mich.: Eerdmans, 1965).

64. Peter Gillquist is a bishop in the Evangelical Orthodox Church and an editor for Thomas Nelson. Several of the leaders in this movement came out of Campus Crusade for Christ.

65. See Ralph Martin, *A Crisis of Truth* (Ann Arbor, Mich.: Servant Books, 1982).

66. This is the magazine of the Assembly of Covenant Churches, which was originally a part of the New Covenant Apostolic Order, the parent body of the Evangelical Orthodox Church. Unlike the last, the Assembly of Covenant Churches seeks consciously to stand in the tradition of the mainstream Protestant Reformation. Among its spiritual leaders is Ray Nethery, an active participant in the Chicago Call conference in May, 1977.

67. For example, it can be shown that I stand partly in both neo-evangelicalism and neo-orthodoxy, even though I belong mostly to catholic evangelicalism.

68. In my opinion, Calvin and Luther are closest to what I have described as a catholic evangelicalism. They sought the reform of the Catholic Church, not the creation of a sect divorced from catholic tradition. Throughout their ministries, moreover, they were concerned for the unity of the whole church. This was more true of Calvin and Melanchthon than of Luther. On the efforts of the mainline Reformers on behalf of church unity see John T. McNeill, *Unitive Protestantism* (Richmond, Va.: John Knox Press, 1964).

69. In his *After Fundamentalism: The Future of Evangelical Theology* (San Francisco: Harper & Row, 1983), Bernard Ramm forcefully argues that Barth's theology can serve as a model for a renewed evangelicalism.

70. See p. 34.

71. See Ronald J. Sider and Richard K. Taylor, *Nuclear Holocaust and Christian Hope* (Downers Grove, Ill.: InterVarsity Press, 1982). Sider is presently working on a new book with the tentative title *What Does It Mean to Be Pro-Life?*

72. J. Gresham Machen, *Christianity and Liberalism* (Grand Rapids, Mich.: Eerdmans, 1923). In my opinion, there are two kinds of Christianity: orthodoxy and heterodoxy. The latter, which contains Christian elements, is moving in the direction of another religion, but it still may be regarded as a variation of Christianity, though a deviant one. When heterodoxy becomes heresy, however, when an unbalanced emphasis becomes a formal repudiation, then we have moved out of the circle of Christian faith. For a further discussion on this subject, see pp. 124–126.

Notes to Chapter IV—Evangelical Disunity

1. Carl Henry, *God, Revelation and Authority* IV (Waco, Tex.: Word Books, 1979), p. 590.

2. The traditional Reformed position on baptism is stated by G. W. Bromiley in his *Children of Promise: The Case for Baptizing Infants* (Grand Rapids, Mich.: Eerdmans, 1979). Paul Jewett, who also belongs to the Reformed family, makes a case for believer baptism in his *Infant Baptism and the Covenant of Grace* (Grand Rapids, Mich.: Eerdmans, 1978). For a book that tries to overcome the gulf between paedobaptists and baptists see Donald Bridge and David Phypers, *The Water That Divides* (Downers Grove, Ill.: InterVarsity Press, 1979, 2nd printing).

3. See Karl Barth, *Church Dogmatics* IV, 4, trans. G. W. Bromiley (Edinburgh: T. & T. Clark, 1969).

4. See note 20, p. 160. It should be noted that Jonathan Blanchard, the first president of Wheaton College, was, for the most part, a postmillennialist.

5. See Robert G. Clouse, *The Meaning of the Millennium: Four Views* (Downers Grove, Ill.: InterVarsity Press, 1977).

6. I am here using "pietism" in its distinctly contemporary meaning, since historical Pietism was noted for its social involvement.

7. This split between personal piety and social concern was not present in earlier evangelicalism. See Donald Dayton, *Discovering An Evangelical Heritage* (New York: Harper & Row, 1976); and David Moberg, *The Great Reversal*, rev. ed. (Philadelphia: J. B. Lippincott, 1977).

8. R. C. Sproul distinguishes between the confessional, presuppositional and classical methods; the last seeks to establish the infallibility of Scripture "on the inductive basis of historical-empirical evidence." In John Warwick Montgomery, ed., *God's Inerrant Word* (Minneapolis: Bethany Fellowship, 1974), [pp. 242–261], p. 250.

9. Augustine can be used to support both groups. Norman Geisler, Gordon Clark and Ronald Nash all appeal to Augustine, though a case can be made that Augustine was much more skeptical of the role of reason in coming to a right understanding of God. See Robert E. Cushman, "Faith and Reason," in Roy W. Battenhouse, ed., *A Companion to the Study of St. Augustine* (reprint ed. Grand Rapids, Mich.: Baker Book House, 1979), pp. 287–314.

10. For a delineation of the increasing divergence of Lutheran orthodoxy from Luther, see Jaroslav Pelikan, *From Luther to Kierkegaard* (St. Louis: Concordia Publishing House, 1950).

11. Kuyper declared that the conviction of faith "is *not* the outcome of observation or demonstration." Abraham Kuyper, *Principles of Sacred Theology* (Grand Rapids, Mich.: Eerdmans, 1954), p. 131. G. C. Berkouwer is representative of this tradition today.

12. Francis Schaeffer, *Escape From Reason* (London: Inter-Varsity Fellowship, 1968).

13. See Brian Gerrish, *Tradition and the Modern World* (Chicago: University of Chicago Press, 1978), pp. 61, 62.

14. It is possible to hold to *ex opere operato* without falling into magic, but only when the rite is united with faith and the Word.

15. See James E. Tull, *The Atoning Gospel* (Macon, Ga.: Mercer University Press, 1982), pp. 190–192.

16. It is a matter of debate whether Charles Hodge can be included among the total inerrancy advocates. He likened what appear to be factual inconsistencies in the text to a speck of sandstone in the Parthenon which was nonetheless built of marble. See Charles Hodge, *Systematic Theology,* Vol. I (New York: Scribner, 1898), p. 170. Hodge, moreover, distinguished between what the writers thought and believed as children of their times and what they genuinely taught under the inspiration of the Spirit. Yet the polemics of his day led him to assert that Scripture can be perfectly harmonized not only with itself but also with the external evidence of science. For a perspicacious critique of Charles Hodge as a "transitional theologian" who prepared the way for the rigid inerrantist position of A. A. Hodge and Benjamin Warfield, see Jack B. Rogers and Donald K. McKim, *The Authority and Interpretation of the Bible* (San Francisco: Harper & Row, 1979).

17. Formerly known as *Present Truth,* this magazine was begun by ex-Seventh-Day Adventists who on rediscovering the Reformation doctrines of *sola gratia* and *sola fide* felt obliged to withdraw from their communion. On its quarrel with the Holiness movement, see *Present Truth,* Vol. 2, No. 1 (February 1973).

18. Paxton has since left Verdict ministries and now works with Lee S. Ferro, Jr., a Florida Presbyterian pastor, in TAP (Theological Assistance Program), but his theological thrust remains the same.

19. See Donald G. Bloesch, *Is the Bible Sexist?: Beyond Feminism and Patriarchalism* (Westchester, Ill.: Crossway Books, 1982).

20. See Letha Scanzoni and Virginia Mollenkott, *Is the Homosexual My Neighbor?* (San Francisco: Harper & Row, 1980).

21. See the statement against weapons of mass extermination drawn up by Arthur C. Cochrane, "Mass Extermination," in *The Reformed Journal,* Vol. 30, Issue 6 (June 1980), pp. 4, 5.

22. For the divergence of attitudes toward war in the evangelical community, see Robert G. Clouse, ed., *War: Four Christian Views* (Downers Grove, Ill.: InterVarsity Press, 1981).

23. Vernon C. Grounds, "An Evangelical's Concern about Evangelical Unconcern," in *MPL Journal,* Vol. III, No. 3 (1982), p. 11. Compare this forthright statement of James R. Cook, spokesman for the Church of God (Anderson, Indiana): "It seems inconsistent for Christians to decry the Nazis' murder of six million Jews and to ignore the implications of our own military build-up. Currently, the United States has enough nuclear warheads deployed or stock-piled to incinerate the world's population eighteen times over. And some American military leaders have spoken publicly about reserving the option for a first strike!" Barry L.

Callen, ed., *The First Century Church of God Reformation Movement,* Vol. 2 (Anderson, Ind.: Warner Press, 1979), p. 794.

We should also, of course, deplore the schizophrenic mind-set of the left which raises an outcry against nuclear weapons development but which is disturbingly silent on the grave evil of abortion, which involves the yearly mass slaughter of millions of unborn children throughout the world.

24. See Billy Graham, "Graham's Mission to Moscow," in *Christianity Today,* Vol. 26, No. 11 (June 18, 1982), pp. 20–23.

25. This is not to dispute the right of church bodies to demand from their adherents a high standard of life, but we must not confuse the moral standards that form part of the revealed law of God with the mores and folkways that have their basis in the dynamics of human culture rather than the mystery of divine revelation.

26. See *Christianity Today,* Vol. 23, No. 5 (December 1, 1978), p. 52.

27. Pierce Beaver also reports that he "has often heard from Asians and Africans the assertion that the scandal of disunity, unbrotherliness, and internecine strife robs the spoken word of power. People of new nations seeking unity and stability fear what they believe to be the inherent divisiveness of Christianity." R. Pierce Beaver, *The Missionary Between the Times* (Garden City, N.Y.: Doubleday, 1968), pp. 11, 12.

28. Paul Holmer, *The Grammar of Faith* (San Francisco: Harper & Row, 1978), p. 2.

29. See Karl Mannheim, *Ideology and Utopia,* trans. Louis Wirth and Edward Schils (New York: Harcourt, Brace & World, 1953). In contrast to Mannheim, I see ideology as encompassing not only the conservative defense of the established order but also its revolutionary opposition.

30. Langdon Gilkey, *Message and Existence* (New York: Seabury Press, 1981), p. 30.

31. Hans Küng, *Does God Exist?,* trans. Edward Quinn (Garden City, N.Y.: Doubleday, 1980), p. 124.

32. For a discerning critique of Reinhold Niebuhr's understanding of ideology, see Dennis P. McCann, "Political Ideologies and Practical Theology: Is There A Difference?" in *Union Seminary Quarterly Review,* Vol. XXXVI, No. 4 (Summer 1981), pp. 243–257. McCann contrasts Niebuhr with the liberation theologian Juan Luis Segundo.

33. Cited by Robert T. Coote, "Carl McIntire's Troubled Trail," in *Eternity,* Vol. 20, No. 5 (May 1969), p. 36.

34. See *Christianity Today,* Vol. 15, No. 1 (October 9, 1970), p. 42.

35. *The Christian Century,* Vol. 86, No. 19 (May 7, 1969), p. 660.

36. See James Davison Hunter, "The New Class and the Young Evangelicals," in *Review of Religious Research,* Vol. 22, No. 2 (December 1980), pp. 155–169.

37. See Peter Berger, *The Sacred Canopy* (Garden City, N.Y.: Doubleday, 1967); "Ethics and the Present Class Struggle," *Worldview,* Vol. 21, No. 4 (April 1978), pp. 6–11; "The Worldview of the New Class: Secularity and its Discontents," in B. Bruce-Briggs, ed., *The New Class?* (New Brunswick, N.J.: Transaction Books, 1979), pp. 49–55; and "The Class Struggle in American Religion," *The Christian Century,* Vol. 98, No. 6 (February 25, 1981), pp. 194–199.

38. For a contemporary scholarly exposition of this ideology, see George Gilder, *Wealth and Poverty* (New York: Basic Books, 1981).

39. H. Richard Niebuhr, "Toward the Independence of the Church," in H. Richard Niebuhr, Wilhelm Pauck and Francis P. Miller, *The Church Against the World* (Chicago: Willett, Clark & Co., 1935), pp. 123–156.

40. Reinhold Niebuhr, *The Contribution of Religion to Social Work* (New York: Columbia University Press, 1932), p. 29.

41. What I call welfare liberalism parallels Peter Berger's "new class" (see note 37), though the latter includes aspects of socialism as well. Welfare liberalism also roughly corresponds to Charles Reich's Consciousness II, whereas classical liberalism would be analogous to his Consciousness I. Reich speaks, too, of Consciousness III, in which harmony with nature takes priority over the quest for mastery over nature. One part of feminist ideology would be in tune with Consciousness III. See Charles Reich, *The Greening of America* (New York: Random House, 1970).

42. Most modern ideologies, including classical liberalism, ably serve the goals of the technological society, though not all are so obviously in harmony with these goals as welfare liberalism.

43. I am including communism and Maoism within the wider ideology of socialism. For a forceful exposition of the socialist creed by an American devotee, see Michael Harrington, *The Twilight of Capitalism* (New York: Simon & Schuster, 1976).

44. David M. Beckmann, *Where Faith and Economics Meet* (Minneapolis: Augsburg Publishing House, 1981), pp. 61–80.

45. Even though holding to the ideal of androgyny, Helen Luke breaks with most feminists by contending that before union is realized the differences between the sexes must be frankly acknowledged:

"Those who assert that the only difference between men and women is biological, and that in every other way they are equal and have the same inborn potentialities, have disastrously missed the point." Helen M. Luke, *Woman Earth and Spirit: The Feminine in Symbol and Myth* (New York: Crossroad Publishing Co., 1981), p. 2. Luke is taken to task for her assertion that there are immutable psychic differences between the sexes by Rita M. Gross in her review of Luke's book in *The Christian Century*, Vol. 99, No. 8 (March 10, 1982), pp. 276–279. In my opinion, the logic of Luke's position leads to an overcoming of the male-female polarity.

Another feminist who tries to maintain the distinctions between male and female is Ann Belford Ulanov. See her *Receiving Woman: Studies in the Psychology and Theology of the Feminine* (Philadelphia: Westminster Press, 1981).

46. Rosemary Ruether, "From Machismo to Mutuality," in Edward Batchelor, Jr., ed., *Homosexuality and Ethics* (New York: Pilgrim Press, 1980), p. 31.

47. See Donald G. Bloesch, *Is the Bible Sexist?: Beyond Feminism and Patriarchalism* (Westchester, Ill.: Crossway Books, 1982).

48. See Naomi Goldenberg, *Changing of the Gods* (Boston: Beacon Press, 1979); Starhawk, *The Spiral Dance: A Rebirth of the Ancient Religion of the Great Goddess* (San Francisco: Harper & Row, 1979); Charlene Spretnak, ed., *The Politics of Women's Spirituality* (Garden City, N.Y.: Doubleday Anchor Books, 1982); Rosemary Ruether, "The Way of Wicca," *The Christian Century*, Vol. 97, No. 6 (February 20, 1980), pp. 208–209; and Virginia Mollenkott, "An Evangelical Feminist Confronts the Goddess," *The Christian Century*, Vol. 99, No. 32 (October 20, 1982), pp. 1043–1046.

49. See Stanley G. Payne, *Fascism: Comparison and Definition* (Madison: University of Wisconsin Press, 1980).

50. Where the present regime in Iran falls short of fascist ideology is in its tendency to subordinate the glory of the state to the cause of the Shiite Moslem faith. Yet it is an open question whether the Iranian state is in fact subordinate to the faith or vice versa. Probably the most accurate picture is that both fascist and theocratic religionist forces are at work in today's Iran and that it is still too early to ascertain which will come out on top.

51. See Arthur C. Cochrane, *The Church's Confession Under Hitler*, 2nd ed. (Pittsburgh: Pickwick Press, 1976).

52. Populism advocates government interference not only in the economic sphere of life (as does socialism) but also in the area of personal

behavior (as does conservatism). Populism, in contrast to fascism, is antielitist, but like fascism it seeks to unite a concern for the common good with the preservation of the national and cultural heritage.

53. See note 41.

54. This is an appropriate, not a mistaken designation. For a first-rate scholarly critique of secular humanism see James Hitchcock, *What Is Secular Humanism?* (Ann Arbor, Mich.: Servant Books, 1982). Hitchcock fails to explore the impact of secular humanism on modern warfare. Another provocative study is Robert Webber, *Secular Humanism* (Grand Rapids, Mich.: Zondervan, 1982). Webber warns against both the secular humanism of the left and the secularism behind growing militarism and nationalism.

55. See Howard A. Snyder, *The Liberating Church* (Downers Grove, Ill.: InterVarsity Press, 1982). See especially pp. 31, 113–114, 139–140, 210–211. Snyder trenchantly develops the dominant characteristics of this life- and world-view.

This underlying ideology or metaideology might also be called "technocratic liberalism" (Robert Bellah), since it realizes the Enlightenment dream of the mastery of nature by practical reason.

56. This position is already anticipated in the social thought of the Enlightenment thinker Jean-Jacques Rousseau, who believed that the will of the people is indestructible and infallible. See Lester G. Crocker, *Rousseau's Social Contract* (Cleveland: Press of Case Western Reserve University, 1968).

57. An instructive book in this connection is Bertram Gross, *Friendly Fascism: The New Face of Power in America* (New York: M. Evans & Co., 1981).

58. Peter L. Berger and Hansfried Kellner, *Sociology Reinterpreted* (Garden City, N.Y.: Doubleday Anchor Books, 1981), p. 144.

59. Cited in *The British Weekly and Christian World*, Vol. XCV, No. 4290 (May 8, 1969), p. 9.

60. The latest secularist intrusion in the public schools is values clarification, "in which children are encouraged to regard all questions of belief as 'open' matters of opinion." The result is to cause children to question the religious and moral beliefs handed down to them by their parents and church. See James Hitchcock, *What Is Secular Humanism?*, p. 108.

61. For a perceptive evangelical critique of the Moral Majority agenda to introduce teacher- or student-directed voluntary religious exercises in the classroom context, see John Warwick Montgomery, "School Prayers: A Common Danger," in *Christianity Today*, Vol. 26, No. 9 (May 7,

1982), p. 59. I see a definite place for teaching the moral values of the Judeo-Christian heritage in the public schools, and our founding fathers would have no objection to this. There can be no such thing as a value-free education.

62. See Karl Barth, *Against the Stream,* trans. E. M. Delacour and Stanley Godman (London: SCM Press, 1954).

63. H. Richard Niebuhr, *The Social Sources of Denominationalism* (New York: Henry Holt & Co., 1929).

64. See note 36.

65. This journal has not, to my knowledge, lent its support to other forms of sexual aberration such as incest and sadomasochism, which are defended by certain segments of the secular liberal community. These criticisms of both *Christianity & Crisis* and *National Catholic Reporter* should not be taken to mean that an authentic prophetic voice can never be heard from their pages. Moreover, when this voice does break through the ideological verbiage, it is one which is seldom available in magazines of a different orientation.

66. For a timely indictment of the World Council of Churches, see Robert Webber, *The Moral Majority: Right or Wrong?* (Westchester, Ill.: Cornerstone Books, 1981), pp. 57–86.

The National Council of Churches is now giving serious consideration to including the Metropolitan Community Church in its membership despite the latter's upholding of a gay life-style. Eastern Orthodox members have rightly objected that because such a life-style conflicts with biblical norms, this must be regarded as "a theological issue."

67. Cf. Paul Vitz: "It is beginning to look as though there is a world-wide fundamental conflict between Christianity and the modern state—a conflict which has little to do with whether the state espouses a leftist or rightist political philosophy." *Psychology as Religion* (Grand Rapids, Mich.: Eerdmans, 1977), p. 114.

68. For an assessment of the Hartford Appeal by eight of its participants, see Peter L. Berger and Richard John Neuhaus, eds., *Against the World For the World* (New York: Seabury Press, 1976).

69. I do not share Tillich's belief that the object of faith is the unconditional beyond all human understanding; instead, it is the incarnate Word of God, Jesus Christ, who enters into our understanding and remolds it. The absolute that I affirm became incarnate in a particular place and time in history.

70. Reformation theology holds that by the action of the Spirit the Bible can indeed transmit the Word of God. There is no absolute equation of the Word of God and the Bible, but there is an inseparable rela-

tion. The Bible is the vessel, the channel, the medium of the Word of God. The infallible criterion in Reformation theology was not the original autographs (as in later fundamentalism) but the unity of the Bible and the Spirit.

71. Dorothy Sayers, *Creed or Chaos?* (New York: Harcourt, Brace & Co., 1949), p. 25. Even though these remarks were made several decades ago, they are surprisingly relevant to the present scene.

72. Cited in G. C. Berkouwer, *A Half Century of Theology,* trans. Lewis B. Smedes (Grand Rapids, Mich.: Eerdmans, 1977), p. 12.

Notes to Chapter V—Pathways to Evangelical Oblivion

1. Karl Barth is helpful in describing the early chapters of Genesis as saga rather than either myth or exact history. Saga is the poetic elaboration of what is essentially divine intervention into history. It is not unhistorical (as is myth) but superhistorical. What it purports to speak about is not accessible to historical investigation.

2. John R. W. Stott, "Are Evangelicals Fundamentalists?" in *Christianity Today,* Vol. 22, No. 21 (September 8, 1978), pp. 44–46. Stott reveals his break with evangelical rationalism by contending that instead of embracing the Aristotelian golden mean or either one of the extremes, we should "hold fast to both extremes, so long as they are equally biblical, even if our human mind cannot reconcile or systematize them. For biblical truth is often stated paradoxically and the attempt to resolve all the 'antinomies' of Scripture is misguided because impossible." Stott is here endorsing Charles Simeon's advice. John R. W. Stott, *Christ the Controversialist* (London: Tyndale House, 1970), p. 46.

3. Restorationist evangelicals should take note of Geddes MacGregor's *The Nicene Creed Illumined by Modern Thought* (Grand Rapids, Mich.: Eerdmans, 1981). MacGregor, who tends to endorse an emanationistic monism, is still a devout defender of the Nicene Creed. Because ancient creeds can be defended by modern liberals and others who stray into heterodox and heretical modes of thinking, such documents cannot serve as the confession of faith that is needed in our time.

4. Those who hold to apostolic succession believe that the authority in the Christian church is derived from the apostles through an unbroken succession of bishops, and unless one receives the rite of laying on of hands from a bishop who stands in this succession, one is not validly ordained.

5. In his later speculation, John Nevin, Mercersburg theologian, moved toward the position of a hierarchical order that proceeds down from Christ through the bishops to the people. He appealed to Cyprian

in support of this view. This theory of hierarchy was at variance with the views that both Nevin and Schaff had previously expressed. See James Hastings Nichols, *Romanticism in American Theology* (Chicago: University of Chicago Press, 1961), pp. 275–276.

6. Note that in the encyclical *Vehementer* of Pope Pius X (1906), the church was defined as "an unequal society," ruled by pastors and teachers, in which the "multitude of the faithful" had "no other right than that of allowing itself to be led, and, as a docile flock to follow its shepherds." Wilhelm Pauck, *The Heritage of the Reformation* (Glencoe, Ill.: Free Press, 1950), p. 193.

7. See Kenneth L. Woodward, "Today's Oxford Movement," *Newsweek,* Vol. 97, No. 2 (January 12, 1981), p. 80.

8. Richard Sibbes, *The Complete Works of Richard Sibbes,* Vol. II, ed. Alexander Balloch Grosart (Edinburgh: James Nichol, 1862), p. 241.

9. Martin Luther, *Luther's Works,* Vol. 41 (Philadelphia: Fortress Press, 1966), p. 114.

10. For examples of recent ecumenical Roman Catholic writing in which the Reformation is treated appreciatively, see Harry J. McSorley, *Luther: Right or Wrong?* (Minneapolis: Augsburg Publishing House, 1969); Hans Küng, *Justification,* trans. Thomas Collins, Edmund Tolk and David Granskou (New York: Thomas Nelson, 1964); Louis Bouyer, *The Spirit and Forms of Protestantism,* trans. A. V. Littledale (Westminster, Md.: Newman Press, 1961); Stephen Pfürtner, *Luther and Aquinas on Salvation,* trans. Edward Quinn (New York: Sheed & Ward, 1964); and John Murray Todd, *Luther, a Life* (New York: Crossroad Publishing Co., 1982).

11. See Karl Barth, *Ad Limina Apostolorum,* trans. Keith R. Crim (Richmond, Va.: John Knox Press, 1967), pp. 27–28; 35–37; 39–40.

12. See George M. Marsden, "Scotland and Philadelphia: Common Sense Philosophy from Jefferson to Westminster," in *The Reformed Journal,* Vol. 29, No. 3 (March 1979), pp. 8–12. Also see the discussion on the Common Sense philosophy in Jack B. Rogers and Donald K. McKim, *The Authority and Interpretation of the Bible* (San Francisco: Harper & Row, 1979), pp. 235–248.

13. John Warwick Montgomery, *The Shape of the Past: A Christian Response to Secular Philosophies of History* (Minneapolis: Bethany Fellowship, 1976), pp. 143, 293–295.

14. See Ronald H. Nash, *The Word of God and the Mind of Man* (Grand Rapids, Mich.: Zondervan, 1982). Nash, following the evangelical rationalism of Gordon Clark and Carl Henry, asserts that our knowl-

edge of God is univocal, not merely analogical, and that the propositions in Scripture are identical with divine revelation. He criticizes my position for undercutting cognitive revelation, though he acknowledges that I affirm it. Against the evangelical rationalists, I contend that although we find the truth of revelation in Scripture, this revelation is not to be identified with the very words of Scripture, for this is to confuse the infinite and the finite.

15. In a letter to *The Christian Century*, Vol. 96, No. 6 (February 21, 1979), p. 197.

16. Paul L. Holmer, *The Grammar of Faith* (San Francisco: Harper & Row, 1978), p. 162.

17. Paul Tillich, *Systematic Theology*, Vol. I (Chicago: University of Chicago Press, 1951), p. 8.

18. See Paul Feinberg, "The Meaning of Inerrancy" in Norman L. Geisler, ed., *Inerrancy* (Grand Rapids, Mich.: Zondervan, 1979), [pp. 265–304], pp. 272–276.

19. Carl Henry, "What Must We Do To Save the Day?" in *Eternity*, Vol. 21, No. 12 (December 1970), p. 24.

20. The Christian is enjoined to break fellowship with an erring brother or sister both to maintain the purity and integrity of the church and to bring the erring one back into the fold. See I Cor. 5:1–5, 11–13; II Thess. 3:14, 15.

21. In Walter Nigg, *Great Saints*, trans. William Stirling (Hinsdale, Ill.: Henry Regnery Co., 1948), p. 216.

22. Cited in A. Skevington Wood, *The Inextinguishable Blaze* (Grand Rapids, Mich.: Eerdmans, 1960), p. 188.

23. The Presbyterian Church (U.S.A.), perhaps more than any other denomination today, impresses me as being two churches under one umbrella. The shadow of schism lies over this as well as several other mainline denominations. As the evangelical movement becomes stronger, the tensions between liberals and conservatives will multiply.

24. H. G. Haile, *Luther* (Garden City, N.Y.: Doubleday, 1980), p. 248.

25. Charismatics who are separatists have an affinity to the ancient Gnostics and Montanists, who distinguished between grades of believers. In these sects, the psychics were those who lived by carnal standards, whereas the pneumatics were those who lived in the full dispensation of the Spirit.

26. Karl Barth, *The Christian Life*, trans. Geoffrey W. Bromiley (Grand Rapids, Mich.: Eerdmans, 1981), p. 194.

27. This is by no means to suggest that all Seventh-Day Adventists have been sectarian. Brinsmead has observed that while Seventh-Day Adventism began as a heresy, it is one of the few churches today that is steadily moving toward orthodoxy.

28. Robert Brinsmead, "The Gospel versus the Sectarian Spirit," *Verdict,* Vol. 4, No. 3 (March 1981), p. 16.

29. Ibid.

30. Other church leaders and scholars in recent times who have felt called to sever their ecclesiastical connections include Martin Marty, Jaroslav Pelikan, James Boice, R. C. Sproul, Charles Keysor, and Paul and Elizabeth Achtemeier.

31. See Richard Quebedeaux, *The Worldly Evangelicals* (San Francisco: Harper & Row, 1978).

32. See Shailer Mathews, *The Faith of Modernism* (New York: Macmillan, 1924); and William R. Hutchison, *The Modernist Impulse in American Protestantism* (New York: Oxford University Press, 1982).

33. P. T. Forsyth, *The Principle of Authority,* 2nd ed. (London: Independent Press, 1952), p. 51.

34. Ibid., p. 348.

35. Ibid., p. 382.

36. Arnold Dallimore, "Whitefield and the Testimony of the Eighteenth Century," *Banner of Truth,* No. 79 (April 1970), p. 21. Also see Arnold Dallimore, *George Whitefield,* Vol. I (London: Banner of Truth Trust, 1970), p. 137.

37. Karl Barth, *Church Dogmatics* IV, 1, ed. G. W. Bromiley and T. F. Torrance, trans. G. W. Bromiley (Edinburgh: T. & T. Clark, 1956), p. 709.

38. A. W. Tozer, *Born After Midnight* (Harrisburg, Pa.: Christian Publications, 1959), p. 141.

39. Cited in David J. Fant, Jr., *A. W. Tozer: A Twentieth Century Prophet* (Harrisburg, Pa.: Christian Publications, 1964), p. 150.

40. Karl Barth, *Against the Stream,* trans. E. M. Delacour and Stanley Godman (London: SCM Press, 1954), p. 228.

41. Søren Kierkegaard, *The Last Years: Journals 1853–1855,* ed. and trans. Ronald Gregor Smith (New York: Harper & Row, 1965), pp. 136–137.

42. P. T. Forsyth, *The Justification of God* (London: Independent Press, 1948), p. 38.

43. John Calvin, *Sermons on the Epistle to the Ephesians* (Edinburgh: Banner of Truth Trust, 1975), p. 140.

44. See Paul Tillich, *The Courage to Be* (New Haven: Yale University Press, 1952).

45. Søren Kierkegaard, *Søren Kierkegaard's Journals and Papers,* Vol. I, A–E, ed. and trans. Howard V. Hong and Edna H. Hong (Bloomington, Ind.: Indiana University Press, 1967), p. 217.

46. For a trenchant critique of the religious right, with its uneven blend of a bastardized Puritanism and nationalism, see Dale Vree, "Ideology versus Theology," in Peter Williamson and Kevin Perrotta, eds., *Christianity Confronts Modernity* (Ann Arbor, Mich.: Servant Books, 1981), pp. 57–78.

Ronald Wells sees a similar fusion of chauvinistic Americanism and latter-day Calvinism in Francis Schaeffer's *A Christian Manifesto* (Westchester, Ill.: Crossway Books, 1981). See Ronald A. Wells, "Francis Schaeffer's Jeremiad," in *The Reformed Journal,* Vol. 32, No. 5 (May 1982), pp. 16–20. Both Vree and Wells fail to do justice to the genuinely biblical foundations of the Calvinist and Puritan vision of a holy community, but they have good reason to be apprehensive of the association of this ideal with the American dream. For a thoughtful retort to Wells in defense of Francis Schaeffer, see Wayne G. Boulton, "A Different Schaeffer," *The Reformed Journal,* Vol. 32, No. 8 (August 1982), pp. 3, 4. Boulton contends that Wells gives away too much in his assertion that Protestantism is "the religious form of Renaissance humanism." Boulton prefers the way Schaeffer states the problem: "*Liberal* theology is only humanism in theological terms" (p. 4). Though I can empathize with Boulton and Schaeffer in their warnings against liberalism and humanism, I cannot go along with Schaeffer's blanket condemnation of liberal theology. To contend that all liberal theology is covert humanism is a gross oversimplification.

For an in-depth study of the concept of "manifest destiny," which has been used to justify American imperial ambitions, see Albert K. Weinberg, *Manifest Destiny: A Study of Nationalist Expansionism in American History* (Baltimore: Johns Hopkins University Press, 1935). Also see Robert Jewett, *The Captain America Complex: The Dilemma of Zealous Nationalism* (Philadelphia: Westminster Press, 1973). For Jewett, the source of modern American "zealous nationalism" lies in radical millenarian Puritanism and Social Darwinism.

47. Cf.: "The ministry is not meant to be a social and philanthropic institution, to organise and run all kinds of movements and campaigns for the external reform of mankind. It is intended to be the soul of the

world, not its arms and feet; an inspirer, a teacher, a healer, not an engineer." Forsyth is here endorsing a statement in the *Missionary Record of the United Free Church of Scotland.* In P. T. Forsyth, *The Church and the Sacraments* (London: Independent Press, 1947), p. 186.

48. Søren Kierkegaard, *Søren Kierkegaard's Journals and Papers* I: 359.

49. *Karl Barth's Table Talk,* ed. John D. Godsey (Edinburgh: Oliver & Boyd, 1963), p. 19.

50. Cited in *Decision,* Vol. 11, No. 1 (January 1970), p. 13.

51. David Tracy, *Blessed Rage for Order* (New York: Seabury Press, 1978), p. 32. Tracy also speaks of the "dramatic confrontation, the mutual illuminations and corrections" between the contemporary consciousness and a reinterpreted Christianity, but it seems that confrontation and mutual correction serve the goal of a possible rapprochement.

52. Langdon Gilkey, *Catholicism Confronts Modernity* (New York: Seabury Press, 1975), p. 60.

53. Søren Kierkegaard, *The Last Years,* p. 124.

54. P. T. Forsyth, *The Principle of Authority,* p. 334. Cf.: "The classic type of Christianity is the experience of moral redemption and not merely ethical reform. Or rather it is the experience of a redeemer. Because it is not the *sense* of the experience that is the main matter, but the *source* of the experience, and its content. It is not our experience we are conscious of—that would be self-conscious piety—but it is Christ. It is not our experience we preach, but the Christ who comes in our experience." P. T. Forsyth, *Positive Preaching and the Modern Mind* (London: Independent Press, 1953, 4th impression), p. 45.

55. Karl Barth and Eduard Thurneysen, *Come Holy Spirit,* trans. George W. Richards, Elmer G. Homrighausen and Karl J. Ernst (Grand Rapids, Mich.: Eerdmans, 1978), p. 63.

56. H. Richard Niebuhr, *Christ and Culture* (New York: Harper & Row, 1951).

57. Jerry Falwell, despite his tacit alliance with the political right, shares this vision more than many of his evangelical and liberal detractors, who often seem content to abandon the world to secularism. Falwell would come closer to the Puritan and Calvinist vision if he would expand his conception of holiness to include the social righteousness of the Old Testament prophets in which the plight of the poor takes priority over both business expansion and national security.

NOTES TO CHAPTER VI—Toward the Recovery of Evangelical Faith

1. Evangelical Christianity as an empirical phenomenon in history is the preeminent vessel of the holy catholic church, but it is not to be equated with the very body of Christ itself. As an earthen vessel, it is not absolutely indispensable to the being or the advancement of the holy catholic church.

2. According to Heppe, both the older Reformed and Lutheran theology clearly distinguished between the Word of God and Holy Scripture, though this was mainly a historical rather than a dogmatic judgment. Heinrich Heppe, *Reformed Dogmatics,* trans. G. T. Thomson (London: Allen & Unwin, 1950), pp. 14, 15.

3. See Donald G. Bloesch, "The Legacy of Pietism" in his *The Evangelical Renaissance* (Grand Rapids, Mich.: Eerdmans, 1973), pp. 101–157.

4. The Reformation applied all of its energies to the task of church reform and consequently was not able to do justice to the imperative of evangelism.

5. See Heiko Oberman, *The Harvest of Medieval Theology* (Grand Rapids, Mich.: Eerdmans, 1967).

6. Brian A. Gerrish, "Historical Theology and Some Theologians," in *Criterion,* Vol. 21, No. 2 (Spring 1982), pp. 8–14.

7. Schaff also argues that the Catholic Church in the Counter-Reformation gave up catholicity in favor of particularity. See Philip Schaff, *The Principle of Protestantism,* ed. Bard Thompson and George H. Bricker (Philadelphia: United Church Press, 1964), pp. 73, 74.

8. This is also Schaff's thesis. See Philip Schaff, *Christ and Christianity* (New York: Scribner, 1885), pp. 126, 132, 133.

9. The Second Vatican Council affirmed the universal call to discipleship in its "Decree on the Apostolate of the Laity." See *The Documents of Vatican II,* ed. Walter M. Abbott and Joseph Gallagher (New York: America Press, 1966), pp. 489–525.

10. Luther and Calvin nonetheless made a place for the special ministry of the Word and sacraments, but this special ministry differs from the general ministry only in function, not in spiritual status or priestly quality.

11. Robert Schuller, who combines aspects of New Thought with evangelical tradition, not surprisingly keeps himself at a distance from the Reformation of the sixteenth century. He accuses the Reformers of leading a reactionary movement, whereas what is needed today is a rec-

onciling movement. Robert Schuller, *Self Esteem: The New Reformation* (Waco, Tex.: Word Books, 1982), pp. 39, 146, 162, 174, 175. Interestingly, Clark Pinnock sees promise in this book, believing that Schuller helps us to find a point of contact between the gospel and modern man—the cultural pursuit of self-esteem (on jacket cover). For a trenchant critique of Schuller's book, see Carl F. H. Henry's review in *Eternity,* Vol. 33, No. 10 (October 1982), pp. 42, 43.

12. David Schaff comments: "Defective as Savonarola's exegesis was, the biblical element was everywhere in control of his thought and descriptions." Savonarola saw himself as a biblical preacher and teacher: "I preach the regeneration of the Church, taking the Scriptures as my sole guide." David S. Schaff, *History of the Christian Church,* Vol. VI (Grand Rapids, Mich.: Eerdmans, 1957), p. 689.

13. This statement is cited in the Augsburg Confession in support of the position of the Reformation. See Theodore G. Tappert, ed. and trans., *The Book of Concord* (Philadelphia: Fortress Press, 1959), p. 32.

14. Thomas Aquinas, *Commentary on Saint Paul's Epistle to the Ephesians,* trans. Matthew L. Lamb (Albany, N.Y.: Magi Books, 1966), p. 96. Thomas nonetheless made a place for merit after the first grace. With the aid of justifying and sanctifying grace, the Christian is able to merit glory.

15. See Bengt R. Hoffman, *Luther and the Mystics* (Minneapolis: Augsburg Publishing House, 1976).

16. See Robert Webber and Donald Bloesch, eds., *The Orthodox Evangelicals* (Nashville: Nelson, 1978).

17. Donald G. Bloesch, *Essentials of Evangelical Theology,* Vol. II (San Francisco: Harper & Row, 1982, 2nd printing).

18. I first enunciated this distinction in *Essentials of Evangelical Theology,* Vol. II, pp. 270–275.

19. Cited in Gerhard Maier, *The End of the Historical-Critical Method,* trans. Edwin W. Leverenz and Rudolph F. Norden (St. Louis: Concordia Publishing House, 1977), p. 59. Hollaz could not break free from scholastic rationalism, but he did make a place for the dynamic element in revelation. It should be noted that Maier affirms the infallibility and verbal inspiration of Scripture but not "anthropological inerrancy" (p. 72).

20. Richard Sibbes, *The Complete Works of Richard Sibbes,* ed. Alexander Balloch Grosart (Edinburgh: James Nichol, 1862–64), VII: 197.

21. Sibbes, *The Complete Works of Richard Sibbes* IV: 383.

22. Philip Schaff, *Christ and Christianity,* p. 171.

23. Ibid., p. 135.

24. Philip Schaff, *The Principle of Protestantism,* pp. 106, 225.

25. Arthur Holmes rightly protests against "the limitation of knowledge to what fits a scientific model, whether in the narrow rationalism of a Cartesian deductive system or in the narrow empiricism of Locke and his positivistic descendants." Arthur F. Holmes, *Christian Philosophy in the Twentieth Century* (Nutley, N.J.: Craig Press, 1969), p. 71.

26. The Bible does not negate history but points beyond history to Eternity. Revelation enters into history, but it does not become bound to history. History is the vessel of Eternity but not an aspect of Eternity. To believe otherwise is to abandon supernaturalism in favor of either naturalism or idealism. History is the occasion but not the source of our knowledge of the messianic identity of Christ as attested in Matthew 16:17. The cross of Christ is not simply a noteworthy event in history but an event in which Eternity impinges upon time or in which time opens up to Eternity. It signifies the fulfillment of time (*kairos*), not simply another moment in time.

27. Barth's approach is also to be contrasted with Van Til, who asserts that we should come to the Bible with the presuppositions of classical Calvinism. For Barth we should come only with simple faith, keeping our own system open-ended and tentative. Here we see the difference between presuppositionalism and confessional theology. Arthur Holmes reveals his distance from Van Til in his *Christian Philosophy in the Twentieth Century,* p. 239.

28. This is the basic position of Calvin, and it seems to be reaffirmed by Karl Barth in his *The Christian Life,* trans. Geoffrey W. Bromiley (Grand Rapids, Mich.: Eerdmans, 1981), pp. 122 ff.

29. "When I thought of You," he said, "it was not as of something firm and solid. For my God was not yet You but the error and vain fantasy I held." *Confessions* IV, Chap. VII, No. 12. Quoted by Henri Bouillard in his "A Dialogue with Barth: The Problem of Natural Theology," in *Cross Currents,* Vol. 18 (Spring 1968), p. 215.

30. Harry Blamires, *The Secularist Heresy* (Ann Arbor, Mich.: Servant Books, 1980), p. 50.

31. In Carnell's view, "Men could know God if they would only will to know him, for the divine tribunal reveals itself in both conscience and the judicial sentiment." He refers to the judicial sentiment as "the narrow point of contact between God and man." Edward John Carnell, *Christian Commitment* (New York: Macmillan, 1957), pp. 209, 237. In his later writings, Carnell increasingly distanced himself from the per-

sonalistic idealism of the Boston school and showed a growing appreciation for existentialist and neo-orthodox theologies.

32. Norman L. Geisler, *Options in Contemporary Christian Ethics* (Grand Rapids, Mich.: Baker Book House, 1981), p. 32.

33. Donald K. McKim in his critique of Bruce A. Demarest, *General Revelation* (Grand Rapids, Mich.: Zondervan, 1982) perceptively asks: "But is this not actually incipient Semi-Pelagianism in which one prepares oneself, through reason, to receive the gift of faith?" *Reformed Review,* Vol. 36, No. 2 (Winter 1983), pp. 103–104.

34. Robert Webber and Donald Bloesch, eds., *The Orthodox Evangelicals,* p. 13.

35. Karl Barth, *Church Dogmatics* III, 4, ed. G. W. Bromiley and T. F. Torrance (Edinburgh: T. & T. Clark, 1961), pp. 78–79.

36. John Calvin, *Institutes of the Christian Religion,* Vol. I, ed. John T. McNeill, trans. Ford Lewis Battles (Philadelphia: Westminster Press, 1960), Book II, viii, 48, p. 412.

37. Philip Schaff, *Christ and Christianity,* p. 18.

38. John Calvin, *Sermons on the Epistle to the Ephesians* (Edinburgh: Banner of Truth Trust, 1973), p. 199.

39. See Emil Brunner, *The Misunderstanding of the Church,* trans. Harold Knight (Philadelphia: Westminster Press, 1953).

40. John Calvin, *Sermons on the Epistle to the Ephesians,* p. 175.

41. An admirable statement on the theological significance of the Eucharist is John Nevin's *The Mystical Presence* (Philadelphia: United Church Press, 1966).

42. Avery Dulles, *Models of the Church* (Garden City, N.Y.: Doubleday, 1974), pp. 31–42, 179 ff.

43. Philip Schaff, *Christ and Christianity,* p. 16. My one reservation is that it is not clear whether Schaff sees theological variety in the service of confessional unity.

44. Cited in Geoffrey Bromiley, *Historical Theology* (Grand Rapids, Mich.: Eerdmans, 1978), p. 263.

45. Cited in David S. Schaff, *The Life of Philip Schaff* (New York: Scribner, 1897), p. 89. Even while regarding Anglo-Catholicism as "an entirely legitimate and necessary reaction against rationalistic and sectaristic pseudo-Protestantism," Philip Schaff faults it for "its utter misapprehension of the divine significance of the Reformation, with its consequent development, that is, of the entire Protestant period of the church." *The Principle of Protestantism,* pp. 158, 160.

46. Cited in James Hastings Nichols, *Romanticism in American Theology* (Chicago: University of Chicago Press, 1961), p. 206. It should be noted that Philip Schaff opposed the idea that the unity and catholicity of the church could be achieved by a return to a past period of church history.

47. See Anders Nygren, *Agape and Eros,* trans. Philip Watson (Philadelphia: Westminster Press, 1953).

48. This kind of mysticism is present in certain strands of liberation theology where the accent is on the struggle of the proletariat to wrest power from the bourgeoisie. It is also evident in neotranscendentalism (Unity, New Thought, Christian Science, Psychiana), which emphasizes the need for developing self-esteem with its dividends of health and prosperity.

49. See Kenneth C. Russell, "Matthew Fox's Spiritual Trilogy," in *New Catholic World,* Vol. 225, No. 1348 (July-August 1982), pp. 189–192. Leading figures in the intellectual world who prepared the way for the new mood include Friedrich Nietzsche, Walt Whitman, William Blake and Carl Jung.

50. In evangelical perspective, a monastery will function as a training center for mission rather than a testing ground to prepare oneself for heaven. Its goal will be not the ascent to divinity but the apostolate to the nations.

51. P. T. Forsyth, *The Justification of God* (London: Independent Press, 1948), p. 117.

52. My position is diametrically opposed to that of Joseph Fletcher: "A fetus is a parasite, tolerable ethically only when welcome to its hostess. If a woman doesn't want a fetus to remain growing in her body, she should be free to rid herself of the unwelcome intruder." In a letter to Charles Fager in Charles Fager, "So Who's the Radical?" in *National Catholic Reporter,* Vol. 9, No. 18 (March 2, 1973), p. 12.

Much more Christian is the position of Lewis Smedes, who sees the fetus or conceptus in the early stages of pregnancy as on the way to becoming a person, though not yet a full-fledged person. Yet because human personhood is latent in all fetal life, this life must be treated with the utmost respect. Biological life and a human person are not identical, but the first is the life-support system for the second. Smedes therefore takes a strongly antiabortion stance, but he stays clear of the absolutist position that sees all abortion after conception as equivalent to infanticide (which is implied by Francis Schaeffer and C. Everett Koop). Lewis Smedes, *Mere Morality* (Grand Rapids, Mich.: Eerdmans, 1983), pp. 124ff., 263.

53. I agree with Karl Barth that human life needs to be protected, but because human life is not an absolute value, this protection cannot be absolute. Geoffrey Bromiley gives an apt summary of Barth's position on legitimate abortion: "The criteria of legitimate abortion are life for life, scrupulous calculation in responsibility before God, and action in faith." Geoffrey Bromiley, *An Introduction to the Theology of Karl Barth* (Grand Rapids, Mich.: Eerdmans, 1979), p. 168.

54. Even in Roman Catholicism, opposition to abortion is not always unequivocal. According to one Catholic scholar, "Catholic teaching allows abortion for ectopic pregnancies (through removal of part or all of the fallopian tube), uterine cancer (through removal of the uterus), and pregnancy due to rape (through dilation and curettage within a short time after rape). In none of these cases is abortion construed as murder but as a procedure for maintaining the health of a woman by severing the tie between her and a fertilized ovum, embryo or fetus." She goes on to say: "In pregnancies due to rape the dilation and curettage is accomplished before it is known whether the woman is pregnant." See Mary B. Mahowald, "Abortion: Towards Continuing the Dialogue," in *Cross Currents,* Vol. XXIX, No. 3 (Fall 1979), pp. 334, 335.

55. My medical friends tell me that there are some very rare occasions when newly born children might face a very short life in considerable pain, so I am not dealing here with a hypothetical possibility. But neither am I making this a principle that must be adhered to in every case. What I am pleading for is to have each case decided on its own merits; a blanket condemnation of all abortion precludes the remote but still real possibility that permission for an abortion may be included in God's commandment.

I also do not believe that the life of the child should in every case be sacrificed for the life of the mother. Here, too, much wrestling in prayer is necessitated in order to discover the divine commandment.

In comparing abortion with suicide, both fall under the commandment against killing. Yet the Bible gives several examples of where the act of suicide (or an act tantamount to suicide) seems to be in accordance with the will of God (cf. Judg. 16:28–30; Jon. 1:12–16; Dan. 3:16–18).

56. I here have in mind what is called passive euthanasia, in which artificial supports are withdrawn from a life deemed by medical experts as hopeless.

57. J. Van Zytveld calls for a partial disarmament in which America would divest itself of all offensive nuclear weapons. J. Van Zytveld, "Back From the Brink," *The Reformed Journal,* Vol. 32, No. 7 (July 1982), pp. 2, 3. See also Arthur Macy Cox, "Reagan Trading Deterrence Policy for a Chance to Win Nuclear War," *Des Moines Register*

(November 3, 1982), p. 12. A. Cox urges a return to the policy of nuclear deterrence as opposed to a policy of "decapitation," involving the development of first-strike weapons capable of obliterating the entire enemy state. Most nuclear pacifists would support all proposals to pare down our nuclear arsenal provided that they are seen as stepping-stones to universal nuclear disarmament.

58. Jim Wallis, *The Call to Conversion* (San Francisco: Harper & Row, 1981), p. 107.

59. See Jacques Ellul, *To Will and To Do,* trans. C. Edward Hopkin (Philadelphia: Pilgrim Press, 1969), pp. 73–110.

60. See Reinhold Niebuhr, *An Interpretation of Christian Ethics* (New York: Seabury Press, 1979), pp. 84–122; *Discerning the Signs of the Times* (New York: Scribner, 1946), pp. 145–151.

61. Flo Conway and Jim Siegelman, *Holy Terror* (Garden City, N.Y.: Doubleday, 1982).

62. Ibid., p. 347.

63. For a critical appraisal of Moral Majority informed by biblical faith, see Richard Neuhaus, "Religion and . . . : Addressing the Naked Public Square," *Worldview,* Vol. 25, No. 1 (January 1982), pp. 11–12. I have already referred to the timely critiques of Robert Webber and Gabriel Fackre. See pp. 154, 158.

64. See Elémire Zolla, *The Androgyne: Reconciliation of Male and Female* (New York: Crossroad Publishing Co., 1981). Mary Daly defends androgyny in her *Beyond God the Father* (Boston: Beacon Press, 1973), though she later abandons this position. Others who favor an androgynous interpretation include Rosemary Ruether, Helen Luke, Thomas D. Parker, and Matthew Fox. Ruether writes: "Both the woman's movement and the gay movement are moving from the psychology of complementarity to the psychology of androgyny. Although the term itself retains all too clearly its dualistic origins, what it means is that both males and females contain the total human psychic essence." Edward Batchelor, Jr., ed., *Homosexuality and Ethics* (New York: Pilgrim Press, 1980), p. 30.

65. In *The Politics of Jesus* (Grand Rapids, Mich.: Eerdmans, 1978), John Howard Yoder ably demonstrates that the biblical concept of revolutionary subordination is the law of the kingdom of God and is therefore demanded of all Christians. This principle as well as that of representative headship is deeply imbedded in biblical faith, and ideological feminists show their contempt for biblical authority by repudiating both.

66. Loving assistance does not always or necessarily entail obedience. In some cases the wife as a sister in Christ may have to thwart her hus-

band out of concern for his best interests and also out of fidelity to the divine commandment (cf. Gen. 27:1–17).

We should also note that the apostle Paul makes a place for mutual subordination in the framework of holy matrimony. The subordination of the husband to his wife takes the form of his love (see Eph. 5:21–33).

67. Some feminists (albeit a minority) also acknowledge immutable psychic differences between the sexes. See Helen M. Luke, *Woman Earth and Spirit: The Feminine in Symbol and Myth* (New York: Crossroad Publishing Co., 1981), pp. 2, 3. Rita M. Gross takes issue with Luke on this point in her review of Luke's book in *The Christian Century*, Vol. 99, No. 8 (March 10, 1982), pp. 276–279. Yet it should be remembered that Luke also emphasizes androgyny over complementarity. In her view, the woman must be able to live by and for herself before she can relate meaningfully to men.

68. For the biblical and theological basis for women's ordination see Paul K. Jewett, *The Ordination of Women* (Grand Rapids, Mich.: Eerdmans, 1980); and Donald G. Bloesch, *Is the Bible Sexist?: Beyond Feminism and Patriarchalism* (Westchester, Ill.: Crossway Books, 1982), pp. 41–60.

69. Dietrich Bonhoeffer, *Prisoner for God*, ed. Eberhard Bethge, trans. Reginald Fuller (New York: Macmillan, 1954), p. 37.

70. See especially Deut. 32:11, 18; Ps. 131:2; Job 38:29; Isa. 49:14, 15; 42:14; 66:13; Matt. 23:37. Despite his very fine contribution to the discussion on feminism and his defense of biblical language in speaking of God, Vernard Eller fails to consider that in addition to the prevailing masculine symbolism for God in the Bible, there are other forms of symbolism, including the feminine. I also have difficulty with Eller's inclination to view "Father, Son and Spirit" as referring to God only in his relationship to the creature and not also to God as he is in himself. See Vernard Eller, *The Language of Canaan and the Grammar of Feminism* (Grand Rapids, Mich.: Eerdmans, 1982).

71. W. A. Visser't Hooft, *The Fatherhood of God in an Age of Emancipation* (Geneva: World Council of Churches, 1982), p. 133.

72. Ibid.

73. My recommendation is that in public prayers we should generally follow the wisdom of church tradition and address God in the masculine imagery of the Scriptures, in the awareness that the masculine contains the feminine. On the other hand, in private devotions it may be appropriate on occasion to address God in the person of his Word or Spirit as

"Holy Mother, Wisdom of God," or something similar, a practice that has some basis in the church fathers as well as in Scripture.

It is also permissible, in my opinion, to refer to God at times by more inclusive symbolism such as "the all-determining reality" and "infinite ground and depth of all being," but these must always be subordinated to the more personal symbolism of the Bible—Father, Son and Spirit. The latter are closer than the former to the real meaning of who God is.

74. Visser't Hooft points to Anselm's prayer to St. Paul and Jesus as an example of the use of creative imagination in personal devotions. After referring to the apostle as his "sweet nurse, sweet mother," Anselm then asks: "And you Jesus, are you not also a mother? Are you not the mother who like a hen gathers her children under her wings?" He concludes: "Then both of you are mothers. Even if you are fathers, you are also mothers. . . . Fathers by your authority, mothers by your mercy." *The Fatherhood of God*, p. 133. See St. Anselm of Canterbury, *The Prayers and Meditations of St. Anselm,* trans. Benedicta Ward (Harmondsworth, Middlesex: Penguin Books, 1973), pp. 152–155.

75. It is well to note that the conflict with feminism on this point parallels the battle of the Confessing Church with the "German Christians," who sought to accommodate the faith to the ideology of National Socialism. They did not hesitate to reject parts of the Bible they disagreed with and pressed for the resymbolization of the faith.

76. Schleiermacher saw the preacher as a spiritual guide or tutor who enables his hearers to proceed on their mystical journey inward. See Friedrich Schleiermacher, *On Religion: Speeches to its Cultured Despisers,* trans. John Oman (New York: Harper & Row, 1958), pp. 91, 123, 153–155, 173–175.

77. See Myron Simon and Thornton Parsons, eds., *Transcendentalism and Its Legacy* (Ann Arbor, Mich.: University of Michigan Press, 1966); Catherine Albanese, *Corresponding Motion: Transcendental Religion and the New America* (Philadelphia: Temple University Press, 1977); J. Stillson Judah, *The History and Philosophy of the Metaphysical Movements in America* (Philadelphia: Westminster Press, 1967); George F. Whicher, *The Transcendentalist Revolt Against Materialism* (Boston: Heath, 1949); and Charles Braden, *Spirits in Rebellion* (Dallas: Southern Methodist University Press, 1963).

78. James Hastings Nichols, *Corporate Worship in the Reformed Tradition* (Philadelphia: Westminster Press, 1968), p. 32.

79. John R. W. Stott gives eloquent testimony to this theme in his *Between Two Worlds: The Art of Preaching in the Twentieth Century* (Grand Rapids, Mich.: Eerdmans, 1982). Stott contends "that our mes-

sage must be God's Word not ours, our aim Christ's glory not ours, and our confidence the Holy Spirit's power, not ours" (p. 335). Stott is to be commended for his stress on study as a necessary preparation for the preaching of the Word of God.

80. It can be said that Jesus Christ is already Creator-Lord of the universe, but he is Redeemer-Lord only of the church in that this is where his Lordship is acknowledged and confessed. He is Lord of all, but Savior only of some.

81. For a trenchant critique of the popular interpretation of "principalities and powers" as socio-political structures in human society, see Peter O'Brien, "Principalities and Powers and Their Relationship to Structures," *Evangelical Review of Theology*, Vol. 6, No. 1 (April 1982), pp. 50–61.

82. I agree with Emil Brunner that our claim to be Reformed is based not on loyalty to a particular historical tradition but on the fact that the holy catholic faith was rediscovered and proclaimed anew by the Reformers.

83. Philip Schaff declares, "There is, indeed, a negative liberalism which is indifferent to the distinction between truth and error; but there is also a positive liberalism or genuine catholicity which springs from the deep conviction of the infinite grandeur of truth and the inability of any single mind or single church to grasp it in all its fullness and variety of aspects." *Christ and Christianity*, p. 308. Schaff, like Nevin, was not immune to the spell of romantic idealism which dominated that age, but he was able to resist the pull of Romanticism by his deep grounding in biblical faith.

Both Schaff and Nevin often referred favorably to Schleiermacher, but it is unfair to accuse them of being followers of that renowned liberal theologian (as did Charles Hodge). In his preface to his *Anti-Christ: Spirit of Sect and Schism* (Taylor, 1848), John Nevin denied that he was guilty of following the errors of either Schleiermacher or Hegel, notwithstanding the help these men gave to him (p. 4). In his retort to Hodge in a series of articles in the *Messenger* (May 24–August 9, 1848), he made clear that while learning much from Schleiermacher, he objected to the inwardness and subjectivity which characterized Schleiermacher's theology. See Luther J. Binkley, *The Mercersburg Theology* (Lancaster, Pa.: Franklin and Marshall College; Manheim, Pa.: Sentinel Printing House, 1953), p. 99. Significantly Nevin introduced his book *The Mystical Presence* with an essay by Carl Ullman which sought to correct Schleiermacher on sin and forgiveness. *The Mystical Presence: A Vindication of the Reformed or Calvinistic Doctrine of the Holy Eucharist* (Philadelphia, 1846), pp. 26–27.

On Schaff's indebtedness to German idealistic philosophy, particularly as found in Hegel, see Klaus Penzel, "The Reformation Goes West: The Notion of Historical Development in the Thought of Philip Schaff," in *The Journal of Religion,* Vol. 62, No. 3 (July 1982), pp. 219–241. See also Penzel, "Church History in Context: The Case of Philip Schaff," in *Our Common History as Christians,* ed. John Deschner et al. (New York: Oxford University Press, 1975), pp. 217–260. Penzel acknowledges that Schaff severely criticized both Hegel and Richard Rothe for idolizing the state.

84. P. T. Forsyth, *Positive Preaching and the Modern Mind* (London: Independent Press, 1953, 4th impression), p. 143. Forsyth nevertheless affirmed that kind of liberalism characterized by the spirit of self-criticism and willingness to remain open to new truth. He definitely sided with a true liberalism over obscurantism.

85. Philip Schaff, *Christ and Christianity,* p. 152.

86. Ibid., p. 297.

Bibliography of Author's Books

AUTHOR OR EDITOR

Centers of Christian Renewal. Philadelphia: United Church Press, 1964.

The Christian Life and Salvation. Grand Rapids, Mich.: William B. Eerdmans Publishing Co., 1967.

The Crisis of Piety. Grand Rapids, Mich.: William B. Eerdmans Publishing Co., 1968.

The Christian Witness in a Secular Age. Minneapolis, Minn.: Augsburg Publishing House, 1968.

Christian Spirituality East and West. Chicago: Priory Press, 1968. (co-author)

The Reform of the Church. Grand Rapids, Mich.: William B. Eerdmans Publishing Co., 1970.

The Ground of Certainty: Toward an Evangelical Theology of Revelation. Grand Rapids, Mich.: William B. Eerdmans Publishing Co., 1971.

Servants of Christ: Deaconesses in Renewal. Minneapolis, Minn.: Bethany Fellowship, 1971. (editor)

The Evangelical Renaissance. Grand Rapids, Mich.: William B. Eerdmans Publishing Co., 1973. Published in London, England, by Hodder & Stoughton, 1974.

Wellsprings of Renewal: Promise in Christian Communal Life. Grand Rapids, Mich.: William B. Eerdmans Publishing Co., 1974.

Light a Fire. St. Louis, Mo.: Eden Publishing House, 1975.

The Invaded Church. Waco, Texas: Word Books, 1975.

Jesus Is Victor!: Karl Barth's Doctrine of Salvation. Nashville, Tenn.: Abingdon Press, 1976.

The Orthodox Evangelicals. Nashville, Tenn.: Thomas Nelson, 1978. (co-editor)

Essentials of Evangelical Theology: God, Authority and Salvation, Vol. I. San Francisco: Harper & Row, 1978.

Essentials of Evangelical Theology: Life, Ministry and Hope, Vol. II. San Francisco: Harper & Row, 1979.

The Struggle of Prayer. San Francisco: Harper & Row, 1980.

Faith and Its Counterfeits. Downers Grove, Ill.: InterVarsity Press, 1981.

Is the Bible Sexist? Westchester, Ill.: Crossway Books, 1982.

The Future of Evangelical Christianity. Garden City, N.Y.: Doubleday & Company, 1983.

CONTRIBUTOR

"Rethinking the Church's Mission" in *Berufung und Bewährung: Internationale Festschrift für Erick Wickberg*. Geissen, Basel: Brunnen Verlag, 1974. English title: *Vocation and Victory*.

"The Basic Issue," in *Christ Is Victor*. Ed. W. Glyn Evans. Valley Forge, Pa.: Judson Press, 1977 (pp. 27–30).

"A Call to Spirituality," in *The Orthodox Evangelicals*. Ed. Robert Webber and Donald Bloesch. Nashville, Tenn.: Thomas Nelson, 1978 (pp. 146–164).

"The Challenge Facing the Churches" in Peter Williamson and Kevin Perrotta, eds., *Christianity Confronts Modernity*. Ann Arbor, Mich.: Servant Books, 1981 (pp. 205–223).

"Pietism" in *Beacon Hill Dictionary of Theology*. Ed. Richard S. Taylor. Kansas City, Mo.: Beacon Hill Press, 1983.

"A Christological Hermeneutic" in Robert Johnston, ed., *The Use of the Bible in Theology: Evangelical Options*. Atlanta: John Knox Press, 1984.

"Frank Buchman" in *Evangelical Dictionary of Theology*. Ed. Walter Elwell. Grand Rapids, Mich.: Baker Book House, 1984.

"Conversion" in *Evangelical Dictionary of Theology*, 1984.

"Descent into Hell (Hades)" in *Evangelical Dictionary of Theology*, 1984.

"Fate" in *Evangelical Dictionary of Theology*, 1984.

"Peter T. Forsyth" in *Evangelical Dictionary of Theology*, 1984.

"Sin" in *Evangelical Dictionary of Theology*, 1984.

Indexes

SUBJECT INDEX

NAME INDEX

SCRIPTURE INDEX